With *Dwelling in the Word*, Bob has pt
and compelling devotional guide for tl
groups alike will find this a useful tool for learning, praying, and spending special
time in God's Word. This work will bless many.

John and Darla deSteiguer
Oklahoma Christian University, Edmond, Oklahoma

It has been my privilege to know Bob Young for a number of years. There are few
folks that are as dedicated to evangelizing Latin America as Bob Young. He works
tirelessly to spread GOD's Word in the Spanish-speaking world. How he found the
time to author the book you have in your hand is beyond amazing. This book will
bless you as it has blessed me. It is obviously written by someone who has loved
the Word of GOD his entire life, and this series of devotionals will demonstrate that
love and the insights gained from his long-time study of the Word.

Jerry C. Lawlis
Gospel Preacher, Executive Director, Red River Family Encampment

Dr. Bob Young, an accomplished biblical scholar, reveals in this book another aspect of his versatile life and ministry: he is a deeply spiritual man. For almost a
decade, he has been developing a daily devotional on each of the 260 chapters in
the New Testament. Arranged in quasi-chronological order, each devotional provides a brief introduction of the chapter, a focused textual thought, discussion
questions, an application to life, and a prayer. The author has based the key text
from each chapter on his own translation from the Greek. Noted for excellence in
his work, these devotionals measure up to the author's high standards.

Howard W. Norton
Retired Bible and Missions Professor, Harding University

Bob Young has created a tool that gives various ways to engage in reading the
books of the New Testament. With each reading there is a text from the New Testament and a brief reflection on the text along with a prayer. The reflections on
the text are insightful and offer much for the reader to consider. As the title suggests, the goal is not just reading the books of the New Testament, it is learning to
dwell with God's Word so that it might impact daily living. *Dwelling in the Word* is
a great tool that I hope many will use.

Brian Sturtz
Senior Minister, Harmony Christian Church, Choctaw, OK

Bob Young's knowledge of and love for the biblical text shines in his new devotional
book. Written for multiple study formats and possible uses, *Dwelling in the Word*
promises to be a rich study tool that will encourage personal and collective spiritual
growth.

Jerry and Lynn Jones
Marriage Matters Conferences

Dwelling in the Word by Bob Young will serve as a thought-provoking and spiritual resource for individuals, couples, families, and all types of church classes and groups. Bob's biblical insights and vast kingdom and mission experiences truly informed the nature of this work. Each chapter is concise, clear, and consistently evokes thinking and discussion. Above all, this work is "focused on the Word of God."

Alan M. Martin, Ph.D.
Vice President, Academic Affairs, African Christian College

I like this devotional guide in that it focuses on the texts seen in the broader context of a Biblical book, and beyond – to the context of the entire New Testament. It encourages the reader to dive in more deeply. In the Reflecting and Thinking sections, the goal is the heart, the heart of God and our hearts -- how ours might be shaped by His. There are many light and fluffy devotional books sold which are based on the author's interests or the recent talking points in contemporary culture. I would strongly recommend this book over them as it is text-based and helps one grasp better "all the counsel of God" [KJV] or "the whole will of God" [NIV] (Acts 20:27), the objective of Paul in his proclamation to Christians at Ephesus.

In the religious world preachers often follow a lectionary which seeks to provide a broad treatment of texts over the course of a year. I prefer preaching through the Bible in a year or preaching through the New Testament in a year in conjunction with the church reading through the Bible or the New Testament together. A preacher could encourage his congregation to read this book together, use this book as a guide, and preach on Sunday what the congregation was to read on Monday or what they had read on Friday. This method of preaching keeps the congregation focused on the text. In following a schedule, the preacher will address those difficult topics often avoided.

Dr. Steve Teel, President
Baxter Institute, Tegucigalpa, Honduras

Dwelling in the Word is an excellent devotional manual for anyone who has a desire to be edified by God's Spirit through a balanced combination of scholarly insight and devotional sensitivity. This combination characterizes the contents of *Dwelling in the Word*. Bob Young has poured into the writing of this book a lifetime of commitment to the exegetical study of the Scriptures and to the teaching and application of the principles that he has mined from Scripture.

Carlos Ulate, M.Ed.
Universidad Nacional de Costa Rica, ESP Teacher
Bammel Church of Christ, Missionary in Costa Rica

Dr. Bob Young's book *Dwelling in the Word* provides an extremely practical, insightful and enjoyable resource for daily devotions. It is concise enough not to bog down the reader while providing excellent details on the scripture selections. It is ideal for personal, family or even small group Bible studies.

Dr. Bob Stephens
Retired President, Ohio Valley University

Dwelling in The Word is truly a devotional book that is fit for the babe, the scholar, and everyone in between. Highlighting a specific biblical text in every chapter of the New Testament creates a desire in the reader to investigate the rest of the chapter. Bob Young encourages the "not so" zealous student to "study to show himself approved unto God." Each daily devotional ending with a prayer is the essence of communicating with God, for He talks to us through the Word and we speak to Him through prayer. I believe this book is one of many tools to aid in the fulfillment of Colossians 3:16: "Let the word of Christ dwell in you richly."

      Antoine N. Holloway, Minister
      Northside church of Christ, Tucson, Arizona

We are excited to be involved in the publication of this unique devotional reading guide. For those who strive to read with understanding, Bob Young provides several optional sequences of study, thus making this book a valuable yearly resource for individual students, Bible classes, and entire congregations. Especially helpful for study and preparation are the overviews of each book through the insightful chapter titles Bob has given each reading.

      Derek and LaDonna Bullard
      Tulsa, Oklahoma

Thanks so much for sending a copy of the book. It is special that you would take the time to share what you have gleaned from a lifetime of study. You are using well the unique gifts that God has given you.

     The five-day, no calendar plan is a great idea. This really works for me as I start plans then get Spirit-led (or side-tracked) by an additional topic of study. You did a great job of coming up with a variety of application questions. On some of the more confrontational passages about sins we all face, you handled your questions very positively. You are more in-depth...in your outlook which helps my study perspective. Your prayers were right on target with the Word presented.

      Dianna Teel
      Missionary, First Lady of Baxter Institute, Tegucigalpa, Honduras

WHY THIS BOOK?

This book is unique among devotional reading guides. Each chapter is placed in its biblical context, exploring questions such as "What does this chapter contribute to the message of the author?" and "How does this chapter fit into the message of the New Testament?"

This book is unique—

because it includes new translations of selected passages.

because of the reading sequence that is used.

because of the five-days-per-week reading plan.

because of the application questions that are included.

because the prayers reflect the message of each reading.

because of its flexibility and variety.

because it does not use a calendar year – begin any time!

because the reading checklists that are included help track progress.

This book can be used again and again with various reading sequences.

DWELLING IN THE WORD

A DEVOTIONAL GUIDE FOR READING AND UNDERSTANDING THE NEW TESTAMENT

Bob Young

Jon & Karen:
Best wishes—
Bob Young

James Kay Publishing

Dwelling in the Word: A Devotional Guide for Reading and Understanding the New Testament
1.2. Copyright © 2020 by Robert J. (Bob) Young.
All right reserved.

Published by James Kay Publishing, Tulsa, Oklahoma
www.jameskaypublishing.com
e-mail: sales@jameskaypublishing.com

James Kay Publishing is committed to excellence in publishing. The opinions expressed by the author are not necessary those of James Kay Publishing.

Book cover design © 2020. All rights reserved.
Cover design by JKP. Cover photo 123RF.com/balazschristina
Author photo by Jan Young.

Published in the United States of America

ISBN: 978-1-943245-61-1

Other Books by the Author

EARLY LETTERS
Helps for Reading and Understanding the Message

PRISON LETTERS
Helps for Reading and Understanding the Message

PASTORAL LETTERS
Helps for Reading and Understanding the Message

HEBREWS
Helps for Reading and Understanding the Message

GENERAL LETTERS
Helps for Reading and Understanding the Message

EVANGELISMO
Energizando y Equipando a la Iglesia
Taller y lecciones para En pos de la verdad

Introductory Matters and Tables of Contents

With a basic understanding of the unique organization and features of this book, the reader will discover many different ways to use it. Three reading plans are possible. The reading plan used in this book is explained below and is reflected in the first Table of Contents. The explanation and the Table of Contents are placed on single openings for ease of reference.

The second Table of Contents follows the New Testament order and includes titles for each devotional. A third possibility for reading or studying the New Testament is to use a personalized plan based on interests or other studies. The reading checklist provided in the back of the book will be especially helpful in personalized or random reading.

Several copies of the reading checklist are provided, making it possible to use this book for several years with different reading plans. Alternately, the reading checklists make it possible for several family members to use this devotional book at the same time.

Table of Contents for Introductory Matters

THE READING PLAN USED IN THIS BOOK

Matthew. Over a month is allotted to reading the book of Matthew. The Gospel of Matthew is about 12% of the New Testament. A good way to introduce a New Testament reading plan is to begin where the New Testament begins – with the Gospel of Matthew. Matthew has numerous Old Testament quotations. Beginning the reading plan with a gospel seems natural -- reading the story of Jesus. Readers who use a red-letter edition of the Bible for personal study will notice that Matthew is a book that has a lot of red letters — the book contains many of Jesus' teachings. Matthew is one of four gospels in the New Testament.

James, Hebrews, and Romans. A goal of this Bible reading plan is to provide variety in the type of literature being read. After reading Matthew, three books written by three different authors are read. These books were written by James, an unidentified author, and Paul.

The letter of James has only five chapters. James, probably written around AD 50, shows how Jesus' teachings were applied in the early church.

The book of Hebrews, written 30-40 years after Jesus' death and resurrection, reflects a time when the church was undergoing persecution. Jewish Christians were tempted to return to Judaism. Hebrews focuses on Jesus, describing the purpose of Jesus' coming and showing how Jesus is superior to the Old Testament system. The message of the book is to remain faithful in the midst of difficulties.

Romans contains doctrinal teachings. In Romans, Paul sets forth God's plan for salvation.

Luke-Acts. Reading Luke and Acts requires almost three months. Luke is about 13% of the New Testament, Acts is also about 13% of the New Testament. Combined, these two books represent about one-fourth of the New Testament. After reading Luke, it is logical to follow Luke Vol. 1 with Luke Vol. 2, the book of Acts.

Galatians, 1-2 Thessalonians, 1-2 Corinthians. Having read Luke's accounts of Jesus and the history of the early church, the next readings are the earliest of the books of the New Testament, the next books in the chronological sequence—Galatians, 1-2 Thessalonians, and 1-2 Corinthians.

In the early church, for the first two to three decades, applying the teaching of the apostles was tricky and difficult. In the 50s, Paul wrote five letters to help the early church clarify its teachings and to apply those teachings to the Christian life.

Mark. After reading the earliest letters of the New Testament, the reading returns to another gospel – Mark is probably the earliest of the gospels.

Ephesians, Philippians, Colossians, Philemon. These four letters known as Prison Letters were written by Paul in the early 60s.

1 Timothy, Titus, and 2 Timothy. Paul wrote these three short letters to church workers in the 60s: 1 Timothy, Titus, and 2 Timothy. The readings follow the order in which the books were written.

1-2 Peter, Jude. In the General Letters are three letters that are usually dated in the 60s.

John, 1-2-3 John, Revelation. John's writings are usually dated as among the last of the New Testament books. The Gospel of John, three letters that are found among the General Letters, and the book of Revelation complete the reading. John's writings make up approximately 20% of the New Testament.

May God richly bless your reading and study of his Word!

TABLE OF CONTENTS
READING PLAN

TABLE OF CONTENTS
NEW TESTAMENT ORDER WITH CHAPTER TITLES

HOW TO USE THIS BOOK IN A LOCAL CHURCH

Get a copy of the book for each member or each family. One advantage of this book is that all family members can use the same book.

Choose the reading plan and communicate regularly with the church!
- The reading plan in the book is recommended. Using this plan will let members simply read through the book in order.
- Reading the New Testament in order is also a popular approach.
- A specific reading plan can be developed in the local church.

Regardless of the reading plan used, the 5-readings-per-week will have to be identified and shared with the church – on a monthly calendar, special handout or bookmark, or in a weekly bulletin or information sheet.

Integrate the reading plan into the teaching of the local church

The most popular and effective way to do this is in the sermon. The preacher either reviews past readings or anticipates future readings. In some churches, this has been done each week during a calendar year. Advantages of this approach is that the members are more likely to continue in the readings and the preacher is encouraged to preach "the whole counsel of God" since every chapter of the New Testament passes across the preaching calendar as a possibility. (See below for suggested topics.)

Integrating the Bible readings and the preaching can also be done with a monthly sermon that reflects the devotional studies being read by the church members.

A weekly correspondence of readings and church Bible studies has maximum impact. If this is not done through the sermons, it is possible to let the congregational Bible readings inform the lessons used in a Bible class, in a weekly (or monthly) small group, or in Sunday night or Wednesday sermons or devotionals.

The purpose of integrating the readings and other congregational studies is repetition. It has been shown that people remember more of what they study with repeated exposure.

Repetition is also the reason that the book is designed to be used year after year, with multiple formats and reading sequences.

Experience has shown that counting and publishing the number of "daily Bible readers" increases participation in any Bible reading project or emphasis.

Coordinate sermons or studies with the readings

The number of weeks devoted to each book (and thus the number of sermons or classes available for each book) can be calculated by dividing the number of chapters in the book by five (number of reading days each week). The chart below shows approximately how many weeks are devoted to each book. The numbers can be adjusted, depending on the day of the week that the reading program is initiated.

For the Gospels and Acts, themes are suggested to illustrate the process. In the letters, one could choose a specific devotional to be expanded, or lessons which summarize the messages of the books could be developed.

Gospel of Matthew (5 sermons)
- Identity of Jesus
- Early ministry of Jesus; teaching, preaching, and healing; Sermon on the Mount
- Climax of Jesus' ministry – increasing hostility, the feeding of the 5000, Peter's confession
- Characteristics of genuine kingdom life
- The events of the week before Jesus' crucifixion and resurrection

Gospel of Mark (3)
- Who is Jesus?
- Who can be a disciple of Jesus? Who can see?
- The events of the final week, crucifixion and resurrection

Gospel of Luke (5)
- Identity narratives
- Jesus' ministry; predictions of his death
- Forgiveness for everyone
- The universality of the gospel
- The final week, crucifixion and resurrection, the Emmaus road

Gospel of John (4)

In John's gospel, one option is to select four narratives that summarize the book. Themes that could be preached include the cosmic Christ, belief, life, love, and worlds in conflict.

Book of Acts (6)

The book of Acts naturally divides with six summary statements. One approach would be to use these statements to guide the development of the sermons or classes during the reading of Acts (6:7; 9:31; 12:24; 16:5; 19:20; 28:31).

The Letters

The suggested number of weeks is given in the parentheses. If no number is given, the readings will be completed in approximately one week with time for only one sermon or class.

Romans (3)	1 Corinthians (3)	2 Corinthians (2)	Galatians
Ephesians	Philippians	Colossians, Philemon	1 Thessalonians
2 Thessalonians	1 Timothy	2 Timothy	Titus
Hebrews (3)	James	1-2 Peter, Jude (2)	1-2-3 John (2)
Revelation (4)			

A WORD FROM THE AUTHOR

A number of factors have converged in my life as influences on my method of Bible study and Bible teaching. My undergraduate training in Bible and biblical languages served as the foundation for my first twenty-five years of full-time preaching ministry.

When I decided to pursue graduate education, I already loved teaching from an exegetical viewpoint, paying close attention to the historical-cultural context and the grammatical-syntactical features of the biblical text. I had seen first-hand the way in which people respond positively to thoughtful efforts to explain and apply the message of the Bible. I used the same kind of detailed Bible study in my sermon preparations. My graduate training helped me expand my understanding of the dynamics of ministry and integrate academic studies with practical applications. Combining graduate work and full-time ministry, I had a "laboratory" for testing and applying what I was learning.

My years of teaching and administration in Christian higher education coupled with increased involvement in the world of missions made me aware of the need to view the Bible outside one's own social, cultural, experiential, and religious backgrounds. My teaching and preaching are influenced by my training and experience. I want to understand the biblical context, the historical-cultural context, and the literary context—vocabulary, genres, grammar, and syntax. I try to understand the original message of the author and the purpose of the text as first steps toward understanding the message of the text in today's world. I want to know what the text said and what it meant, so that I can know what it says and what it means today.

My approach to Bible study has influenced the development of this book. As I wrote, I constantly asked myself, "What would I want in a devotional guide?" Guided by that question, I established these goals: (1) become aware of the larger context of each chapter, (2) identify a limited text for deeper study, a passage that helps capture the essence of the chapter, (3) explore the message of the text, why it was written, and what it said and meant in the original context, (4) explore ways to transfer and apply that message and meaning to contemporary life applications, and (5) use the text to guide a deeper prayer life. I have used these ideas to develop a brief and practical devotional guide that includes an explanation of what the text says, what the text means, how the text can be applied, and a prayer to guide the spiritual journey.

May God bless you in your desire and your efforts to read, understand and apply the message of the Bible!

--Bob Young
Tulsa, Oklahoma

PREFACE

In 2011, I began writing a series of devotionals as part of my annual journey through the New Testament. My initial efforts have been edited several times over the past decade. I envisioned devotionals that could serve as a study guide with several unique features. First, there are **five devotional readings per week**. Five devotionals each week for 52 weeks covers the 260 chapters in the New Testament in a year.

Second, **each devotional covers a chapter**, designed to reflect the content of the chapter and its contribution to the message of the New Testament. For each chapter, my translation of a selected reading is augmented by an explanation of the message and questions to assist with the application of the message, along with a prayer based on the chapter and reading.

Third, the suggested order of readings in this book **generally follows New Testament chronology**. The order of readings alternates between different sections of Scripture and different types of New Testament literature, rather than consecutively reading the Gospels or the letters of Paul.

A fourth feature is **flexibility**. At least three reading plans are possible.

First, follow the order suggested in this guide. By following the suggested order, the reader will follow the general chronology of the New Testament while alternating between different sections and literary types of the New Testament.

Second, study the chapters of the New Testament through in order. Those who prefer to study or read through the New Testament in order (Matthew to Revelation), five chapters per week, will finish the study of the New Testament in one year. (A table of contents and a reading guide are provided to help those who want to use this method.)

Third, use a different method or read randomly. Using a reading guide will help those who want to follow a different plan and those who want to read randomly, checking off or circling the chapters read.

While many people begin reading the New Testament at the beginning of the year, the flexibility of this book allows one to begin at any time during the year. At the back of the book, pages are provided to help track progress. When multiple family members use the book at the same time, each can track progress on a separate page.

Fifth, **the translations are new**. The goal of translation is to communicate the message of the biblical text in an understandable way. The translations in this book often retain the word order of the original text. Due to the frequent use of participles in the original language, some passages use sentences that are longer and more complex than is normal in English. When the same Greek word appears repeatedly in a passage, an effort is made to identify an English word or phrase that adequately conveys the meaning in each occurrence. An example is the use of the phrase "set aside as useless" in 1 Cor. 13:8-11, translating four occurrences of the same Greek word with the same English phrase. Such translations are at times awkward, but the repetition in the original language is made clearer. My hope is that your Bible study will be refreshed as you read these new translations.

INTRODUCTION

I do not remember my first attempt to read the Bible through. One Christmas when I was in high school, I received a new Bible. It was my first Bible with summaries of the books and comments. I was intrigued. I better understood what I was reading. At the beginning of the New Year, I made the typical resolution to read the Bible. As often happens, I failed to keep my resolution. I believe I know why many people have read Genesis and Matthew more than any other books in the Bible.

The first time I read the New Testament through, cover to cover, was when I was a student at Wichita State University. Our on-campus Christian student group received permission to distribute copies of *Good News for Modern Man* New Testaments in the student center. We gave away hundreds of copies. We had many conversations with fellow students about the Bible.

At the same time, I belonged to an academic club that hosted a campus version of *College Bowl*, a competition between fraternities, sororities, and other student groups. (*College Bowl* was a televised academic competition in the 1960s, similar to *Jeopardy*.) A group of us students wrote the questions for the competition, covering various academic disciplines. I served as student moderator of the on-campus competition, so I had to become familiar with all of the questions and answers. With campus visibility, I was asked lots of questions during the New Testament distribution, many about how I could maintain a strong, informed academic posture and at the same time accept Christianity.

Because of the questions from fellow students, and because some churches were upset that a Christian campus group was distributing a "modern" version of the New Testament, I decided to read *Good News for Modern Man*." I did it in less than a week! The New Testament that had seemed so big was within my grasp! Our campus sponsor, Maurice Hall, liked to say that we were distributing a Bible that college students might actually read: "Anything that will cause students to read the Bible cannot be all bad."

Later, during my undergraduate studies at Oklahoma Christian, I read large sections of both the Old Testament and New Testament. I remember reading the Psalms in a night of prayer and meditation. Another night, I gulped down the book of Proverbs. What was formerly a chore was becoming enjoyable.

My first ministry was with a small church in southwest Arkansas. I became a voracious reader. My reading schedule included the New Testament. I kept one of my business cards in my Bible; on the reverse side I had written out a reading schedule that would let me read the New Testament in a month. I maintained that schedule for more than ten years. While I failed to finish a few times, during that time I read the New Testament through over 100 times. Later I committed to reading the entire Bible through every year. As new translations became available, I used my annual Bible reading to read the newer translations.

The Bible is readable and understandable. Many people long to read and understand the Bible. Their struggle is reflected in the question Philip asked the eunuch, "Do you understand what you are reading?" It is not much fun to read if you do not understand what you are reading. This devotional reading guide is my effort to help you experience what I have experienced, to enjoy what I have enjoyed. I want you to read with understanding. I want you to succeed in your desire to read, understand, and apply God's word. I want that word to be your companion and guide as you pray.

I am thankful to the preachers and teachers who have made the message and meaning of the Bible available to me. I pray that this book will be a blessing to others even as I have been blessed by those who have guided and encouraged me.

Matthew 1: God with Us -- Savior and Messiah

Selected Biblical Text

18 The birth of Jesus Christ happened like this. His mother Mary was betrothed to be married to Joseph. Before they came together, she was found to be pregnant from the Holy Spirit. 19 Joseph her husband, being a just man, and not wanting to call attention to her, he intended to send her away privately. 20 After he had thought on these things, an angel of the Lord appeared to him in a dream and said: "Joseph son of David, do not fear to take Mary as your wife, for that which is conceived in her is from the Holy Spirit. 21 She will give birth to a son, and you will call his name Jesus, for he will save his people from their sins." 22 All this happened so the word of the Lord by the prophet might be fulfilled: 23 "The virgin will conceive and will give birth to a son, and they will call his name Immanuel, which means God with us." 24 When Joseph arose from his sleep, he did as the angel of the Lord had commanded him and he took her as his wife. 25 But he did not know her until she gave birth to a son, and he called his name Jesus. (Matthew 1:18-25)

Reflecting and Thinking

Matthew is one of three Synoptic Gospels (along with Mark and Luke). Matthew is unique because of its Jewish background --numerous Old Testament quotations, prophetic notes, and fulfillment statements. The three Synoptic Gospels can be outlined with three major sections: (1) identity stories that introduce the gospel, (2) the ministry of Jesus, including three predictions of his death, and (3) the events of the Last Week, beginning with the Triumphal Entry and concluding with the Resurrection, followed by a brief description of the time between the Resurrection and the Ascension.

Today's chapter introduces Matthew's identity stories. The reading says something about who Jesus is. In Matthew, the identity stories appear in the first four chapters and include a genealogy, Jesus' identity as Jesus-Immanuel-Christ, a contrast of two kinds of kings, the "Son out of Egypt" prophecy, his baptism, and his temptation.

The name Jesus signifies "Savior." What do you think of when you think of salvation? What did the Jews think of or anticipate (for example, deliverance from oppression by other nations)? Today's text refers to "salvation from sins." Contemplate the importance of the name "Jesus" and try to connect the name with the concept of salvation more often when you hear it or read it. The name Immanuel means "God with us." What does it mean to you that God is with us through Jesus? Contrast this passage from Chapter 1 with the Great Commission in Chapter 28 when the disciples wonder if Jesus' departure will mean that God will no longer be present with them. (Jesus' promise in the last words before his ascension is that he will always be with them.) The designation Christ in 2:4 (Christ is the Greek

1

word, Messiah in Hebrew, anointed in English) suggests another aspect of Jesus' identity. What does it mean to you that Jesus is the "anointed one?" Considering that Matthew's description of Jesus is sometimes summarized as "Servant King," how do these various descriptions connect with his royalty?

Prayer

Dearest Father, God, help me understand more clearly the identity of Jesus. Help me not to take for granted the meanings that are communicated when he is called Jesus, Immanuel, or Christ. Thank you for salvation through him, thank you for being with me on this earthly pilgrimage, thank you for his conquest and his Kingdom reign. Thank you most of all for giving me access to your throne through prayer in his name, as I raise this prayer in Jesus' name and by his power, Amen.

Matthew 2: A Different Kind of King

Selected Biblical Text

1 After Jesus was born in Bethlehem in Judea in the days of Herod the King, wise men from the east came to Jerusalem, 2 asking: "Where is the one who has been born to be king of the Jews? We saw his star in its rising and have come to worship him." 3 When King Herod heard this, he was troubled, and all Jerusalem with him. 4 Calling together all the chief priests and law experts of the people, he asked them where the Christ was to be born. 5 They said to him: "In Bethlehem in Judea, for thus it has been written through the prophet: 6 'And you, Bethlehem, of the land of Judah, in no way are least among the rulers of Judah; for from you will come a ruler who will shepherd my people Israel.'" (Matthew 2:1-6)

Reflecting and Thinking

Matthew's Gospel describes a "Servant King" who comes to fulfill God's promises and prophecy. The contrast between a "servant king" and a "power-driven political king" is clear in today's reading. Wise men come to worship the new king whose star has arisen in the East. They first go to the reigning political king who reigns by coercion and force, with intrigue and manipulation. Jesus comes as a different kind of king. He is a king who reigns in the hearts and lives of those who willingly accept him as king. His is a reign characterized by drawing people to him and by shepherding them with protection and care. He is a different kind of ruler. His entry into the world was planned by God (note the three parallel "fourteen generations" in the genealogy and the references to dreams in the first two chapters). God is at work already--and in Jesus He will do even greater things.

Think about the contrasts between Herod the King and Christ the King. How many contrasts can you identify based on this chapter? What would happen if Jesus were a coercive king? How would this advance (or damage) his kingdom? What aspects of Jesus' kingdom make you want to follow him as King? What aspects of Jesus' kingdom present the greatest challenges to would-be followers? Based on today's reading, why did the Jews fail to see Jesus as the promised Messiah?

Prayer

Dear Heavenly Father, we worship today the one you sent as King in the kingdom. We ascribe honor and glory and praise to him, because through him we are able to see and understand you. Help us be loyal subjects in the kingdom. Strengthen us as we devote ourselves to doing the will of the King, as we adopt his priorities as our priorities. Thank you for demonstrating your love and providing us an alternative way of living and interacting with others. Develop in us the heart of Jesus, we pray in his name, Amen.

Matthew 3: The Baptism of Jesus -- Son of God

Selected Biblical Text

1 In those days came John the Baptist, preaching in the desert area of Judea 2 saying: "Repent, for the kingdom of heaven has come near." 3 He is the one spoken about through the prophet Isaiah when he says: "A voice crying out in the wilderness, 'Prepare the way of the Lord, make straight his paths.'"
13 Then Jesus came from Galilee unto the Jordan to John to be baptized by him. 14 John tried to refuse him by saying: "I have need to be baptized by you, and you come to me?" 15 Jesus answering said: "Let it happen now, for thus is it proper for us to fulfill all righteousness." Then John agreed.
16 After Jesus was baptized, as soon as he arose from the water, heaven was opened, and he saw the Spirit of God coming down as a dove and landing on him, 17 and a voice out of heaven saying: "This is my beloved Son, in whom I am well pleased." (Matthew 3:1-3, 13-17)

Reflecting and Thinking

Matthew declares Jesus' identity in ways that would speak to a Jewish audience as he describes John the Baptist's preaching as the fulfillment of Isaiah's prophecy and as he recounts the voice from heaven at Jesus' baptism, "This is my Son whom I love; with him I am well pleased." In the early chapters of Matthew, Jesus' identity is set forth clearly: as Son of David, Savior, Immanuel (God with us), Christ (anointed, king), fulfillment of Old Testament prophecy, Son of God (see also 2:15, "Out of Egypt I called my son;" and 4:3,6 in the context of the temptation), and as a human being (in the temptation of Chapter 4, see also "Son of Man" in 8:20, 9:6; 10:23, and 11:19).

On a normal day, what do you think of when you think about Jesus? How often do you think about Jesus? The descriptions we are discussing may seem technical and theological -- what practical descriptions of Jesus are most meaningful to you (friend, intercessor, etc.)? On a scale of 1 to 10, how sure are you that Jesus is the divine Son of God? What would help increase that confidence (as applicable)?

Prayer

Dear God, we thank you for clearly revealing yourself in your Son. We are grateful for the clarity with which you have made him known. We are not dependent on one or two pieces of evidence to believe in Jesus and understand his identity -- you have provided us many different ways to see and know him. Help us be more confident in sharing the message of Jesus with others. We pray in Jesus' name, grateful that he provides for us also the way to approach your heavenly throne, Amen.

Matthew 4: "From That Time" -- Teaching, Preaching and Healing

Selected Biblical Text

17 From that time Jesus began to preach, saying: "Repent, for the kingdom of heaven has come near."
23 Jesus went about throughout Galilee, teaching in their synagogues, preaching the gospel of the kingdom, and healing every disease and sickness among the people. 24 The report about him went forth into all of Syria, and they brought to him all those having various diseases and torments, afflicted with severe pain, being demon-possessed, having seizures, and being paralyzed, and he healed them. 25 So large crowds followed him from Galilee, the Decapolis, Jerusalem, Judea and the area across the Jordan. (Matthew 4:17, 23-25)

Reflecting and Thinking

Matthew's Gospel has several interesting literary characteristics. Previously mentioned are the parallel ideas in 1:23 ("God with us") and 28:20 ("I will be with you always"). These two texts serve as bookends or parentheses in the book. Matthew contains five major discourses or teaching sections (Chapters 5-7, 10, 13, 18, and 24-25). We will explain these teaching sections in future devotionals. Matthew divides the ministry of Jesus into two sections with the repeated phrase, "from that time" (see 4:17 and 16:21). These two verses introduce two major textual sections. The first section describes how Jesus came teaching, preaching and healing; the second section focuses on the truth that Jesus came to die. These two verses provide a structural frame for Matthew's description of the Messiah. The Jews had certain Messianic expectations -- that Jesus came teaching, preaching, and healing was only slightly inconsistent with their expectation of a political and militant king; that the Messiah came to die was utterly impossible!

For disciples of Jesus, what is the importance of the statement that Jesus came teaching, preaching, and healing? What would we do if we wanted to be like him? (The basic meaning of "disciple" is one who is a learner and is becoming like the Master.) How are the actions of Jesus an indication of the presence of the kingdom? Based on today's reading, why does the good news of the kingdom, the gospel of Jesus, not spread more rapidly today? What causes the gospel to spread? What kind of false expectations do people in the world today have about Jesus? What kind of false expectations exist in the church? How would you personally explain why Jesus came, using his actions to explain why he came?

Prayer

Heavenly Father, we seek you again this day, wanting to know you better, affirming your presence in this world and in our lives, seeking your power that we might serve others. Help us imitate Jesus as we share Good News and seek healing and help for the hurts of the world. Thank you for your word and its revelation of Jesus, in the name of the one who came teaching, preaching, and healing, Jesus the Christ, Amen.

Matthew 5: Sermon on the Mount -- Turning Things Upside Down

Selected Biblical Text

1 When Jesus saw the crowds, he went up on the mountainside. When he had sat down, his disciples came to him, 2 and opening his mouth he began to teach them, saying: 3 "Blessed are the poor in spirit, because theirs is the kingdom of heaven. 4 Blessed are those who mourn, because they will be comforted. 5 Blessed are the meek, because they will inherit the earth. 6 Blessed are the ones hungering and thirsting for righteousness, because they will be satisfied. 7 Blessed are the merciful, because they will be shown mercy. 8 Blessed are the pure in heart, because they will see God. 9 Blessed are the peacemakers, because they will be called children of God. 10 Blessed are the ones having been persecuted because of righteousness, because theirs is the kingdom of heaven.

11 "You are blessed when people insult you, persecute you and say every evil thing against you because of me. 12 Rejoice and be glad, because your reward is great in heaven, for in this way they persecuted the prophets who were before you." (Matthew 5:1-12)

6

Reflecting and Thinking

Today's reading is the first chapter of the first discourse in Matthew -- the Sermon on the Mount (Chapters 5-7). Jesus describes a different way of living. Life in the kingdom is different than the life many people see as normal -- values are changed, expectations are different, attitudes are altered. Blessings come from unexpected sources. What matters is redefined as life is seen in a new light. Misunderstandings are swept away. Jesus begins to turn understandings upside down in the Beatitudes and he continues throughout Chapter 5 with six paragraphs that begin, "You have heard it said but I tell you...." The fulfillment of God's purpose in our lives is not measured by technical legalities that convince us that we have successfully jumped through the right hoops. God's purpose in our lives is measured by change that begins in the heart, changing our thinking, our attitudes, and our lives.

Do you find it easy or hard to read the Sermon on the Mount? Do you find it easy or hard to apply these teachings of Jesus? Take a few moments to reflect on the "why" of your answers. One way to appreciate this section of Jesus' teaching is to trace the occurrences of the word "righteous" or "righteousness." What is Jesus saying about righteousness in this chapter?

Prayer

Heavenly Father, we are overwhelmed by how unchanged our lives are on some days. We long for power and strength that will help us be light and salt and leaven. We want to make a difference even though we are worn out by the tasks of getting through the day and taking care of the little stuff of life. Instill in us a changed heart as we read and reflect upon your word. Touch us, remake us, mold us and change us, through Jesus we pray, Amen.

Matthew 6: Sermon on the Mount -- Focusing on What Matters

Selected Biblical Text

19 "Do not save up for yourselves treasures on earth, where moths and eating away consume, and where thieves break in and steal. 20 But save for yourselves treasures in heaven, where neither moths nor eating away consume, and where thieves do not break in and steal. 21 For where your treasure is, there will be also your heart.

22 "The lamp of the body is the eye. If your eye is healthy [generous], your whole body will be full of light. 23 But if your eye is unhealthy [stingy], your whole body will be full of darkness. If then the light that is within you is in fact darkness, how great will be that darkness! 24 No one is able to serve two masters. Because you

will hate the one and will love the other, or you will hold to the one and despise the other. You cannot serve both God and wealth.

33 But seek first the kingdom and its righteousness, and all these things will be given to you. 34 Do not anxiously be concerned about tomorrow, because tomorrow can be concerned about itself. Sufficient for each day is its own trouble." (Matthew 6:19-24, 33-34)

Reflecting and Thinking

Here is a good question: what really matters in life? Many Christians today would say that what they do in service to Christ is what really matters. Certainly, Jesus commends the one who both hears and acts (see Matt. 7:24-27, Jesus' teaching about the wise builder and the foolish builder), but first he cautions against "acts of righteousness" that call attention to oneself more than to God. There is a certain danger in prayer, self-denial, and giving. That danger is that our hearts may stray, and our attitudes may falter. The way to focus on what matters is to invest our lives and resources in the most important things, because our hearts follow our treasure. Jesus contrasts two attitudes in verses 22-23: the attitude of generosity and the attitude of stinginess. (These are the basic meanings of the words "healthy" and "unhealthy.") The priority of life lived in the kingdom is made clear in verse 33: seeking his kingdom and his righteousness takes care of everything else!

How can you know what is important to another person? Looking at your life, what would others say is important to you? How well does your life reflect your priorities? Make a list of the things that matter to you. (You may want to think about your life in categories to identify the one or two most important things in each category.) Those who study human behavior say that reviewing your list regularly will help keep you on target in your desire to focus on the most important things. How can we avoid the "tyranny of the urgent?" How can we keep from investing the entirety of our lives in trivial things? (Hint: One answer is to do the things that are most important first!)

Prayer

Father God, focus our attention today on the things that really matter. Help us seek Jesus' kingdom and his righteousness above all. Focus our attention on kingdom things more than worldly things. In Jesus' name and by his power we ask it, Amen.

Matthew 7: Sermon on the Mount -- Making Right Choices

Selected Biblical Text

21 "Not everyone who says to me, 'Lord, Lord,' will enter the kingdom of heaven – only the one doing the will of my Father who is in heaven. 22 Many will say to me on that day: 'Lord, Lord, did we not prophesy in your name and in your name cast out demons, and in your name do many powerful things?' 23 Then I will declare plainly to them, 'I never knew you. Depart from me, you workers of lawlessness.'
24 "Therefore everyone who hears these words of mine and practices them will be like a wise man who built his house on the rock. 25 The rain came down and the rivers flowed, and the winds blew and beat against that house; but it did not fall because it had foundations on the rock. 26 But everyone who hears these words of mine and does not practice them will be like a foolish man who built his house on sand. 27 The rain came down and the rivers flowed, and the winds blew and beat against that house, and it fell; and its fall was great."
28 It happened that when Jesus had finished these words, the crowds were amazed at his teaching, 29 because he taught them as one having authority, and not as their law experts. (Matthew 7:21-29)

Reflecting and Thinking

It is not easy to make decisions. Some people muddle through life because they cannot make timely decisions. Many people fail because of poor decisions. Today's chapter is filled with a long list of options: narrow gate or wide gate, narrow road or broad road, life or destruction, truth or falsehood, grapes or thorns, figs or thistles, good fruit or bad fruit, good trees or bad trees, obedience or disobedience, God's will or my will, rock or sand, wisdom or foolishness, hearing and doing or merely hearing. These are not a dozen decisions -- in reality, they are descriptions of only one decision. A well-known preacher observed that on Sunday mornings faithful Christians do not have to decide again and again each week whether to go to church. He explained by noting that faithful church attendance is the result of a single decision that one makes when one gives one's life to Christ. So it is! The one choice to seek the king in his kingdom and his righteousness takes care of a lot of little choices.

Why are we sometimes tempted to break life down into a series of small decisions? How can it be that some would appear to be doing good things in Jesus' name and yet be lost? (Think about the principles set forth in the Sermon on the Mount.) Are you committed to doing the will of God in every aspect of your life? Is today the day to "remake" your decision for faithful discipleship?

Prayer

Dear God, we believe that following Jesus surely cannot be as hard as we make it some days. Constantly remind us of our decision to follow him -- regardless. Guide us as we continually recommit to doing your will rather than ours. Help us not to be caught up in the spectacular and in self-glory. Make us humble wise servants, we pray in Jesus' name, Amen.

Matthew 8: Healing the Hurting

Selected Biblical Text

14 When Jesus came to Peter's house, he saw Peter's mother-in-law bed-ridden and feverish. 15 He touched her hand and the fever left her. She got up and began to serve the guests. 16 When it was evening, they brought to Jesus many who were demon-possessed, and he cast out the spirits with a word and all those having illnesses he healed. 17 In this way was fulfilled what was spoken through Isaiah the prophet when he said: "He carried our weaknesses and bore our diseases." (Matthew 8:14-17)

Reflecting and Thinking

Today's text is part of the section that describes how Jesus came teaching, preaching and healing (compare 4:23 and 9:35). After teaching and preaching in the Sermon on the Mount, we might expect a series of healing stories. Matthew 8 gives us just that. Jesus cures a man with leprosy (8:1-4), heals the servant of a centurion (8:5-13), heals Peter's mother-in-law and heals many others who were brought to him (8:14-17). In typical fashion, reminding us of the Jewish emphasis of this Gospel, Matthew observes that this is a fulfillment of prophecy, citing Isaiah 53:4. Later in the chapter, Jesus heals two demon-possessed men (8:28-34) and we find out that not everyone is happy with a Teacher who heals, especially if it threatens their sense of "normal" and their customary way of life. Not everyone is ready for a new "normal." Some people enjoy hurting -- some enjoy the attention and the focus on self.

How has Jesus "healed" your life? (Consider that healing may be physical, emotional, spiritual, and social, or that it may take various other forms.) Phrasing the question another way, how has Jesus made a difference in your life? What is he calling you to do for others today? How could you be his representative in touching, helping, and serving others? How could you imitate the one who came teaching, preaching, and healing?

Prayer

Dear Heavenly Father, we ask you to increase our faith, strengthen our commitment, and empower our ministry in the kingdom. Help us be more confident as we point others to Jesus, confident that he can heal their infirmities and change their lives. May we reflect the changed lives he makes possible, in Jesus' name, Amen.

Matthew 9: Seeing the Harvest through Compassionate Eyes

Selected Biblical Text

35 Then Jesus went through all the towns and villages, teaching in their synagogues, proclaiming the gospel of the kingdom and healing every disease and sickness. 36 Seeing the crowds, he had compassion on them, because they were bewildered and helpless, as sheep not having a shepherd. 37 Then he said to his disciples: "The harvest is plentiful, but the workers are few. 38 Pray then to the Lord of the harvest to send out workers into his harvest field." (Matthew 9:35-38)

Reflecting and Thinking

That Jesus came teaching, preaching and healing is mentioned again in today's text (compare 4:23). Jesus' actions reveal the essence of kingdom commitment. Here is the very nature of the kingdom -- the good news of the kingdom is proclaimed, minds and attitudes are changed, people are made whole. Jesus speaks to his disciples about the plentiful harvest and the limited number of workers. He urges prayer for the workers and for the harvest. He sees the harvest because he looks at the people with compassion. He sees them as harassed and helpless, hopeless, hapless and homeless. He sees them as sheep without a shepherd -- with no one to care, to comfort, to nourish and guide. He sees them as having lost direction. When we ask how God wants us to see the world and what he wants us to do about the hurts of the world, this text shouts a powerful answer. Pray for workers who will reap the harvest!

It seems that many in our world today have given up on the kingdom harvest of souls. Some believe that few are interested in spiritual things. We will do well to ask ourselves: How often am I following Jesus' instructions to pray for the harvest and for more workers? Could it be that we do not see the harvest because we do not look at the world through spiritually compassionate eyes? Consider the difference between seeing the physical needs of people and seeing the spiritual needs of people. How often does the modern church do ministry or mission work focused almost exclusively on benevolence and physical needs? Does the harvest fail because there is nothing to harvest, or because of the lack of workers? Remember that Jesus says the harvest is plentiful.

Prayer

Dear Heavenly Father, help us see the harvest through compassionate eyes. Help us see those you see, help us love those you love, help us serve those Jesus died for. Bring to our hearts the love of Jesus for others, and help us live out that compassionate love, even as he loved us. We pray today for the harvest and for more workers. As always, we pray in Jesus' name, Amen.

Matthew 10: Who Can Be a Follower?

Selected Biblical Text

32 "Whoever confesses me before others, I will also confess before my Father in heaven. 33 But whoever denies me before others, I will deny also before my Father in heaven. 34 Do not think that I came to bring peace on the earth. I did not come to bring peace, but a sword. 35 I came to turn 'a man against his father, a daughter against her mother, and a daughter-in-law against her mother-in-law.' 36 The enemies of a man will be the members of his own household.

37 "One who loves father or mother above me is not worthy of me; and one who loves son or daughter above me is not worthy of me. 38 Whoever does not take up their cross and follow after me is not worthy of me. 39 The one finding his life will lose it, and the one losing his life because of me will find it." (Matthew 10:32-39)

Reflecting and Thinking

Today's chapter is the second major discourse (teaching section) of Matthew's Gospel. As Jesus sends out the Twelve, he gives them the instructions recorded in this chapter. The mission of the Kingdom will begin with the people of Israel -- preaching the kingdom, serving the sick and needy, sharing good news and blessings (verses 5-8). (Eventually the mission of the Kingdom will be expanded to include both Jews and Gentiles, but that detail is not included in today's reading due to Matthew's focus on the Jews.)

When the question of mission and outreach comes up, a companion question also arises: Who can be a follower? Matthew's concern in this chapter is not the inclusion of both Jews and Gentiles in the kingdom. Matthew's focus is on the necessity of owning Jesus, confessing faith, acknowledging Jesus, and being willing to pay the price of discipleship. These require establishing new priorities that may exclude the things and the people previously loved and cherished. Anything less is not acceptable. The result is a total redefinition of life. The old "normal" must be rejected — the new "normal" must take over. That is the way of Jesus -- that is the way of the cross.

Because of the severity of the requirements, passages such as to-day's text are often cast off as irrelevant and not applicable in today's world. Does following Jesus really require rejecting family? Does following Jesus really require the way of the cross -- the way of sacrifice and death to self? Is genuine life to be found by losing what we value in return for gaining what may appear to be little value? How does one square finding life to lose it and losing life to find it? These are not easy questions -- they are worthy of our thoughtful prayer this day. And finally, the ultimate question is not about who can be a follower. The ultimate question is whether I am a faith-ful follower!

Prayer

Dear Heavenly Father, we seek this day to find life abundant, genuine and full. We recommit ourselves to that goal, even as we are hesitant to take up our cross, we affirm that we are willing to follow wherever is necessary. We seek his righteousness and his way, in Jesus' name, Amen.

Matthew 11: Taking Up the Yoke of Jesus

Selected Biblical Text

25 At that time, answering, Jesus said: "I thank you, Father, Lord of heaven and earth, because you have hidden these things from wise and insightful people, and have revealed them to little children. 26 Yes, Father, for this was well-pleasing to you. 27 All things have been entrusted to me by my Father. No one knows the Son except the Father, and no one knows the Father except the Son and the one to whom the Son wishes to reveal him. 28 Come to me, all you who are weary and burdened, and I will give rest to you. 29 Take my yoke upon you and learn from me, because I am gentle and humble in heart, and you will find rest for your lives. 30 For my yoke is easy and my burden is light." (Matthew 11:25-30)

Reflecting and Thinking

Today's chapter has three major paragraphs: Jesus' teachings about John the Baptist, woe to the cities that did not repent, and Jesus' instructions to take up his yoke. It is difficult to capture the entire chapter in a brief devotional thought. Today's devotional centers on the last section of the chapter.

Rob Bell has popularized the idea that being a disciple of Christ, in response to Jesus' command to "take up my yoke," means to become a fol-lower of the Teacher and to take up his teaching. Bell says that a rabbi's interpretations and teachings were called his "yoke" and that to "take up his yoke" was to accept his teachings with the goal of becoming like the rabbi, learning and explaining his yoke (teachings) to others. Whether this is accurate is much discussed and doubtful. Jewish teachers spoke of the "yoke" of the Torah and the yoke of the commandments, but no record exists of a Jewish teacher telling another person to "take up my yoke." Paul called the law a yoke of bondage.

The text suggests that many yokes are wearisome and burdensome, but that Jesus' yoke is different. The text also says that taking Jesus' yoke allows us to learn from him, become like him, and find rest in his easy yoke and light burden. The yoke allowed pulling a burden with less stress and strain, and a good yoke made the work easier. The most obvious application is that Jesus helps us to bear the burdens of life more easily.

What aspects of life are most difficult for you personally? How does Jesus make these areas of life easier to bear? What aspects of Christianity are most difficult for you? How do you reconcile difficulties in the Christian life with Jesus' promise of an easier yoke and lighter burden? Does the text suggest that one of our problems may be that we have not yet clearly seen the things God is revealing through Jesus?

Prayer

Dear Father, we are grateful for your revelation and want above all else to seek and know your way. Strengthen us as we walk the Christian life and help us understand the easier yoke and lighter burden, not for our own benefit, but so that we can share the message of Jesus effectively in the world around us. Again, we pray in Jesus' name, Amen.

Matthew 12: Fulfilling Prophecy

Selected Biblical Text

13 Then he said to the man: "Stretch out your hand," and he stretched it out and it was restored, as healthy as the other. 14 After they left him, the Pharisees plotted against him how they might kill him.

15 Jesus, knowing their plans, went away from that place. Great crowds followed him, and he healed them all. 16 He admonished them not to make him known, 17 so it might be fulfilled what was spoken through Isaiah the prophet when he said: 18 "Behold my servant whom I have chosen, the one loved by me, in whom I delight; I will put my Spirit upon him, and he will proclaim just judgment to the nations. 19 He will not quarrel or cry out; nor will anyone hear his voice in the streets. 20 A bruised reed he will not break, and a smoldering wick he will not extinguish, until he sends out judgment to victory. 21 In his name the nations will hope." (Matthew 12:13-21)

Reflecting and Thinking

Today's chapter contains five paragraphs: (1) Jesus demonstrates that he is Lord of the Sabbath by healing the man with a withered hand; (2) Jesus is identified as God's chosen servant who fulfills Isaiah's prophecy by the power of God's Spirit; (3) Jesus answers the charge of the Pharisees that he is empowered by Beelzebub; (4) Jesus addresses the Pharisees' desire for a sign; and (5) then he speaks about his mother and brothers. In Matthew's Gospel, the identity of Jesus is never far from view; it is always in the near background. That Jesus fulfills Isaiah's prophecy concerning God's chosen servant -- loved, a source of delight to God, Spirit-filled and Spirit-empowered to proclaim justice and hope -- provides an obvious contrast to the accusations and challenges of the Jewish leaders.

Jesus is a teacher of a different sort, especially when compared to the average Jewish rabbi or teacher of his day. Jesus not only taught; he healed. He taught with authority. He taught with compassion. He taught to make life easier, not harder. He focused on the heart, not external actions; he presented a different model for life. He exalted spiritual relationships over physical, and internal heart change over external adherence to the law. One's life must be more than a vacuum where nothing bad exists -- life is to be filled with goodness and mercy, wisdom and value. One cannot be content to evacuate all the evil. One must take a stand for goodness and truth. Justice and victory and hope spring forth in no other way.

Prayer

Dear Father in Heaven, fill us this day with your power, presence, mercy and love. Give us a measure of your wisdom. Focus our hearts on doing your will so that we may indeed be brothers and sisters of Jesus, in his name, Amen.

Matthew 13: Revealing Kingdom Realities -- Changing Expectations

Selected Biblical Text

31 He gave them another parable, saying: "The kingdom of heaven is like a mustard seed, which a man took and sowed in his field. 32 On one hand it is the smallest of all seeds, but when it has grown, it is the largest plant in the garden plants and becomes a tree, so that the birds of the sky come and lodge in its branches."

33 He spoke to them another parable: "The kingdom of heaven is like yeast that a woman took and mixed into three measures of flour [about 50 pounds] until it was all leavened." 34 All these things Jesus spoke in parables to the crowds; and he spoke nothing to them without a parable. 35 Thus was fulfilled what was spoken through the prophet, saying: "I will open my mouth in parables, I will announce things that have been hidden since the foundations of the world." (Matthew 13:31-35)

Reflecting and Thinking

In Matthew's Gospel, the third major discourse (teaching section) of Jesus is a group of parables. Parables, by their very nature, reveal hidden truths. The nature of the kingdom was not immediately obvious in Jesus' day, nor is it obvious in our day. Some things are hidden, invisible until one takes a closer look. The nature of the kingdom is easily misunderstood. We tend to think in normal patterns rather than seeking meaning in life by changing our expectations. Jesus came to help people change their expectations. Life can be better than we thought. We can escape tedium and find fruitfulness; we can endure difficulties knowing that God is in control. These new possibilities are of such great value that those who see them will pay virtually any price to obtain them.

The two parables in the selected text show the power of small beginnings. Parables turn reality upside down. Parables reflect new, never-before-seen realities. Parables say that things do not have to be the way they always have been. Parables integrate life, combining what is with what can be.

On a scale of 1 to 10, how would you rate the "expectancy quotient" of your life? Do you tend to expect only a little change or a lot of change? How hopeful are you that Jesus can turn around the difficult parts of your life or the difficult things in the lives of your family and loved ones? Do you expect the "same old same old" or do you expect things to be different? What commitments would you be willing to make if things could really change? The reality of Jesus' kingdom, what is not always visible and easily seen, is that God's power can change our lives. Praise Him!

Prayer

Dear God, thank you for revealing yourself to us. Forgive us when we are stubborn, hard-headed and unchangeable. Mold us and make us new, into the image of Jesus, reflecting kingdom realities which are different than what we have known previously. Give us wisdom to see, even as the disciples of Jesus needed an explanation. We pray in Jesus' name, Amen.

Matthew 14: Kingdom Mission -- Keeping the Mission in Focus

Selected Biblical Text

13 Jesus, hearing of this, privately went away from that place by boat to an isolated place. When the crowds heard of it, they followed him on foot from the towns. 14 When Jesus went forth, he saw a large crowd and he had compassion on them and healed the infirm among them. 15 When evening came, the disciples came to him, saying: "This place is isolated, and the hour is already late. Send away the crowds,

so they can go into the villages and buy food for themselves." 16 Jesus said to them: "They do not need to go away. You give them something to eat."

17 But they said to him: "We have nothing here except five loaves of bread and two fish." 18 And he said: "Bring them here to me." 19 And he commanded the crowd to sit down on the grass. Taking the five loaves and the two fish and looking unto heaven, he gave thanks. Breaking the loaves, he gave them to the disciples, and the disciples to the crowd. 20 They all ate and were satisfied, and there were left over of the broken pieces twelve full baskets. 21 And those having eaten were about five thousand men, without counting women and children.

22 Immediately Jesus made the disciples get into the boat to go ahead of him to the other side, while he sent the crowd away. 23 And having sent the crowd away, he went up on the mountain alone to pray. (Matthew 14:13-23a)

Reflecting and Thinking

This chapter reflects a turning point in Jesus' ministry. We are about to move from increasing crowds to increasing doubt, from increasing popularity to increasing animosity. The death of John the Baptist touched Jesus deeply. John was a near relative as well as a friend, supporter, and herald. Jesus withdrew. When the crowds followed him, Jesus compassionately fed them. We know from John's Gospel that this event caused the crowds to want to crown Jesus as their king. Perhaps the disciples also bought into the idea, because verse 22 uses a strong word when it says Jesus MADE the disciples get into the boat. Once the disciples are gone, Jesus can more easily dismiss the crowd with their ill-conceived idea and plan.

There comes a time in every life (sometimes many such times come) when it is easy to get one's mission and purpose out of focus. Mission easily becomes fuzzy. Mission drifts. We forget why we are here and what we are to do. We are easily sidetracked, especially when others are pleased or served. We can justify a variety of detours.

After the events recounted in today's selected reading, Jesus comes walking to the disciples on the water and the disciples are terrified. The question surfaces again: Who is Jesus? Is this really Jesus? When all has calmed down, the validating affirmation should hit us full force: "Truly you are the Son of God" (14:33). Jesus is the one he claims to be! He is therefore able to do what God sent him to do. How sad would it be if Jesus were to get off-mission? How sad is it today when God's people get off-mission! Take time today to pray about what God is doing in your life and pray for clarity that you might understand his mission in your life.

Prayer

Dear God, keep us on mission in our Christian lives. So many good things beckon. Help us choose what is best. May we not be satisfied with being mediocre; may we not be satisfied with less than all you desire in our lives, in Jesus' name, Amen.

❖ ❖ ❖

Matthew 15: Getting to the Heart of the Matter

Selected Biblical Text

10 Calling the crowd to him, he said: "Listen and understand. 11 That which enters the mouth does not make a person unclean, but that which comes out of the mouth, that makes a person unclean."
12 Then the disciples came to him and said: "Do you know that the Pharisees were displeased when they heard this?" 13 He answered: "Every plant that my heavenly Father did not plant will be uprooted. 14 Leave them; they are blind guides of the blind. If a blind person leads a blind person, both will fall into a hole."
15 Peter said to him: "Explain to us the parable." 16 Jesus said: "Are you still undiscerning? 17 Do you not know that whatever enters the mouth goes into the stomach and is eliminated in the latrine? 18 But the things that come out of a person's mouth come from the heart, and these make the person unclean. 19 For out of the heart come hurtful arguments, murder, adultery, fornication, stealing, false testimony, and slander. 20 These things make a person unclean; but to eat with unwashed hands does not make a person unclean." (Matthew 15:10-20)

Reflecting and Thinking

The Jews were very concerned with cleanliness, especially in their desire to define what was ceremonially clean or unclean. In fact, an extensive tradition had developed in Judaism with numerous man-made rules and regulations to govern cleanliness. The problem with the rules was that they were superficial and external, failing to address the matter of the heart which is the heart of the matter. No wonder Jesus used the words of Isaiah's prophecy to accuse the Jews of dishonoring God, distancing themselves from God, and vain worship.

When Jesus says that cleanliness is not defined in physical matters but rather in internal thoughts that are reflected in what one says, the Pharisees are offended. Peter asks for an explanation of Jesus' words in verse 11, calling the teaching a parable. Jesus makes clear what matters in verses 17-20 of the today's text.

What matters most to you? In your Christian life, do you focus more on external measurements like what you do or on internal matters such as the condition of your heart (thoughts, attitudes, feelings, desire, will)? What is the importance of Jesus' statement that evil actions begin in the evil thoughts of the heart? How can we most effectively address behavioral problems? Do we change behavior, or do we change our hearts? Why were the Pharisees offended? Are the words of Isaiah's prophecy ever applicable to us in our lives (honor given only with lips, distanced hearts, vain worship, man-made rules)?

Prayer

Dear God, help us focus on what really matters so that our lives will bring you glory and honor and praise. Help us develop hearts that care about important things. Help us develop the mind of Christ. Help us understand how unimportant some of the trivial matters that we emphasize may be. Cleanse and purify our hearts as we obediently seek your will and way, we pray in Jesus' name, Amen.

Matthew 16: "From That Time"-- Dying

Selected Biblical Text

21 From that time on Jesus began to explain to his disciples that it was necessary for him to go to Jerusalem, to suffer many things from the elders, the chief priests and the law experts, to be killed and on the third day to be raised. 22 Peter took him aside and began to rebuke him, saying: "May God have mercy, Lord! By no means shall this ever happen to you." 23 Turning around, he said to Peter: "Get behind me, Satan. You are a stumbling block to me; you are not considering the things of God, but the things of human beings."
24 Then Jesus said to his disciples: "If anyone wants to come after me, such a person must totally deny self and take up his cross and follow me. 25 For whoever wants to save their life will lose it, but whoever loses his life for my sake will find it. 26 What does it benefit a person to gain the whole world and yet lose his life? What will a person give in exchange for his life? 27 The Son of Man is about to come in the glory of his Father with his angels, and then he will reward each person according to what he has done. 28 In truth I say to you that some of those standing here will not experience death before they see the Son of Man coming in his kingdom." (Matthew 16:21-28)

Reflecting and Thinking

Today's reading introduces a second description of Jesus' ministry: Jesus came dying. The second aspect of Jesus' ministry is solidly built on the identity of Jesus as confessed by Peter: "the Christ, the Son of the living God" (16:16). Matthew summarizes the first part of Jesus' ministry as "teaching, preaching and healing" (4:23). In today's text, he summarizes the second part of Jesus' ministry as "suffering and dying." Because of our familiarity with the gospel story, we may not realize how unbelievable was the idea that the Messiah could become victorious by dying. Jesus answers Peter's impetuous response by contrasting the things of God and the things of men. We must ask ourselves the same question: where is our focus? Are we looking at the things of God or the things of men?

Not only will Jesus die -- all who follow him are also called to die. It is in dying that we truly live. Life is found and saved by losing it; life is lost by seeking to save it, using human standards and desires. Jesus' death will usher in the kingdom, even during the lifetime of some of those who were present and listening to the words of Jesus.

What are some of the human concerns that Peter had in mind? What "things of men" do we today tend to focus on? What specific examples can you give of Christians or churches that consider human things and priorities more than the things of God? What does it mean for us to deny ourselves and take up crosses? In what ways are we called to die?

Prayer

Dear celestial Father, today we want to focus on spiritual things more than on our own things. We do not totally understand the wisdom of your plan, but we willingly follow, committing ourselves to give our all as faithful followers of the King. Help us understand more clearly how we are called to deny self and take up our crosses. We pray in Jesus' name, Amen.

Matthew 17: Son of God -- God Speaks Again

Selected Biblical Text

1 After six days Jesus took aside Peter, James, and John the brother of James, and led them up a high mountain by themselves. 2 He was transfigured before them. His face shone like the sun, and his clothes became as white as the light. 3 Then Moses and Elijah appeared to them, talking with Jesus. 4 So Peter said to Jesus: "Lord, it is good for us to be here. If you want, I will make three shelters -- one for you, one for Moses and one for Elijah."
5 While he was yet speaking, a bright cloud surrounded them, and a voice from the cloud said: "This is my beloved Son; with him I am well pleased. Listen to him." 6 When the disciples heard this, they fell down on their faces, very alarmed. 7 But Jesus came, and touching them he said: "Get up. Do not be alarmed." 8 When they looked up, they saw no one except Jesus alone.
9 As they came down the mountain, Jesus commanded them, saying: "Do not tell anyone what you saw, until the Son of Man has been raised from the dead." (Matthew 17:1-9)

Reflecting and Thinking

By now we have come to expect affirmations of Jesus' identity in Matthew's Gospel. At the Transfiguration, God again speaks from heaven, affirming Jesus as his loved and well-pleasing Son. That Jesus' identity is not to be shared seems to connect with the necessity of his death so that he can fulfill God's plan. Would people respond to Jesus differently if they really understood who he is? Would we be changed by a clearer perception of Jesus? Would our friends and neighbors, cities and communities, nation and world be changed if the real identity of Jesus as God's Son was so clear as to be undeniable?

When have you seen Jesus' identity most clearly? Do you think peo-ple would believe if they heard a voice from heaven affirming Jesus as the only way? Why or why not? What could we as Christians do to make the message of Jesus clearer? Given that some do not believe in Jesus because they have never heard the gospel message, what could we do to help the message go to all who are willing to believe? (You might begin to answer this question by remembering Jesus' instruction to pray for the harvest and pray for workers in Matthew 9. Do not stop there. What could we do besides pray?)

Prayer

Father God, in Jesus' name and by his power we seek to make known the gospel. Give us wisdom and understanding to know how we can best ad-vance the Kingdom around the world. We pray again today for the harvest and for workers. Because Jesus is the Christ, the Son of God, we come be-fore your throne in his name and by his authority, Amen.

Matthew 18: The Kingdom Community

Selected Biblical Text

1 At that time the disciples came to Jesus asking: "Who is the greatest in the king-dom of heaven?" 2 Calling a little child to him, Jesus had him stand among them. 3 And he said: "In truth I say to you, unless you reverse your thinking and become as little children, you will never enter the kingdom of heaven. 4 Whoever then hum-bles himself as this child, that one is the greatest in the kingdom of heaven."

12 "What do you think? If someone has a hundred sheep, and one of them wanders away, will he not leave the ninety-nine on the mountains and go look for the wan-dering one? 13 And if he finds it, in truth I tell you, he rejoices in that one sheep more than in the ninety-nine that did not wander. 14 In the same way your Father in heaven is not willing that any of these little ones perish.

15 "If your brother sins, go and admonish him, between him and you only. If he listens to you, you have regained your brother. 16 If he will not listen, take with you now one or two others, so that 'every matter may be made to stand upon the testimony of two or three witnesses.' 17 If he refuses to listen to them, tell the church; and if he refuses to listen to the church, let him be to you as a Gentile or a tax collector."

21 Then Peter came to him and asked: "Lord, how many times can my brother sin against me and I forgive him? As many as seven times?" 22 Jesus said to him: "I say to you, not seven times, but seventy-seven times." (Matthew 18:1-4, 12-14, 15-17, 21-22)

Reflecting and Thinking

Life in the community of the kingdom is not lived by the same standards as life in the social settings of the world. Matthew 18 is the fourth of the Jesus' major discourses (teaching sections) in this gospel. It contains four related paragraphs. (The selected reading today includes the introductions to each of these paragraphs.) The kingdom community (1) measures greatness differently than the world, (2) cares for others sincerely and joyfully, (3) seeks meaningful, open fellowship and relationships, and (4) forgives more times than duty demands. The principles that govern the kingdom community avoid the kind of internal bickering and positioning that the question of the disciples reflects (verse 1).

On a scale of 1 to 10, how would you rate the fellowship in the kingdom community where you attend church? What factors cause you to give the assessment you give? To what extent did you consider Jesus' factors -- exalting the lowly, caring for all, transparent relationships, continual forgiveness? How could the modern church improve in its goal to be a genuine community of faith and a community of the Kingdom?

Prayer

Dear God, bind together your people in faith communities that help us toward faithfulness and Kingdom realities. Take away from us bickering and infighting. Teach us humility, compassion, transparency, and forgiveness. Help us reflect the nature of the Kingdom to the world about us by the way we live with one another in the Kingdom, we pray in Jesus' name, Amen.

Matthew 19: Kingdom Values

Selected Biblical Text

16 Then someone came up to Jesus and asked: "Teacher, what good thing must I do to obtain eternal life?" 17 But Jesus asked him: "Why do you ask me concerning what is good? There is One who is good. If you want to enter life, keep the commandments."

18 He said: "Which ones?" Jesus replied: "Do not murder, do not commit adultery, do not steal, do not give false testimony, 19 honor your father and mother, and love your neighbor as yourself." 20 The young man said: "All these I have observed. What do I still lack?" 21 Jesus answered him: "If you want to be perfect, go sell your possessions and give the money to the poor, and you will have treasure in heaven. Then come back here and follow me."

22 When the young man heard this word, he went away sorrowing, because he had great wealth. 23 Then Jesus said to his disciples: "In truth I tell you, only with great difficulty does a rich person enter the kingdom of heaven. 24 Again I say to you, it is easier for a camel to go through the eye of a needle than for a rich person to enter the kingdom of God." 25 The disciples, upon hearing this, were greatly

astonished and said: "Who then can be saved?" 26 Jesus looked at them and said: "For a human being this is impossible, but with God all things are possible."
27 Then Peter answered him: "We have left everything and followed you. What will there be for us?" (Matthew 19:16-27)

Reflecting and Thinking

We now understand from Matthew's gospel that life in the kingdom is different -- in its attitudes, priorities, and choices; in its commitments, expectations, and purpose; in its actions and values. Life and goodness are not measured by commandment-keeping but by values of the heart. If this change in attitudes and values seems humanly impossible, the good news of the gospel of the kingdom is that God makes possible what is impossible with human beings. We must understand, however, that escaping the world's way of thinking and the world's value system is not easy. After witnessing the encounter between Jesus and the rich young man and hearing Jesus' teaching, Peter's question seems to revert to the same self-centered approach to life: What will we get? What will there be for us? These questions echo through the ages and continue to plague Christianity. People still attend church and seek Christian connections because of what they can get. People still buy into and respond to the health and wealth promises of religious charlatans. Living out the values of the kingdom -- self-denial, cross-bearing, and sacrifice -- is never easy.

How can the church help Christians avoid the "what's in it for me" attitude? How does the church inadvertently or unknowingly buy into the attitude reflected in Peter's question? What are some examples of more appropriate Christian values? If you had to make a list of kingdom values, what things would you include? (Try to reflect some of the concepts we have studied in Matthew's gospel in your answer.) What are some of the values advanced by the world that are inconsistent with the Christian value system?

Prayer

Dear God, we seek today an understanding of your priorities and values so that we will make appropriate commitments and choices. Teach us unselfishness as we seek to follow Jesus, in his name, Amen.

Matthew 20: What Will WE Get?

Selected Biblical Text

19:30 Many who are first will be last, and the last first.
1 For the kingdom of heaven is like a landowner who went out early in the morning to hire workers for his vineyard. 2 After agreeing with the workers for a denarius

for the day, he sent them into his vineyard. 3 And going out three hours later [at nine in the morning], he saw others standing in the marketplace without work. 4 He said to those, you also go into the vineyard, and whatever is fair I will pay you. 5 So they went. He went out again about noon and about three in the afternoon and he did the same thing. 6 When he went out about five in the afternoon, he found some others standing around and he said to them, why have you been standing here all day without work? 7 They said to him, because no one has hired us. He said to them, you also go to the vineyard. 8 When evening came, the owner of the vineyard said to his manager, call the workers and give them their pay, beginning with the last ones to the first.

13 And the landowner replied to one of them: "Friend, I am not being unfair with you, friend. Did you not agree with me for a denarius? 14 Take what is yours and go. I want to give to the last person the same as to you. 15 Am I not permitted to do what I want with what is mine? Are you envious because I am generous?"

16 In this way, the last will be first, and the first last. (Matthew 19:30; 20:1-8, 13-16)

Reflecting and Thinking

Today's text begins and ends with the same affirmation: the first will be last and the last will be first. The parable of the workers in the vineyard is Jesus' expansion of his answer to Peter's question: what will we get? (19:27, see the Matthew 19 devotional study).

Peter says, "We have left all -- what will there be for us?" Jesus' response is that while they have left everything, they have left nothing. One cannot out give God. There will be future abundance and position (19:30).

Another question arises: What about fairness? In today's reading, the landowner responds to the complaining workers by pointing out that he has done what he promised (20:13). The point is that God is generous to all, regardless of performance, ability or inability to perform.

Later in today's chapter, James and John reflect the same attitude: What will we get? Jesus responds: Do you really want what I am going to get? Their affirmative response belies their misunderstanding. Jesus is challenging their basic values. Jesus came to serve and to give his life (20:26-28). A differing set of values applies to kingdom work: Jesus calls many people (20:3-6); he pays "what is right" (20:4); he is generous but not "fair" (20:13-15); he is not "fair" because he errs on the side of giving too much rather than too little; he gives "his life as a ransom for many" (20:28). These values contradict many of the contemporary cultural values that Christians and churches tend to use in the work of God.

Chapters 19 and 20 contain several well-defined paragraphs. Think through and describe the connection between the stories of the rich young man, Peter's question, the parable of the workers, Jesus' prediction of his death, the request of James and John, and Jesus' affirmation of his purpose to serve rather than being served.

24

Prayer

Heavenly Father, help us see the world through fresh eyes. Help us follow Jesus for right reasons and not out of self-serving motives. Help us imitate Jesus as we seek to serve rather than to be served. In the name of the Christ who willingly sacrificed everything to serve as our ransom, Amen.

Matthew 21: The King is Coming

Selected Biblical Text

1 Now when they approached Jerusalem and came to Bethphage, unto the Mount of Olives, Jesus sent two disciples, 2 telling them: "Go into the village that lies ahead of you, and at once you will find a donkey tied there, with her colt with her. Untie them and bring them to me. 3 If anyone says anything to you, say, 'the Lord needs them,' and he will send them at once." 4 This happened to fulfill what was spoken through the prophet: 5 "Tell the inhabitants of Zion, 'Look, your king comes to you, gentle and riding on a donkey, and on a colt, the foal of a donkey.'"
6 Then the disciples went and did as Jesus had instructed them. 7 They brought the donkey and the colt and placed their cloaks on them, and he sat on them. 8 A very large crowd spread their cloaks on the road, and others cut branches from the trees and spread them on the road. 9 The crowds going ahead of him and following him kept shouting: "Hosanna to the Son of David! Blessed is the one who comes in the name of the Lord! Hosanna in the highest heights!"
10 As Jesus entered Jerusalem, the whole city was troubled, asking: "Who is this?" 11 The crowds answered: "This is the prophet Jesus from Nazareth in Galilee." (Matthew 21:1-11)

Reflecting and Thinking

Yet another identity statement! The Triumphal Entry narrative declares that Jesus is the kingly fulfillment of Old Testament prophecy. King, prophet, Jesus. Prophet, priest, and king. This chapter is filled with narratives designed to support the claim of Jesus' identity. The final week has begun. The encounters with the Jewish leaders will intensify and eventually result in Jesus' death on the cross. Meanwhile, for a few moments today, relish the truth that Jesus is King.

Why did the Jewish leaders have so much trouble recognizing Jesus as King? Why do people today have trouble recognizing Jesus for who he is? What is an appropriate response for those of us today who want to recognize Jesus as king? How should we treat him? How can we honor our king?

Prayer

Heavenly Father, we praise you again today for the glory of creation, the merciful kindness of your sustaining hand, and the gracious gift of salvation you have given us through Jesus. We marvel at how he came as prophet, priest, and king, declaring truth, saving us and connecting us with God, guiding and shepherding us through life. We are grateful for the power of the gospel in our lives and pray for that power to come to our world. We offer this praise and ask these things through Jesus' name, Amen.

Matthew 22: Love God, Love Your Neighbor

Selected Biblical Text

34 The Pharisees, hearing that Jesus had silenced the Sadducees, assembled together. 35 One of them, a law expert, asked a question to test him: 36 "Teacher, which commandment is the greatest in the Law?" 37 Jesus answered him: "'You shall love the Lord your God with all your heart and with all your being and with all your mind.' 38 This is the first and greatest commandment. 39 And the second is like it, 'you shall love your neighbor as yourself.' 40 On these two commandments, all the Law and the Prophets depend." (Matthew 22:34-39)

Reflecting and Thinking

Boil it down to the simplest version possible. What do you see? Jesus said the entirety of the Old Testament Law and Prophets hinged on two great commandments: love God, love your neighbor. Admittedly, the question was designed as a trick question, but Jesus' answer was accurate. The words are easy. Many can quote a fairly accurate version of Jesus' response. But consider more carefully what Jesus says. Love for God must be entire and complete: all your heart, all your soul, all your mind. Loving neighbor to the extent Jesus describes is not all that easy: as we love ourselves.

These are #1 and #2. The order is essential. Number One is our pearl of great price, the treasure hidden in a field. Christianity is a treasure hunt. We are on a treasure hunt. To understand and practice this kind of love for God, seeing him and responding to him, is our #1 priority. Number Two is a lot easier when #1 is in place. In fact, #2 is impossible unless #1 is present. Loving others, serving others, giving self for others, caring for others -- these are empowered by God's love and presence within us.

Have you seen the Christian life more often as a treasure hunt or as a rescue mission? If our #1 task is finding and loving God, how does this change the way you live life from day to day? What can you do today to express more clearly or openly your love for God? What can you do today to express more clearly your love for your neighbor or fellow human beings? Pray about the commitment you need to make in order to obey more completely these two commandments.

Prayer

Father God, I love you and adore you. I want to hold back nothing of my being. My heart, mind, body, and very being are yours. Help me understand more completely the obedient love that pleases you. Help me love the unlovable ones around me, recognizing that I am not all that lovable at times. Thank you for the love you demonstrated in the gift of Jesus. I love you because you have loved me. Teach me your ways. In Jesus' name and by his power I ask it. Amen.

Matthew 23: When Down is Up -- Escaping Wrong Priorities

Selected Biblical Text

1 Then Jesus spoke to the crowds and to his disciples: 2 "The law experts and the Pharisees sit on Moses' seat. 3 Therefore you should do and observe everything they tell you. But do not do according to what they do, for they speak and do not do it. 4 They tie up heavy loads that are hard to carry and put them on the shoulders of others, but they themselves are not willing to lift a finger to move them. 5 All of their actions they do so that others will see: They enlarge their phylacteries wide and lengthen their tassels; 6 they love the place of honor at banquets and the most important seats in the synagogues; 7 the public greetings in the marketplaces and to be called 'Rabbi' by the people. 8 But you are not to be called 'rabbi,' because for you there is one Teacher, and all of you are brothers. 9 Do not call your 'father' anyone on earth, for you have one heavenly Father. 10 Nor are you to be called 'teachers,' for you have one Teacher, the Christ. 11 Whoever is greatest among you will be your servant. 12 Whoever exalts himself will be humbled, and whoever humbles himself will be exalted." (Matthew 23:1-12)

Reflecting and Thinking

Depending on the Bible you use for your Bible reading, you may have noticed -- lots of red words! Most of chapters 23-24-25. The words of Jesus. Preparing for the end. What does one say when one knows the end is near? No need to hold back about things that are wrong -- speak clearly about the things that are not as they should be. And in Jesus' day, there was a lot more wrong with the Pharisees than there was right. Misuse of authority, bad examples, inconsistent practices, burdensome interpretations, hypocritical glory-seeking. They had totally missed it. The way up is down; the way down is up. The humble are exalted; the self-exalted will be humbled. Service is greatness; greatness by any other standard is nothingness. The kingdom is not defined by positions and titles. What is needed is a brand-new set of priorities -- to focus on others more than self; to live out compassion, humility, service, love.

What impresses you as you read Jesus' woes against the Pharisees? With whom do you identify? Do you identify with Jesus -- thinking about some people you would like to tell these very things? Do you identify with the crowds and disciples? They are the ones Jesus is addressing. Do you identify with the religious leaders who have missed the whole point of following God? Is Jesus saying anything at all to you, to us, in this chapter? What are some of the applications we should make?

Prayer

Dear God, help us hear your word. When it stings and hurts, let us hear it anyway and change our lives. Help us hear what we need to hear. We know that our priorities get confused. We know that we are at times self-seeking and self-serving. We know also that we can be harsh taskmasters in those areas of life we think we have under control. Develop in us the heart of Jesus, we pray in Jesus' name, Amen.

Matthew 24: The End is Coming

Selected Biblical Text

1 As Jesus exited the temple courts, his disciples approached him to show him the temple buildings. 2 He said to them: "Do you see all these things? In truth I tell you, not one stone will be left here upon another, all of them will be thrown down." 3 As he was sitting on the Mount of Olives, his disciples came to him privately and said: "Tell us, when will these things be, and what will be the sign of your coming and the end of the age?"

4 Jesus answered them: "Watch out that no one deceives you. 5 For many will come in my name, saying, 'I am the Christ,' and they will deceive many. 6 You are about to hear of wars and rumors of wars; pay attention so you will not be alarmed. Such things must happen, but it is not yet the end. 7 Nation will rise against nation, and kingdom against kingdom. There will be famines and earthquakes in various places. 8 All these are the beginning of sorrows.

9 Then they will hand you over for persecution and they will kill you, and you will be hated by all the pagan nations because of my name. 10 Then many will be caused to stumble [away from the faith] and they will betray one another and hate one another. 11 Many false prophets will be raised up and deceive many. 12 Because of the increase of wickedness, the love of many will grow cold. 13 The one who stands firm to the end will be saved. 14 And this gospel of the kingdom will be proclaimed in the whole world as a testimony to all the nations, and then the end will come." (Matthew 24:1-13)

Reflecting and Thinking

This chapter and the next are the fifth and final great discourse (teaching section) in Matthew's Gospel. Life lived in the kingdom is a life of expectant sojourning. The kingdom in the here and now points to a future reality -- the kingdom in the "there and then." In this chapter, Jesus speaks of "the end." As he describes his future coming, he actually speaks of several "comings" and several "endings." We can clearly see references to the end referring to the destruction of the temple structure and the end of the age. We read of the end of Judaism; we read about the end of the world. Many have studied and written about the meaning of this chapter and it is beyond the few words available here to provide a complete explanation. Suffice it to say in this devotional reflection that many of the events described were immediate and would occur in the lifetime of those who heard Jesus. Other events were more distant, and their timing was unknown.

The truth is even clearer when the two chapters are taken as a single discourse. In the kingdom, life is to be lived knowing that the end will come. No need to buy, renting is sufficient, because this world is not the ultimate goal. In this physical realm, we are not eternal. Nothing here is eternal, for the earth is temporal (time-limited or constrained). Only the spiritual being housed in the physical body is eternal. Life here will not be easy; difficulties and challenges will come, false teachers and distressing days. Nations rise and fall, but God controls.

Do you live with the end in view? How would you need to change your life to be able to say that you live knowing that the end is coming? What goals of your church would you describe as worldly? Are goals focused in this world valid? Why or why not? Think of some examples of spiritual goals the church could adopt. What are valid goals for your life, keeping in mind that the end is coming? What is the ideal version of your life given the truths presented in this chapter?

Prayer

Dear God, help me live with the end in view. Give me the strength to endure the challenges of this life as I journey toward the ultimate kingdom goal, in Jesus' name, Amen.

Matthew 25: The King is Coming -- Use Your Opportunities

Selected Biblical Text

1 "At that time kingdom of heaven will be like ten virgins who took their lamps and went out to meet the bridegroom. 2 Five of the virgins were foolish and five were wise. 3 Now the foolish ones took their lamps but did not take enough lamp oil with them. 4 The wise ones took lamp oil in jars along with their lamps. 5 When

the bridegroom was delayed, they all became drowsy and fell asleep. 6 At midnight the shout came: 'Behold! the bridegroom is here! Come out to meet him!' 7 Then all those virgins got up and trimmed their lamps. 8 The foolish ones said to the wise, 'Give us some of your oil; our lamps are going out.' 9 But the wise ones replied, 'No, lest there not be enough for us and for you. Instead, go to those selling lamp oil and buy for yourselves.' 10 But as they were going to buy lamp oil for themselves, the bridegroom arrived. The virgins who were ready entered with him into the wedding, and the door was shut. 11 Later the rest of the virgins came saying, 'Lord, Lord, open for us!' 12 But he replied, 'In truth I tell you, I do not know you.' 13 Therefore keep watch, because you do not know the day or the hour." (Matthew 25:1-13)

Reflecting and Thinking

This chapter is part of the fifth discourse (Chapters 24-25). (Some people believe we should limit the fifth discourse to Chapter 25.) There are three generally well-known sections: the parable of the ten virgins (today's selected text), the parable of the talents, and the judgment scene where the sheep and goats are separated. The point of each of these stories is similar -- the bridegroom-owner-King is coming back so you should use the opportunities of today well. To take advantage of the opportunities of the present is to be prepared for the return of the King.

Perhaps one of the biggest problems with opportunities is that they go unrecognized. Some opportunities do not look much like opportunities. They sometimes come in disguise; they sometimes look unimportant or useless. Because we think there will be other opportunities, we miss the urgency of the moment. The three narratives of this chapter bring into focus all of these human tendencies and more. What spiritual opportunities have you missed in the past? Will you resolve today to look for opportunities and take full advantage of them?

Prayer

Dear God, give me today sensitivity to the opportunities and the open doors you provide. Help me see the potential of those moments so that I can respond in the spirit and love of Jesus. Help me discern the times so that I will be prepared, having used the resources you gave. Help me accomplish the will of Jesus my King, I pray in his name, Amen.

Matthew 26: Covenant Forgiveness and the Kingdom

Selected Biblical Text

20 When it was evening, Jesus was reclining at the table with the Twelve. 21 And while they were eating, he said: "In truth I tell you, one of you will betray me." 22 They were very sorrowful and began to say to him one by one: "Surely not I, Lord?"

23 He replied: "The one who has dipped his hand into the bowl with me will betray me. 24 The Son of Man will go as it is written about him. Woe to that man by whom the Son of Man is betrayed! It would be better for him if he had not been born." 25 Then Judas, the one who would betray him, answered: "Surely not I, Rabbi?" Jesus said: "You yourself said it."
26 While they were eating, Jesus, taking bread and giving thanks, broke it, gave it to his disciples, and said: "Take, eat; this is my body." 27 Taking the cup and giving thanks, he gave it to them, saying: "Drink from it, all of you, 28 for this is my blood of the covenant, which for many is poured out for the forgiveness of sins. 29 I tell you: 'From now on, I will not drink from this fruit of the vine until that day when I drink it new with you in the kingdom of my Father.'" (Matthew 26:20-29)

Reflecting and Thinking

Jesus the Messiah came to die -- this is Matthew's summary of the second half of Jesus' ministry. In his death and the shedding of his blood, Jesus established a covenant of forgiveness. The covenant, established by blood, is "for the forgiveness" of sins. This is an interesting phrase; its meaning has been much discussed. The same phrase appears in Acts 2:38 where some say it means "because of the forgiveness" of sins. The phrase occurs three other times in the New Testament (see Mark 1:4; Luke 3:3; 24:47). A reading of the other passages where the phrase occurs suggests that forgiveness is the result, not a preexisting condition. Certainly, Jesus did not shed his blood because sins had already been forgiven.

The New Testament covenant, established by the shedding of Jesus' blood, is the basis of God's forgiveness of sins. This covenant and the sacrifice that established it were remembered weekly by the early church in the Lord's Supper. Only those in the covenant can experience covenant benefits. One can also describe this as the kingdom covenant, for it is the basis of Jesus' kingdom. Appropriating the saving blood of Jesus in our lives provides forgiveness; it also ushers us into the kingdom of the King.

To what extent have you previously connected forgiveness and the covenant in your study and thinking? In your previous Bible studies, have you connected forgiveness and Jesus' blood? Have you studied the connection between the covenant and the Lord's Supper in the early church? (In your study of the passages mentioned above including today's selected text, consider whether these teachings point toward a future forgiveness or a past forgiveness already accomplished.)

Prayer

Dear God, we are grateful today for forgiveness through the blood that Jesus shed in his death on the cross. We find the extent of his suffering on our behalf virtually incomprehensible. We hardly grasp it, even when we consider it deeply and soberly. Thank you for providing what we could not provide for ourselves. Thank you for loving us. We pray in Jesus' name, Amen.

Matthew 27: The Son of God -- Crucified

Selected Biblical Text

50 Then Jesus crying out again in a loud voice, gave up his spirit. 51 At once the curtain of the temple was torn in two from top to bottom. The earth shook, the rocks split 52 and the tombs were opened. The bodies of many holy people who had died were raised. 53 (When they came out of the tombs after Jesus' resurrection, they went into the holy city and appeared to many.) 54 When the centurion and those with him who were guarding Jesus saw the earthquake and all that happened, they were extremely terrified, and exclaimed: "Truly this one was the Son of God." (Matthew 27:50-54)

Reflecting and Thinking

The events of Jesus' final hours (Chapters 26-27) tell a story of deceit and suffering -- Gethsemane, the betrayal by Judas, Jesus' arrest, the trial before the Sanhedrin, the denial by Peter, the appearance before Pilate, mocking, crucifixion, and death. With a loud voice, Jesus died. The events that the text describes in the next three verses (27:51-53) provide evidence of heaven's disgust and power. The testimony of the centurion and those with him in verse 54 -- another statement of Jesus' identity -- is an unmistakable witness: "Surely he was the Son of God!"

Jesus was the Son of God! The cross is the story of the Son of God crucified. Jesus came dying so that we might live. He came dying so that we might be forgiven. How does this make you feel? How would you respond to such love? What impact does this story have on your faith?

Prayer

Father God, we hardly comprehend your all-surpassing love. We hear the story again and again, we seek to engrave it firmly in our minds, but some aspects of it continually escape us. Help us see more clearly, help us believe and be changed. In Jesus' name and by his power we pray, Amen.

Matthew 28: Resurrected with All Authority -- Go Share the News

Selected Biblical Text

8 So the women left the tomb quickly, with fear and great joy, and ran to tell his disciples. 9 At once Jesus met them and said: "Greetings." They came to him, took hold of his feet, and worshiped him. 10 Then Jesus said to them: "Do not be afraid. Go and tell my brothers to go to Galilee; there they will see me."
16 So the eleven disciples went to Galilee, to the mountain which Jesus had appointed. 17 When they saw him, they worshiped him; but some of them doubted.

18 Then Jesus came to them and said: "All authority in heaven and on earth has been given to me. 19 Therefore, as you are going forth, make disciples of all nations, baptizing them in the name of the Father and of the Son and of the Holy Spirit, 20 teaching them to obey everything which I commanded you. Remember: I am with you always, to the end of the age." (Matthew 28:8-10, 16-20)

Reflecting and Thinking

The good news is so good that it is unbelievable! Who would have thought it? Can it really be true? The first messengers of the resurrection are a small handful of women. They share the good news, the disciples believe, and in Galilee the eleven receive instructions which the church honors even until this day.

Go share the news! As you are going, wherever you go from day to day in your life, identify and teach others about discipleship, baptizing them, and teaching them obedience to the commandments of the King. In this task, Jesus remains present with his church. The resurrected King has all authority -- he is our power and our guide. He is our authority and our example.

We have finished our journey through Matthew. Matthew leaves no doubt about Jesus' identity. This book of Matthew, probably written in the last quarter of the first century, possibly to the Jewish community in Antioch, declares again and again the identity of Jesus. We can be fully assured of the truth. With this confidence, we go forth to proclaim the gospel. How would you rate the church's efforts in sharing the gospel today? Is the church doing poorly, less than desired, average, pretty good, or great? If you answered that the effort is average or below, how could the church become a more effective witness? (Remember to pray for the harvest and for workers.)

Prayer

Dear God, we want to tell the good news of Jesus more effectively and more powerfully. Help us know with confidence Jesus' presence in our lives as we accept this commission. Help us avoid distractions and doubt. May the gospel make a difference in our lives so that we can share it and make a difference in the lives of others. Again, we pray in Jesus' name, Amen.

James 1: The Testing of Faith

Selected Biblical Text

2 Count it a real joy, my brothers, whenever you fall into various kinds of trials, 3 because you know that the testing of your faith produces endurance. 4 Let endurance do its work completely so that you may be complete and whole, not lacking anything. 5 If anyone among you lacks wisdom, let that person ask God who gives generously to all without reproach, and it will be given to him. 6 But let him ask in faith, not at all doubting, because the one who doubts is like a wave of the sea, blown and tossed by the wind. 7 So that person should not expect to receive anything from the Lord, 8 a double-minded person, unstable in all his ways. 9 Let the poor brother take pride when he is raised up, 10 but the rich person in being humble, since he will pass away like a flower of the grass. 11 For the sun rises with its heat and withers the grass; its blossom drops, and it loses its beauty. In the same way also, the rich person in his daily pursuits will fade away.
12 Blessed is the one who endures a trial, because after being tested, that person will receive the crown of life that God promised to those who love him. (James 1:2-12)

Reflecting and Thinking

Considering the goal of this devotional series -- to reflect the content of each chapter of the New Testament and its overall contribution to the message of Scripture -- the little book of James presents unique difficulties. James has characteristics much like the literary genre of wisdom literature and treats many different themes. Some have referred to it as a New Testament version of Proverbs. It is difficult to find a single overarching message in each chapter.

An important theme in James 1 is what to do when trials come and faith is tested. Faith is tested in many ways. Among the topics James 1 connects to the testing of faith are trials of various kinds, doubt, poverty and riches, temptation, anger, evil, forgetfulness, lack of action, and speech. James says that the testing of faith builds the kind of perseverance and endurance necessary to receive the crown of life.

Perhaps no question is more important than the question of faith. Are we people of faith? Do we have faith? Do we have the right kind of faith?

When has your faith been tested? How did you respond? Did it make you stronger or weaker? How can both poverty and riches test faith (1:9-11)? Is the testing of our faith always obvious? What are some examples of times when the testing of our faith may not be obvious?

Prayer

Father God, we want to be people of great faith. When the situations of life test our faith, we want to grow and overcome. Teach us your ways. Strengthen us in the face of temptation. Provide that which we need to escape. In Jesus' name and by his power I ask it, Amen.

James 2: The Results of Faith

Selected Biblical Text

14 What profit is it, my brothers, if someone claims to have faith but has no works? Such faith cannot save him, can it? 15 If a brother or a sister is without clothing and daily food, 16 and if anyone of you says to them: "Go in peace; be warmed and be filled," but you do not give them physical necessities, what profit is it? 17 In the same way, faith by itself, if it does not accompany works, is dead.

18 But someone will say: "You have faith; I have works. Show me your faith without works, and I will show you my faith by my works." 19 You believe that God is one. You do well. Even the demons believe and shudder.

20 Do you want evidence, you empty person, that faith without works is useless? 21 Was not our father Abraham justified by works when he offered his son Isaac on the altar? 22 You see that his faith was working together with his works, and his faith was made perfect by his works. 23 And the scripture was fulfilled that says: "And Abraham believed God, and it was credited to him for righteousness, and he was called a friend of God." 24 You see that a person is justified by works and not by faith alone. (James 2:14-24)

Reflecting and Thinking

Some days we wonder if we really have faith. Sometimes when trials and difficulties come, our faith appears so weak that we wonder if it exists. James says that faith has certain results. These results help us see and measure our faith. James uses the phrase "rich in faith" (2:6).

Holding the faith of Christ correctly avoids favoritism. Faith is the foundation of love for neighbor. In today's reading, faith is coupled always with action. Real faith is active. Inactive "belief" hardly qualifies as biblical faith (2:19). Faith is more than mere belief. To believe in the existence of God is not faith. Faith acts on what it believes. In today's chapter, Abraham is James's example of active faith. Faith and action combine to complete or perfect faith.

As you think about your life, on a scale of 1 to 10, how active is your faith? According to today's biblical text, what kinds of activities reflect faith in Jesus? According to the general message of the Christian church today, what activities reflect faith in Jesus? What could you do today to demonstrate your faith? What would keep you from doing it?

Prayer

Dear God, increase our faith. Show us the things we can do to reflect our faith. Help us take our faith from a mental exercise to spiritual applications in the pathways of our lives. Help us live out our faith. We admit that we are weak and often incapable in this area, and we ask your blessing and help, in Jesus' name, Amen.

James 3: Wisdom and the Tongue

Selected Biblical Text

9 With the tongue we bless the Lord and Father and with it we curse human beings who have been made in God's image. 10 From the same mouth come out blessing and cursing. These things should not be, my brothers. 11 Does the spring, from the same opening, pour out the fresh and the bitter water? 12 My brothers and sisters, can a fig tree produce olives or a vine produce figs? Neither can a salt spring produce fresh water.

13 Who is wise and understanding among you? Let him show, by good conduct, his works done with gentleness that comes from wisdom. 14 But if you have bitter jealousy and selfishness in your hearts, do not boast about it and tell lies against the truth. 15 This wisdom does not come down from above but is earthly, carnal, demonic. 16 For where there is jealousy and selfishness, there is disorder and every evil practice.

17 But the wisdom that comes from above is first of all pure; then peaceable, gentle, easily persuaded, full of mercy and good fruit, impartial and unhypocritical. 18 The fruit of righteousness is planted in peace by those who make peace. (James 3:9-17)

Reflecting and Thinking

In this middle chapter of the book, we find two related concepts -- the tongue and wisdom. (The middle chapter of the book may reveal the primary focus and message of James, considering the possibility of a chiastic structure for the book.) There are two ways to use the tongue; there are two kinds of wisdom. Both the tongue and wisdom are powerful beyond what is at first apparent. The two concepts are related -- the tongue reveals whether the wisdom that guides our life is earthly or heavenly. There is a wisdom that is informed by the principles of this world, but it ultimately comes to nothing. Any advancement it brings is temporary. The wisdom from above may seem little capable of moving any cause forward, but its presence and practice reaps a great harvest of righteousness.

James suggests the tongue is a major part of hypocrisy -- what other factors play a part in our tendencies toward hypocrisy? The tongue is involved in many sins. Make a list of some of the sins that are related to the tongue. Which one of the sins you listed will you work on today?

What could you do to cultivate God's wisdom in your life? Which characteristic of heavenly wisdom (wisdom from above) will you work on today?

[Note: The suggested exercises for today's reflection give you both positives and negatives to work on -- may God bless your efforts to apply your knowledge in your daily life.]

Prayer

Dear God, help us be both hearers and doers of your word. Help us as we strive today to avoid a negative related to the tongue and to build a positive related to heavenly wisdom. Make us this day peacemakers, ready to harvest. Help us use our tongue in positive ways to encourage others. We pray for your presence and power this day, in Jesus' name, Amen.

James 4: The Submission of Faith

Selected Biblical Text

7 Submit yourselves, then, to God. Resist the devil and he will flee from you. 8 Come near to God and he will come near to you. Wash your hands, you sinners, and purify your hearts, you double-minded. 9 Grieve and mourn and wail. Change your laughter into mourning and your joy into gloom. 10 Humble yourselves before the Lord, and he will lift you up.

11 Do not speak against one another, brothers. The one speaking against a brother or judging his brother speaks against the law and judges the law. When you judge the law, you are not a doer of the law but a judge. 12 There is only one Lawgiver and Judge, the one who is able to save and destroy. So, who are you to judge your neighbor? (James 4:7-12)

Reflecting and Thinking

Faith can be tested because faith yields results. Faith is reflected in how we use our tongue and how we develop and live out the wisdom from above. Even though the word "faith" is not used in James 3, the connection is clear. Neither does the word "faith" appear in James 4, but James is giving instructions about how faith is lived out in our submission to God.

In the text (4:7-10) is a series of imperatives (command forms): submit, resist, draw near, wash, purify, grieve, mourn, wail, change, and humble yourselves. These may appear in a 2-3-3-2 pattern. If so, (1) submit and resist are a set; (2) draw near, wash, and purify belong together; (3) grieve, mourn and wail are connected; and (4) changing laughter to mourning and humbling self are a set. [The way these imperatives focus the message of this chapter is worthy of additional contemplation and thought.] The message may be outlined as instruction in dependence, response, repentance, and self-renunciation.

The rest of the chapter makes clear that faith submits. Faith seeks God's will and way before selfish pleasures and desires. Faith submits to the one Lawgiver and Judge. Faith does not run ahead but waits to understand God's will. Faith does not brag and boast.

In our culture of individual rights, how hard is it for the modern church to hear the message of submission? (Use a 1-10 scale to answer.)

Why is submission difficult for us in the 21st century? How are slander, gossip, and judging related to a lack of submission? Our difficulty in submitting to God (his will, way, and word) is reflected in our difficulty in submitting to one another. People who will not submit to God will not submit to others. Think through some of the ways these two ideas connect.

Prayer

Heavenly Father, help us develop the submissive spirit of Jesus, reflecting his servant heart and his love for people. Help us understand your way; help us be your friends. Teach us dependence and penitent response as we seek your face and humbly submit ourselves to you. In the name of Jesus, Amen.

James 5: The Triumph of Faith

Selected Biblical Text

13 Anyone among you who is suffering, let him pray. Anyone of good cheer, let him sing praises. 14 Anyone who is weak among you, let him call the elders of the church and let them pray over him, anointing him with oil in the name of the Lord. 15 And the prayer of faith will save the weakened person and the Lord will raise him up. And if he has committed sins, they will be forgiven to him. 16 So confess sins to one another and pray for one another so you may be healed.
The prayer of a righteous person works with much force. 17 Elijah was a human being just as we are, and he prayed earnestly that it would not rain, and it did not rain on the land for three and a half years. 18 Again he prayed, and the heavens gave rain, and the land brought forth its fruit.
19 My brothers, if anyone of you wanders from the truth and someone turns him around, 20 know this: the one who turns around a sinner from the error of his way will save him from death and cover a multitude of sins. (James 5:13-20)

Reflecting and Thinking

Faith comes full circle. Faith when it is tested becomes stronger and more visible. Faith in our lives influences how we act and what we do. Because faith seeks God's wisdom, faith readily submits to God. The climactic, resounding result is that faith triumphs. Yes, ours is a world of oppression and injustice. Yes, suffering is ever-present, and patience is difficult. Such has it been from the beginning.

Faith that is activated by prayer and based on God's authority and God's purpose will ultimately triumph. Have no doubt! Prayer is powerful because God is powerful. Prayer does not depend on us -- even on our righteousness. Prayers offered in faith, even by the frailest of human beings, when coupled with God's power, bring about the most astounding results—

joy in the midst of trouble, healing, forgiveness, and salvation. What greater victory can we want?

Why is it so hard for us to believe that faith will ultimately triumph? Have you ever given up on praying? What caused you to stop? If you have resumed praying, what caused you to begin again? What do verses 19-20 say about the importance of our efforts and prayers on behalf of those who have wandered away from the Lord?

Prayer

Heavenly Father, teach us to pray. Teach us the ultimate triumph of faith. Strengthen our faith, help us develop more patience and perseverance. Today we pray for those who are on our hearts (make your own list), and we ask you to hear our prayers, through Jesus we pray, Amen.

Hebrews 1: Getting a Clear View of Jesus -- Son of God

Selected Biblical Text

1 After God spoke in various parts and various ways in the past to our ancestors through the prophets, 2 in these last days he has spoken to us by a son, whom he appointed heir of all things, and through whom also he made the universe. 3 This one, being the radiance of God's glory and the exact representation of his essence, sustaining all things by his powerful word, having made purification for sins, sat down at the right hand of the Majesty on high. 4 By becoming much better than the angels, he has inherited a name surpassingly better than theirs. (Hebrews 1:1-4)

Reflecting and Thinking

When a believer walks away from practicing the faith, most often that person, little by little, also walks away from Jesus. When a Christian is tempted to give up on Jesus, the first line of defense is to make certain that Jesus' identity is clearly understood. The text makes seven affirmations about Jesus. The chapter concludes with seven Old Testament citations supporting the supremacy and superiority of Jesus over the angels. Jesus is without equal. Before him, there had never been one like him, nor should we expect one like him to appear in the future.

As Son of God, Jesus is heir, creator, glory of God, exact essence, sustainer, purifier, and the one who reigns. Take a moment to reflect upon the significance of each of these descriptions. Each of them has implications for our lives.

In-depth study: find the seven Old Testament citations in Hebrews 1 and look them up in your Bible, read them, and use them to reflect upon the uniqueness of Jesus.

Prayer

Father God, you know that some days we struggle with our faith. Some days, it is hard to focus on Jesus and it is hard to keep Jesus in focus. Some days he seems all but absent. Help us today to see and appreciate the beauty of your plan for us, the glory of the gift of your Son, and the potential of his power at work with us. In Jesus' name and by his power I ask it, Amen.

Hebrews 2: Jesus -- Son of Man

Selected Biblical Text

14 Therefore, since the children share flesh and blood, he also shared in their humanity so that by his death he might destroy the one who holds the power of death, that is, the devil, 15 and set free those who by the fear of death throughout

all their lives were held in slavery. 16 For surely it is not angels he helps, but he helps Abraham's descendants. 17 Wherefore, he had to be made like his brothers in every way, so he could become a merciful and faithful high priest in the things of God, to make atonement for the sins of the people. 18 And in what he himself suffered when he was tempted, he is able to help those who are being tempted. (Hebrews 2:14-18)

Reflecting and Thinking

I found it difficult to select a text from this chapter. Every section is pertinent and powerful. In today's devotional time, I urge you to take time to read the entire chapter carefully and slowly. Here is a brief summary to help you read with understanding. God gave to his human creation a unique position. Jesus came and participated in the human experience; he experienced suffering and death to bring human beings to glory. This truth makes Jesus a part of the human family, exalting and protecting and delivering us. We are mere mortals who participate in flesh and blood. The conclusion of the first two chapters -- Jesus as one sharing God's nature, and Jesus as one sharing human nature -- is that Jesus has become a merciful and faithful high priest, making atonement for sins, and helping and ministering to those who are tempted.

How do you explain the significance of the dual nature of Jesus? Why is it important? If he is "merciful" high priest as a result of his participation in and understanding of the human dilemma, what does that mean to you as you live life each day? Since he is "faithful" high priest as a result of being God's Son, how important is it to you to know that you have this kind of faithful high priest?

Prayer

Dearest Heavenly Father, we stand in awe and amazement at the beauty and wisdom of your eternal plan. We are amazed because in Jesus you anticipated our every need -- for atonement and forgiveness, and for help and support and encouragement in the temptations of this life. Thank you that Jesus provides both in an amazing evidence of your divine wisdom and plan. Thank you that we can come before you in His name, Amen.

Hebrews 3: A Faithful High Priest

Selected Biblical Text

1 Therefore, holy brothers, sharers in a heavenly calling, carefully consider Jesus, the apostle and high priest of our confession, 2 who is faithful to the one who appointed him, as Moses was also in his [God's] house. 3 Jesus has been counted worthy of greater glory than Moses, just as the builder of a house has greater honor

than the house itself. 4 For every house is built by someone, but the builder of all things is God. 5 Now Moses was faithful as a servant in all God's house, as a testimony to the things that would be spoken. 6 But Christ is faithful as a son over God's house, whose house we are if indeed we hold firmly to our confidence and the glory of our hope. (Hebrews 3:1-6)

Reflecting and Thinking

The high priest in Judaism functioned as a bridge or go-between, linking God and human beings. The writer of Hebrews will soon point out that the difficulty in this plan was not the ability or inability of the high priest to identify with the people, but was that the high priest had to offer sacrifices for his own sins before he could enter God's presence on behalf of the people. Jesus can be our faithful high priest because he is God's Son. As a Son, he is greater than the servants in God's house. Lest the reader doubt the frailty and inability of the former system, the writer reminds the readers that Moses' leadership in the wilderness resulted in rebellion, unbelieving hearts, disobedience, and departure from God. Those who rebelled were those Moses had led out of Egypt. The only antidote to the human dilemma is to share Christ, maintaining a firm hold on confidence, courage, and hope.

Why did the people in the wilderness turn away from God? Where was the flaw or fault? Was it with God, Moses, or their hearts? Based on today's text, why do Christians today turn away from God? How do you react to the suggestion that the problem is failure to fix one's thoughts firmly on Jesus as the one sent to serve as our high priest? How confident can we be in our relationship with God under the high priesthood of Jesus? Are the writer's admonitions to courage and hope just empty words, or is he reflecting something we need to learn? Write down three great lessons you want to remember from today's devotional reading.

Prayer

Dear God, thank you for sending Jesus as your presence and representative, as your son and our high priest. Help us grow in faith and obedience. Rescue us when we are tempted to swerve away from our hope and calling. Help us keep our thoughts fixed on Jesus, even as we pray in his name, Amen.

Hebrews 4: A Merciful High Priest

Selected Biblical Text

14 Having then a great high priest who has passed through the heavens, Jesus the Son of God, let us hold fast to our confession. 15 For we do not have a high priest who is not able to sympathize with our weaknesses, but one who has been

tempted in every way, just as we are, yet without sin. 16 Let us then with boldness approach the throne of grace, so that we may receive mercy and find grace to help us in any time of need. (Hebrews 4:14-16)

Reflecting and Thinking

A word of warning as we begin today -- let us be careful not to miss the point because of the complexity of the writer's train of thought. The chapter begins with lots of details -- the unfulfilled promise of rest, the importance of hearing the gospel by faith, the problem of disobedience. Against this background, we usually read the text of 4:12-13 as a threat -- God knows everything about us, the word of God lays bare and judges our thoughts, nothing is hidden from God, and everyone must give an account. In the context, however, one must at least consider the possibility that the words of 4:12-13 are designed to give comfort. In the challenges of this life, with the incredible promise of God as the source of our hope, should we not be grateful that God understands our hearts? Should we not be grateful that he is aware of our weaknesses and has nonetheless provided us confident access to the throne of grace where we find strength and help just when we need it most?

Our need is for both a faithful high priest who in fulfilling his priestly responsibilities on our behalf provides for us atonement, and for a merciful high priest who understands our sin dilemma, our weaknesses, our temptations, and our need for grace, mercy, and support. Summarizing the book of Hebrews to this point, we have learned that in Jesus Christ, we have exactly what we need. He provides us access to God because he is Son of God (chapter 1), but he also identifies with God's human creation as Son of Man (chapter 2). This uniquely qualifies him as faithful high priest (Chapter 3) and merciful high priest (Chapter 4). As you think today about the beauty of God's plan, take a few moments to contemplate these two unique aspects of Christ's nature, and think about how he understands us and has access to God to intercede for us.

Prayer

Heavenly Father, we cannot but marvel at the wisdom and beauty of your plan for us as frail human creation. Most days, we desperately feel the separation and distance in our human experience, and we are grateful for the promise that Jesus walks beside us, understands our needs, is able to nourish us, and provides prayer access to your throne of grace and forgiveness. Thank you for hearing us today, in the name of Jesus who is the Christ, the one who explains everything, Amen.

Hebrews 5: Grow Up -- The Goal Is Maturity in Christ!

Selected Biblical Text

7 During the days of his life on earth, Christ, having offered up prayers and suppli-
cations with fervent cries and tears to the one who was able to save him from
death, was heard because of his reverent devotion. 8 Although he was a son, he
learned obedience from what he suffered, 9 and being made perfect, he became
the source of eternal salvation for all who obey him, 10 having been designated by
God as high priest in the order of Melchizedek.

11 Concerning this we have much to say, but it is hard to explain because you have
become slow to hear. 12 for though you should be teachers by this time, you again
need someone to teach you the elementary truths of God's utterances, so you have
come back to needing milk not solid food. 13 For everyone who lives on milk is
unskilled in the message of righteousness, because such a person is an infant. 14
But solid food is for the mature, for those who by constant practice have their per-
ceptions trained to distinguish good and evil. (Hebrews 5:7-14)

Reflecting and Thinking

Chapter 5 does two things to advance the argument of the writer.
First, the summary of Jesus' high priesthood (5:1-10) foreshadows what is
to come in Chapters 7-9. Perhaps a brief preview will help orient us. The
Hebrew writer will make three points in Chapters 7-9. In Chapter 7, he will
explain how Jesus is a different kind of priest, not in the Levitical order but
in the order of Melchizedek. In Chapter 8, he will claim that this is the only
source of eternal salvation. In Chapter 9, he will point out that this perfect
system addresses the weaknesses of the former system. These points are
clearly in view in 5:9-10, but in reverse order.

Second, the admonition to "grow up" (5:11-14) introduces a
lengthy bridge which continues into Chapter 6, making clear that faithfulness is not dependent on human power, but on God's faithful and certain
promise. (The bridge or parenthesis can be easily seen by comparing 5:10
and 7:1.)

*Today, let us have confidence in God's divine plan and wisdom, and
let us focus on our response. Some things are hard to understand because
we are not mature thinkers in Christ. We see problems that do not exist in
God's mind and plan. We struggle with challenges that he has already conquered. We have doubts that he has taken out of the way. The simple
version of our challenge says, "Grow Up!" A longer version reminds us that
we are to be constant learners, sharers of truth, willing to bite into the solid
meat of Scripture, discerning hearers, and capable, discerning Christians because of our constant thinking and training in spiritual matters. The
opposites are telling. Too often we merely sample Bible truths from time to
time, seldom share our faith, go back to the same old truths and go over the
same material again and again, can hardly discern how to integrate newly*

discovered texts into our previous system of thinking, are less than constant in our study, and disinterested in training that equips us. What changes do you need to make in your life to continue to mature spiritually?

Prayer

Heavenly Father, we are glad you know our struggles. We admit that we at times resemble the description of today's text. Bring us closer to you today, through Jesus we offer this prayer, Amen.

Hebrews 6: Keep Growing

Selected Biblical Text

1 Therefore, leaving behind the elementary teaching of Christ, let us move forward to maturity, not laying again the foundation of repentance from dead works and faith in God, 2 teaching about baptisms, laying on of hands, resurrection of the dead, and eternal judgment. 3 And this we will do, if God allows.

19 We have this hope as an anchor for the soul, sure and steadfast, hope that reaches the interior sanctuary behind the curtain, 20 where our forerunner, Jesus, entered on our behalf, becoming a high priest forever in the order of Melchizedek. (Hebrews 6:1-3, 19-20)

Reflecting and Thinking

Most Christians start their Christian lives with high hopes. I have never known anyone who began by wondering when they could quit. Yet, quitting and falling away is an all too common experience among Christians. The writer does not doubt that some will fall away -- even of those who have known the truth, the gift of God, the presence of the Holy Spirit, and hope for the future. In fact, some will fall away with little or no hope of restoration. The point of today's chapter is that our faithful perseverance is a shared challenge -- certainly we work and love and are diligent with faith and patience. But the promise is secured not by our actions but by God's nature. Our hope is secure because of our high priest.

When have you felt insecure in your Christian life? What were you looking at in those times of insecurity? How much of your thinking was focused in the problems of life, and how much was focused on the hope and rescue God provides in Christ? On a scale of 1-10, how dependable do you think God is?

Prayer

Our heavenly Father God, thank you for doing for us what we could not do for ourselves. Thank you for providing a firm anchor of hope and certainty concerning your promise. Help us keep on growing every day, help us not regress, and help us depend on Jesus, not only for our salvation, but also for our strength in daily living. In the name of Jesus, who makes the invisible visible, Amen.

Hebrews 7: A Better Priest

Selected Biblical Text

18 On the one hand, it happens that a former command is set aside because of its weakness and inefficacy, 19 for the law made nothing perfect. On the other hand, a better hope is introduced through which we draw near to God.

20 And this was not without an oath. They became priests without an oath, 21 but he became a priest with an oath, by the one who said to him, The Lord has sworn and will not change his mind. You are a priest forever. 22 Because of this, Jesus has become the guarantee of a better covenant. 23 Now, on the one hand, those who have become priests are many, because they were prevented by death from continuing to serve; 24 but because Jesus remains forever, he has a permanent priesthood. 25 Thus is he able to save completely those who come to God through him, because he always lives to intercede for them. 26 Now such a high priest is fitting for us, holy, innocent, undefiled, set apart from sinners, exalted above the heavens. 27 He has no need every day to do as did the high priests, to offer sacrifices, first for their own sins and then for the sins of the people. This he did once for all when he offered himself. 28 For the law appoints as high priests men who have weakness; but the word of the oath, which came after the law, appointed a son who had been made perfect forever. (Hebrews 7:19-28)

Reflecting and Thinking

The selected text for today provides a good summary. Jesus was declared an eternal priest by God. The Old Testament quotation is from Psalm 110:4. The promise of Psalm 110 comes after the Old Testament law given in Exodus and therefore supersedes it. The result is a better covenant, complete salvation, and Jesus' intercession on our behalf. These are possible because Jesus serves as a high priest based on his sinless perfection, his perfect sacrifice, his strength, and his position as Son of God.

What kind of confidence ought we to have knowing that we have perfect and complete access to God's throne through Jesus our High Priest? What does it mean to your confidence that Jesus intercedes on your behalf?

46

Prayer

Dear God, today we come with renewed boldness, not because we are good, but because of your promise that Jesus intercedes for us, that when we come through him we come with sins forgiven, and that our access and relationship do not depend on our own perfection. Thank you again for this marvelous gift, in Jesus' name, Amen.

Hebrews 8: The Shadow Has Been Replaced by the Real

Selected Biblical Text

1 Now the main point of what we are saying is this: We have such a high priest, who sat down at the right hand of the throne of the Majesty in heaven, 2 a minister of the holies [who serves in the Holy of Holies, the inner sanctuary], the true tabernacle which the Lord, not a man, set up. 3 Now every high priest is appointed to offer both gifts and sacrifices, so it was necessary for this one also to have something to offer. 4 Now if he were on earth, he would not be a priest, since there are already those who offer the gifts required by the law. 5 They serve in a sanctuary that is a prototype and shadow of heavenly things, just as Moses had been divinely instructed when he was about to finish the tabernacle: See that you make everything according to the model shown you on the mountain. 6 And now the ministry Jesus has attained is superior, as much as also the covenant he mediates is better, which has been enacted on better promises. (Hebrews 8:1-6)

Reflecting and Thinking

The typology of Hebrews is not easy to understand -- one must take time to think it through. First, one must understand the words. The type is not the real thing; the real thing is the antitype. This seems backward to many people. Think about a typewriter or the now antiquated process of typesetting. The type is not the real thing -- the type is a reverse image which leaves a correct imprint (the real thing) when it touches the paper. The writer of Hebrews is saying that what we see here on earth is a copy or shadow (a type) of the real thing which is in heaven. The real throne of God was not in the earthly tabernacle, it is in heaven. The pattern given on Mount Sinai was based on the real thing in heaven. So it is also with Jesus' high priesthood, access to the heavenly throne, Jesus' ministry, Jesus' mediation, the new covenant, and the better promises. What we see here on earth is merely a reflection or copy of the real thing!

In view of this chapter, consider how easy it is to become satisfied with less than the real thing. What areas of your life can you think of where you have accepted something less than God's ultimate plan for you? Think of other applications of this principle in your own Christian life.

Prayer

Dearest heavenly Father, how incredible that we can come before your real throne in heaven as a result of Jesus' high priestly function! How incredible that we do not merely come to a physical location where you exist, but that we come into your very presence through Jesus. Help us to see what is real, and to celebrate the fact that most of what we see here is only a support system for this temporary world. Help us even in the here and now to understand better the beauty of the real thing. In the name of Jesus we pray, Amen.

Hebrews 9: A Better Sacrifice

Selected Biblical Text

23 So it was necessary, then, for the prototypes of the heavenly things to be purified with these sacrifices, but the heavenly things themselves with better sacrifices than these. 24 For Christ did not enter into the holies [that is, the Holy of Holies, or, the Most Holy Place] made with human hands, a figure [literally, antitype] of the true one; but into heaven itself, now to appear in the presence of God for us. 25 And he did not enter to offer himself again and again, as the high priest enters the holies [the Most Holy Place] every year with blood that is not his own. 26 For then Christ would have had to suffer again and again since the foundation of the world. But now he has appeared once for all at the completion of the ages to cancel sin by the sacrifice which he offered. 27 Just as people are appointed to die once, and after this will come judgment, 28 in the same way also Christ, having been offered once to bear the sins of many, will appear a second time to those who are waiting for him, not to bear sin but to bring salvation. (Hebrews 9:23-28)

Reflecting and Thinking

The contrast between the first covenant with its regulations and the second covenant in which Jesus enters the perfect heavenly tabernacle is like the contrast between daylight and dark. Everything has changed. Everything is better. Consciences are cleansed. The promise is secured. The ransom is consistent with the reward. The copies could be purified with merely physical sacrifices. Not so the real thing! Jesus has entered the very throne room of God, not to appear annually to deal with sin, but once and for all to do away with sin forever. He appears continually in God's presence FOR US. He came to this earth once to provide the eternal sin sacrifice; when he comes again it will be to claim those who eagerly await him. That is indeed good news!

How often do you think about the coming of Jesus with an attitude of eagerness? What obstacles are in your life that keep you from eager anticipation? Which ones can you begin to handle today? Which ones do you need to cast on God?

Prayer

Heavenly Father, the beauty of Jesus' better sacrifice is overwhelming. It shines so brightly that all else pales. How incredible to think that you have given us insight into your nature and throne in such physical representations. Help us not to value the copy more than the original. Give us insight to see and believe, to worship, and to act. We pray for your help, in Jesus' name, Amen.

Hebrews 10: Better Followers

Selected Biblical Text

19 Therefore, brothers, since we have confidence to enter the holies [the Most Holy Place] by the blood of Jesus, 20 [entering] by a new and living way that he inaugurated for us through the curtain, that is, through his flesh, 21 and since we have a great priest over the house of God, 22 let us draw near with a sincere heart, in full assurance of faith, our hearts having been sprinkled [to cleanse us] from a guilty conscience, and our bodies having been washed with pure water. 23 Let us hold unwaveringly to the hope we confess, for the one who promised is faithful. 24 And let us carefully consider one another to stimulate [each other] to love and good works, 25 not forsaking our own assembling, as is the custom of some, but encouraging one another all the more, as much as you see the day drawing near. (Hebrews 10:19-25)

Reflecting and Thinking

The first part of this chapter (10:1-18) concludes the argument of Chapters 7-9. Jesus' new and different priesthood, reflecting the heavenly realities and not the mere physical copies of this world, gives believers genuine access to God through the better sacrifice. Where genuine forgiveness exists, there is no need for a continuing sacrifice for sin. The most incredible part of the story begins to unfold in today's text. The better promises, ministry, and sacrifice lead to better followers. Jesus' followers are confident in their access to God, sincere in heart, assured in faith, cleansed and hopeful, not because of their own efforts but because the one who promised is faithful. The result is renewed fellowship, communion, shared meetings, and encouragement. The text describes two possibilities: those who "get it" and those who do not "get it."

Those who understand the significance of what Jesus has done per-severe. The promise is "not yet." Perseverance is essential to receive the promise. Some will shrink back and give up. This is no different than the wilderness experience described in Chapter 3. But that some would shrink back and give up after Jesus has come is incomprehensible! What specific encouragement do you find in this chapter to help you cope with dark days and difficult challenges?

Prayer

Thank you, Father, for the confidence you provide. May we today draw near to your throne with confidence and with cleansed, pure hearts. Thank you for doing what we most needed, so that we do not veer off course and lose sight of our hope. Help us to care for one another in the house of God, knowing that what we see here is a replica of the heavenly reality. In the name of Jesus our Savior, who opened our way to you through his blood, Amen.

Hebrews 11: Examples of Faithful Endurance

Selected Biblical Text

39 These were all commended for their faith, but they did not receive the promise. 40 God had planned something better pertaining to us, so that they would not be made perfect without us. (Hebrews 11:39-40)

Reflecting and Thinking

Today's reading is familiar and well known. Some call it the "Faith Chapter." Others refer to it as the "Hall of Faith." We celebrate the Old Testament examples of faith. The pattern becomes automatic, "by faith." Those who are mentioned could not see what is now visible. They did not receive what was promised. They led the way; they provide us examples of faith; they persevered despite the obstacles they faced -- obstacles that have now been overcome in Jesus. These Old Testament heroes are now a part of us; or better said, we are a part of them. We are sharing together the victory.

Can you imagine what it would have been like to have lived in diffi-cult times during the Old Testament? What does it mean for you to faithfully endure? How long does God want us to endure? What has God provided so that we can endure?

50

Prayer

Heavenly Father, we are amazed at the perseverance of those who lived by faith before Jesus came. We so much want to see; it is hard for us to imagine living faithfully when we cannot see. Help us grow in faith -- in our confidence in your existence, and in our confidence in your reward for diligent seekers. Thank you for Jesus, in His name we pray, Amen.

Hebrews 12: Reasons to Persevere

Selected Biblical Text

1 Therefore, having such a great cloud of witnesses surrounding us, and casting aside every weight and the sin that is all around us, let us run with endurance the race that lies before us, 2 keeping our eyes on Jesus, the pioneer and perfecter of faith, who because of the joy that was before him, endured the cross, disdaining its shame, and has sat down at the right hand of the throne of God. 3 Now think about the cost for the one who endured such opposition from sinners, so that you in your lives will not grow weary and give up. (Hebrews 12:1-3)

Reflecting and Thinking

This chapter, as many of the chapters in Hebrews, is too complex to summarize in a few verses. In the faith examples and the cloud of witnesses, and in the example of Jesus who exemplifies faith, joy and endurance, we find hope and rescue from weariness. God is working on our behalf. The blessings of the new covenant -- God's presence, renewed joy, confidence, the possibilities for holiness, and the certainty of God's grace (12:22-24) -- provide a stark contrast to the untouchable, dark mountain of the previous covenant.

Reread or scan this chapter looking for "reasons to persevere." How many can you find? How many of the reasons you list were not available or were not clearly in view under the first covenant? The chapter concludes with a confident assertion that the kingdom we are receiving is unshakeable, with admonitions to worship and be grateful.

Prayer

Dear God, thank you for putting us in an unshakeable kingdom, thank you for giving us so many reasons to persevere, thank you for working in our lives to meet our needs. Accept our joyful hearts as we are filled with worship and gratitude. In the name of the One who is the source and perfecter of our faith, Amen.

Hebrews 13: Pilgrim Calling

Selected Biblical Text

13 Then let us go to him outside the camp, bearing his disgrace. 14 For here we have no enduring city, but we are looking for the city that is to come. 15 Through Jesus, then, let us continually offer to God a sacrifice of praise, that is, the fruit of lips that confess his name. 16 And do not neglect doing good and sharing, for with such sacrifices God is pleased.

20 Now may the God of peace who by the blood of the eternal covenant brought back from the dead the great shepherd of the sheep, our Lord Jesus, 21 equip you with every good thing for doing his will, working in us what is pleasing before him, through Jesus Christ, to whom be glory forever. Amen. (Hebrews 13:13-16, 20-21)

Reflecting and Thinking

The admonition of verse 13 probably represents a final call to leave Judaism and return to Christ. For us today, it is a call to leave all that is comfortable so that we will follow Jesus regardless of the consequences. We are pilgrims in this world just as certainly as were those Old Testament heroes who were looking for the city to come. And even if we are not called to sacrifice our physical lives, we daily present ourselves to God as living sacrifices of praise, confession, good works, and unselfish sharing.

What God has done through the eternal covenant far surpasses the possibilities under the first covenant. The resurrection of Jesus is promise of our future. He equips us, works in us, protects us, and guides us. As we conclude the book of Hebrews today, take a moment to consider how God is at work in your life, and praise and thank him for those blessings.

Prayer

Heavenly Father, today we reflect upon your eternal goodness and reality, wanting to see beyond the challenges we face in this world. Teach us your ways and protect us as we journey toward our eternal home, in the name of our Lord Jesus, the great Shepherd, Amen.

Romans 1: The Gospel -- I Am Obligated, Eager, and Unashamed

Selected Biblical Text
14 I am a debtor both to Greeks and to barbarians, both to the wise and to the foolish. 15 So I am eager to preach the gospel also to you who are in Rome. 16 For I am not ashamed of the gospel, for it is the power of God for salvation to everyone who believes, to the Jew first and also to the Greek. 17 For in it the righteousness of God is revealed from faith to faith, as it is written: "The righteous one will live by faith." 18 For the wrath of God is revealed from heaven against all ungodliness and unrighteousness of people who by their unrighteousness suppress the truth. (Romans 1:14-18)

Reflecting and Thinking
The book of Romans is Paul's great salvation treatise. His description of Jesus in 1:1-6 is incredibly complete given its brevity. Paul's letters were personal and occasional (intended for a specific group of readers at a specific time for a specific situation). They contain both teaching (doctrine) and applications.

In today's text Paul makes three personal affirmations: I am debtor (obligated), I am eager (ready) to preach, I am not ashamed of the gospel. These affirmations were true for Paul because of what God had revealed to him. In the gospel God's righteousness is revealed, but God's wrath against sin is also visible. God's rescue and God's righteousness indignation are Paul's motivation. Paul will return to the theme of the revelation of God's righteousness in 3:20, but first comes a lengthy section concerning God's wrath. An awareness of God's wrath provides motivation for the Christian. Some want to gloss over the message of God's wrath, but Paul sets it forth plainly (the bad news) in order to show just how good, the good news of the gospel is.

The picture of evil painted in the last half of the first chapter is not pretty. Evil enters when God is not recognized. God can be seen, but some do not see him because they do not want to see him.

How does your attitude compare with Paul's? Do you feel obligated to share the gospel, eager or ready to share the gospel, unashamed of the gospel? Are you more motivated by God's wrath or God's righteousness? In your experience, what are the best motivations to encourage those in the world to consider the message of Jesus?

Prayer
Our Heavenly Father, we ask you to work in our hearts today. We want to see and understand more about Jesus, we want to find in the message of Jesus motivation for sharing the gospel, and we want to understand more fully the righteousness you attribute to those who imitate the faith of Jesus in faithful living. Help us see evil for the repulsive reality that it is. Instill in

us a greater desire to turn from evil and to walk in faithful obedience to the truth so that we might know your righteousness, In Jesus' name and by his power I ask it. Amen.

Romans 2: Repentance -- Because God is Good

Selected Biblical Text

4 Or do you take lightly the riches of his kindness, forbearance and patience, not knowing that God's kindness leads you to repentance? 5 But because of your hard and unrepentant heart you are storing up for yourself wrath on the day of wrath—the day of the revelation of God's righteous judgment. 6 He will reward each one according to his works: 7 eternal life to those who by patient endurance in good works seek glory and honor and immortality, 8 but wrath and anger to those who out of selfish ambition do not obey the truth but obey unrighteousness. 9 There will be affliction and distress on everyone who does evil, on the Jew first and also on the Greek, 10 but glory and honor and peace for everyone who does good, for the Jew first and also for the Greek. 11 For there is no partiality with God. 12 For all who have sinned without the law will also perish without the law, and all who have sinned under the law will be judged by the law. 13 For it is not the hearers of the law who are righteous before God, but the doers of the law who will be justified. 14 For when Gentiles, who do not have the law, by nature do the things of the law, these who do not have the law are a law to themselves. 15 They show that the work of the law is written on their hearts with their conscience bearing witness, and their reasonings between themselves either accuse or excuse them, 16 on the day when God judges the secrets of men by Christ Jesus according to my gospel. (Romans 2:4-16)

Reflecting and Thinking

The Good News is that God's gracious mercy and kindness can lead me to repentance. Why would I subject myself to God's wrath when rescue is possible? Law (any legal system) does not bring righteousness; the gospel brings righteousness. Even when I try to do what is right according to the best of my awareness and ability, my conscience still accuses me in my inadequacy and inability to follow through on what I know and want to do.

Some have seen in today's selected text the salvation of those outside of Christ. We must be careful lest we miss the meaning of the illustration. Even those who instinctively meet the requirements of any legal system are at times accused by their own thoughts and consciences. No one can be righteous enough to live by law; everyone needs the gospel. Righteousness will never come by law; for us to be righteousness in God's sight requires more than law.

How often are you inclined to try to live by perfect legal obedience rather than by God's gracious righteousness in the gospel? Why do people

*seek gospel AND law? How does the gospel exclude law? How does law ex-
clude the gospel? Can people who are a law to themselves live good enough
lives to never be accused by God? Explain the meaning of today's text in
your own words.*

Prayer
Dear God, help us to be careful, diligent students of your word. Help us to
see afresh and to escape our preconceived ideas. Thank you for showing us
your mercy in Christ. May we be motivated to repentance and changed lives
today and every day, in Jesus' name, Amen.

Romans 3: From Faith to Faith -- From Jesus' Faithfulness to Our Faith

Selected Biblical Text
21 But now without the law the righteousness of God has been manifested – being
attested to by the Law and the Prophets -- 22 the righteousness of God through
the faithfulness of Jesus Christ unto all who believe. For there is no distinction: 23
for all have sinned and fall short of the glory of God, 24 being justified freely by his
grace, through the redemption that is in Christ Jesus, 25 whom God purposed as a
propitiation [sacrifice] through faith by his blood, in order to show his righteousness in the passing over of previously committed sins 26 in his divine forbearance,
to show his righteousness at the present time, so that he might be just and the
justifier of everyone, by the faithfulness of Jesus. (Romans 3:21-26)

Reflecting and Thinking
After Paul describes the presence of evil in the lives of both unreli-
gious and religious people, he begins his description of God's righteousness
-- attested to and anticipated by the law but now revealed apart from the
law, through the faithfulness of Jesus unto those who imitate Jesus' faith.
This is the concept toward which Paul was pointing in Chapter 1 when he
spoke of the gospel as the revelation of God's righteousness "from faith to
faith."

Paul affirms the presence of sin in every life, demonstrating that all
need salvation. The modern reader may hear religious jargon in Paul's
words, but Paul is using familiar first-century illustrations from the legal system (justified), the slave system (redeemed), and the religious system
(atoned) to describe what God has done through Jesus. God's redeeming
work accomplished through the atoning blood of Jesus demonstrates God's
righteousness -- his commitment to deal with all sins in a way that is consistent with his gracious patience. Justification (righteousness) is God's gift
and action in the lives of those who have the faith of Jesus. Abraham will
provide a clear example -- but that's the story of the next chapter.

In what way did Jesus have "faith" toward God? What does it mean for us to participate in or imitate the "faith of Jesus?" Summarize the contrast Paul is making between law and gospel, between God's wrath and God's justification.

Prayer
Dear God, we want to be people of faith. We want to do more than pay lip service to the truths of your word. We want to live by faith. We want to experience changed lives and genuine freedom from sin. We want to walk in fellowship with you and to experience that fellowship personally. We are grateful for what you have done for us in Jesus, and for the privilege of approaching your throne in prayer through his name, Amen.

❖ ❖ ❖

Romans 4: The Promise Came by Faith

Selected Biblical Text
8 "...blessed is the one against whom the Lord will not charge sin to his account."
9 Then is this blessing only for the circumcised, or also for the uncircumcised? Now we say that faith was credited to Abraham as righteousness. 10 How then was it credited to him? Was he already circumcised, or was he uncircumcised? He was not circumcised, but uncircumcised. 11 He received the sign of circumcision as a seal of the righteousness that he had by faith while he was still uncircumcised, so he would become the father of all who believe but are not circumcised, so that righteousness would be credited to them as well. 12 And the father of the circumcised, who are not merely circumcised, but who also walk in the footsteps of the faith that our father Abraham had when he was still uncircumcised. 13 For the promise to Abraham or his descendants that he would be heir of the world was not through the law but through the righteousness of faith. 14 For if they are heirs through the law, faith has been invalidated and the promise is nullified. 15 For the law brings wrath, and where there is no law neither is there transgression. 16 That is why it is "from" faith, in order to be according to grace, so that promise may be guaranteed to all the descendants, not to the one "from" the law only but also to the one "from" the faith of Abraham, who is the father of us all... (Romans 4:8-16)

Reflecting and Thinking
A great contribution of Paul in Romans is his explanation of the primacy of the promise -- why and how the promise precedes and overrides the Old Testament law which was always intended to be temporary. The law does did not negate the promise; the law is part of God's plan to make the promise available to people who could never deserve God's grace. God does this by declaring that unrighteous people are righteous. This is no flippant or capricious declaration. It is based on God's work in the gospel (3:20-31)

and the faithful response of those who participate in the faith of Jesus (3:26), those who share the faith of Abraham.

That God's gift is based on God's promise does not undo the necessity of response -- promise produces response. The promise, delivered before the law and apart from the law, is an exhibition of grace extended to all of Abraham's spiritual descendants, that is, to all who share faith.

What is God's promise to us? In what way do we participate in God's promise to Abraham? Consider the implications of the statement: grace extends a blessing that can never be deserved or earned. How does this chapter support that statement? Why do some Christians try to earn God's grace? Why do some think grace implies universalism? Why do some believe that grace cannot be received conditionally, that is, that grace extended based on conditions is not really grace? Try to describe the biblical concepts mentioned in this paragraph by using biblical terms and words.

Prayer

Heavenly Father, we praise you this day for your wisdom. We marvel that your love extended grace to the human race when all were sinners and none deserved it. Help us appreciate and live in the grace of the promise. Increase our faith, in the name of the Christ, Amen.

Romans 5: Justified by Faith....Much More!

Selected Biblical Text

1 Therefore, because we have been justified by faith, we have peace with God through our Lord Jesus Christ, 2 through whom we have also obtained access by faith into this grace in which we stand, and we rejoice in the hope of the glory of God. 3 Not only that, but we also rejoice in our sufferings, knowing that suffering produces endurance, 4 and endurance produces character, and character produces hope, 5 and hope does not disillusion, because the love of God has been poured into our hearts through the Holy Spirit who was given to us. 6 For while we were still weak, at the right time Christ died for the ungodly. 7 One would hardly die for a righteous person, but possibly for a good person one would dare to die, 8 but God demonstrates his love for us in that while we were still sinners, Christ died for us. 9 Much more then, having now been justified by his blood, we will be saved by him from the wrath of God. 10 For if while we were enemies we were reconciled to God by the death of his Son, much more, having been reconciled, we will be saved by his life. 11 Not only that, but we also rejoice in God through our Lord Jesus Christ, through whom we have now received reconciliation. (Romans 5:1-11)

Reflecting and Thinking

The great introductory chapters of Romans demand to be read as a unit. They should not be separated, and we do some disservice to them by dividing them for daily devotional reading. Consider this summary. God's action in the gospel of grace has brought wrath to some and righteousness to others. All deserved wrath; but God intervened in Christ to provide justification (righteousness), redemption, and atonement through the faith of Christ. This righteousness did not depend on law and was declared (made known) apart from the law. It was based on the grace extended in the promise, and thus extends to all of Abraham's faithful descendants.

With these things in mind, Paul turns to the confidence that is possible through justification by faith. Faith brings peace, access, confident hope, and God's love. God's action in the gospel -- the death and life (resurrection) of Jesus -- saves from wrath. Whatever may be the circumstances apart from the gospel, the gospel answers every situation. Not only does it answer -- it answers, "much more!"

Make a list of the blessings mentioned in today's text, the blessings that are available to the Christian based on justification by faith.

In depth: If you wish to study the remainder of the chapter in detail, take a piece of paper and record the contrasts and comparisons. You should be able to find at least seven. Hint: some of the comparisons are negative, two things are unlike rather than alike.

Prayer

Heavenly Father, we are grateful that you acted on our behalf when we were undeserving, even before we were born. We do not understand your wisdom. Your gracious action made clear that we deserved and were destined for your wrath and spiritual death. We praise you that your gracious action in the gospel made possible our justification and reconciliation. Through Jesus we pray, Amen.

Romans 6: Baptism -- A Clean Break with Slavery to Sin

Selected Biblical Text

1 What shall we say then? Are we to continue in sin that grace may abound? 2 By no means! How can we who died to sin still live in it? 3 Do you not know that all of us who were baptized into Christ Jesus were baptized into his death? 4 Therefore, we were buried with him by baptism into death, in order that just as Christ was raised from the dead by the glory of the Father, in the same way we may walk in newness of life. 5 For if we have been united with him in the likeness of his death, we will certainly be united with him in the likeness of his resurrection. 6 Knowing this: that our old self was crucified with him so that the body of sin may be made

ineffective, so that we would no longer be enslaved to sin. 7 For the one who has died has been set free from sin.

8 Now if we have died with Christ, we believe that we will also live with him. 9 We know that Christ, being raised from the dead, will never die again; death no longer has mastery over him. 10 For the death he died, he died to sin once for all; but the life he lives, he lives to God. 11 In the same way, you also consider yourselves dead to sin and alive to God in Christ Jesus. 12 Do not let sin therefore reign in your mortal body, leading you to obey its desires. 13 Do not present your members to sin as instruments for unrighteousness but present yourselves to God as those who are now made alive out of death, and your members to God as instruments for righteousness. 14 For sin will have no mastery over you, since you are not under law but under grace.

15 What then? Are we to sin because we are not under law but under grace? By no means! (Romans 6:1-15)

Reflecting and Thinking

The parenthetical construction is easy to miss -- v. 1 and v. 15 are parallel. Or perhaps Paul uses the parallel verses to introduce two separate paragraphs. Regardless, this chapter is a single argument. Having been initiated into a life of grace by baptism, it is unthinkable for Paul that anyone would want to revert to the old nature instead of celebrating newness of life, that anyone would want death instead of life, slavery instead of freedom.

Some have argued that the death of the old person occurs prior to baptism, but that is highly unlike when one considers that we bury dead people. In the context it seems better to understand Paul as saying that our death to sin occurs in our baptism and that newness of life results from our baptism, not before (vv. 1-4). Our participation in Christ's death through baptism is the basis of our certainty of participating with him in resurrection.

The argument of vv. 8-14 is complex but the conclusion is clear. Only grace can free us from the mastery of sin -- law cannot. Law demands wages, but free gifts (v. 23) are freely given and freely received, even though the result is commitment (Paul uses the word "slavery") to God (v. 22). Paul apologizes for such a strong and imperfect illustration (v. 19). The process set in motion by the free gift (grace) freely given and freely received results in slavery to God, holiness, and eternal life.

How many times does Paul refer to death (verb or noun) in this chapter? How does your understanding of this chapter change when you understand the overall topic or theme to be death?

Prayer

Father God, thank you for freeing us from the death that sin brings. Thank you for the free gift of eternal life, in Jesus' name we again say, "thank you," Amen.

Romans 7: New Life in the Spirit

Selected Biblical Text

4 In the same way, my brothers, you also were made dead to the law through the body of Christ, so that you may belong to [literally, become of] another, to the one who was raised from the dead, so we may bear fruit for God. 5 For when we were "in the flesh," the sinful desires aroused by the law were at work in our members to bear fruit unto death. 6 But now we have been released from the law because we died to that which controlled us, so that we serve "in the renewal of the Spirit" and not in the antiquated way of the letter.
7 What then shall we say? That the law is sin? By no means! I would not have known sin except through the law. For I would not have known covetousness, except the law said: "You shall not covet." 8 But sin, seizing opportunity through the commandment, produced in me all kinds of covetousness. But [now] without the Law, sin is dead. (Romans 7:4-8)

Reflecting and Thinking

Even though the argument and application in this chapter are confusing to many, the conclusion is clear: new life is possible in the Spirit (v. 6). The primary question that arises is whether verses 13-25 are a description of Paul's experience in Christ or a description of his life under the law. The latter is contextually sound and appears to be the better choice, understanding that the references to God's law throughout the chapter are to the Old Testament law. Understanding the application of the passage to Paul's experience under the Old Testament law also squares with Galatians 5 where Paul says that those who live in the Spirit do not carry out the desires and actions of the fleshly person.

Those who favor the opposite position (an application to the Christian life) note that many Christians today struggle with the same things Paul describes. Considering the context of the chapter, one might ask, is this an indication that many modern Christians are inclined to live by law and commandment, thus magnifying the influence of the law of sin?

The contrast is clear (vv. 21-25). [Note: the word "law" in v. 21 means principle.] Even when there is a desire to do good and a delight in God's will (v. 21), the principle of sin is at work. This experience, whether under the law or in Christ, is a wretched battle -- the mind and the body are enslaved to two different masters. That such a battle should continue after one is in Christ is hard to argue theologically, but easy to argue experientially. (Note also that this is a continuation of Paul's master-slave illustration from Chapter 6.) Paul will provide more light on his meaning in the first verses of Chapter 8.

[Note: If our reading and study of the text seems broken and discontinuous, remember that Paul did not insert the chapter divisions -- those were added later.]

As you read Chapter 7, note the occurrences of the words "then" and "now" (both written and understood). Do these provide any help in understanding Paul's teaching? The question is not whether a Christian will struggle with sin (see 6:11-14), but what is the nature of that struggle. What is a biblical understanding of the relationship of law and sin? How is it possible for sin to live in a Christian who has died to sin (6:2; 7:17)?

For deeper study: what interpretive dangers exist in this chapter that could lead to adopting a dualistic understanding of body and spirit rather than a holistic understanding?

Prayer

Dear God, you know the power than sin holds over human beings and the struggle that we endure even as we live in Christ. You know the nature of temptation, and we ask your presence and deliverance through Jesus, in his name, Amen.

Romans 8: Living According to the Spirit

Selected Biblical Text

1 Therefore, now there is no condemnation for those who are in Christ Jesus. 2 For the law of the Spirit of life in Christ Jesus has set you free from the law of sin and death. 3 Because what the law could not do because it was weakened by the flesh, God did by sending his own Son in the likeness of sinful flesh, and concerning sin, he condemned sin in the flesh, 4 in order that the righteous requirement of the law might be fulfilled in us who do not live not according to the flesh but according to the Spirit.

5 For those who live according to the flesh set their mind on the things of the flesh, but those who live according to the Spirit [set their mind on] the things of the Spirit. 6 For [following] the mindset of the flesh is death, but [following] the mindset of the Spirit is life and peace. 7 For the mindset of the flesh is hostile to God, for it does not submit to the law of God, it is not able to do so. 8 Those who are in [the mindset of] the flesh cannot please God. 9 You, however, are not "in the flesh" but "in the Spirit," if in fact the Spirit of God lives in you. Anyone who does not have the Spirit of Christ does not belong to him. 10 But if Christ is in you, the body is dying [lit., death] because of sin, but the spirit is living [lit., life] because of righteousness. 11 And, if the Spirit of the one who raised Jesus from the dead lives in you, the one who raised Christ from the dead will give life also to your dying bodies through his Spirit who lives in you.

12 So then, brothers, we are under obligation, not to the flesh, to live according to the flesh 13 (for if you live according to the flesh, you will die), but if by the Spirit you put to death the deeds of the body you will live. 14 For as many as are led by the Spirit of God, these are the sons of God. (Romans 8:1-14)

Reflecting and Thinking

The word "now" shines in 8:1 like a beacon. Whatever may be the case in the previous verses, those in Christ Jesus have escaped condemnation because they have been freed from the law of sin and death (specifically, the Old Testament law, see 8:3) through the sin offering of Jesus. This sacrifice meets the righteous requirements of the law for those who live in the Spirit. Even if the primary application for Paul is to Jews who have been converted to Christ (read 7:1-6), the principle extends to all who are rescued by Christ's death.

The contrast and the options are made clear -- life according to human fleshly desires or life according to the Spirit. In Christ, it is possible to live according to the Spirit and to be controlled by the Spirit living in us rather than by the flesh (8:9). By the way, what might this chapter say about the application of Chapter 7 to Christians? In what way does Chapter 8 serve as commentary on Chapter 7?

How does life through the Spirit impact our lives? What does the presence of the Spirit say about our relationship to God? What does this confidence say about the future, even considering present sufferings, persecution, and weakness? How does the experience of Jesus shed light on our experience?

In depth: can you find five convictions, five affirmations, and five questions in 8:28-34? How do these provide the foundation for the great affirmation of 8:37-39?

Prayer

Dear God, we thank you again today for the deliverance and conquest you provided in Jesus. We are grateful to be freed from sin's grasp and to know your presence in our difficulties. We appreciate the assurance that you are working for good in all things, in Jesus' name, Amen.

Romans 9: God's Sovereign Righteousness -- Children of the Promise

Selected Biblical Text

1 I speak the truth in Christ -- I am not lying; my conscience bears witness to me in the Holy Spirit – 2 I have great sorrow and unceasing anguish in my heart. 3 I could wish that I myself were accursed and cut off from Christ for the sake of my brothers, my fellow countryman according to the flesh, 4 those who are Israelites, to whom belong the adoption as sons, the glory, the covenants, the giving of the law, the worship, and the promises. 5 To them belong the patriarchs, and from them, according to the flesh, is the Christ who is God over all, blessed forever. Amen. 6 Now it is not as though the word of God has failed. For not all of the ones descended from Israel are in fact Israel, 7 nor are all children of Abraham that are his

descendants, rather "through Isaac shall your descendants be named." 8 This means that it is not the children of the flesh who are the children of God, but the children of the promise are counted as descendants. (Romans 9:1-8)

Reflecting and Thinking

Some outlines of Romans suggest that the topic changes in Romans 9-11, but this section can also be understood as an amplification of Paul's treatise on salvation and righteousness (Chapters 1-8). Paul expands his explanation of how God's righteousness will be applied to Israel (3:25-26), demonstrating the justice of God's dealings with Israel.

God has rejected Israel, and rightly so. God made a sovereign choice when he selected Israel (9:1-5). God treated Israel as his children, based on his promise to Abraham and his eternal purpose (vv. 6-13), not because of anything they had done. The question of God's foreknowledge or predestination is not only a New Testament concern -- here the question is raised concerning Pharaoh (vv. 14-18) and is eventually extended to Israel. Was God unjust to elect Jacob over Esau? Has God failed Israel?

God's intent in Israel was to reveal himself in order to reach all whom he prepared for glory and called, not only in physical Israel but in spiritual Israel, including Gentiles (vv. 19-29). Israel's lack of faith and dependence on law and works have excluded them. The Gentiles have found faith and righteousness even though they were not seeking it (vv. 30-33).

[As we will see in the chapters that follow, these are generalizations. Not all physical Israel is excluded and not all Gentiles are included.]

What advantages did Israel have? Why did Israel find it so hard to seek God through the faith of Abraham, choosing instead to depend on righteousness by the law and by works? Based on this chapter, how would you explain that God was not unjust in choosing Isaac over Ishmael, or in choosing Jacob over Esau, or in rejecting Pharaoh?

Deeper study: What does v. 30 say about whether we by faith seek God or merely seek salvation (righteousness)?

Prayer

Dear God, we stand in awe of how far you will go to accomplish your will, raising up and using human beings according to their desires and your purposes, being gracious to all so that your wrath may be seen and your righteousness come to those you call. We pray in Jesus' name, Amen.

Romans 10: Christ Is the Goal of the Law

Selected Biblical Text

1 Brothers, my heart's desire and prayer to God on their behalf is for [their] salvation. 2 For I testify about them that they have a zeal for God, but not according to knowledge. 3 Then, being ignorant of the righteousness of God and seeking to establish their own, they did not submit to God's righteousness. 4 For Christ is the end goal of the law leading to righteousness for everyone who believes.
17 So faith comes from hearing, and hearing through the preached word of Christ. 18 But I ask: "Have they not heard?" Certainly! Their voice has gone out to all the earth, and their words to the ends of the world. 19 But I ask: "Did Israel not understand?" First Moses says: "I will make you jealous of those who are not a nation; with a nation without understanding I will make you angry." 20 Then Isaiah is bold and says: "I have been found by those who did not seek me; I became obvious to those who did not ask for me." 21 But of Israel he says: "All day long I have held out my hands to a disobedient and contrary people." (Romans 10:1-4, 17-21)

Reflecting and Thinking

Today's biblical text (the thought or paragraph begins with 9:30) makes clear the cause of God's rejection of Israel. It is not that Israel has not been zealous for God. It is rather that they are seeking self-attained righteousness based on law, an effort which has limited their ability and willingness to submit to God's righteousness and has blinded them to the law's focus on Christ. Their attitude of exclusivity stands between them and God's ultimate purpose of righteousness for all who believe.

God has rejected Israel because they rejected him. The twelve Old Testament quotations (vv. 5-21) provide evidence that God's plan for righteousness by faith is not something recently developed. [Be careful how you use and apply these Old Testament quotations!] The message has gone forth, and some of Israel has not accepted the gospel (v. 16). Yet, God has been immeasurably patient with Israel (v. 21).

How should we apply this chapter? Do we today ever seek God's salvation or righteousness (the blessings of God) without wanting God? What does it mean to seek God by faith? Israel heard the message but misheard it. Do we ever mishear the message, yet rest confidently as we affirm that we "know" the Bible (v. 17)? What do you think of God's reasons for rejecting Israel? How many of the reasons given also apply to us?

Prayer

Dear God, we want to be more zealous, but we want to be zealous about your will and way and not only for our benefit. Help us seek your righteousness and submit to it. In our more sober moments, we fear that we may seek well and submit poorly. Help us avoid attitudes of exclusivity. Be with us as we seek to bring good news to the entire world, we pray in Jesus' name, Amen.

Romans 11: Israel Saved through the Deliverer from Zion

Selected Biblical Text
26 And this is the way all Israel will be saved, as it is written: "The Deliverer will come from Zion, he will turn away ungodliness from Jacob; 27 and this will be my covenant with them when I take away their sins." 28 With regard to the gospel, they are enemies [of God] for your [Gentiles'] sake, but with regard to election, they are loved for the sake of the forefathers. 29 For the gifts and the calling of God are irrevocable. 30 For just as you were at one time disobedient to God but now have received mercy in their disobedience, 31 so they too have now been disobedient in order that by the mercy shown to you they also may now receive mercy. 32 For God has consigned all to disobedience so that he may have mercy on them all. 33 Oh, the depth of the riches and wisdom and knowledge of God! How unsearchable are his judgments and how inscrutable his ways! 34 For who has known the mind of the Lord, or who has been his counselor? 35 Or who has given a gift to him so it will be repaid? 36 For from him and through him and to him are all things. To him be glory forever. Amen. (Romans 11:26-36)

Reflecting and Thinking
As we come to the last chapter in this subsection of Romans (Chapters 9-11), the good news comes clearly into view. God's plan is that all might be declared righteous through the faith of Christ. God has been perfectly righteous (just) in his sovereignty as he has worked in Israel's history to accomplish his purpose. God was just in his rejection of Israel; Paul lists the causes of that rejection. Good News! God's rejection of Israel is not total, and it is not final. This is seen in three truths: there is a remnant (vv. 1-10), the temporary rejection allowed new branches to be grafted in (vv. 11-24), and God's ultimate saving purpose will be accomplished in the work of the deliverer from Zion who will take away sins and make righteousness a reality (vv. 25-32).

What other response is possible except wonderful words of praise and glory?

Since Paul's point in Chapters 9-11 is that some of Israel has always been excluded based on their own choices (and there are plenty of Old Testament examples in addition to those included in these chapters), how can some now conclude that this passage teaches that all of Israel will be included? In studying these chapters, consider that throughout the book of Romans God's plan is righteousness by faith, extended only to those who believe (participate in the faith of Christ).

In depth: If you have time, reread Chapters 9-11. Try to put the message of these three chapters in your own words.

Prayer

Dear God, thank you that you can work in our lives when we are weak and wrong. Thank you that you use your grace and glory to reveal your wrath and to reveal your righteousness, thus calling us to repentance by your goodness and mercy. Thank you for the amazing wisdom of your plan in our lives. May we learn your ways and your work, we pray in Jesus' name, Amen.

Romans 12: Discerning God's Will -- Members Together

Selected Biblical Text

1 Therefore, I exhort you, brothers, by the mercies of God, to present your bodies as a living sacrifice, holy and well-pleasing to God, which is your reasonable ministry. 2 Do not be conformed to this world, but be transformed by the renewal of your mind, that by testing you may understand what the will of God is, what is good and well-pleasing and perfect. 3 For I say by the grace given to me to every one of you not to think of yourself beyond what you ought to think, but to think with sober thought, as God distributed a measure of faith to each one. 4 For as in one body we have many members, and the members do not all have the same function, 5 so we are many in one body in Christ, and individually members together of one another. (Romans 12:1-5)

Reflecting and Thinking

Many of Paul's letters have two major sections: doctrinal and practical. In this chapter, we turn to the practical applications of life lived in God's righteousness. God's mercy not only calls us to repentance, it calls us to life lived as a worshipful sacrifice presented to God, evidenced by transformed lives, renewed thinking, and restored relationships. Life in the body of Christ allows us to live out God's gracious gifts in fresh ways without worrying about our own capacities.

The picture Paul paints beginning in 12:3, and continuing into Chapter 13, wonderfully portrays the potential and power of an awareness of God's righteousness, not an earned righteousness but the free gift from faith to faith (by the faith of Christ to all who believe).

The text says in 12:5 that we (members of the body, the church) belong to one another. Explore in your meditation and prayer some of the applications of this principle -- what does it mean that other Christians belong to me and that I belong to other Christians?

In depth: In verses 9-18, Paul uses a number of short imperative sentences. Which of these is the most difficult for you? Which ones are easiest?

Prayer

Dear God, help us live out the reality of the transformed life as we renew our minds according to your will and the Spirit's presence. Bind us together and use us to your glory. Thank you for showing us more clearly the righteousness you declare for us, that we can stand justified in your sight by faith. We pray in Jesus' name, Amen.

Romans 13: Put on the Lord Jesus Christ

Selected Biblical Text

11 This is important: knowing the time, it is the hour for you rise up from sleep, for now our salvation is nearer than when we first believed. 12 The night is almost over, and the day is at hand. So then let us put aside the works of darkness and put on the armor of light. 13 During the day, let us walk decently, not in reveling and drunkenness, not in sexual immorality and sensuality, not in quarreling and jealousy. 14 But put on the Lord Jesus Christ and make no provision for the flesh to fulfill its desires. (Romans 13:11-14)

Reflecting and Thinking

Romans 13 is closely connected with Romans 12 -- it is both a continuation and a conclusion. The way we live out our transformed lives in sacrificial living includes both our life with one another and our life in the world. Today's selected text provides a fitting capstone. The challenges are great; let us live in newness; let us live out the presence of God's Spirit and the law of life in Christ rather than returning to the law that appeals to the flesh.

[Note: the "putting on" of the Lord Jesus Christ in this context is different from the "putting on" in Gal. 3:27 where the reference is to baptism, even though the same Greek word is used.]

Looking Ahead. In Chapters 14-15, Paul will turn to a more detailed consideration of how we should behave when the faith we share causes conflicts.

Why are our relationships to governments, authorities, and neighbors important in our life of righteousness? How is today's selected text a summary of Chapters 12-13? Explain some of the possible applications of the admonition to "put on the Lord Jesus Christ" in this context?

Prayer

Dear God, help us live consistently in every part of our lives. Help us demonstrate genuine love in our social responsibilities. Protect us from evil and the deeds of darkness. Focus our hearts on your desires. In Jesus' name, Amen.

Romans 14: Living Together -- By Faith

Selected Biblical Text

15 For if your brother is distressed by what you eat, you are no longer walking in love. Do not, by what you eat, destroy that person for whom Christ died. 16 Do not let what you think is good be spoken against as evil. 17 For the kingdom of God is not defined by eating and drinking but by righteousness and peace and joy in the Holy Spirit. 18 The one who in these things serves Christ is well-pleasing to God and approved by others. 19 So then let us pursue what makes for peace and for building up one another. 20 Do not, for the sake of food, destroy the work of God. All things are clean, but it is wrong for anyone who eats and thus becomes a stumbling block.* 21 It is good not to eat meat or drink wine or do anything that causes your brother to stumble. 22 The faith that you have, keep to yourself before God. Blessed is the one who does not place judgment on himself by what he approves. 23 But the one who doubts is condemned if he eats, because his eating is not from faith. For whatever is not from faith is sin. (Romans 14:15-23)
*(NET, it is wrong to cause anyone to stumble by what you eat; literally, but wrong to the man who through a stumbling block eats).

Reflecting and Thinking

The application of Romans 14 has often challenged the church. What is strong faith and what is weak faith? Who is the weaker brother and who is the stronger brother? Are the "disputable" matters mentioned in this chapter doctrinal questions or mere incidentals? And how does one answer that question when one side says "doctrine" and the other says "optional?" Our understanding of the text is helped by recognizing several truths. First, Paul does not use the Greek word that would be translated "opinion" even though he had access to that word. He uses a word that means thoughts or reasonings, often with an element of doubt. Second, considering the two examples, Paul is not talking about doctrinal matters. Third, Paul basically describes those who can and those who cannot do certain things, based on their own consciences. This may be a more helpful description than asking who is strong and who is weak. Two key words that appear repeatedly in the chapter are not translated consistently in every version. The words are "condemn" (judge) -- the attitude of the weaker (the one who cannot) toward the stronger, and "look down on" or despise -- the attitude of the stronger (the one who can) toward the weaker. In the church at Rome, it appears that both sides were behaving badly. The question is about faith. How does one live by faith? What should we do when your faith and my faith arrive at different understandings? How do we live out God's righteousness by faith when we do not understand everything alike? These instructions from Paul suggest that it is not easy, but it is necessary if we are to be the people God has called us to be.

What topics have you heard included in discussions of Romans 14? Which topics do you think belong, which do not belong? Why? Based on verse 22, "keep these things between you and God," what challenges does the church face in those actions that are by their very nature public and visible?

Prayer

Dear God, help us to love one another as much as you love us. Help us to love one another enough to get self out of the way, especially in matters such as those described in this chapter. Give us insight, wisdom and understanding so that we will know how to apply these words and how to build one another up in faith without judging or arrogance, with placing undue limitations or stumbling blocks. Always we pray in Jesus' name, seeking his authority and will, Amen.

Romans 15: Living in Harmony with One Another

Selected Biblical Text

1 We who are strong ought to endure the scruples of the weak, and not to please ourselves. 2 Let each of us please his neighbor for good, for building up. 3 For even Christ did not please himself, but as it is written: "The reproaches of those who reproached you fell on me." 4 For whatever things were written in times past were written for our instruction, that through endurance and through the encouragement of the Scriptures we might have hope. 5 May the God of endurance and encouragement grant you to think the same way with one another, in accord with [the example of] Christ Jesus, 6 that together you may with one voice glorify the God and Father of our Lord Jesus Christ. 7 Therefore receive one another as Christ has received you, for the glory of God. (Romans 15:1-7)

Reflecting and Thinking

Romans 12-15 has three major sections: transformed living (12-13), living by faith in the midst of differing ideas (14-15:13), and Paul's desire to build on the strong faith of the church in Rome to advance his ministry to the Gentiles (15:14-33).

The short reading today continues the discussion from Romans 14. Focusing on 15:1-7 leaves the important section of 15:14-33 untouched. That demonstrates one of the challenges of writing daily devotional thoughts that are designed to cover entire chapters. What does one do when a chapter contains two distinctly different themes? How does one write briefly but completely? Compromises must be made, and today's compromise excludes an important part of this chapter. I encourage you to read and study it on your own.

Today's text explains more fully the conclusions that should be drawn from Paul's teachings in Chapter 14. All members of the body are obligated to the others (we belong to one another, 12:5), but the strong (with more liberated consciences) have a special obligation to the weak (with restricted consciences). Christ is our example. The Old Testament provides ample examples. Living in harmony brings praise and glory to God. The key teaching is that we should accept one another as Christ has accepted us in our imperfections and frailties.

How hard is it for the contemporary church to live out the teachings of Romans 14-15? A quote: "Churches split over personalities and call it doctrine." Do you agree or disagree? If the "faith" of brothers in Christ does not always agree, what should we conclude?

In depth: To what extent do you think the matters of Chapters 14-15 deal with Jewish-Gentile differences, based on the doctrinal sections (chapters 1-11), the illustrations of chapter 14, and the quotations in 15:9-12?

Prayer
Dear God, bind us together in the body of Christ in fresh and affirming ways, so that we will demonstrate and declare your glory. Give us a spirit that builds unity. Give us a commitment to one another and to you that is bigger than our own personal preferences -- so that we do not seek to please ourselves. Give us the joy, peace, trust, hope, and power for which Paul prays, in Jesus' name, Amen.

Romans 16: Strengthened and Obedient in the Faith

Selected Biblical Text
25 Now to him who is able to strengthen you according to my gospel and the preaching of Jesus Christ, according to the revelation of the mystery that was kept secret for long ages, 26 but now is disclosed, and through the prophetic writings has been made known to all nations, according to the command of the eternal God, to bring about the obedience of faith – 27 to the only wise God, through Jesus Christ, be glory forevermore, Amen. (Romans 16:25-27)

Reflecting and Thinking

Perhaps you already know that Chapter 16 is largely a collection of personal greetings with which Paul closes the book of Romans. The presence of personal greetings is not unusual; other writings of Paul have similar lists. What is unusual in the book of Romans is that the list is so long, especially because Paul had never visited Rome.

Today's text serves as a doxology and conclusion to the entire book. The obedience of faith of 1:5 is reflected in 16:26. The focus is the gospel; the message is Jesus Christ. The purpose of God has not changed -- and that purpose is now made clear. The gospel is to be made known to all nations so that all may be obedient by faith. God's plan is bigger than any person or group of people.

An interesting exercise is to think about how today's text relates to the message of the book. Several of the themes in the three verses of our selected text are echoes of ideas presented throughout the book of Romans. How many connections can you identify?

Prayer

Dear God, we pray that we will understand Romans so that you really rule and reign in our lives. We want to understand and know your way and will, so that we can be full participants in your purpose, experiencing deliverance from sin and new life in Christ. Give us wisdom and understanding, we pray in Jesus' name, Amen.

Luke 1: Getting Ready and Waiting for God's New Work

Selected Biblical Text

1 Forasmuch as many have undertaken to compile a written account of the things that have been accomplished among us, 2 like the accounts that those who from the beginning were eyewitnesses and ministers of the word have given to us, 3 it seemed good to me also, having followed all things closely from the first, to write an orderly account for you, most excellent Theophilus, that you may know with certainty the things you have been taught. (Luke 1:1-4)

51 He has performed powerful deeds with his arm; he has scattered the proud with the arrogant imaginations of their hearts; 52 he has brought down the mighty ones from thrones and exalted the humble ones; 53 he has filled the hungry with good things, and the rich ones he has sent away empty. 54 He has helped his servant Israel, because he remembered his mercy, 55 even as he said to our fathers, to Abraham and to his offspring forever. (Luke 1:51-55)

Reflecting and Thinking

For some, Luke is a favorite gospel. For others, it is the gospel least read. Matthew comes first and is read frequently (thinking of those who resolve each year to read through the New Testament); Mark comes second and is short (for those in a hurry); John is unique and tends to capture our attention. What about the Gospel of Luke? What is distinctive about Luke's Gospel? Where should we begin if we genuinely want to read and understand the "gospel to the Gentiles?"

God is preparing his people for a new work -- something never before seen. Reading between the lines of the introduction to the book (1:1-4), Luke says that while the things that have occurred may seem random, unexplainable, and unorganized, there is a design and purpose that can be discerned when the events are set forth in an orderly way.

The uniqueness of the birth of John the Baptist provides a beginning point for this new work of God. The announcement of the birth of Jesus confirms it. The song of Mary foreshadows the truth that God is getting ready to change the world -- to turn things upside down so that the proud are brought low, the mighty are brought down, the lowly are exalted, the hungry are filled, and the rich are emptied. The text of Luke 1:51-55, one of the first of many "reversal" texts in Luke, introduces us to the flavor of this gospel. God's plan will not be unfolded immediately, but the beginning has come. Patience! "And John the Baptist grew and became strong in spirit, waiting until his public appearance in Israel."

In our instantaneous world, we are not very good at waiting. We are always in a hurry; we seldom give God time to work. We desire instant results. Patience! God is working his work. He is at work among those who are genuinely his people; he is reaching out to include others, even those who seem beyond hope. If we limit ourselves to human resources and human means, we will struggle to see God's unfolding story in our own lives. The story told in Luke's gospel is a story of power and intrigue, a story with plots and subplots. For the next month, we are going to try to read the story anew as though we have never heard it before. Let us pray that we can see new things and ponder them. What is God doing in our world? What does God want to do in your life? Luke's gospel will bring the answer. Let us listen carefully.

Prayer
Dear Heavenly Father, help me to slow down in the coming days, to hear afresh the story of Jesus. Bless my efforts to hear, to marvel, to learn, and to grow. Help me as I seek to grasp what you are already doing, to hear your call for me to join you in your work, and to find my unique place. Help me that I may be a help to others. In Jesus' name and by his power I pray, Amen.

Luke 2: Where It's Happening -- Below the Radar

Selected Biblical Text
8 And there were shepherds in the same area living out in the field, keeping guard over their flock by night. 9 And at once an angel of the Lord appeared to them, and the glory of the Lord shone around them, and they were filled with great fear. 10 And the angel said to them: "Do not be afraid. Listen, I proclaim to you good news, which will be a great joy for all people, 11 because in the city of David a Savior was born to you today, who is Christ the Lord. 12 And this will be a sign for you: you will find a baby wrapped in layers of cloth, lying in a manger."
13 And suddenly there was with the angel a multitude of the armies of heaven praising God and saying: 14 "Glory in the highest to God, and on earth peace among people with whom he is pleased!" (Luke 2:8-14)

Reflecting and Thinking
At the beginning of the century we know as the first century, big stuff was happening among the movers and shakers. Caesar Augustus ordered a census. Quirinius was governing Syria. The common folks merely did what they were told to do. Everyone went to his own town to register for the census. Luke tells the story and reveals to us that God was at work fulfilling Old Testament prophecy.

Look at the some of the players in the storyline. Common people who apparently did not have family members to stay with and could not find a place at the inn. Shepherds, common laborers who were among the lowest level of society, were among the first to receive the good news.

Good news that God is working for his glory and on behalf of every person on earth. Mary, a young lady chosen by God to participate in God's plan; she can only treasure and ponder such marvelous occurrences. The sacrifices associated with the new birth reflect the status of the family among the poor. The story continues -- encounters with Simeon and Anna in the temple; returning to Nazareth; twelve years of growing, developing wisdom and God's grace; all made apparent and brought to a climax in the temple conversations which conclude this amazing chapter.

How can I grasp the amazing story that is unfolding? How can I understand how unique is God's way of initiating his purpose and plan? The readings easily become "old hat" as I read the story again and again. But the message must never become old -- it is always new because it shows me things I have not seen, and it touches those who have not been touched before. Such was the story of Jesus in the first century, such can be the story of Jesus in our day. Why do I have so much trouble seeing it? Why is it so hard to believe that God wants to touch and include people who have never before been included?

Prayer
Dear God, thank you for including me in your plan even though I am undeserving. Thank you for not giving up on me, because I know (as do you) that not every day of my life is a great testimony to your presence and power in my life. Thank you for reaching out to me; help me to accept your desire to reach out to others through me, as I live out the reality of your work in my life. In Jesus' name I gratefully pray, Amen.

Luke 3: Yes, This Is He!

Selected Biblical Text
21 Now when all the people were baptized, and when Jesus also had been baptized and was praying, the heavens were opened, 22 and the Holy Spirit descended on him in a physical shape like a dove; and a voice came from heaven: "You are my beloved Son; with you I am well pleased." (Luke 3:21-22)

Reflecting and Thinking
A certain humor begins this chapter. We get one more look at a list of the movers and shakers who live in the places where things are supposed to happen. But the most important thing that is happening is not happening in the palaces among kings, governors, tetrarch and sub-governors, nor among the high priests and religious leaders. The thing Luke wants us to notice is happening in the countryside and desert.

John the Baptist prepares the way for Jesus by saying one thing: "He is the One!" Jesus is baptized, and one heavenly declaration summarizes the event: "You are my Son whom I love; with you I am well pleased." Jesus begins his ministry, and Luke clarifies once more the heritage of Jesus through a genealogical list which concludes: "...the son of Adam, the son of God."

How would it have felt to have been there? Wouldn't it have been fun to catch a glimpse of what was occurring -- the irony of God working in seemingly unimportant places through unknown people, not through people of renown, but through a simple message that appealed to the large crowds who responded to the hope which resounded in the message: crowds which included tax collectors and soldiers and many others, all wanting to change their lives. As always, some didn't want to change. The message was temporarily stifled but not silenced by the imprisonment of John the Baptist.

God, help me be among those who want to change!

Prayer

Dear God, thank you for the certainty with which you introduced Jesus to this world -- Old Testament prophecy was confirmed with clear declarations and evidence of his identity. Some days it is easy to wonder; days of doubt diminish my ability to live a changed life. Strengthen me in difficult days and help always my unbelief. Help me live life today in full belief in Jesus, in Jesus' name, Amen.

Luke 4: Fresh Beginnings

Selected Biblical Text

14 Then Jesus returned in the power of the Spirit to Galilee, and a report about him went out through all the region. 15 He was teaching in their synagogues, being glorified by all. 16 When he came to Nazareth, where he had been brought up, he went, as was his custom, to the synagogue on the Sabbath day, and he stood up to read. 17 And the scroll of the prophet Isaiah was given to him. Unrolling the scroll, he found the place where it was written: 18 "The Spirit of the Lord is upon me, therefore he anointed me to proclaim good news to the poor. He has sent me to announce deliverance to captives and recovered sight to the blind, to send forth the oppressed with deliverance, 19 to announce the year of the Lord's favor." 20 Rolling up the scroll, he gave it back to the attendant and sat down. And the eyes of all in the synagogue were staring at him. 21 And he began to say to them: "Today this Scripture has been fulfilled in your hearing." (Luke 4:14-21)

Reflecting and Thinking

Luke 4 begins with the story of Jesus' temptation. This narrative belongs with and concludes the identity stories of chapters 1-3. Luke 4 also provides us with a beginning point for Jesus' ministry. Jesus will serve in the power of the Spirit to fulfill Old Testament prophecy. His message will not be accepted by all. In fact, it will generally be rejected by the religious leaders of that day. What an interesting turn of events!

Jesus teaches -- preaching good news, proclaiming freedom and sight, proclaiming the Lord's favor. He casts out evil spirits and heals the sick. He preaches because that is why he came: "I must preach the good news of the kingdom of God to the other towns as well; for I was sent for this purpose."

If you were going to begin a new ministry, how would you begin? Would you go to already existing churches? Would you go to religious people or to non-religious people? What would you teach? What would you proclaim? Jesus' model of ministry breaks many of our preexisting molds and challenges many of our ideas. Jesus faces immediate persecution, yet he is admired, accepted, and sought by the most unlikely of the society. He refuses to "locate," answering the call to preach in every place possible.

What other interesting dynamics can you identify in this narrative of the beginnings of Jesus' ministry?

Prayer

Heavenly Father, in our hearts, we want to serve and minister and make a difference. We want to touch lives but many times we do not know where to begin. We marvel at the example of Jesus and want to know how to follow him more closely. Empower us afresh with your Spirit. In the name of Jesus, Amen.

Luke 5: Mountaintop Prayer -- Power for the Marketplace

Selected Biblical Text

15 But the report about him spread even more, and great crowds gathered to hear him and to be healed of their illnesses. 16 Now Jesus himself was withdrawing to isolated places and praying, 17 and on one of those days, as he was teaching, Pharisees and teachers of the law were there, having come from all the villages of Galilee and Judea and from Jerusalem. And the power of the Lord was upon him to heal. (Luke 5:15-17)

Reflecting and Thinking

Luke describes the first phase of Jesus' ministry as centered in the region around Galilee (4:14-9:17). In the synagogue Jesus declares that he has come to help people (4:18-19, quoting Isa. 61:1-2). The synagogue narrative is followed immediately by a staccato series of "people stories" -- driving out an evil spirit, healing Simon's mother, healing many others, calling disciples, healing a leper, healing a paralytic, and calling Matthew Levi.

Today's text (5:15-17) introduces a continuing rhythm of Jesus' life, a theme which surfaces again and again. Jesus has marketplace power because of his personal time with God (4:42 also suggests his withdrawal to spend quiet time with God). For Jesus, marketplace power comes from mountaintop prayer. This subtheme is consistent with Luke's emphasis on prayer. Jesus was powerful because he was in contact with the source of power. One can only wonder if we are sometimes powerless because we are not in regular contact with the source of power.

Luke's emphasis on prayer is visible in Jesus' prayers before and during major activities or events in his life (today's text in 5:16; the selection of the Twelve in 6:12; 9:18 before Peter's confession, 9:28-29 before the Transfiguration, 11:1, 22:32-41 in Gethsemane, 23:34,46 on the cross). How would our lives change if we were more prayerful? When have you prayed all night? When have you prayed before major events in your life? How did it turn out? When have you failed to pray before major events? How did it turn out?

Prayer
Heavenly Father, we want to walk more closely with you; we ask you to bring us closer to you today. Help us follow through on our desire for daily contact, relationship and fellowship with you. Encourage us with your power as we depend on you. Thank you for your presence in our lives. We pray through Jesus, the One who makes our relationship with you possible, Amen.

Luke 6: Controversy, Choices, and Contrasts

Selected Biblical Text
19 The whole crowd sought to touch him, for power was coming out from him and healing everyone. 20 Lifting up his eyes to his disciples, he said: "Blessed are you who are poor, for yours is the kingdom of God. 21 Blessed are you who are hungry now, for you will be satisfied. Blessed are you who weep now, for you will laugh. 22 Blessed are you when people hate you and when they exclude you and defame you and mention your name as evil, on account of the Son of Man. 23 Rejoice in that day, and leap for joy, for your reward is great in heaven, for their fathers did the same things to the prophets. 24 But woe to you who are rich, for you have already received your comfort. 25 Woe to you who are well satisfied now, for you will be hungry. Woe to you who laugh now, for you will mourn and weep. 26 Woe to you, when all people speak well of you, for their fathers did the same things to the false prophets." (Luke 6:19-26)

Reflecting and Thinking

Luke 6 has three major sections. Jesus' identity as the Lord of the Sabbath is central to a controversy with the Jews; Jesus chooses the Twelve; and Jesus preaches an extended sermon. Luke's account of the Sermon on the Plain has many obvious parallels to Matthew's Sermon on the Mount (Matthew 5-7) and almost certainly refers to the same event. Jesus stood on a level place, perhaps a mountain plateau or a flat overlook. These options would satisfy any perceived discrepancy between the "plain" and the "mount." Of course, there also exists the possibility that Jesus gave similar sermons on different occasions, as still happens with preachers today. The crowds have been attracted by his power. The sermon in Luke begins by contrasting blessings and woes. The woes are point by point answers that correspond to the blessings.

What strikes you about the themes Jesus addresses in this short series of blessings and woes? If you had to paraphrase the sermon in entirely different words, what synonyms and parallel concepts would you use? What themes or common subjects can you identify in the sermon? Or, is this merely a miscellaneous series of topics? How can we apply these teachings of Jesus in our lives each day?

Prayer

Father God, we want to be your followers. We want to recognize you clearly, to walk closely, to understand your will and way, and to participate in your work. Give us wisdom. In the name of Jesus, Amen.

Luke 7: God's Way is Right

Selected Biblical Text

20 When the men came to Jesus, they said: "John the Baptist has sent us to you to ask, 'Are you the one who is to come, or shall we look for another?'" 21 In that same hour he healed many people of diseases, sicknesses, and evil spirits, and he gave sight to many who were blind. 22 And he answered them: "Go and tell John what you have seen and heard: the blind see again, the lame walk, lepers are cleansed, the deaf hear, the dead are raised, the poor have good news preached to them. 23 Blessed is the one who does not stumble because of me." (Luke 7:20-23)

Reflecting and Thinking

In today's chapter, Jesus continues his ministry in the area around Galilee -- healing a centurion's servant, raising the widow's son, sending an encouraging word to John the Baptist, and speaking forgiveness to a sinful woman. The response Jesus sends to John (see selected text above) is especially interesting. Not only does the story qualify as an identity narrative

("Are you the one who was to come, or should we expect someone else?"), it also recaps the introduction to Jesus' ministry from the reading in the synagogue (4:18-19). The diseased, sick, possessed and blind are cured. The blind see, the lame walk, the lepers are cured, the deaf hear, the dead are raised, the good news is preached. For this, Jesus came! Two responses are possible: some fall away because of Jesus; others cling more closely because of Jesus. Jesus pronounced a blessing on the one who abides.

The title of today's devotional comes from 7:29. The people had acknowledged that God's word was right in their desire to be baptized by John. The opposite attitude is reflected in v. 30: the Pharisees had rejected God's purpose for them; they had not been baptized by John. Two different results are described, based on whether one has received and accepted the words of the forerunner (John the Baptist). How important is it that we be pliable when God's word comes to us? Why do some people today not acknowledge that God's way is right? How do these verses serve as a commentary or explanation of what continues to occur today? Based on these verses, what would you do to help someone acknowledge God's way as right? What would you say? What information would you share? What would you teach?

Prayer

Dear God, thank you for blessing our lives with faith. Thank you for helping us to see when we were blind and unseeing. Keep us near you; keep us from falling. Help us to imitate the attitude of Jesus as we go forth with his power to touch, influence, and alter lives. May we help others toward faith. In Jesus' name, Amen.

Luke 8: Jesus' Identity -- Who Is this?

Selected Biblical Text

22 One day he got into a boat with his disciples, and he said to them: "Let us go across to the other side of the lake." They set out 23 and as they sailed, he fell asleep. Now a violent squall came down onto the lake, and they were being swamped and were in danger. 24 They went and woke him, saying: "Master, Master, we are about to perish." So, he got up and commanded the wind and the raging waves. They ceased and it became calm. 25 He said to them: "Where is your faith?" They were afraid and marveled, and said to one another: "Who then is this, that he commands the winds and the water, and they obey him?" (Luke 8:22-25)

Reflecting and Thinking

As Jesus nears the end of his ministry in Galilee (using Luke's timeline as he recounts the story), he travels from place to place, proclaiming the good news of the kingdom (see 4:18-19, he came to preach good news). As crowds assemble, Jesus teaches in parables. Luke places the parable section in a slightly different chronology than Matthew, but the explanation given in contrasting the Sermon on the Plain and the Sermon on the Mount (see Luke 6) again applies: certainly, Jesus used the same teachings and stories more than once during his ministry. The parable narrative in Luke is immediately followed by stories that appear in Matthew's gospel right after the Sermon on the Mount. These chronological difficulties are interesting but are not overwhelming, remembering that the Gospel writers were redactors (editors of existing materials) as much as authors of original material (Luke 1:1-4).

Luke's gospel includes several sections of Jesus' teachings, but it seems that the focus is more on Jesus' personal interactions as he fulfills the Isaiah prophecy (4:18-19). In contrast to the disciples' question concerning Jesus' identity (see 8:25, "Who is this?"), the demon-possessed man, after his healing, wants to tell about Jesus and what Jesus has done for him. The hemorrhaging, unclean woman touches him and is rewarded with healing; the faith of the synagogue ruler is victorious as his daughter is restored to life and made whole.

Assume with me for a moment that one purpose of this chapter is to give us a series of identity narratives. Jesus is traveling about and some women who have been healed and cured are following him and financing him. Do they have faith? Do they understand who he is? Do they have any idea? After he teaches in parables, his identity in relation to his mother and brothers is brought up. What does Jesus' response mean? His disciples raise the question of his identity after he calms the storm. The demon-possessed man cannot withhold his joy. The synagogue ruler does not know where else to turn. Neither does the woman subject to bleeding. Two things go hand in hand: Jesus' identity and our faith. What do you think about Jesus? How is your understanding of Jesus reflected in your life as you live out that faith?

Prayer

Dear God and Father in heaven, we praise you for your majestic greatness and wisdom. We are overwhelmed by your wisdom in sending Jesus to show us your nature and your love. We wonder at our lack of faith. We want more faith. Help us have courage to tell others what Jesus has done for us. In the name of Jesus, we pray, Amen.

Luke 9: Don't Look Back

Selected Biblical Text

57 As they were going along the road, someone said to him: "I will follow you wherever you go." 58 And Jesus said to him: "Foxes have burrows, and birds of the sky have nests, but the Son of Man has no place to lay his head."
59 To another he said: "Follow me." But he said: "Lord, let me first go to bury my father." 60 And Jesus said to him: "Leave the dead to bury their own dead. But as for you, go and preach the kingdom of God."
61 Yet another said: "I will follow you, Lord, but let me first say farewell to those in my household." 62 Jesus said to him: "No one who puts his hand to the plow and looks back is fit for the kingdom of God." (Luke 9:57-62)

Reflecting and Thinking

What a power-packed chapter! Here's a quick overview -- Jesus sends out the Twelve with power, Herod tries to see Jesus, Jesus feeds the 5000, Peter's confession, the first two of three predictions of Jesus' suffering and death, the Transfiguration, Jesus heals a boy with an evil spirit, the disciples argue about greatness, Jesus resolutely sets out for Jerusalem and his crucifixion, and some Samaritans reject Jesus' visit to their village. How do we sort it out?

A key thought to help us tie things together is found in the last section of the chapter. Even after Jesus' identity is firmly established, an important question yet remains. Who will be a follower of Jesus? Some would follow but find the price too high. Some are distracted with personal desires and priorities. Some cannot let go completely of family and possessions and the obligations and rhythms of daily life. For many of us in cultures and societies of the Western World, following Jesus has become very easy (too easy?). The temptation to "look back" is ever present -- never complete erased. Again and again, Christians are tempted to look longingly at the world. Some even to try to integrate their Christian lives into a secular world. Jesus says, "It won't work!"

When have you been tempted to "look back?" Have you ever committed yourself to something for the Lord or in the church, and then changed your mind and withdrawn from the project? Why? What does this verse say to such situations? Have you ever started and then stopped? Why? What does Jesus think about "looking back," based on these verses?

Prayer

Heavenly Father, we marvel at the commitment of Jesus who went forward in your will and plan, knowing what was awaiting him. He himself predicted his death. He purposefully, resolutely, determinedly set out for Jerusalem, even with the end in sight. Help us to appreciate and imitate such commitment. We pray for your help as we count the cost and commit to follow Jesus -- regardless. In Jesus' name we ask this, Amen.

Luke 10: Names Written in Heaven

Selected Biblical Text

17 Then the seventy-two returned with joy, saying: "Lord, even the demons submit to us by your name!" 18 He said to them: "I saw Satan falling out of heaven like lightning. 19 Look, I have given you authority to trample snakes and scorpions, and authority over all the power of the enemy, and nothing will hurt you. 20 Nevertheless, do not rejoice that the spirits submit to you, but rejoice that your names are written in heaven."

21 In that same hour Jesus rejoiced in the Holy Spirit and said: "I thank you, Father, Lord of heaven and earth, that you have hidden these things from the wise and understanding and revealed them to little children; yes, Father, because this was well pleasing to you. 22 All things have been given to me by my Father. No one knows who the Son is except the Father, or who the Father is except the Son and the one to whom the Son chooses to reveal him."

23 Turning to the disciples privately, he said: "Blessed are the eyes that see what you see! 24 For I tell you that many prophets and kings desired to see what you see, and did not see it, and to hear what you hear, and did not hear it." (Luke 10:17-24)

Reflecting and Thinking

We previously observed that Luke locates Jesus' early ministry in Galilee (Luke 4-9). We know from the other Gospels that Jesus went to Caesarea Philippi prior to Peter's confession and the Transfiguration (Luke 9). Near the end of Luke 9, Jesus sets out for Jerusalem. The journey theme in Luke may be as much spiritual as physical. Nonetheless, by the end of Luke 10, Jesus has arrived in Bethany, about two miles from Jerusalem, perhaps only for a brief visit. The recurring theme of Jesus' journey to Jerusalem will surface throughout Luke until Jesus arrives at Jerusalem for his crucifixion.

While the parable of the Good Samaritan is probably the most well-known section of Luke 10, I want to turn our attention to a theme that also deserves a high priority in our understanding of today's reading. The Samaritans (9:51-56) are not the only ones opposing Jesus. In the narrative that describes the sending out the 72 (or 70, if one reads the textual variant), Jesus notes that the demons also oppose him but that they are being overcome by the ministry of his followers! The events for which the prophets and kings have been waiting are at hand and are being fulfilled. Jesus is the fulfillment of the Old Testament prophecies, and the plan and purpose of God are slowly but surely advancing.

Notice how easy it is to get caught up in the enthusiasm and excitement of the present moment and lose sight of the things that really matter -- the things that have long-term value. We are no different today than were the 72. They were thrilled to see firsthand the power they had been given. Even the demons were submitting to them. To see and experience such things was certainly reason for rejoicing, but the greater benefit was eternal -- their names were written in heaven. How easily we overlook the blessing of seeing and knowing with certainty! Many through the years have longed to see but could not.

Prayer

Thank you, Father, for blessing us in ways that those people of faith who lived long ago were not able to be blessed. Thank you for giving us your power and showing us how everything will come out. May we live and walk in faith. In Jesus' name, Amen.

Luke 11: Blessed by Hearing and Obeying God's Word

Selected Biblical Text

14 He was casting out a demon that was mute. When the demon had gone out, the mute man spoke, and the crowds marveled. 15 But some of them said: "By Beelzebul, the prince of demons, he casts out demons." 16 Others, testing him, kept seeking from him a sign from heaven. 17 But he, knowing their thoughts, said to them: "Every kingdom divided against itself comes to naught; and a divided household will fall. 18 So also, if Satan is divided against himself, how will his kingdom stand? You say that I cast out demons by Beelzebul. 19 But if I cast out demons by Beelzebul, by whom do your sons cast them out? Therefore, they will be your judges. 20 But if it by the finger of God I cast out demons, then the kingdom of God has come upon you. 21 When a strong man, fully armed, guards his own palace, his possessions remain at peace; 22 but when a stronger man attacks him and conquers him, he takes away his armor on which he relied and distributes the plunder. 23 Whoever is not with me is against me, and the one not gathering with me is scattering. 24 "When the unclean spirit has gone out of a person, it goes through waterless places seeking rest, and when it finds none it says, 'I will return to my house from which I came.' 25 And when it comes, it finds the house swept clean and decorated. 26 Then it goes and brings seven other spirits even more evil than itself, and they enter and live there. And the last situation of that person is worse than the first." 27 As he said these things, a woman in the crowd raised her voice and said to him: "Blessed is the womb that bore you, and the breasts at which you nursed." 28 But he said: "Blessed rather are those who upon hearing the word of God keep it." (Luke 11:14-28)

Reflecting and Thinking

Today's chapter is part of a longer section of Luke's gospel that is unique. In the extended section (chapters 10-18), Luke shares many events and teachings from Jesus' life that are not recounted in the other Gospels. More than in any other part of Luke's Gospel, in this section we read the teachings of Jesus.

Jesus' teachings in Luke make clear that we are in a spiritual battle. The battle involves prayer, the Holy Spirit, loyalties, and perseverance. It involves repentance and attitudes. Many details of the spiritual battle are difficult to discern, but one truth is abundantly clear: God blesses those who hear and keep the word of God!

Can success in the spiritual battle really be so easy -- simply hear and obey God's Word? Are we among those who want some difficult or amazing thing, as did Naaman in the Old Testament (2 Kings 5)? Are we among the throngs who seek the spectacular? Are we less than satisfied with the simple admonition to keep the word of God? Notice how this theme continues in the next paragraph which describes those who would prefer to see miraculous signs rather than to accept the simple teaching of the Bible.

Prayer

Heavenly Father, we ask your help as we wage the spiritual battle that surrounds us. We ask your strength so that we will hear and keep your word. We ask your presence as we seek to develop the mind of Christ. We humbly repent, believing that your word convicts us, and we ask your forgiveness, in Jesus' name, Amen.

Luke 12: Interpret the Times -- Discern What Is Right

Selected Biblical Text

54 He also said to the crowds: "When you see a cloud rising in the west, you say at once, 'A heavy rainstorm is coming,' and it rains. 55 And when you see the south wind blowing, you say, 'There will be scorching heat,' and there is. 56 You hypocrites! You know how to discern the appearance of earth and sky. How is it that do you not know how to discern the present season? 57 Why can you not judge for yourselves what is right? 58 As you go with your accuser before the magistrate, on the way make an effort to settle with him, lest he drag you to the judge, and the judge hand you over to the officer, and the officer put you in prison. 59 I tell you that you will never get out until you have paid the very last penny." (Luke 12:54-59)

Reflecting and Thinking

     Today's chapter is the second of three consecutive chapters that contain many of Jesus' teachings. (If you have a Bible with Jesus' words in red, you will see all of the red letters!) Each chapter contains several smaller thought sections. Today's chapter can be summarized like this: "Be careful about false teaching, do not be afraid of those who oppose you, be on your guard against greed, do not worry, be watchful and ready, be wise and discern what is right." Each of these admonitions provides instruction for the spiritual battle described in the previous chapter. Luke emphasizes the Holy Spirit and the presence of spiritual realities. The theme of spirituality runs through Luke as a thread, but in the teachings included in today's chapter, it is as though Luke develops an entire tapestry which shows how spiritual realities intersect daily life.

     How often do you think about spiritual things on an average day? Make a list of areas of your life that should be included in a list of "spiritual concerns." (Make your list before you read on!) Jesus' list includes at least the following: what we say and teach, hypocrisy, possessions or wealth, worry -- especially about physical needs, inattention, short-cuts, family, priorities, and reconciliation. What does the idea of correctly "interpreting the times" mean to you? How does one do this? What are some ways that one can go astray in this matter?

Prayer

Dear Father God, help us interpret the times correctly. Help us know and do what is right. In the pressure of daily life, it is easy to lose sight of spiritual realities. It is easy to let down our guard and let things slip. Help us develop the spiritual side of our lives, so that we focus on spiritual, eternal matters more than on physical, mundane concerns. We are grateful for the privilege of prayer, and we confidently approach your throne in the name of Jesus, Amen.

Luke 13: Teaching with Emotion

Selected Biblical Text

31 In the same hour, some Pharisees came and said to him: "Get away from here because Herod wants to kill you."

32 And he said to them: "Go and tell that fox, 'Look, I am casting out demons and doing healings today and tomorrow, and the third day I finish my work. 33 Nevertheless, it is necessary for me to go on my way today and tomorrow and the day following, for it cannot be that a prophet should perish outside of Jerusalem.' 34 O Jerusalem, Jerusalem, the city that kills the prophets and stones those who are sent to it. How often I have wanted to gather your children together as a hen gathers

her brood under her wings, and you would not. 35 Look, your house is forsaken. And I tell you, you will not see me until you say, 'Blessed is the one coming in the name of the Lord!'" (Luke 13:31-35)

Reflecting and Thinking

When I think of Luke 13, I think of a chapter filled with emotion. One can hear the pathos in Jesus' voice as he teaches about repentance and fruitfulness. How did Jesus feel when people were humiliated, or when people delighted in evil? Does he not hope that some among his listeners will catch on when he talks about the kingdom as mustard seed and yeast? Is that sorrow we hear in his voice as he describes the narrow door? Despite the need to answer Herod's emissaries, the sorrow crescendos to an unmistakable forte as Jesus weeps over Jerusalem.

What things fill you with emotion? When have you been deeply sorrowful about a spiritual matter? How would you describe your attitude toward those around you who are lost? Are you concerned about the fruitfulness of other Christians? Do you pray about the lack of effectiveness of the church? What personal applications could you make from our reading or from this chapter?

Prayer

Heavenly Father, teach us to care like Jesus cared. Help us to hear his heart so we can become like him. Help us to weep about our world's separation from and departure from you. Help us understand more clearly the stakes involved and help us to find meaningful emotional involvement with those we can touch for Jesus. We pray in His name, Amen.

Luke 14: Who Can Be a Disciple? Who Will Be a Disciple?

Selected Biblical Text

25 Now great crowds accompanied him, and he turned to them and said: 26 "If anyone comes to me and does not hate his own father and mother and wife and children and brothers and sisters, yes, and even his own life, he cannot be my disciple. 27 Whoever does not carry his own cross and come after me cannot be my disciple."
33 "In the same way, therefore, any one of you who does not renounce all his possessions cannot be my disciple. 34 Salt is good, but if salt loses its saltiness, how can it be used as seasoning? 35 It is of no use either for the soil or for the manure pile. It is thrown away. The one having ears that can hear, let him hear." (Luke 14:25-27, 33-35)

Reflecting and Thinking

We have noted that Luke 10-18 includes many stories and teachings that are unique to Luke's Gospel. An interesting way to analyze the stories is to note who is present and to whom Jesus is speaking. Following is a simple analysis of these chapters. The groups he addresses most often are his disciples, the crowd, and the Pharisees. The text usually notes that Jesus' teachings are directed at one or more of these groups. The following list of hearers makes this easier to see.

11:1, disciples; 11:14, crowd; 11:29, crowd; 11:37, Pharisees

12:1, disciples; 12:13, crowd; 12:22, disciples; 12:54, crowd

13:1, crowd/people; 13:31, Pharisees

14:1, Pharisees/banquet guests; 14:25, crowd

15:1, Pharisees; 16:1, disciples; 16:14, Pharisees; 17:1, disciples

The teachings of Luke 14 should be read with the original audience in view. The "cost of discipleship" teachings are spoken to the crowds. In a day when many were willing to be "group followers," Jesus describes what it means to be a committed individual disciple. There is no value in piling up huge amounts of tasteless salt. One cannot find a good use for it, and it must ultimately be discarded. Do you get the point? ("He who has ears to hear, let him hear.")

On a scale of 1-10, how well do you think Christians today are able to hear and apply these teachings? What challenges do we face in today's world in accurately hearing these words? What do you think of the idea that some churches may be piling up lots of useless "unsalty salt?" What personal challenge do you feel in the statement that saltiness cannot be restored? How could this chapter help the church reconsider its priorities?

Prayer

Heavenly Father, on some days, we fear that our version of discipleship is too insipid to make much difference in our world. Help us to hear afresh today the words of Jesus, and to renew our commitment to apply these words in our lives. Increase our love for your word and our desire to do your will. Forgive us when we are less than committed and help us so that we never lose our saltiness. In the name of Jesus who is the Christ, Amen.

Luke 15: Lost and Found

Selected Biblical Text

1 Now all the tax collectors and sinners were coming near to hear him. 2 And the Pharisees and the law experts grumbled, saying: "This man welcomes sinners and eats with them." 3 He told them this parable: 4 "Which one of you, having a hundred sheep and losing one of them, does not leave the ninety-nine in the pasture,

and go look for the lost one until he finds it? 5 And when he finds it, he places it on his shoulders, rejoicing 6 as he goes home. He calls together his friends and his neighbors and says to them, 'Rejoice with me, I found my sheep that was lost.' 7 I tell you that, in the same way, there will be more joy in heaven over one sinner who repents than over ninety-nine righteous persons who do not need to repent. 8 Or what woman, having ten silver coins, if she loses one coin, does not light a lamp and sweep the house and search carefully until she finds it? 9 Then when she has found it, she calls together her friends and neighbors, saying, 'Rejoice with me, for I have found the coin that I had lost.' 10 In the same way, I tell you, there is joy in the presence of the angels of God over one sinner who repents."

32 To celebrate and to be glad was fitting, because this your brother was dead and is alive; he was lost and is found. (Luke 15:1-10, 32)

Reflecting and Thinking

Well-known stories must be studied more closely. Volumes have been written about the prodigal son. The parable was spoken to the Pharisees and teachers of the law. Did they get the point? Do we get the point? Lostness is reversible. Lostness is not a perpetual state. Lost things can be found -- sheep and coins. In this parable, the restoration of a lost person requires the involvement of the person -- awareness, repentance, decision, and action. Some who should rejoice when sinners are restored do not rejoice. Even family members can be cold and hard, demanding, and unforgiving. God and the angels in heaven rejoice when lostness becomes foundness.

What does this parable say to God's people today? Where should the church see itself in the parable? Do we miss the point? Are we the Pharisees? Are we the elder brother? Are we the wayward son? Would we go out of our way to help others find their way home?

Prayer

Heavenly Father, help us develop your heart within us, caring for those you care for, rejoicing when you rejoice, seeking to find those who are lost. Help us imitate Jesus more completely, seeking and saving the lost. Soften our hearts until we develop caring compassion. Open our eyes to the opportunities. Bring us closer to you today, through Jesus we offer our prayer, Amen.

Luke 16: "Stuff" Gets in the Way

Selected Biblical Text

10 "One who is trustworthy with very little is also trustworthy with much, and one who is dishonest with very little is also dishonest with much. 11 If then you have not been trustworthy with worldly riches, who will entrust to you the true riches?

12 And if you have not been trustworthy in that which belongs to another, who will give you that which belongs to you? 13 No servant can serve two masters, for either he will hate the one and love the other, or he will be devoted to the one and despise the other. You cannot serve God and worldly riches."

14 The Pharisees, who were lovers of money, heard all these things, and they ridiculed him. 15 And he said to them: "You justify yourselves before men, but God knows your hearts. For what is highly valued among men is detestable idolatry in the sight of God." (Luke 16:10-15)

Reflecting and Thinking

A theme frequently mentioned in studies of Luke's writings is his interest in the poor and the rich. Luke has much to say about wealth and poverty. The theme is reflected in numerous passages -- many of the references to poverty and wealth are found in the "reversal texts" of Luke. For example, consider the "debt parables," the parable of the Good Samaritan, the parable of the Rich Fool, and the tax collector narratives [Zacchaeus is only one of several].

Today's chapter and reading reflect Luke's focus on wealth. In the parable of the shrewd manager Jesus does not exalt the misuse of the boss's funds. Jesus' conclusion advances the principles of trust and honesty. (It is important to study carefully and distinguish the parable from Jesus' conclusions and teachings.) The things people of the world value are of no value at all before God -- in fact, Jesus says they are detestable and abominable.

The story of the rich man and Lazarus is also a story about wealth and poverty. Money reveals much about our life -- our emphases, priorities, and major focus. Money also reveals our heart. We can fool ourselves, justify our actions, and deceive ourselves, but God is not deceived.

What has been your previous understanding of the parable of the shrewd manager? (Many have struggled to understand and apply this parable.) What is an appropriate use of worldly wealth? What does it mean to be shrewd in financial dealings? When is shrewdness acceptable and when is it not acceptable? Considering the context, who was the shrewd manager serving? Was he serving God or money? What other 'money' texts are you aware of in Luke's Gospel?

Prayer

Our heavenly Father God, thank you for the many blessings you have given us. Thank you for the physical blessings we have; thank you for the spiritual blessings we have. We are grateful for those blessings we see, and also for those we do not see. Help us to use every blessing we receive to your honor and glory. Help us not to set up false gods from the resources you have given us. Give us wisdom. Help us keep our hearts focused on serving only you. In the name of Jesus, we pray, Amen.

Luke 17: The Coming of the Kingdom

Selected Biblical Text

20 When he was asked by the Pharisees when the kingdom of God would come, he answered them: "The kingdom of God does not come with signs that can be seen, 21 nor will they say, 'Look, it is here!' or 'It is there!' For indeed the kingdom of God is among you." (Luke 17:20-21)

Reflecting and Thinking

The kingdom! Today's text is a small section in a much longer chapter. Other themes in this chapter are equally worthy of note -- sin, repentance, faith, duty, and gratitude. What is Jesus saying in today's selected biblical text? Several possibilities come to mind. He is saying that it is easy to miss the kingdom. Some look for the kingdom in the wrong places. It is easy to misidentify the kingdom. Some think they have found the kingdom when they have not. They point here or there, thinking the kingdom is within their grasp, but they are wrong. They are missing the kingdom. Some will try to study their way to the kingdom by observing the signs and times, but the kingdom is not advanced or brought to fruition by such careful observations. Some will become overly enamored by timing questions, always wanting to know the "when" and missing the "what" and the "why." The presence of the kingdom is subtle because it is not an external reality to be identified. The kingdom is not physical and external. It is spiritual and internal. The kingdom is not a visible entity or reality. Jesus claims that the kingdom is already among them (through his presence among them) and that they have missed it. They have failed to see it.

When have you missed the kingdom? That is, when has the kingdom been present but you failed to see it at first? How do you measure the presence of the kingdom? Are the measurements you use external and visible, or internal and invisible? How do your answers measure up in view of the teaching of Jesus in this passage?

Prayer

Dear God, we so desperately want to see and experience kingdom realities; we at times are tempted to buy into external measurements and evidences. Help us focus on authentic kingdom realities and biblical kingdom values. Help us understand what it means to advance the things of the kingdom, beginning with our firm allegiance to the King and his will. Help us avoid the distractions and misunderstandings that so commonly beset us. We pray in the name of King Jesus, Amen.

Luke 18: Humility

Selected Biblical Text

31 Then taking the Twelve aside, he said to them: "Look, we are going up to Jerusalem, and everything that is written about the Son of Man by the prophets will be accomplished. 32 For he will be delivered to the Gentiles. He will be mocked, violently abused, and spit upon. 33 And after flogging him, they will kill him, and on the third day he will rise." 34 But they understood none of these things. This saying was hidden from them, and they did not grasp what Jesus had said. (Luke 18:31-34)

Reflecting and Thinking

Humility. Easy to say, hard to achieve. A man said he planned to write a book, *Humility and How I Achieved It*. His effort is dead in the water, even before he begins. Humility puts self out of the way. Humility does not care for reputation, what others think, or self-interests. The persistent widow keeps asking -- regardless of what the judge thinks. Two men in prayer represent two opposite extremes -- humility and pride. Become as little children: the admonition connects humility and entering the kingdom. The rich ruler had multiple problems -- a big one was his lack of humility. "Look at me; I have done it all, I kept all of the commands, and I did it better than most." A blind beggar can cry out and call attention to his plight only when he overcomes embarrassment and pride.

Our selected biblical today is Jesus' third and final passion prediction before the cross. Read between the lines. Jesus is the ultimate example of humility -- he will go to the cross, he will be mocked, insulted, made fun of, passed from one to another like mere chattel. He will not stand up for his own self-interests; he will not pay back in kind; he will in humbling himself pay the price for our sins and transgressions.

Why is humility so hard? What would you say in response to the suggestion that one opposite of gratitude is pride? How could we develop a greater humility in our own lives? To what extent is our problem with humility based in the cultural values around us -- independence, self-reliance, and personal rights?

Prayer

Dearest heavenly Father, help me learn humility. Help me see myself correctly; help me not to think of myself more highly than I should. Help me also to see others as persons made in your image and likeness, with potential and value in your eyes. Thank you for Jesus and his sacrifice. Thank you that he was willing to go humbly to the cross for me, emptying himself to become a servant. Make me a servant. In the name of Jesus, I pray, Amen.

Luke 19: The King Is Here!

Selected Biblical Text

37 By this time he was approaching the road that went down from the Mount of Olives -- the entire group of his disciples began to praise God joyfully with a loud voice for all the mighty works that they had seen, 38 saying: "Blessed is the King who comes in the name of the Lord! Peace in heaven and glory in the highest!" 39 And some of the Pharisees in the crowd said to him: "Teacher, rebuke your disciples." 40 He answered: "I tell you, if they keep silent, the stones themselves will cry out." 41 Now as he approached and saw the city, he wept over it, 42 saying: "If only you had foreseen this day, the things that lead to peace! But now they are hidden from your eyes. 43 For the days will come upon you when your enemies will set up a barricade around you and surround you and hem you in on every side 44 and tear you down to the ground, you and your children within your walls. And they will not leave one stone upon another in you, because you did not recognize the time of God's help."
45 Entering the temple courts, he began to drive out the sellers, 46 saying to them: "It is written, 'My house will be a house of prayer,' but you have made it a den of robbers." 47 And he was teaching each day in the temple. The chief priests and the law experts were seeking to put him to death, along with the leaders of the people, 48 but they did not find an opportunity to do it, for all the people were listening closely to his words. (Luke 19:37-48)

Reflecting and Thinking

Analyzing Luke 19, we have no indication that Zacchaeus thought Jesus was a king. Some who assembled, perhaps outside the door of Zacchaeus's house, listened to Jesus' parable of the minas (similar to the parable of the talents in Matthew) because they thought the kingdom of God was going to appear immediately. The clearest indicators that the story of Jesus is reaching a climax are the Triumphal Entry and the temple confrontation. The Pharisees are upset that Jesus is being declared a King -- "Blessed is the King who comes in the name of the Lord." When they ask him to quiet the throngs, Jesus says there is no way to keep the message quiet. How sad! They did not recognize the time of God's coming to them.

Have you ever failed to recognize God's presence? In the world today, most do not have any personal experience with kings and queens. What does it mean to you that Jesus is king? Do you think Jesus would consider our church buildings as places of extraneous activities more than as places of prayer?

Prayer

Heavenly Father God, we praise and honor you for your wisdom in sending Jesus to be King over a spiritual kingdom. Help us to grasp what that means. Help us to strengthen our commitment to the King. Help us to do his will more completely. As we read these stories about Jesus, we wonder how we would have responded. We pray for your help as we live life as subjects of the King in His kingdom, in Jesus' name, Amen.

Luke 20: Jesus is Supreme

Selected Biblical Text

41 But he said to them: "How can they say that the Christ is David's son? 42 For David himself says in the book of Psalms, 'The Lord said to my lord, sit at my right hand, 43 until I make your enemies a footstool for your feet.' 44 David calls him Lord, so how can he be his son?" 45 As all of the people were listening, he said to his disciples: 46 "Beware of the law experts who like to walk around in long flowing robes; they love special greetings in the marketplaces and the most important seats in the synagogues and the places of honor at feasts. 47 They devour widows' houses and for a show pray long prayers. They will receive a greater judgment." (Luke 20:41-47)

Reflecting and Thinking

For some chapters of the Bible, writing a devotional thought that reflects the contents of the chapter is very difficult. Luke has especially long chapters so that in some chapters the overarching themes are difficult to discern, plus there are often subthemes and subplots. This chapter, however, seems clear. The events of this chapter clearly declare Jesus' supremacy. Jesus has authority; he is the son of the vineyard owner in the parable. When his opponents seek to hand him over to the authority and power of the politicians, he effectively positions himself above those earthly powers as he declares their limited arena of authority. He is the teacher without equal, he is the one who stands in the lineage of David; he soundly criticizes the abuses of the teachers of the law. Believers today may tend to take Jesus' authority, power, and supremacy for granted, but many people do not accept his authority, even though the Bible affirms it again and again. Let us hear the Word afresh and be strengthened!

What are some evidences that we sometimes take the supremacy of Jesus for granted? Why do we do that? This chapter is a good example of how Scripture reinforces a basic truth by a series of narratives, all of which point in the same direction. What impact do you think this series of events had on the people? on the disciples? on the Pharisees and Jewish leaders?

Prayer

Thank you, Father, for your revelation. Thank you for making it possible for us to know who Jesus is. Thank you for revealing his power and majesty, his splendor and supremacy. Help us to hear and to apply your truth. In the name of the One who is truth, Amen.

Luke 21: The "End" is Coming

Selected Biblical Text

1 Looking up, Jesus saw the rich putting their gifts into the offering box, 2 and he saw a poor widow put in two small copper coins. 3 He said: "In truth, I tell you, this poor widow has put in more than all of them. 4 For they all gave from their abundance, but she out of her poverty put in all she had to live on."
37 Every day Jesus was teaching in the temple courts, but at night he went out and stayed on the Mount of Olives. 38 And all the people early in the morning came to him in the area of the temple to hear him. (Luke 21:1-4, 37-38)

Reflecting and Thinking

The Olivet Discourse of this chapter is an important teaching. It tells about the future destruction of the temple by the Roman army in AD 70. It puts the coming of the kingdom into a specific time perspective and anticipates a sudden end and a time of judgment. The chapter is worthy of in-depth study and should not be passed over lightly (the parallel passages are found in Matthew 24 and Mark 13).

In the middle of such a challenging study, it is easy to lose sight of the "parentheses" that are included in Luke's Gospel -- the story that introduces the chapter and the story that concludes the chapter. First, the story of the widow's offering (21:1-4) is one final nail in the coffin of the Jewish leaders. They are anything but leaders -- they are leeches who take advantage of and abuse the neediest persons in Jewish society. Second, the last two verses of the chapter (21:37-38) reflect the mountain place-marketplace rhythm of Jesus' life that we observed in Luke 5. Jesus' time with God at night on the mount empowers his temple teaching. Important principles are here -- authentic leadership, sacrifice, generosity, and time alone with God. Pick one specific principle or concept from these verses to pray about today. Keep it in mind, think about it, and pray about it throughout the day to strengthen your Christian walk.

Which of the concepts in our text do you most need to focus on in your Christian life? Thinking of that one specific area, what outcomes do you desire? What kind of personal growth would you like to experience? How will working on the area you have identified change your life?

Prayer

Dearest Heavenly Father, Creator God, bless my life this day as I strive to become more like Jesus. Teach me your ways, guide my paths. Instill me with a greater desire for time together with you, empower my life with your presence. In Jesus' name and by his power I ask it. Amen.

Luke 22: Into Their Hands

Selected Biblical Text

47 While he was still speaking, a crowd and the one called Judas, one of the Twelve, approached him. He approached Jesus to kiss him, 48 Jesus said to him: "Judas, would you betray the Son of Man with a kiss?" 49 Those around Jesus, seeing what was happening, said: "Lord, shall we strike with swords?" 50 And one of them struck the bondservant of the high priest and cut off his right ear. 51 But Jesus said: "That's enough of this!" And he touched his ear and healed him. 52 Then Jesus said to those who had come near to him, the chief priests and officials of the temple and the elders: "Have you come out as you would against a robber, with swords and clubs? 53 Day after day when I was with you in the temple courts, you did not lay hands on me. But this is your hour, and the power of darkness." (Luke 22:47-53)

Reflecting and Thinking

As we approach the end of Luke's Gospel, the wheels of God's plan are turning more and more rapidly. Several things happen in today's chapter: (1) Judas agrees to betray Jesus, (2) at the Last Supper Jesus talks about many things -- his love for his disciples, the future kingdom, betrayal, leadership, and denial, (3) in Gethsemane Jesus draws strength from prayer, (4) his arrest is described as "darkness reigning," (5) Peter disowns him, (6) the guards mock him, and (7) Jesus is hustled off to appear before the Jewish council and then before Pilate and Herod. Finally, the enemies of Jesus conspire to seize him, and the chapter provides a vivid description of Jesus' delivery "into their hands."

How do you think you would have responded had you been present at the events described in this chapter? Can you read the story while maintaining the suspense? Most of us have heard and known the story for a long time. Because we know the outcome, it is hard to read it in fresh, new, and challenging ways. Try to read the selected text (or the chapter) through the eyes of someone who is hearing the story for the first time and does not already know the ending.

Prayer

Dear God, thank you again for the sacrifice of Jesus. I am thinking today, not only about his sacrifice on the cross, but about the emotional turmoil he endured during the events of this chapter -- knowing in advance about the betrayal, denial, and scattering of his followers. I think about his fore-knowledge of his deliverance into the hands of his enemies. I cannot fully grasp the depth of his pain and suffering. Even in my inability to under-stand, however, I am grateful for his love. My heart can only express gratitude, because I know that the penalty was really mine, in Jesus' name, Amen.

Luke 23: Into the Father's Hands

Selected Biblical Text

44 It was now about the sixth hour [noon], and there was darkness over the whole land until the ninth hour [three in the afternoon] 45 because the sun's light failed. And the curtain of the temple was torn in two. 46 Then Jesus, calling out with a loud voice, said: "Father, into your hands I commit my spirit!" And having said this he breathed his last. 47 Now when the centurion saw what had taken place, he praised God, saying: "Certainly, this man was innocent!" 48 And all the crowds that had come together to see this spectacle, when they saw what had taken place, returned home beating their breasts. 49 And all those who knew Jesus stood at a distance, with the women who had followed him from Galilee, watching these things. (Luke 23:44-49)

Reflecting and Thinking

Jesus' delivery into the hands of his enemies was temporary at best -- almost less than real -- for Jesus was always in the Father's will. The cru-cifixion narrative climaxes in today's text. Darkness came, the sun stopped shining, the curtain of the temple was torn, and Jesus made clear his de-pendence on the Heavenly Father: "Father, into your hands I commit my spirit." The centurion witnessed the events and stated his conclusion: "Surely this was a righteous man." Joseph of Arimathea, a member of the Jewish council and one who was waiting for the kingdom of God, took care of the details of Jesus' burial. We can rest secure in the knowledge that Jesus has been delivered into the Father's hands, not into the hands of evil men. We rest secure and wait!

How are the events of this chapter a validation of the identity of Jesus? (Remember that he has not yet been resurrected.) How aware do you think Jesus was of the Father's constant care during this time? How does it make you feel to know that you are resting in the Father's hands?

Prayer

Dear God, help us sense your everlasting arms beneath us, help us know that your hands surround and support us. May we know your presence more fully. Buoy our spirits in difficult days as we turn to you. Thank you for the example of Jesus, for the privilege of approaching your throne in his name and by his authority, and for the certainty that you hear us, Amen.

Luke 24: Risen! New Beginnings for the Good News

Selected Biblical Text

44 Then he said to them: "These are my words that I spoke to you while I was still with you, that everything written about me in the Law of Moses and the Prophets and the Psalms must be fulfilled." 45 Then he opened their minds so they would understand the Scriptures, 46 and said to them: "Thus it has been written, that the Christ would suffer and would rise from the dead on the third day, 47 and that repentance and forgiveness of sins would be preached in his name to all nations, beginning from Jerusalem. 48 You are witnesses of these things. 49 Look, I am sending forth the promise of my Father upon you. Remain in the city until you have been endued with power from on high." 50 Then he led them out as far as Bethany and lifting up his hands he blessed them. 51 While he blessed them, he departed from them and was taken up into heaven. 52 So they worshiped him and returned to Jerusalem with great joy, 53 and were continually in the temple courts blessing God. (Luke 24:44-53)

Reflecting and Thinking

Sometimes the end is the beginning. That is certainly true in Luke's gospel. The storyline will continue in the book of Acts: Luke--Volume 2. The Old Testament prophecies have been fulfilled; it is time for a new beginning. It is time to preach repentance and forgiveness of sins through the name of Jesus in every nation. The promise is about to be fulfilled; the power is about to be granted. Jesus must go away so that the power of the Comforter can come. All doubt has been removed. The truth is clearly in view. No wonder his disciples worshiped him, were filled with joy, and continually blessed and praised God.

[Note: If you are following the order of the readings in this daily devotional series, we will immediately jump to Luke's second volume, continuing in the Book of Acts. Get ready for some very good news!]

When have you received something special that had been promised to you? How did you feel when the promise was made? How did you feel when the promise was fulfilled? Think about how special the apostles must have felt when they received the promise. What kind of anticipation would they have felt? Consider also how they must have felt as Jesus left them.

How would you describe that feeling? How aware are you today that the gospel proclaimed is in fact very good news? How committed are you to telling that good news to others?

Prayer
Heavenly Father, we thank you for giving us a written record of Jesus' life. Help us understand the story; help us appreciate how good the good news is. Help us participate more fully in the proclamation of the good news. Thank you for loving us, thank you for saving us. We pray in the name of Jesus the Christ, Amen.

Acts 1: Waiting -- Getting Ready to Spread the Good News

Selected Biblical Text

8 "But you will receive power when the Holy Spirit has come upon you, and you will be my witnesses in Jerusalem and in all Judea and Samaria, and to the end of the earth." 9 And after he had said these things, while they were watching, he was lifted up, and a cloud took him up out of their sight. 10 And while they were staring into heaven as he went, suddenly, two men stood beside them in white clothing, 11 and said: "Men of Galilee, why do you stand looking into heaven? This Jesus, who was taken up from you into heaven, will come in the same way as you saw him go into heaven." 12 Then they returned to Jerusalem from the Mount of Olives, which is near Jerusalem, a Sabbath day's journey away. 13 When they had entered Jerusalem, they went up to the upstairs room, where they were staying, Peter and John and James and Andrew, Philip and Thomas, Bartholomew and Matthew, James the son of Alphaeus and Simon the Zealot and Judas the son of James. 14 All these, being of one mind, were devoting themselves to prayer, together with the women, and Mary the mother of Jesus, and his brothers. (Acts 1:8-14)

Reflecting and Thinking

Acts 1 is a story of waiting. Few things are more difficult. Why do we often dislike the times of preparing, getting ready, and anticipating? Why is it so hard to wait? In Acts 1, God's people are waiting for the promise -- they are devoted to and joined together in prayer, they listen to Scripture, and they replace Judas with the person of God's choice. The events of Acts 1 are more than miscellaneous details to get us ready for Acts 2.

We want to start immediately. We like action and activity. It is not easy to learn the lesson that God works in God's time. God's work is seldom done according to our timetable -- even less is it done according to our expectations. We call it wasting time -- God sees it differently. God understands that waiting can be a time for equipping and empowering us as we learn patience. Consider some options -- "not enough time to pray" vs. "I must pray to get everything done," "not enough time for a daily dose of God's Word" vs. "having the right word at the right time." Take time today to contemplate what is happening in Acts 1. Do not jump ahead to the next chapter (which many of us know quite well). Ask yourself what is happening in today's chapter. Think about how Luke unfolds the story. The gospel will go forth -- Jerusalem, Judea, Samaria, the uttermost parts of the earth (1:8). It will happen within the lifetime of some of those assembled, within 30 years or so. We are in a hurry and the work doesn't get done. Wait on God. His work will be done by his people in his way in his time. Not an easy message to hear in our modern world.

When have you been tempted to run ahead of God? When have you been amazed to see God work when you thought all hope was gone? Use your answers to guide your prayer time today.

Prayer

Father God, teach us this day to wait. Help us learn your ways -- renew us and empower us. Teach us patience, teach us holiness. We pray for the accomplishment of your will. We want you to use us in accomplishing your will. Equip us for the task and use us for your glory. In Jesus' name and by his power we ask it. Amen.

Acts 2: The Good News Is Preached -- A New Community Is Born

Selected Biblical Text

36 "So then, let all the house of Israel therefore know with certainty that God made him both Lord and Christ, this Jesus whom you crucified."
37 When they heard these words, they were greatly distressed and said to Peter and the rest of the apostles: "What should we do, brothers?" 38 Peter said to them: "You should repent, and every one of you should be baptized in the name of Jesus Christ for the forgiveness of your sins, and you will receive the gift of the Holy Spirit. 39 For the promise is for you and for your children and for all who are far away, everyone whom the Lord our God calls to himself." 40 With many other words he testified and continually exhorted them: "Save yourselves from this crooked generation." 41 Then those who accepted his message were baptized, and about three thousand were added on that day.
42 And they devoted themselves to the apostles' teaching and the fellowship, to the breaking of bread and to prayer. 43 Reverent fear was on every person, and many wonders and miraculous signs were done by the apostles. 44 And all the believers were together and had everything in common. 45 They sold their possessions and belongings and distributed the proceeds to everyone, as anyone had need. 46 Every day they were assembling together in the temple courts; they were breaking bread in their homes receiving their food with glad and generous hearts, 47 they were praising God and having favor before all the people. And the Lord was adding those being saved every day to their group. (Acts 2:36-47)

Reflecting and Thinking

The coming of the Holy Spirit upon the apostles empowered them to communicate with those assembled in the different languages represented among the hearers. Peter addresses the entire crowd. The Pentecost sermon is the first "gospel" sermon. Peter's message is that what is occurring was predicted by the prophets and is according to God's will. The sermon concludes in verse 36: "God has made Jesus both Lord and Christ." The text tells us that those who received these words were baptized and a new community was born. The new community, knowing salvation from sin and having received the gift of the Holy Spirit, committed itself to teaching and sharing, praise and prayer. Their reputation spread among the people and the community grew every day by God's power.

As we read this description of the first Christian community, would it be fair to use this text as a model against which to compare the contemporary church? Why or why not? How would the church where you attend stack up against this description? Would it be fair to use this text as a model for contemporary Christians? How would you come out in such an evaluation? What areas would you most need to work on?

Prayer

Dear God, we marvel at the powerful way in which the church began on the Day of Pentecost. We wonder about our own struggles and challenges. Why does the modern church not experience a Pentecost revival? Help us find newness as we preach and live the good news; help us discover anew the power of devotion and commitment. Bind us together in deeper fellowship. Make us more aware of your presence through the gift of your Spirit, we pray in Jesus' name, Amen.

Acts 3: More Good News -- A Crippled Man Healed

Selected Biblical Text

9 And all the people saw him [the man who had been lame] walking and praising God, 10 and knew that he was the one who sat at the Beautiful Gate of the temple, asking for donations. And they were filled with astonishment and amazement at what had happened to him.
11 While he was hanging onto to Peter and John, all the people, utterly astounded, ran together to them in the colonnade called Solomon's Portico. 12 When Peter saw this, he spoke to the people: "Men of Israel, why do you marvel at this, why are you staring at us as though by our own power or godliness we have made him walk? 13 The God of Abraham, the God of Isaac, and the God of Jacob, the God of our fathers, glorified his servant Jesus, whom you delivered over and disowned in the presence of Pilate, when he had decided to release him. 14 But you disowned the Holy and Righteous One and asked that a murderer be given to you. 15 You killed the Author of life, whom God raised from the dead. Of this we are witnesses. 16 And upon faith in Jesus' name, his name has made strong this man whom you see and know. The faith that is through Jesus has given him complete healing in the presence of you all." (Acts 3:9-16)

Reflecting and Thinking

In today's chapter, Luke tells us about one of the first miracles in the early church. The impact of this miracle on the new community must have been astounding. People who were not aware of recent events must have taken note. Unbelievers were astounded. Peter saw the occasion as a preaching opportunity, affirming Jesus as the Christ, the one by whose power the healing had occurred. The miracle declared God's existence; it also revealed how God's plan was being fulfilled in the Good News of Jesus. Most of the chapter is devoted to summarizing Peter's sermon. The main point of Peter's sermon is the resurrection of the dead in Jesus. The words recorded in Acts 3 are only a summary and seem to end abruptly. In the next chapter, we will learn that Peter and John were interrupted by the Jewish leaders.

How many people would believe if they saw a miracle? Would everyone believe? Why would some possibly not believe? Why do you believe (or not believe) in Jesus? On a scale of 1 to 10, how good is the "good news" for you?

Prayer

Dear God, we marvel that on some days the Good News doesn't seem all that good to us. We marvel that we can be so nonchalant and uninvolved. We sometimes think that more visible activity and evidence of your presence would convince us, but we are not sure even of that. Increase our faith. Help us see you in the world around us today. In Jesus' name, Amen.

Acts 4: Persecution -- The Community Grows

Selected Biblical Text

31 And when they had prayed, the place in which they were gathered was shaken, and all of them were filled with the Holy Spirit and began speaking the word of God with boldness. 32 Now the entire group of the believers were of one heart and mind, and no one said that any of his possessions were his own, but to them all things were shared. 33 And with great power the apostles were testifying to the resurrection of the Lord Jesus, and great grace was upon them all. 34 There was not a needy person among them, because those who were owners of lands or houses were selling them. Then they brought the proceeds of what was sold 35 and laid it at the apostles' feet, and it was distributed to each as anyone had need. (Acts 4:31-35)

Reflecting and Thinking

The sermon of Acts 3 was apparently interrupted by the Jewish authorities. The Jewish authorities understood the power of the message contained in the sermon -- something we may easily miss as we read the Bible through 21st century eyes. The seizure of Peter and John did not stop the spread of the message. Many hearers believed and the number of believers grew (4:4). Peter's defense and declaration of Jesus as power for healing and power for salvation impressed even the opponents. There is little to say when the man who has been healed is standing right there (4:14). The only recourse for the Jewish leaders was to warn and threaten Peter and John. The people had obviously already been won over.

Peter and John returned to the group of believers where their report and shared prayer yielded the results reported in verse 31 of the text. The community was growing through bold proclamation, clear evidence of changed lives, prayer, the presence of the Spirit, and sharing the message of Jesus. The testimony of the apostles was empowered. Persecution was not an obstacle -- rather it brought the early church together and encouraged its growth.

What do you think would happen today if the church experienced severe persecution? How many would continue to be faithful? How many would give up? Would persecution make the modern church stronger or weaker? How can today's church powerfully declare the resurrection of Jesus? If the church returned to an "on center" message of Jesus' crucifixion and resurrection, avoiding the peripheral issues that tend to surface, what do you think the result would be?

Prayer

Heavenly Father, give us wisdom as we teach and proclaim your word. Help us to focus on the things that matter more than those that do not. Help us know the difference. Give us boldness in the face of difficulties; bring us to prayerful dependence on you. We pray that you will work in us and through us to help the church grow powerfully again. In the name of the resurrected Christ, Amen.

Acts 5: More Problems -- The Community Keeps Growing

Selected Biblical Text

11 Great fear came upon the whole church and upon all who heard of these things. 12 Now many signs and wonders were regularly done among the people by the hands of the apostles. And they were all together in Solomon's Portico. 13 None of the rest dared join them, but the people held them in high esteem. 14 And more than ever believers were added to the Lord, multitudes of both men and women.... 41 Then they left the presence of the council, rejoicing that they were counted worthy to suffer dishonor for the name. 42 And every day, in the temple and from house to house, they did not cease teaching and preaching Jesus as the Christ. (Acts 5:11-14a; 41-42)

Reflecting and Thinking

This chapter describes two major problems that arose in the early church -- one internal and the other external. First, the church had to deal with the situation brought about by Ananias and Sapphira and their deception concerning the sale and gift of their land. Their sudden deaths brought great fear to the church, but believers were continually added to the Lord.

The second problem was more persecution from the Jewish leaders. The apostles were arrested and jailed, miraculously released from jail by an angel with the admonition to go preach and teach, then returned to appear before the Jewish council, and finally given a stern warning not to preach. Their response was, "We must obey God rather than men" (5:29). Although their claims before the council resulted in more fury from the Jewish leaders, Gamaliel's wise advice to the council prevailed and the apostles continued preaching unceasingly.

What hinders the church today? Are most of our problems and challenges internal or external? Can the church grow in the midst of problems? What does it take for the church to grow when there are severe challenges? What do you think it means that they were teaching every day? How many days a week does your church teach and preach Jesus as the Christ? If there is a difference in your answer and what the Bible says, could that difference explain why the church often fails to grow today?

Prayer
Heavenly Father, we marvel again and again at the experiences of the early Jerusalem church. The story is astounding -- many of us have become unimpressed as we have heard the story repeatedly. Teach us how to avoid the distraction of internal problems and how to surmount external problems, so that the church might spread the Good News. May believers be attracted and added to your kingdom, through Jesus we pray, Amen.

Acts 6: A Problem Solved -- The New Community Establishes Priorities

Selected Biblical Text
1 In those days when the disciples were increasing in number, a complaint arose from the Hellenists [Grecian Jews] against the Hebrews [Hebraic Jews] because their widows were being overlooked in the daily food distribution. 2 So the Twelve, calling together summoned the entire group of the disciples, said: "It is not right that we should leave [the ministry of] the word of God in order to serve at the tables. 3 Brothers, you select from among you seven men with a good reputation, full of the Spirit and of wisdom, whom we will put in charge of this necessity. 4 But we will devote ourselves to prayer and to the ministry of the word."
5 This advice pleased the entire group, and they chose Stephen, a man full of faith and of the Holy Spirit, Philip, Prochorus, Nicanor, Timon, Parmenas, and Nicolas, a proselyte from Antioch. 6 These they set before the apostles who prayed and laid their hands on them. 7 And the word of God continued to spread, the number of the disciples in Jerusalem multiplied greatly, and a large group of the [Jewish] priests became obedient to the faith. (Acts 6:1-7)

Reflecting and Thinking

The new problem that the church faces in today's chapter is internal and multi-faceted. In every church, there are lots of people with lots of needs. There is jealously and complaining. Differences are emphasized. There exists a sense of inequality. In Acts 6, there is also the danger that the apostles will become distracted from their primary task. The church must clearly establish its priorities, or the daily pressures of life will overwhelm it.

In the early church, the problem was solved by selecting servants who were given responsibility for the task. The result was that the word of God continued to spread, the number of disciples increased, and more were converted from Judaism, even from among the priests.

Note: because the Greek word *diakonos* can be translated as servant, minister, or deacon, it is difficult to know how to describe the Seven. I have chosen not to translate the word as "deacon" in this context because of the various official meanings of that word in modern church organization.

When you have been aware that a church problem was resolved successfully? What factors contributed to the positive result? Do you think the church today is distracted by problems and its failure to establish priorities? Based on this chapter, what priorities did the early church choose?

Prayer

Father God, we pray for the ability to move forward in the midst of distractions and difficulties. Help us to establish right priorities in our individual lives and in the church. Help us to learn from your word so that our lives and the lives of others are changed. In the name of Jesus, Amen.

Acts 7: A Sermon Can Get You Killed

Selected Biblical Text

54 Now when they heard these things, they were exasperated, and they ground their teeth at Stephen. 55 But he, full of the Holy Spirit, looked intently into heaven and saw the glory of God and Jesus standing at the right hand of God. 56 He said: "Behold I see the heavens opened and the Son of Man standing at the right hand of God." 57 Crying out with a loud voice, they covered their ears and all together they rushed him. 58 After driving him out of the city, they began to stone him. And the witnesses laid their clothes at the feet of a young man named Saul. 59 And as they continued to stone Stephen, he prayed: "Lord Jesus, receive my spirit." 60 Falling to his knees, he cried out with a loud voice: "Lord, do not hold this sin against them." And when he had said this, he died. (Acts 7:54-60)

Reflecting and Thinking

Most of today's chapter is a summary of Stephen's speech to the Sanhedrin. The speech provides an excellent overview of Old Testament history. Stephen begins with Abraham's call; then in detail he speaks of the covenant with Abraham, the sojourn in Egypt, deliverance through Moses, and rebellion in the wilderness despite God's continuing presence in the Tabernacle. He quickly mentions Joshua, David, and Solomon, and concludes by accusing the Jews -- including the members of the Sanhedrin -- of continuing rebellion. His boldness is his undoing -- at least so far as physical life is concerned. The outcome is described in the last verses of the chapter (see the selected textual reading above).

When have you found it difficult to tell people what they really needed to hear about the Lord? What would it take to make you bolder in such situations? What is your reaction to the historical narrative Stephen shared? Do we tend to tell the story today in the same way or differently? What should we learn?

Prayer

Dear God, we want to be more diligent and to be bolder in telling the story of Jesus. We want to seize the opportunities you provide. We want to be wise and yet dependent on you and your power in our lives. This day, help us see the opportunities. In Jesus' name, Amen.

Acts 8: Persecution -- The Message Spreads

Selected Biblical Text

1 Saul was in agreement with killing Stephen. Now there was from that day a great persecution against the church in Jerusalem, and they were all scattered throughout the regions of Judea and Samaria, except the apostles. 2 Devout men buried Stephen and made great lamentation over him. 3 But Saul was wreaking havoc with the church, entering house after house. Dragging off men and women, he was putting them in prison. 4 Now those who were scattered went around preaching the word.
39 And when they came up out of the water, the Spirit of the Lord snatched away Philip, and the eunuch did not see him anymore, but continued his journey rejoicing. 40 But Philip found himself at Azotus, and as he journeyed along, he preached the gospel in all the towns until he came to Caesarea. (Acts 8:1-4; 39-40)

Reflecting and Thinking

In the world today, we would hardly think that the best way to get the message of Jesus proclaimed to the world would be for intense persecution to arise. That is not the subject of our prayers: "Lord, please help the message spread by sending us persecution." But that is exactly what happened in today's reading. After the death of Stephen, the church in Jerusalem suffered even greater persecution so that the Christians were scattered throughout Judea and Samaria. Luke notes that the apostles stayed in Jerusalem. (We should not miss the fact that Saul was a major factor in the persecution in Jerusalem.)

The result of the persecution and scattering was the spread of the message. The believers who went forth from Jerusalem preached the word. Philip went to Samaria and many of the Samaritans, along with Simon the sorcerer, believed and were baptized. Peter and John went to Samaria and preached the gospel in many Samaritan villages. Philip is called south; encountering a eunuch from Ethiopia, he teaches and baptizes him. After the baptism of the eunuch (8:39-40, see selected text above), Philip preaches the gospel as he travels to Caesarea. The impact of the persecution is the spread of the message -- to Samaria and Judea (remember Acts 1:8), and to the African continent through the eunuch.

As the gospel spreads and Christian preaching moves away from Jerusalem, the gospel goes to Samaritans (intermarried Jews who were rejected by those who claimed a pure Jewish lineage). The gospel had previously gone to proselytes (Gentiles who had converted to Judaism) but taking the gospel to the Samaritans was a new step. The gospel goes to an Ethiopian eunuch (also a Gentile proselyte). Do you think the gospel could spread in this way today? That is, by one person telling another person who would tell another person? How can the modern church best help the gospel go into new regions and areas? Is it more effective to go on "mission trips" or to take the gospel to those places where we are going anyway?

Prayer

Dearest heavenly Father God, we marvel at the way in which the gospel spread in the early years of the church. We are amazed that the message continued to go forth despite adverse circumstances and that many received the word. Our world is as much in need of the gospel as was the first century world. Help us to dream afresh about the ways in which we can spread the word. In the name of Jesus, we pray, Amen.

Acts 9: Conversion of Saul --
Getting Ready to Take the Good News Further

Selected Biblical Text

15 But the Lord said to him [Ananias]: "Go, because he [Saul] is my chosen instrument to carry my name before the Gentiles and kings and the people of Israel. 16 For I will show him how much he must suffer for the sake of my name." 17 So Ananias departed and entered the house. Laying his hands on him, he said: "Brother Saul, the Lord Jesus who appeared to you on the road by which you came has sent me so that you may see again and be filled with the Holy Spirit." 18 And immediately something like scales fell from his eyes. He could see again, and getting up, he was baptized. 19 After taking food, he was strengthened. For several days he was with the disciples in Damascus 20 and immediately he began to preach Jesus in the synagogues: "This man is the Son of God." 21 And all who heard him were amazed and said: "Is not this the man who was making havoc in Jerusalem of those who call on this name, the one who came here to bring them in bonds to the chief priests?" 22 But Saul was becoming stronger and he confounded the Jews who lived in Damascus by proving that Jesus is the Christ. (Acts 9:15-22)

Reflecting and Thinking

Most Bible students have heard of Saul's conversion. A tremendous change occurred when a persecutor of the church became a Christian. This Saul, mentioned in the previous two chapters, will become the great apostle Paul. God chooses Paul to be an apostle to the Gentiles. Paul began by teaching the Jews in Damascus, but in the face of a plot against his life he fled to Jerusalem where he was accepted by the disciples because of the recommendation of Barnabas. Later Paul taught among the Grecian Jews who also tried to kill him, so he fled to Caesarea and then to Tarsus. The church continued to grow. (Acts 9:31 is one of six summary statements in Acts, see 6:7; 9:31; 12:24; 16:5; 19:20; and 28:31.)

The rest of today's chapter focuses on Peter's travels to Lydda where he heals a paralytic named Aeneas and to Joppa where he raises Dorcas. The Christians are encouraged, many more turn to the Lord and believe in the Lord. As we get ready for "the rest of the story" in the next chapter, Peter stays in Joppa at the house of Simon the tanner.

[Note: Since much of the book of Acts is a historical account, some of the "reflecting" sections of these devotionals will, in addition to focusing on specific interests and applications, also provide summaries of the historical events and travels.]

Who do you know that you would consider the most unlikely prospect to become a Christian? Have you considered that Saul was probably on someone's "most unlikely" prospect list? Will you continue to pray about the salvation of even the unlikely ones? Note the phrase, "encouraged by the Holy Spirit", in 9:31. What do you think that means? Can the church today be encouraged by the Holy Spirit? If so, what impact would that have?

Prayer

Heavenly Father, help us see the world through your eyes. Help us see the possibilities that exist even in the "least likely ones." Bind us together with genuine fellowship that empowers bold speech. We pray for your help, in Jesus' name, Amen.

Acts 10: Good News to the Gentiles

Selected Biblical Text

34 Then Peter began speaking: "Now I understand the truth that God does not show favoritism, 35 but in every nation one who fears him and does what is right is welcomed with him. 36 Regarding the word that he sent to the people of Israel, preaching good news of peace through Jesus Christ who is Lord of all, 37 you yourselves know the message that came into all of Judea, beginning from Galilee after the baptism that John proclaimed: 38 Jesus of Nazareth, whom God anointed with the Holy Spirit and with power, went about doing good and healing all who were oppressed by the devil, for God was with him."
44 While Peter was yet speaking these words, the Holy Spirit fell on all who were hearing the message. 45 And the Jewish believers [those from among the circumcised] who had come with Peter were amazed, because even upon the Gentiles the gift of the Holy Spirit was poured out, 46 for they heard them speaking in tongues and magnifying God. 47 Then Peter asked: "Can anyone withhold water for these to be baptized, who have received the Holy Spirit as we did?" 48 And he commanded them to be baptized in the name of Jesus Christ. Then they asked him to remain for several days. (Acts 10:34-38, 44-48)

Reflecting and Thinking

It is fair to say that the next step in the spread of the gospel was difficult. We may miss the difficulty due to our familiarity with the text. Paul is chosen as an apostle to the Gentiles. It is now clear that the gospel is also for the Gentiles. The spread of the gospel into the entire world will not be limited to Jews. The gospel is for all. How do you convince separatist Jews that the Gentiles can be included and can receive the gospel? Peter was convinced by the miraculous vision he received on the rooftop. Peter's sermon in this chapter declares God's impartiality. Those who accompanied Peter to the house of Cornelius were convinced by a different kind of miracle -- the coming and presence of the Holy Spirit on the Gentiles. This miraculous outpouring served as a sign; what happened was not the norm in the early church. In this case, after receiving the Holy Spirit, the Gentiles still needed to be baptized. They still needed to be saved. We must not err by making a special occasion the pattern for all occasions. Each text must be understood in its context, and the context for Acts 10 must include the salvation stories in the rest of the book of Acts.

Does the modern church ever limit the gospel by refusing or failing to take the gospel to those God wants to reach? Where does God want the gospel to go today? What places or people are within your reach, your sphere of influence, or your daily routines? Are you willing to be God's instrument to take the gospel to those places?

Prayer
Thank you, Heavenly Father, for your love and mercy extended to me and to the entire world through Jesus. Help me be like Jesus by doing good. Help me see those in my path today who need the gospel. Please be present with me as I share the Good News. In the name of Jesus, the One who is at the center of the Good News, Amen.

Acts 11: To Antioch -- The Good News Keeps Spreading

Selected Biblical Text
19 Now those who were scattered because of the persecution that arose over Stephen traveled as far as Phoenicia and Cyprus and Antioch, speaking the word to no one except Jews. 20 But there were some of them, men of Cyprus and Cyrene, who when they came to Antioch began to speak to the Greeks also, preaching the gospel of the Lord Jesus. 21 And the hand of the Lord was with them, and a great number of those who believed turned to the Lord.
22 This news came to the attention of the church in Jerusalem, and they sent Barnabas to Antioch. 23 When he came and saw the grace of God, he rejoiced and he encouraged them all to persevere in the Lord with steadfast hearts, 24 for he was a good man, full of the Holy Spirit and of faith. And a large group of people was added to the Lord. 25 Then Barnabas left for Tarsus to look for Saul, 26 and when he found him, he brought him to Antioch. For a whole year Barnabas and Saul met with the church and taught a large group of people. And in Antioch the disciples were first called Christians. (Acts 11:19-26)

Reflecting and Thinking
News about the baptism of Cornelius and his household and the reception of the word by Gentiles traveled quickly. When Jews in Judea became aware of the happenings in Caesarea, Peter went up to Jerusalem to explain what had happened. In the first half of today's chapter, Peter recounts the events at the house of Cornelius, providing many helpful details as we compare Acts 10 and Acts 11.

In the second part the chapter, those scattered by the persecution traveled to Phoenicia, Cyprus and Antioch, but the gospel was shared only with Jews. After the conversion of Cornelius, some who came to Antioch spoke to the Gentiles and many Gentiles became believers. Again, the news reached Jerusalem, and the response this time was to send Barnabas to Antioch. Barnabas rejoiced to see the work of God. He encouraged the new Christians (as they soon came to be called) and brought Paul from Tarsus to Antioch. If Gentiles were coming to faith in Antioch, and if Paul was to be an apostle to the Gentiles according to God's commission, Antioch was a good place for Paul to be.

This chapter shows the providence of God in several ways. The gospel will spread more rapidly into the whole world if it is being spread by both Jews and Gentiles. Although Antioch had the second largest concentration of Jews in the eastern Mediterranean, preaching to the Gentiles in Antioch was probably easier than in Jerusalem. No better ambassador could have been chosen than Barnabas; he was from Cyprus, the home region of some of the first preachers to the Antiochian Gentiles. How did Barnabas know to go get Paul? Perhaps Paul had told Barnabas the story of his conversion and the words of the Lord (chapter 9). Barnabas had been one of Paul's first supporters in Jerusalem. When news of famine problems in Jerusalem reached the church in Antioch, the church (including some Gentiles) decided to send aid to Jerusalem. Barnabas and Saul were charged with delivering the help. How interesting that the Jerusalem church needed and received aid from Antioch so quickly. God's providence is not always easy to see. The value of this chapter as evidence of God's providence is often overlooked.

When have you overlooked God's providence, only to later look back on events and clearly see God's hand?

Prayer
Heavenly Father, we thank you for your constant involvement in our lives. We marvel at your work; by faith we answer your call depending on you to work for good in our efforts. May we today see those who need and want you, in Jesus' name, Amen.

Acts 12: God at Work

Selected Biblical Text
1 About that time Herod the king, wishing to do harm, laid hands on certain ones from the church. 2 He killed James the brother of John with the sword. 3 When he saw that it pleased the Jews, he in addition arrested Peter as well. This was during the feast of the Unleavened Bread. 4 And when he had seized him, he put him in prison, delivering him to four squads of soldiers to guard him, planning to bring him out to the people after the Passover. 5 So Peter was kept in prison, and fervent

prayer was being offered to God by the church for him. 6 When Herod was about to bring him out, that same night, Peter was sleeping between two soldiers, bound with two chains, and guards before the door were securing the prison. 7 Then suddenly an angel of the Lord stood beside him, and a light shined in the cell. The angel touched Peter's side and awakened him, saying: "Get up quickly." And the chains fell from his hands. 8 And the angel said to him: "Put on your belt and your sandals." Peter did so. And the angel said to him: "Put your cloak around you and follow me." 9 Peter went out and followed him. He did not know that what was happening by the angel was real, but thought he was seeing a vision. 10 When they had passed the first and the second guard, they came to the iron gate leading into the city. It opened for them automatically [by itself], and they went outside and went down a street, and immediately the angel left him. 11 When Peter came to himself, he said: "Now I know for certain that the Lord has sent his angel and rescued me from the hand of Herod and from everything the Jewish people were expecting."

24 So the word of God increased and multiplied. 25 And Barnabas and Saul returned to Jerusalem when they had finished their ministry, bringing with them John Mark. (Acts 12:1-11, 24-25)

Reflecting and Thinking

In the previous chapter, we noted that God was at work behind the scenes. In this chapter, his work is more clearly seen. Peter's arrest by Herod is short-lived (as is Herod!) because God delivers Peter from prison by an angel. The intrigue and surprising twists continue as we meet the praying believers doubtful of Peter's release (for which they have been praying). Herod steps over the line in claiming to have divine power and God strikes him dead. Meanwhile, the work of God increases more and more, and Barnabas and Saul return to Antioch from Jerusalem along with John Mark. We are ready for the next step in the spread of the gospel -- "into all the world."

Two miraculous events in this chapter are concluded with the simple observation that the word of the Lord was increasing and multiplying. What was the purpose of the miraculous events? Can the word go forth without miraculous support? Think about some of the ways God is at work in this chapter. How is God at work in your life and in the life of the church today?

Prayer

Our God and Father, impress upon us afresh the power of prayer. Teach us dependence; teach us humility. Work among us and in us and through us so that your word may spread with great power today. Help us reflect your glory, in the name of Jesus, Amen.

Acts 13: Good News to Cyprus and Pisidian Antioch

Selected Biblical Text

1 Now there were in the church in Antioch prophets and teachers -- Barnabas, Simeon called Niger, Lucius of Cyrene, Manaen a childhood friend of Herod the tetrarch, and Saul. 2 While they were ministering to the Lord and fasting, the Holy Spirit said: "Set apart for me Barnabas and Saul for the work to which I have called them." 3 Then after fasting and praying and laying their hands on them, they sent them off. 4 Being sent out by the Holy Spirit, Barnabas and Saul went down to Seleucia, and from there sailed to Cyprus. 5 When they arrived in Salamis, they preached the word of God in the synagogues of the Jews. And they had John as an assistant.

13 Now Paul and his companions set sail from Paphos and came to Perga in Pamphylia, but John left them and returned to Jerusalem. 14 They, going on from Perga, came to Antioch in Pisidia. Entering the synagogue on the Sabbath day, they sat down. 15 After the reading from the Law and the Prophets, the leaders of the synagogue sent a message to them, saying: "Brothers, if you have any word of encouragement for the people, you are invited to speak." (Acts 13:1-5, 13-15)

Reflecting and Thinking

The gospel spreads into new territory when the congregation in Antioch sends forth messengers. The decision did not happen accidentally -- they were praying and fasting. The first stop for the missionary team was Cyprus where they began their work by proclaiming the word in the Jewish synagogues (as was Paul's custom). On Cyprus, the opposition of Elymas the sorcerer was overcome, and the governor believed. The continuation of the journey found John returning to Jerusalem while Paul and Barnabas continued on to Antioch of Pisidia (named for the Roman ruler, Antiochus). They went again to the synagogue where they were (at first) warmly received. The sermon recorded in today's chapter is a masterful summary of Old Testament history and a clear declaration of God's work. In Antioch of Pisidia, the opposition that developed was too much, and the chapter ends with the departure of Paul and Barnabas from the city.

In today's reading, the gospel is going where it has not gone before. Are there places today the gospel has not gone? What could the church do to help the gospel go into all the world to every creature? Paul's sermon gives a historical summary which concludes by focusing on Jesus. In your observation, how much of the preaching in the church today focuses on Jesus? How much of it focuses on peripheral matters? Are the typical sermons in local churches today evangelistic? Why or why not?

Prayer

Heavenly Father, we are grateful for mission work and missionaries. We want to take the gospel to the whole world, especially we want to take it where it has not gone. Help us know how to share the message more effectively. Teach us what matters. Help us develop sacrificial hearts so we are willing to pay the price. In the name of the One who sacrificed himself for us, Amen.

Acts 14: Good News in Galatia -- To Iconium, Lystra, and Derbe

Selected Biblical Text

20 But after the disciples gathered about him, he got up and went back into the city, and the next day he went with Barnabas to Derbe. 21 After they had preached the gospel to that city and had made many disciples, they returned to Lystra, to Iconium and to Antioch, 22 strengthening the souls of the disciples, encouraging them to continue in the faith, and saying: "Through many afflictions we must enter the kingdom of God." 23 And when they had appointed elders for them in the churches, with prayer and fasting they committed them to the Lord in whom they had believed. 24 Then they passed through Pisidia and came into Pamphylia. 25 And when they had spoken the word in Perga, they went down to Attalia, 26 and from there they sailed to Antioch, where they had been committed to the grace of God for the work that they had now finished. 27 When they arrived and gathered the church together, they declared all that God had done with them, and that he had opened a door of faith to the Gentiles. 28 And they remained with the disciples quite a while. (Acts 14:20-28)

Reflecting and Thinking

The experience of the missionaries was different in each of the three Galatian cities mentioned in today's chapter. In Iconium, they preached among the Jews and the message was received by many Jews and Gentiles, but a death threat eventually drove them from town. In Lystra, as a result of their healing a crippled man, they were mistaken for gods and were thus received readily, until some opponents from Antioch and Iconium came and stoned Paul, leaving him for dead. The next day Paul and Barnabas traveled to Derbe and preached the word. The return trip from Derbe through Lystra, Iconium, and Antioch was apparently with less opposition as they strengthened and encouraged the new disciples and appointed leaders in the churches. Retracing their journey (except they did not visit Cyprus), they returned to Antioch and reported what God had done, especially focusing on God's work among the Gentiles.

What do you think the church today would do if it faced the kind of opposition Paul and Barnabas faced? What would preachers today do in the face of such threats? In your opinion, does the gospel spread better (does

114

the church grow faster) with or without opposition? If it is God who opens doors of faith, do you think our evangelism or mission efforts today are too dependent on our own efforts and not dependent enough on God? What does it mean to you that they had been commended "to the grace of God" for this work?

Prayer
Heavenly Father, we praise you today for your majesty and greatness, even as Paul described your care for your creation in the sermon in Lystra. We are grateful that you have revealed yourself to us and claimed us as your children. By your grace, show us our place in your work and empower us to do your will. In the name of Jesus who is the Christ, Amen.

Acts 15: Solving Another Problem -- Who Can Receive the Good News?

Selected Biblical Text
1 Now some men came down from Judea and were teaching the brothers: "Unless you are circumcised according to the custom of Moses, you cannot be saved." 2 After Paul and Barnabas had quite an argument and debate with them, they appointed Paul and Barnabas and some of the others from among them to go up to Jerusalem to the apostles and the elders about this question. 3 Being sent out by the church, they passed through both Phoenicia and Samaria, describing in detail the conversion of the Gentiles, bring great joy to all the brothers. 4 When they came to Jerusalem, they were welcomed by the church and the apostles and the elders, and they declared all that God had done with them. 5 But some who had become believers from the party of the Pharisees stood up and said: "It is necessary to circumcise them and to command them to keep the law of Moses." 6 The apostles and the elders gathered together to consider this matter.
22 Then it seemed good to the apostles and the elders, with the whole church, to choose men from among them and send them to Antioch with Paul and Barnabas— Judas called Barsabbas and Silas, leaders among the brothers-- 23 with this letter: "From your brothers, the apostles and the elders, to the Gentile brothers in Antioch and Syria and Cilicia, greetings. 24 Since we have heard that some to whom we gave no orders have gone out from us and troubled you with their words, upsetting your minds, 25 it seemed good to us, being in total agreement, to choose men to send to you with our beloved Barnabas and Paul, 26 men who have risked their lives for the name of our Lord Jesus Christ. 27 Therefore, we have sent Judas and Silas, who will themselves personally tell you the same things...."
30 So when they were sent off, they went down to Antioch, and having gathered the entire group together, they delivered the letter. 31 And when they had read it, they rejoiced because of its encouragement. (Acts 15:1-6, 22-27, 30-31)

Reflecting and Thinking

Acts 15 is a good study of problem-solving. The addition of Gentiles to the church generated a doctrinal problem -- whether circumcision was essential to be a Christian. It was not a small issue. Some traveled long distances to debate the issue. Finally, a conference was held in Jerusalem to consider the matter. The problem was resolved, information was sent to the churches, and the result was that the churches were strengthened and encouraged.

How often do our problem-solving efforts result in encouragement and rejoicing? What could we learn from this text concerning how to approach problem-solving? What changes to current practices would you suggest so that the contemporary church could more effectively solve problems and resolve conflict? What problem-solving principles can you identify from this passage?

Prayer

Heavenly Father, we celebrate the reconciliation you have brought to us in Christ Jesus. We want to live in peace; we want to be peacemakers. Some things seem so important in the emotion of the moment. Help us learn how to model the spirit of Jesus as we deal with conflicts. Through Jesus we offer this prayer, Amen.

Acts 16: A Call to Macedonia -- God Guides

Selected Biblical Text

1 [Then] Paul also came to Derbe and to Lystra. A disciple named Timothy was there, the son of a Jewish woman who was a believer, but his father was a Greek. 2 He was well spoken of by the brothers in Lystra and Iconium. 3 Paul wanted Timothy to accompany him, and he took him and circumcised him because of the Jews who were in those places, for all of them knew that his father was a Greek. 4 As they went through the cities, they delivered [the letter] for them to observe the decisions that had been reached by the apostles and elders in Jerusalem. 5 So the churches were strengthened in the faith and were increasing in number daily. 6 And they went through the region of Phrygia and Galatia, having been forbidden by the Holy Spirit to speak the word in Asia. 7 And when they came up to Mysia, they attempted to go into Bithynia, but the Spirit of Jesus did not permit them. 8 So, passing by Mysia, they went down to Troas. 9 And a vision appeared to Paul in the night: a man of Macedonia was standing there and urging him, saying: "Come over to Macedonia and help us." 10 And after Paul had seen the vision, immediately we sought to go to Macedonia, concluding that God had called us to preach the gospel to them. (Acts 16:1-10)

Reflecting and Thinking

Acts 16 begins what is commonly referred to as the second missionary journey. Paul traveled again through the churches he had established -- Derbe, Lystra, and Iconium, but his long-range plan was to take the gospel to new regions. The missionaries reached a point where they could not go into the regions they had hoped to visit. Stopping in Troas, Paul had a vision, "the Macedonian call," that caused him to conclude with certainty that God was guiding them and calling them to Macedonia. The verb that is translated "we concluded" means "to brings things together, to coalesce or knit together, to make this and that agree, and thus to conclude." The word suggests a process of bringing various details or factors together so that a new reality emerges. The rest of today's chapter is the story of how the decision came out -- a story of Macedonian travels and gospel preaching, beginning in Philippi.

When have you had to sort through a variety of factors and details to decide the direction God wanted you to go? Paul and Silas ended up in jail in Philippi. Do you think Paul was tempted to question his "conclusion?" What does God want from you today? This week? This year? How have you reached that conclusion? What will you do now?

Prayer

Father God, in the name of Jesus, we ask your guidance in the decisions of life. We want to do what you call us to do. Help us see the direction to go, the opportunities, the open doors, and the way in which you are leading us. In Jesus' name, Amen.

Acts 17: Good News to Achaia

Selected Biblical Text

1 After passing through Amphipolis and Apollonia, they came to Thessalonica, where there was a synagogue of the Jews. 2 And Paul went in to them, as was his custom, and for three Sabbaths he reasoned with them from the Scriptures, 3 explaining and proving that it was necessary for the Christ to suffer and to rise from the dead, and saying: This Jesus, whom I proclaim to you, is the Christ. 4 Some of them were persuaded and joined Paul and Silas, a large group of the God-fearing Greeks and quite a number of the leading women.

10 The brothers immediately sent Paul and Silas away to Berea by night, and when they arrived, they went into the synagogue of the Jews. 11 Now these Jews were more open to learning than those in Thessalonica; they received the word eagerly, examining the Scriptures daily to see if these things were so. 12 Therefore many of them believed, with quite a few prominent Greek women and men.

16 Now while Paul was waiting for them at Athens, his spirit was upset within him as he saw that the city was full of idols. 17 So he reasoned in the synagogue with

the Jews and the God-fearing Greeks, and in the marketplace every day with those who happened to come there.

32 Now when they heard the resurrection of the dead, some mocked, but others said: "We will hear from you again about this." 33 So Paul left their midst. 34 But some people joined him and believed, among whom were Dionysius the Areopagite, a woman named Damaris, and others with them. (Acts 17:1-4, 10-12, 16-17, 32-34)

Reflecting and Thinking

The gospel did not go forward without problems and challenges. Problems in Thessalonica sent Paul and Silas to Berea by night. When the opposition followed Paul and Silas to Berea, Paul was whisked away to Athens. At Athens he preached as he waited for his companions to join him, but those who believed were few, and some mocked him.

What is your attitude toward the rapid way the gospel spread in the first century? Are we ever guilty of "glorifying" the Pentecost results and the Jerusalem experience that followed while ignoring the great challenges the gospel faced as it moved into Asia Minor and Macedonia? On a scale of 1 to 10, how would you rate the magnitude of the problems described in this chapter? How would you compare them to the challenges the church faces today?

Prayer

Dear God, give us courage as we live our Christian lives. Give us courage when we have opportunities to speak to others about Jesus. Help us keep going when things are difficult. We have not suffered as Paul and Silas did in today's reading. We ask your presence with us today, in Jesus' name, Amen.

Acts 18: The Good News Spreads in Corinth

Selected Biblical Text

1 After this Paul left Athens and went to Corinth. 2 And he found a Jew named Aquila, a native of Pontus, recently come from Italy with his wife Priscilla, because Claudius had ordered all the Jews to leave Rome. And he went to see them, 3 and because he had the same trade, he stayed with them and worked with them, for they were tentmakers by trade. 4 And he reasoned in the synagogue every Sabbath and tried to persuade both Jews and Greeks. 5 When Silas and Timothy arrived from Macedonia, Paul was totally occupied with the word, testifying to the Jews that Jesus was the Christ. 6 And when they opposed him and spoke evil of him, he shook out his clothes [taking exception] and said to them: "Your blood be on your own heads. I am innocent. From now on I will go to the Gentiles."

7 And he left there and went to the house of a man named Titius Justus, a God-fearer whose house was next door to the synagogue. 8 Crispus, the ruler of the synagogue, believed in the Lord, together with his entire household, and many of the Corinthians who heard Paul believed and were baptized. 9 And the Lord said to Paul one night in a vision: "Do not be afraid; speak and do not be silent, 10 for I am with you, and no one will attack you to harm you, for I have many people in this city." 11 So he stayed a year and six months, teaching the word of God among them. (Acts 18:1-11)

Reflecting and Thinking

Paul spent a year and a half in Corinth, despite some early difficulties with the Jews in that city. Paul's ministry in Corinth resulted in the establishment of a church in that heathen city. Paul stayed there in the midst of difficulties because God was guiding him, and he was confident of God's presence. Wanting to visit Jerusalem again, he accompanied Priscilla and Aquila as far as Ephesus and then traveled on to Caesarea and Jerusalem. After visiting Jerusalem, he went to Antioch and then through the areas of Galatia and Phrygia, eventually arriving back in Ephesus.

Paul's eighteen months in Corinth is the longest "ministry" he has had to this point in the book of Acts. What are some of the reasons for Paul staying longer in Corinth? What options do we have when we face opposition? Do you think the best prospects today -- those who are willing to hear the gospel -- are unchurched people or churched people? How easy or difficult is it for you to reach out to "God-fearers" who are not religious and are not churched?

Prayer

Dearest heavenly Father, we are intrigued by the spread of the gospel in the first century. We want to share Jesus with those around us, and we want to do it in the most effective way. We admit that we fail to act sometimes because we do not know how to proceed. We ask your wisdom and guidance as we look for those who will believe and respond to the message of Jesus. In the name of Jesus, we pray, Amen.

Acts 19: Ephesus -- Success and Opposition

Selected Biblical Text

8 For three months he entered the synagogue and spoke boldly, reasoning and persuading them about the kingdom of God. 9 But when some became stubborn and refused to be persuaded, speaking evil of the Way before the congregation, he withdrew from the synagogue, took the disciples with him, and was reasoning daily in the lecture hall of Tyrannus. 10 This continued for two years, so that all who lived in Asia heard the word of the Lord, both Jews and Greeks. 11 God was doing

extraordinary miracles by the hands of Paul, 12 so that even handkerchiefs or aprons that had touched him were carried away to the sick, and their diseases left them, and the evil spirits came out of them.

23 About that time there was quite a disturbance concerning the Way. 24 For a man named Demetrius, a silversmith, who made silver shrines of Artemis, brought a great amount of business to the craftsmen. 25 These he gathered together, with the workmen in similar trades, and said: "Men, you know that our wealth comes from this business. 26 And you see and hear that not only in Ephesus but in almost all of Asia this Paul has persuaded and turned away large crowds, saying that gods made with hands are not gods." (Acts 19:8-12, 23-26)

Reflecting and Thinking

This chapter is a reminder that the gospel went forth in the first century with both success and opposition -- sometimes in the same city! In Ephesus, Paul taught twelve disciples who had known only John's baptism; perhaps it was this success that emboldened him to preach in the synagogue. Facing considerable stubbornness and unbelief among the Jews, he turned to teaching publicly in a different forum, a private school. Two years of teaching reached both Jews and Greeks so that the gospel went forth into all of Asia, perhaps through the converts Paul made. God was at work in extraordinary ways and the message echoed forth.

Opposition came not only from the Jews, but also from artisans who provided idols for the worship of Diana, a temple goddess who was popular among the Ephesians. Paul's success in teaching about Jesus and turning people from idol worship had a negative influence on the business of the artisans. The uproar that followed was enough reason for Paul to decide to leave Ephesus and journey to Macedonia.

What are the most serious sources of opposition to the gospel today? Why doesn't the church today spend more time preaching and teaching in public forums away from the church building? Why does the preaching of the gospel not disturb more people today? Is it because the gospel is not heard or because the gospel is not perceived as a threat? How could the preaching of the gospel confront people more directly?

Prayer

Heavenly Father, encourage us when we do not succeed and help us not to be satisfied when success comes. Give us wisdom to know how to deal with opposition. Lift our eyes to see the possibilities for sharing the gospel beyond our traditional methods and places. We pray for your help in living by faith and proclaiming Jesus, in Jesus' name, Amen.

Acts 20: Paul Visits Macedonia and Greece -- One Last Time

Selected Biblical Text

1 After the disturbance stopped, Paul sent for the disciples, and after encouraging them and saying goodbye, he departed for Macedonia. 2 When he had gone through those regions and encouraged them with many words, he came to Greece 3 where he spent three months, and when a plot was made against him by the Jews as he was about to sail for Syria, he decided to return through Macedonia. 4 Sopater the Berean, son of Pyrrhus, accompanied him; and of the Thessalonians, Aristarchus and Secundus; and Gaius of Derbe, and Timothy; and from the province of Asia, Tychicus and Trophimus. 5 These went on ahead and were waiting for us at Troas, 6 but we sailed away from Philippi after the days of Unleavened Bread, and after five days we came to them at Troas, where we stayed for seven days. 7 On the first day of the week, when we gathered together to break bread, Paul spoke to the people, intending to depart the next day, and he prolonged his speech until midnight. (Acts 20:1-7)

Reflecting and Thinking

Today's chapter briefly summarizes Paul's trip through Macedonia to Greece. He decides to make the return trip overland through Macedonia as a result of a threat against his life. At Troas he lingers a week in order to meet with the church on Sunday. In the last half of the chapter he meets with the Ephesian elders at Miletus, deciding not to visit Ephesus personally so that he could be in Jerusalem by Pentecost. Paul's words to the elders from Ephesus (20:18-35) provide a valuable study of leadership for those who want to understand how the first century church was organized.

Why are so many people accompanying Paul on this part of his journeys? [Hint: might it have to do with the fact that he is working to deliver an offering for the poor saints in Jerusalem?] What does verse 7 say about the weekly gatherings of the early church? [Note that the verb, "break bread," has a plural subject in verse 7, referring to the entire church, and a singular subject in verse 11, referring only to Paul.] How might Paul have felt as he visited Macedonia and Achaia, probably knowing that this would be his last visit with these Christians? [Compare similar words that Paul spoke to the Ephesian elders in verse 38.]

Prayer

Thank you, Father, for every blessing you bring to our lives. Thank you for the church and for the opportunity to share worship in the Christian community each Sunday. Thank you for the communion feast whereby we remember the sacrifice of Jesus on our behalf. Thank you for the examples you provide in your word so we can understand your will and plan for us. Bless us as we strive to be your faithful people, in Jesus' name, Amen.

Acts 21: Problems in Jerusalem

Selected Biblical Text

26 Then Paul took the men the next day. He purified himself with them and went into the temple, giving notice of the completion of the days of purification when the sacrifice would be offered for each one of them. 27 When the seven days were almost completed, the Jews from Asia, seeing him in the temple, stirred up the whole crowd and laid hands on him, 28 crying out: "Men of Israel, help. This is the man who is teaching everyone everywhere against the people and the law and this place. Besides, he brought Greeks into the temple and defiled this holy place."
29 Previously having seen Trophimus the Ephesian with Paul in the city, they supposed that Paul had brought him into the temple. 30 Then all the city was stirred up and the people ran together. Seizing Paul, they dragged him out of the temple, and immediately the gates were shut. 31 While they were trying to kill him, word went up to the commanding officer of the cohort that all Jerusalem was in confusion. 32 He immediately took soldiers and centurions and ran down to them. When they saw the commanding officer and the soldiers, they stopped beating Paul. 33 Then the commanding officer came up and arrested him and ordered him to be secured with two chains. He asked who he was and what he had done. (Acts 21:26-33)

Reflecting and Thinking

Paul's trip to Jerusalem was without problems even though it was coupled with tears for what awaited him -- especially in view of the prophetic words that he would be bound and imprisoned. Shortly after his arrival in Jerusalem, a plan to soften the attitude of the Jews toward him and to correct a misconception concerning his teaching was developed in a meeting with James and the Jerusalem elders. Our text recounts what happened next. False accusations by some Asian Jews resulted in an uproar so great that it got the attention of the Roman authorities. Paul ended up under arrest and bound, as prophesied.

In chapter 15 we discussed the wisdom of the Jerusalem elders in devising a plan to address the inclusion of Gentiles in the church. In this chapter we have another example of a plan devised by the Jerusalem elders. What do you think went awry on this occasion? Was the fault in the plan or elsewhere? Could the problems have been foreseen and avoided? Is this merely fulfillment of prophecy, an evidence of God at work to fulfill his plan for Paul? A frequently discussed matter from this chapter is to what extent Christians with backgrounds in Judaism continued to participate in certain Jewish practices and customs. How do you understand and explain Paul's participation in temple activities?

122

Prayer

Dear Heavenly Father, we again ask wisdom as we study your word and contemplate lessons for our lives. We wonder why the Bible does not give us enough details to understand exactly what occurred in this chapter. We want to do what is right. We ask you to guide us as we go forth into the world as your ambassadors. In Jesus' name and by his power we pray these things, Amen.

Acts 22: Paul's Defense

Selected Biblical Text

21 "And he said to me, 'Go, for I will send you far away to the Gentiles.'" 22 They listened to him up to this word. Then they raised their voices and said: "Away with this man from the earth! For he should not be allowed to live." 23 And as they were shouting and throwing off their cloaks and tossing dust into the air, 24 the commanding officer ordered Paul to be brought into the barracks, instructing that he should be examined by flogging to find out the reason they were shouting against him like this. 25 But when they had stretched him out for the thongs, Paul said to the centurion standing by: "Is it legal for you to flog a man who is a Roman citizen before he is sentenced?"
26 When the centurion heard this, he went to the commanding officer and reported, saying: "What are you about to do? For this man is a Roman citizen." 27 So the commanding officer came and said to Paul: "Tell me, are you a Roman citizen?" And he said: "Yes." 28 The commanding officer answered: "I bought this citizenship for a large sum." Paul said: "But I was actually born a citizen." 29 Immediately those who were about to examine him withdrew from him, and the commanding officer was afraid for he realized that Paul was a Roman citizen and that he had bound him. 30 The next day, wanting to know the real reason he was being accused by the Jews, he unloosed him and commanded the chief priests and all the Sanhedrin council to come together, and he brought Paul down and stood him before them. (Acts 22:21-30)

Reflecting and Thinking

Think about the contents of this chapter. Paul is allowed to address the crowd. Because he speaks to them in Hebrew, they listen to him as he recounts the events of his encounter with Jesus and his conversion. (This is the second time Paul's "conversion story" appears in the book of Acts.) The crowd listens until Paul mentions that he was sent to the Gentiles. Almost as though the word Gentiles was a "trigger" word, the turmoil resumes and Paul is returned to the barracks for flogging, an effort to force him to reveal the cause of the problem. When Paul mentions his Roman citizenship, it becomes apparent that the flogging would be illegal. The only alternative before the Roman government was a face to face meeting between Paul and his accusers, a meeting which the Roman tribune set for the following day. Therefore, as the chapter concludes, Paul is seated before a meeting of the chief priests and the council (Sanhedrin).

In this chapter, what evidences do you see that God is at work in Paul's life? How is God's purpose for Paul being developed? What should we think when things that seem to be bad turn out for the good? Paul's Roman citizenship serves him well on this occasion. When have specific aspects of your life turned out to be for the good and especially suited for the situation you found yourself in?

Prayer

Dear God, we believe you are at work in the world today, and we ask you to help us see the ways we can effectively join you in accomplishing your will and purpose. We ask you for boldness, courage and confidence in the face of life's difficulties and challenges. We pray for opportunities to share our faith, in Jesus' name, Amen.

Acts 23: Testifying in Jerusalem -- On to Caesarea

Selected Biblical Text

1 Looking directly at the Sanhedrin council, Paul said: "Brothers, I have lived my life before God in all good conscience up to this day." 2 And the high priest Ananias ordered those standing near Paul to strike him on the mouth. 3 Then Paul said to him: "God will strike you, you whitewashed wall! You sit judging me according to the law, and yet acting contrary to the law you order me to be struck?" 4 Those standing nearby said: "Would you insult the high priest of God?" 5 And Paul said: "I did not know, brothers, that he was the high priest, for it is written, 'You shall not speak evil of a ruler of your people.'" 6 When Paul noted that one part were Sadducees and the other Pharisees, he cried out in the Sanhedrin council: "Brothers, I am a Pharisee, a son of Pharisees. I am facing judgment regarding the hope of the resurrection of the dead." 7 After he had said this, a dispute arose between the Pharisees and the Sadducees, and the assembly was divided. 8 For the Sadducees say that there is no resurrection, nor angel, nor spirit, but the Pharisees acknowledge them all. 9 So there was a great commotion, and some of the law experts of the Pharisees' party stood up and contended strongly: "We find nothing wrong in this man. What if a spirit or an angel spoke to him?" 10 Because the controversy was so intense, the commanding officer, fearing that Paul would be torn to pieces by them, commanded the soldiers to go down and take Paul away from among them by force and bring him into the barracks. 11 The following night the Lord stood by Paul and said: "Have courage, for as you have testified about me in Jerusalem, it is necessary for you to testify also in Rome." (Acts 23:1-11)

Reflecting and Thinking

Paul's hearing before the council does not accomplish the purpose which the Roman authorities had hoped. In fact, Paul divides the council over a doctrinal difference between the Pharisees and the Sadducees. The meeting turns violent and the Romans again rescue Paul and return him to the barracks. A night vision from the Lord reveals to Paul that what is happening is part of God's plan -- that he would testify in Jerusalem and again in Rome. Paul now knows the ultimate end of this journey, but the first step is a covert journey to Caesarea under Roman guard in order to avoid another plot against his life.

What lessons do you see in this chapter for Christians today? How can you apply this text in your own life today? What do you see as God's long-term plan for your life? How has God used "baby steps" to get you where you are spiritually?

Prayer

Dear God, we praise you today for your majesty and splendor, for your love and mercy extended in the gift and sacrifice of your Son, Jesus Christ, as atonement for our sins. Help us as we commit our lives to you today and strengthen us for the journey. Again, we pray in Jesus' name, Amen.

Acts 24: In Caesarea -- Before Felix

Selected Biblical Text

22 But Felix put them off, knowing with some accuracy the facts concerning the Way: When Lysias the commanding officer comes down, I will decide your case. 23 Then he gave orders to the centurion that Paul should be guarded but have some liberty, and not to keep his friends from attending to his needs. 24 Some days later, Felix came with his wife Drusilla, who was Jewish, and he sent for Paul and listened to him speak about faith in Christ Jesus. 25 As Paul reasoned about righteousness, self-control and the coming judgment, Felix became alarmed and said: "Go away for now. When I have a better time, I will call for you." 26 At the same time he hoped that money would be given him by Paul. Therefore, as often as possible, he sent for him and talked with him. 27 After two years, Felix was succeeded by Porcius Festus. Wanting to do the Jews a favor, Felix left Paul in prison. (Acts 24:22-27)

Reflecting and Thinking

Paul's journey to Caesarea protects him from some Jews with evil intentions but accomplishes little else except to put him in a new location for another hearing. After five days, Ananias the high priest, some Jewish elders, and an orator named Tertullian arrive in Caesarea from Jerusalem to accuse Paul. Paul is allowed to speak for himself in his defense. Felix has an awareness of Christianity and quickly sees that there are no serious charges against Paul. But Felix was also a politician who desired to appease both sides. Rather than deciding the case immediately, he put it off while waiting for a Roman authority to come and verify the events. Paul was given liberty to receive visitors, but Felix left Paul in prison to appease the Jews. On at least one occasion, Felix sent for Paul and heard him speak about faith in Jesus -- a message which apparently touched Felix's conscience. The text says that it was because Felix hoped to receive money from Paul that Paul remained in prison for two years, frequently conversing with Felix. After two years, Felix was replaced by Festus.

Today's text provides a good example of a time when God's plans and purposes unfolded slowly. God had already told Paul what the outcome would be. Two years is a long time to wait in prison with no relief in sight. It must be hard to wait when it is apparent that no one is working very seriously to move the case forward. How do you think Paul felt about the periodic conversations with Felix? Did he see an opportunity? Did he feel used? Did he tire of the routine? When have you had to wait for God to unfold the next phase of his plan for your life? Was it easy or hard?

Prayer
Heavenly Father, our human nature seems to push us forward constantly. We want things to happen; we are impatient. It is hard to imagine what Paul experienced as he waited for Felix to act for an entire two years. Teach us your ways. Help us through this day as we wait for you; help us act when opportunities come. In the name of Jesus, the Christ, Amen.

Acts 25: In Caesarea -- Before Festus

Selected Biblical Text
13 After some days had passed, Agrippa the king and Bernice arrived at Caesarea to welcome Festus. 14 As they were staying there several days, Festus laid out Paul's case before the king, saying: "There is a man left prisoner by Felix, 15 and when I was at Jerusalem, the chief priests and the elders of the Jews informed me about him, asking for a sentence of condemnation against him. 16 I answered that it was not the custom of the Romans to hand over any person until the accused met the accusers face to face and had the opportunity to make his defense concerning the accusation. 17 When they accompanied me here, I did not delay, but the next day I sat on the judgment seat and ordered the man to be brought. 18 When the accusers stood up, they brought no charge of evil actions as I had supposed. 19 Rather they had some points of disagreement with him about their own religion and about a certain Jesus, who had died, but whom Paul claimed was alive. 20 Being undecided about how to investigate these questions, I asked if he was willing to go to Jerusalem and there to be tried concerning these things.

21 But when Paul appealed to be kept in custody for a hearing before the emperor, I ordered him to be kept in custody until I could send him to Caesar." (Acts 25:13-21)

Reflecting and Thinking

Almost as soon as Festus began his work, the accusations of the Jews against Paul resurfaced. Festus initially refused to send Paul to Jerusalem; he heard the case again in Caesarea with Paul defending himself. When it appeared that the case might be sent to Jerusalem where Paul perceived his life would be in danger, Paul appealed to Caesar. Perhaps Paul remembered the words of the Lord that he would testify also in Rome. Regardless, the die is cast, and Paul will go to Caesar's court.

Meanwhile, a visit from King Agrippa gives Festus an opportunity to give his account of the events (see selected text for today). The visit also gives Paul an opportunity to present his case again.

Do you think Paul had in mind God's vision and the prediction that he would testify in Rome when he appealed to Caesar? Festus admits that there were no sustainable charges against Paul but only questions related to religious disputes. Why would Festus not decide to release Paul? What dynamics of the Roman efforts to keep the Jews at peace might be reflected in the decision of Festus?

Prayer

Heavenly Father, we know that you work in mysterious ways in this world. We do not understand your wisdom or your timing. We are grateful that you are with us as you were with Paul. Bring us closer to you today, through Jesus we offer this prayer, Amen.

Acts 26: In Caesarea -- Before Agrippa

Selected Biblical Text

19 "Therefore, King Agrippa, I was not disobedient to the heavenly vision, 20 but declared first to those in Damascus, then in Jerusalem and in all the region of Judea, and to the Gentiles, that they should repent and turn to God, performing deeds consistent with their repentance. 21 For this reason, the Jews seized me in the temple courts and tried to kill me. 22 Having met with God's help to this day, I stand here testifying to both small and great, saying nothing but what the prophets and Moses said would happen: 23 that the Christ would suffer and be the first to rise from the dead, in order to proclaim light both to our people and to the Gentiles."

24 And as he was saying these things in his defense, Festus said with a loud voice: "Paul, you are out of your mind; your great learning is driving you out of your mind." 25 But Paul said: "I am not out of my mind, most excellent Festus, but I am

speaking true and rational words. 28 For the king knows about these things, and to him I speak boldly. For I am convinced that none of these things has been hidden from him, for this has not been done in a corner. 27 King Agrippa, do you believe the prophets? I know that you believe." 28 And Agrippa said to Paul: "In a short time would you persuade me to become a Christian?" (Acts 26:19-28)

Reflecting and Thinking

Paul begins his defense before Agrippa by telling once again the story of his encounter with Jesus and his conversion (the third account of Paul's conversion in the book of Acts). This account includes his commission to the Gentiles "to open their eyes, so that they may turn from darkness to light and from the power of Satan to God, and so that they may receive forgiveness of sins and a place among those who are sanctified by faith in me." The selected biblical text for today immediately follows Paul's account of his conversion.

Festus gave his account of the events in the previous chapter; today's text provides an overview of Paul's version of the events. Festus thinks Paul is out of his mind, but Paul's appeal is not to Festus but to Agrippa. Paul did not fumble this opportunity to share the gospel with kings and those in highest authority. Agrippa says Paul could have been released had he not appealed to Caesar, but God's purpose is being fulfilled.

Have you ever had the opportunity to share the gospel with someone who would be considered important or of high position in the eyes of the world? What could we conclude from Paul's failure to persuade Agrippa? Do we ever fail to act because we fear failure? What could encourage us to try even though we do not know how it will turn out?

Prayer

Father God, we try to understand your word, but we often miss subtle points. Paul has spent a lot of time in prison in Caesarea -- probably almost three years. Did he become tired? Discouraged? Doubtful? Was he patient as he waited so long? Was he disappointed that he could not be more evangelistic? Help us learn how to live out our faith regardless of the circumstances in which we find ourselves, in Jesus' name, Amen.

Acts 27: On to Rome

Selected Biblical Text

20 When neither sun nor stars appeared for many days, and a large storm continued to beat upon us, we gave up all hope of being saved. 21 Because many had gone without food for a long time, Paul stood up among them and said: "Men, you should have listened to me and not have set sail from Crete to avoid this damage

and loss. 22 But now I urge you to have courage, for there will be no loss of life among you, but only loss of the ship. 23 For on this very night there stood before me an angel of the God to whom I belong and whom I worship, 24 and he said, 'Do not be afraid, Paul; you must stand before Caesar. God has graciously granted you all those with you.' 25 So have courage, men, for I believe God that it will be exactly as I have been told. 26 But we must run aground on some island." 27 When the fourteenth night had come, as we were being driven across the Adriatic Sea, about midnight the sailors suspected that they were nearing land. 28 When they took a sounding, it was twenty fathoms. A little farther on they took a sounding again and it was fifteen fathoms. 29 And fearing that we might run aground in a rocky place, they let down four anchors from the stern and wished for day to come. (Acts 27:20-29)

Reflecting and Thinking

The journey to Rome was by ship, begun very late in the year when the sailing season was almost past. The result was a shipwreck -- at least Paul's fourth since he had previously written to the Corinthians that he had been shipwrecked three times (2 Cor. 11:25). Luke's account provides interesting details. Although hope is all but gone based on the situation, Paul speaks about hope as he recounts his encounter with an angel of God. Paul will indeed appear before Caesar. Those on the ship will be saved although the ship will run aground. The text makes an interesting observation: As the water grows shallower, they prayed for daybreak to come. We should not make too much of this statement -- we do not know to whom they were praying. Perhaps they were indeed praying to Paul's God. Certainly, Paul's influence and example of faith is made clear in this passage.

When have you been especially aware of God's presence? When have others been aware of God's presence because of your attitude or your words? What are some of the ways Christians can communicate their faith without words? What are some situations in which you would be hesitant to speak up or share your faith? How can you increase your confidence and boldness?

Prayer

Dear God, we are grateful for your providence and care. We do not always see evidence of your loving protection, but we are grateful for every blessing from your hand--even those we do not see or cannot know. Help us as we go forth this day to represent you as your emissaries sent into the world, help us reflect our commitment to you and our dependence on you. Thank you for your grace; thank you that you took the initiative to reestablish relationship with us when we were lost in sin. In Jesus' name, Amen.

Acts 28: Without Hindrance -- The Gospel Continues to Spread

Selected Biblical Text

23 Having agreed to a day with him, they came to him where he was living in even greater numbers. From morning till evening, he explained to them, testifying about the kingdom of God and trying to convince them about Jesus from both the Law of Moses and the Prophets. 24 Some were convinced by the things being said, but others did not believe. 25 And disagreeing among themselves, they departed after Paul had made one statement: "The Holy Spirit was right in saying to your fathers through Isaiah the prophet: 26 'Go to this people, and say, You will hear with hearing but never understand, and you will look with looking but never see. 27 For the heart of this people has become dull, and with their ears they barely hear, and their eyes they have closed; lest they should see with their eyes and hear with their ears and understand with their heart and turn, and I would heal them.' 28 Therefore let it be known to you that to the Gentiles this salvation of God has been sent; they will listen." [29 When he had said these words, the Jews departed, having a great disagreement among themselves.] 30 He lived there two whole years at his own expense, and welcomed all who came to him, 31 proclaiming the kingdom of God and teaching about the Lord Jesus Christ with all boldness unhinderedly. (Acts 28:23-31)

Reflecting and Thinking

Paul's arrival in Rome is met with none of the Jewish opposition that he seems to have anticipated. The Jewish community in Rome had received no negative news about Paul. In fact, the Jews in Rome were anxious to hear what he had to say. The time was set, and Paul's message was on target -- the kingdom of God, Jesus the King. Some could not overcome their "Jewish understandings," an obstacle which Paul reflects in quoting Isaiah. The gospel will go to the Gentiles. For two years, Paul kept proclaiming the kingdom and Jesus Christ. The book of Acts ends with an interesting statement: "the gospel is continuing to go forth without hindrance." Many forces may seek to hinder or stop the gospel message, but it spreads anyway. Such words encourage us because they are still true today. The preaching of the kingdom and Jesus Christ is not by human power but by God's power. The power of the gospel is unchanged. May we be bold; may the gospel go forth to every corner of the world "without hindrance."

The last Greek word in Acts may be translated "unhinderedly." What does it mean to you that the gospel goes forth without hindrance? What part does Paul's boldness play in this summary? What part of this summary is due to the power of God's message? What happens if we get the message wrong? What happens if our message gets "off target?" Should we decide who to tell and who not to tell based on whether we think they will accept the message? Will you include in your personal prayers a prayer for the continued spread of the gospel into all the world?

Prayer

Dearest heavenly Father, we pray for the spread of the gospel. We never want to stand in the way. We seek your power to proclaim boldly. We ask for understanding so that we will proclaim accurately the message that is life changing. May it continue to change our lives. May it change the lives of others. In the name of Jesus, we pray, Amen.

Galatians 1: The "Too Hard" Gospel Is No Gospel at All

Selected Biblical Text

6 I am astonished that so quickly you are turning away from the one who called you in the grace of Christ to an entirely different gospel – 7 there is not another gospel, but some are troubling you and wanting to distort the gospel of Christ. 8 But even if we or an angel from heaven should preach to you a gospel contrary to the one that we preached to you, let him be accursed. 9 As we have said before, now I say again: "If anyone is preaching to you a gospel contrary to the one you received, let him be accursed." 10 Should I agree with people or with God? Or am I trying to please people? If I were still trying to please people, I would not be a slave of Christ. 11 For I make known to you, brothers, that the gospel that was preached by me is not of human origin. 12 For I did not receive it from any person, nor was I taught it, but I received it through a revelation of Jesus Christ. (Gal. 1:6-12)

Reflecting and Thinking

An interesting framework for approaching the book of Galatians is to think of the book in "Goldilocks" terms. Paul presents three options: legalism, license, and liberty. I like to label these the "too hard" gospel, the "too soft" gospel, and the "just right" gospel.

The "too hard" gospel was a big problem in Galatia. Unfortunately, many Christians today continue to seek God through law, seeing the Bible as a law code or system of commandments. Paul says that the "too hard" gospel is no gospel at all. Legalism is not good news. A law code that is beyond our capacity to keep, one that will always end in separation from God, is not good news.

Paul himself had at one time tried to approach God through law. For Paul, the antidote to legalism is justification by faith in Christ. Righteousness through Christ is the ultimate declaration of God's grace and is more than sufficient reason for rejecting any version of the gospel that belongs in the "too hard" category.

When have you experienced a "too hard" version of the gospel? How would you describe the gospel Paul sets forth in Galatians? (I know we have not studied this point yet -- just a question to help you establish your baseline; and your answer is only between you and God!) Why would the Jews tend to think that Paul's message to the Gentiles was too soft? Is the too hard gospel sometimes a reaction against the opposite extreme?

Prayer

Father God, we want to understand the gospel correctly. We want to share it effectively. We do not want to make it too hard for those who are interested in following Jesus; neither do we want to make it too easy. Help us live in the realm of joyous liberty, confident of the life that is ours because Christ is living in us. In Jesus' name and by his power I ask it. Amen.

❖ ❖ ❖

Galatians 2: The "Lived-Out" Gospel

Selected Biblical Text
20 I have been crucified with Christ; no longer do I live, but Christ lives in me. And the life I now live in the flesh I live by faith in the Son of God, who loved me and delivered himself over for me. 21 I do not invalidate the grace of God, for if righteousness were possible through the law, then Christ died for nothing. (Gal. 2:20-21)

Reflecting and Thinking
　　Another possible description of the gospel Paul shares is the "lived out" gospel. This descriptive phrase, "lived out," may not mean what you initially think. Chapter 2 is Paul's description of how the gospel has changed his life. He makes clear that it is not always easy to "live out" the gospel. Even Peter was tempted to compromise some details of faith, and good-hearted Barnabas was led astray by Peter's example.
　　The lived-out gospel has consequences we may not like. When we live out the gospel and are willing to be justified by Christ (instead of our own works), our sin becomes very evident. Living out the gospel is not a description of perfect actions; it is Paul's description of perfect submission to Christ, allowing Christ to control our lives and to live through us. Living out the gospel shows that I am weak and sinful, incapable and inconsistent. The good news is that the weak, sinful person is crucified with Christ and no longer exists in God's sight, since life is now lived by faith in the Son of God. The grace of God does not make me better. The grace of God declares me better and I no longer have to be righteous in myself since I am righteous through Christ.
　　What does it mean to you to be crucified with Christ? How hard is it to live so that Christ is the total explanation of how we live, allowing him to live in us? What are some ways we could nullify the grace of God today? What are some specific ways we nullify the gospel by seeking righteousness through our own efforts? Why does a merit and demerit version of Christianity nullify the gospel?

Prayer
Dear God, help me do right for the right reasons. Help me know with confidence that my faith in Christ justifies me, and not the good things I can do. Help me integrate these two concepts correctly, so that faith is primary, and my actions follow. May Christ live more fully in me and through me is my prayer in his name, Amen.

Galatians 3: The Law Is Not the Gospel

Selected Biblical Text

11 That by the law no one is justified before God is evident, for "the righteous shall live by faith." 12 Therefore the law is not of faith, but "the one doing these things shall live by them." 13 Christ redeemed us from the curse of the law by becoming a curse for us. It is written: "Cursed is everyone who hangs on a tree," 14 so that in Christ Jesus the blessing of Abraham would come to the Gentiles, so we receive the promise of the Spirit through faith. 15 Brothers, I give a human example: once a covenant is ratified, even though it is a human contract, no one annuls it or adds to it. 16 Now the promises were spoken to Abraham and his descendant [literally, seed]. It does not say, "And to descendants," referring to many, but referring to one, "And to your descendant," who is Christ. 17 I am saying this: "The law, coming four hundred thirty years afterward, does not invalidate a covenant previously ratified by God, so as to make the promise of no effect." 18 For if the inheritance comes by the law, it no longer comes by promise; but God gave it to Abraham through a promise. (Galatians 3:11-18)

Reflecting and Thinking

Paul's introduces his description of the "just right" gospel, the gospel that undergirds genuine freedom and liberty in Christ, with a contrast of faith and law. The law is not of faith. The presence of law denies the gospel. Dependence on law eliminates appreciation for the promise. The promise came first, and the law was added to deal with transgressions until the promise could be fulfilled in the Seed who is Christ. The law was temporary, pointing toward Christ. In Christ we find genuine freedom, sonship, and inheritance.

Why do people seek to guarantee their relationship with God through legal means, that is, by keeping a law code? How was Abraham justified? What was the purpose of the Old Testament law?

Prayer

Dear God, help us understand the beauty of the good news of Jesus and live our lives by its power rather than our own feeble efforts to measure up. Build our faith as we wear Christ's riches through baptism. Help us recognize our own filthy rags (our own works) as the blot that they are on the gospel message. Thank you for the "just right" gospel of Jesus. In Jesus' name, Amen.

Galatians 4: The "Just Right" Gospel of Maturity

Selected Biblical Text

1 I mean that the heir, as long as he is a child, is no different from a slave, though he is the owner of everything, 2 but he is under guardians and managers until the date set by his father. 3 So we also, when we were children, were enslaved to the beginning principles of the world. 4 But when the fullness of the time had come, God sent forth his Son, born of a woman, born under the law, 5 to redeem those who were under the law, so that we might receive adoption as sons. 6 And because you are sons, God sent forth the Spirit of his Son into our hearts, crying, "Abba! Father!" 7 So you are no longer a slave but a son, and if a son, also an heir through God. 8 Formerly, when you did not know God, you were enslaved to things that by nature are not gods. 9 But now that you have come to know God, or rather to be known by God, how can you turn back again to the weak and worthless beginning principles of the world, do you want to be enslaved again as at the beginning? 10 You observe days and months and seasons and years. 11 I am fearful for you lest I have labored in vain for you. (Gal. 4:1-11)

Reflecting and Thinking

The application of the "just right" gospel is often difficult. Paul is concerned about the Galatians because right starts are easily followed by wrong moves. False teaching (the "too hard" gospel?) easily enslaves because it requires jumping through numerous hoops. Paul's illustration in this chapter centers on the contrast between Hagar and Sarah. Law and gospel cannot coexist. The "too hard" gospel enslaves. Mature Christians recognize the power of the promise and live in the power of the Spirit.

In thinking about applications of Paul's instructions in the text, what kinds of things tend to enslave Christians today? What kinds of artificial "laws" do Christians sometimes honor or want others to follow? How can we live lives of genuine freedom in the "just right" gospel?

Prayer

Heavenly Father, bring us closer to your will and way, and help us avoid the detours and temptations that appear in our path. Help us grow toward a mature faith in Christ as your sons and daughters. Help us live in and experience freedom in Christ. In the name of the resurrected Christ, Amen.

Galatians 5: Be Careful About the "Too Easy" Gospel

Selected Biblical Text
13 For you were called to freedom, brothers, only do not use your freedom as an opportunity for the flesh, but through love serve one another. 14 For the whole law has been summarized in one saying: "You shall love your neighbor as yourself." 15 If you constantly bite and devour one another, be careful that you are not consumed by one another. 16 But I say, live by the Spirit, and you will not fulfill the desires of the flesh. 17 For the desires of the flesh are opposed to the Spirit, and the desires of the Spirit are opposed to the flesh, for these are stand against each other in opposition, so you will not do the things you want to do. 18 But if you are led by the Spirit, you are not under the law.
19 Now the works of the flesh are evident: sexual immorality, impurity, licentiousness, 20 idolatry, sorcery, enmities, strife, jealousy, fits of anger, selfish rivalries, dissensions, divisions, 21 envy, drunkenness, carousing, and similar things. I warn you, as I warned you before, that those who do such things will not inherit the kingdom of God. 22 But the fruit of the Spirit is love, joy, peace, patience, kindness, goodness, faithfulness, 23 gentleness, and self-control; against such things there is no law. 24 Now those who belong to Christ Jesus have crucified the flesh with its strong physical passions and desires. 25 If we live by the Spirit, let us also walk by the Spirit. 26 Let us not become conceited, provoking one another, envying one another. (Gal. 5:13-26)

Reflecting and Thinking
One warning remains. Moving away from legalism can easily land one in the opposite ditch of license. Paul warns against both extremes. The presence of God's Spirit controls our Christian life -- avoiding the works of the flesh which Paul associates with license and unbridled living. God's Spirit yields a life of true liberty, where love, joy, peace, patience, kindness, goodness, faithfulness, gentleness, and self-control exist. The fruits of the Spirit are not forced; they exist in our lives because that is who we are. The "too easy" gospel has its own unique set of traps; only liberty in Christ sets us free to be all that God has called us to be and all that he empowers us to be.

Paul addresses both gospel extremes in this chapter – legalism and license. Which is the greatest threat to the church today in your opinion? Do Christians tend toward too much restriction or too much license? What advice would you give to someone who is seeking to live a balanced life and to walk in Christian liberty, celebrating life in the Spirit?

Prayer
Heavenly Father, walk beside us as we seek to live out the love principle. Guide and guard us -- from both extremes. May we walk in your way by the Spirit, through Jesus we pray, Amen.

❖ ❖ ❖

Galatians 6: Living Under the Cross of Jesus

Selected Biblical Text

14 May I never boast except in the cross of our Lord Jesus Christ, through which the world has been crucified to me, and I to the world. 15 Neither circumcision is anything nor uncircumcision; only a new creation matters. 16 Upon all who conform to this standard, peace be to them and mercy, even to the Israel of God. 17 From now on, let no one cause me trouble, for I bear on my body the marks of Jesus. 18 The grace of our Lord Jesus Christ be with your spirit, brothers. Amen. (Galatians 6:14-18)

Reflecting and Thinking

When all is said and done, what really matters in the Christian life? Paul's answer to the Galatians, as they sought to live a life that accurately reflected the gospel was this: what matters is a new creation! What counts is that we are new, remade, and reborn. The power for newness does not come from a legalistic alignment with commandments that we cannot humanly keep. The power for newness does not come from a lack of guidance that makes everything acceptable. The power for newness is from God through Christ, through faith in Christ, and through the presence of God's Spirit within us.

What kind of outward signs are often used to measure the Christian life? What makes one a good Christian? What are the biblical markers of a Christian? Paul says that what matters is newness! What would happen if a church only accepted members that are willing to be constantly renewed? What would happen in our own lives if we took seriously this measurement: I am obligated to reflect my newness in Christ?

Prayer

Father God, we want to live in the cross, we want to boast only in the cross, we want that power to guide us as we live renewed lives. Help us to understand what matters and what you want. In Jesus' name, Amen.

1 Thessalonians 1: Developing Faith in a New Church -- Expectant Living

Selected Biblical Text

4 We know, brothers beloved by God, that he has chosen you, 5 because our gospel did not come to you only with words but also with power, with the Holy Spirit and deep conviction, just as you know how we lived among you for your sakes. 6 You became imitators of us and of the Lord, when you received the message in much affliction with joy from the Holy Spirit. 7 In this way, you became a model to all the believers in Macedonia and Achaia. 8 For from you the message of the Lord echoed forth not only in Macedonia and Achaia, but in every place your faith toward God has been reported so that we have no need to say anything, 9 for they themselves report what kind of entrance we had to you, and how you turned to God from idols to serve the living and true God, 10 and to wait for his Son from heaven, whom he raised from the dead, Jesus the one rescuing us from the coming wrath. (1 Thess. 1:4-10)

Reflecting and Thinking

The book of First Thessalonians is among the earliest writings of the New Testament. Paul established the Thessalonian church on his second missionary journey (Acts 17) and was forced to leave very quickly. This letter to an infant church is his response when he received the good news of their faithful perseverance.

How does faith develop in a newly planted church? Several key words and phrases appear in our text: gospel, power, Holy Spirit, conviction. The church in Thessalonica faced suffering almost immediately after its establishment. In the face of opposition, they became an example of faith throughout the region. Their faith developed quickly in trying circumstances. The gospel message became the power for their lives.

An interesting description of how and why this was possible appears in the last two verses of today's chapter. From their past idol worship, they had turned to God so that their present tense was a life of service to God. The power for their faith was found in their eager anticipation of Jesus' coming. Rescue brings gratitude. Expectant, hopeful living grew out of their intense awareness of how bad their former life had been, and how good the future could be.

When have you been rescued? If you do not have a personal experience to think about, think of a situation you have known in which a rescue occurred. What does it feel like to be rescued? How does one's outlook on life change? How does one's life change? Do you think the contemporary church would live life differently if there were a greater sense of gratitude for the rescue that has been made possible through Jesus?

In your observation, do older churches or newer churches grow faster? Why? What explanation would you give for the reasons behind your answer? How could we build a more meaningful faith in our lives as Christians? On a scale of 1 to 10 (10 is the highest), how would you rate the presence of the following in your life: gospel, power, Holy Spirit, conviction?

Prayer

Father God, thank you for the gospel. Thank you for the power of your word and the continuing presence of the Holy Spirit in our lives. Help us to live convicted lives in your service. Help us remember our rescue so that we will continually appreciate what it means that we have been saved. Help us live expectant lives, in Jesus' name and by his power I ask it. Amen.

1 Thessalonians 2: Ministry in a New Church -- Building Relationships

Selected Biblical Text

3 For our exhortation does not come from deceit, impurity, or subtilty. 4 Rather, as we been approved by God to be entrusted with the gospel, so we speak, not to please people but God who examines our hearts. 5 For we neither came with flattering words, as you know, nor covering up our greed -- God is our witness, 6 nor seeking praise from people, from you or from others. 7 As apostles of Christ we could have asserted authority, but we were as little children among you. Even as a nursing mother cares for her own children, 8 with the same caring affection, we were delighted to share with you not only the gospel of God but also our own lives. 9 You remember, brothers, our labor and toil; working night and day in order not to be a burden to any of you, we preached the gospel of God to you. 10 You are witnesses as is God, of how we were holy, righteous and blameless to you who believe. 11 As you know, to each one of you, as a father with his own children, 12 we were exhorting you, encouraging and urging you to live worthy of God, who calls you into his kingdom and glory. (1 Thess. 2:3-12)

Reflecting and Thinking

One of the things that concerned Paul was that he did not know how the infant church in Thessalonica had received his ministry. Had opponents infiltrated the infant church and brought Paul's motives into question after his departure? In today's text, Paul describes his ministry in Thessalonica. He says it was a ministry based on God's truth and pure motives, pleasing God without flattery or greed. He uses two illustrations to describe his work: a nursing mother (v. 7) and a father (v. 11). Later in the chapter he speaks of being orphaned from them by his untimely, forced departure.

Paul's fatherly ministry among the Thessalonians was one of sacrifice and example. Based on close relationships, he desired for them encouragement, comfort, and exhortation. This chapter provides excellent instruction for church leaders who work in the church, especially for those who work in newly planted churches. It also provides instruction for Christians who want to help new brothers and sisters grow in faith. It suggests attitudes and actions to help us help others toward growing faith.

How could you help a new Christian grow in faith? What kind of things could you do to encourage a brother or sister? Try to be specific and pay close attention to the words of the text -- encourage, comfort, exhort. How could you encourage? How could you comfort? How could you exhort? How could you help others build more firmly on the truth of the gospel as the word of God?

Prayer

Dear God, we pray today for new churches and new Christians around the world. We pray for those who work in ministry situations with new churches and new Christians. We pray for missionaries who share the good news and are involved in the first stages of faith for new Christians. We ask you to help us see how we can influence others toward Jesus, and how we can be part of the process by which their faith grows. We pray in Jesus' name, Amen.

1 Thessalonians 3: Hope for a New Church -- Awaiting Good News

Selected Biblical Text

4 For in fact, when we were with you, we kept predicting to you that we would be persecuted, just as also it happened as you know. 5 For this reason, when I could stand it no longer, I sent to find out about your faith, lest the tempter somehow had tempted you and our labor had been in vain. 6 But now Timothy has come to us from you, bringing us good news about your faith and love, and that you have good memories of us always, longing to see us just as we also long to see you. 7 For this reason, brothers, we were encouraged about you in all our distress and persecution, because of your faith. 8 Now we live, if you stand firm in the Lord. 9 How can we give God enough thanks for you, for all the joy with which we rejoice because of you, in the presence of our God? 10 Night and day we pray fervently to see you in person and to restore what is lacking in your faith. (1 Thess. 3:4-10)

Reflecting and Thinking

What keeps us going in difficult days or in the face of persistent persecution? Many people who have endured difficult situations point to hope as the most important factor. Paul did not know how the Thessalonians had fared in the face of challenges to their fledging faith. He had high hopes that they had faithfully endured. In today's chapter, we learn that he sent Timothy to check on them and that he wrote the first letter to the Thessalonians after receiving the good news of their continuing faith and love. His spirit was buoyed by the deep faith that had been established in such a short time. Paul's life was full because of the firm faith of the Thessalonians (v. 8). His hope for them reflected his deep love for them and motivated constant prayer on their behalf.

Hope is a powerful influence in the life of a Christian. Have you ever been hopeful of something in the sense described in this text -- hopeful about the spiritual progress or well-being of another person or group of people? Think about that situation and describe how that hope influenced your prayer life? What did you do to stay informed about the situation? To what lengths will we go to bring hope to reality?

Prayer

Dear God, we want to live by faith, but it is hard when we do not know the details of situations that are important to us. We trust you to provide, but we still want to know what is happening. We want foundations for our hope. You know the specific things we hope for today -- in the lives of family, children, friends, other Christians, neighbors, and our world. We depend on you to be present and to provide in these situations, and to present to us the opportunities to be used in your service to make a difference. In Jesus' name, Amen.

1 Thessalonians 4: Struggles in a New Church -- Living with the End in View

Selected Biblical Text

1 Finally then, brothers, we ask and exhort you in the Lord Jesus, that as you received instruction from us, how you ought to live and please God, even as you are living, may you abound more and more. 2 For you know what instructions we gave you through the Lord Jesus.
3 This is God's will, your sanctification....
9 Now about brotherly love, you have no need for anyone to write to you, for you yourselves are taught by God to love each other....
11 ...to strive to lead a quiet life.
13 We do not want you to be uninformed, brothers, about those who sleep [in death], so that you do not grieve like the rest who have no hope. 14 For since we believe that Jesus died and rose again, we also believe that God will lead forth with Jesus those who have fallen asleep in him. (selected passages from 1 Thess. 4:1-14)

Reflecting and Thinking

The letter of First Thessalonians is characterized by references to Jesus' return. A reference to the coming of Jesus occurs near the end of every chapter. Paul lived with the coming of Jesus in view and he urged his converts to live in the same way. Enduring struggles is easier when we are confident that the time is limited and that the ultimate outcome will be deliverance. Paul, along with other New Testament writers, wrote with the end in view. After 2000 years, it is harder for the contemporary church to affirm the imminent coming of Jesus. (Imminent means soon, or that it could happen at any time.) Paul sought to encourage and instruct the Thessalonians in how to live with the end in view. Such awareness provides motivation for obedience, purity, love, simplicity, and hope.

On a scale of 1-10, how aware are you that Jesus could come today? Do you live your life with such an attitude -- seldom, sometimes, usually, almost always? How would your life change if you were more aware of the coming of Jesus? How does confidence concerning Jesus' coming change the grieving process?

Prayer

Heavenly Father, we are grateful for Jesus' first coming without sin unto salvation, so that we can be redeemed and restored to relationship with you. We anticipate his second coming in hope. We want to live lives that reflect that hope. We ask from you power and strength. Instill in us a more constant awareness of your presence and plan in our lives. In the name of the resurrected Christ who will come again, Amen.

1 Thessalonians 5: The Maturing of a New Church -- Advice for New Christians

Selected Biblical Text

11 Therefore encourage one another and build each other up, just as you are doing. 12 Now we ask you, brothers, to acknowledge those who labor among you, preside over you in the Lord, and admonish you. 13 Esteem them highly in love because of their work. Live in peace with one other. 14 And we urge you, brothers, admonish the undisciplined, encourage the discouraged, help the weak, be patient with everyone. 15 See that no person pays back wrong for wrong, but always pursue what is good for each other and for all. 16 Always rejoice, 17 unceasingly pray, 18 in everything give thanks; for this is the will of God for you in Christ Jesus. 19 Do not quench the Spirit. 20 Do not belittle prophesying 21 but examine all things; hold on to what is good. 22 Stay away from every kind of evil. (1 Thess. 5:11-22)

Reflecting and Thinking

How amazing that some think the rules for developing spiritual maturity change as we mature in Christ. The same things that start us on a path to spiritual maturity will keep us on that path and keep us growing in Christ. The instructions Paul writes to the Thessalonians apply to all Christians in every place in every time in every situation. Here are instructions for relationships, leadership, work and activity in the church, spiritual development, spiritual living, and purity of heart. The selected text above contains at least 18 instructions. Choose two or three of those most relevant to your life and make a special effort to work on them today.

Which of the instructions above are hardest for Christians to follow? Which are for you the easiest? Are you surprised by the list Paul writes? Why or why not? How well does the church where you worship do in following these instructions?

Prayer

Heavenly Father, we want to grow up in Christ through your power and presence. Help us discern those things that are most important and strengthen us as we develop spiritual lives to your glory. Help us as we encourage one another. We want to walk closer to you today and we ask your presence as we pray through Jesus, Amen.

2 Thessalonians 1: Anticipating His Coming -- Persecution and Problems

Selected Biblical Text

3 We ought always to thank God for you, brothers, and rightly so, because your faith is growing incredibly, and the love all of you have for one another is ever greater. 4 Therefore, we ourselves boast about you in the churches of God, for your perseverance and faith in all the persecutions and afflictions you are enduring, 5 which are evidence of the righteous judgment of God, so you will be counted worthy of the kingdom of God, for which you are suffering. 6 It is just for God to pay back affliction to those who trouble you, 7 and to you who are troubled, to give [you] rest with us, at the revealing of the Lord Jesus from heaven with his powerful angels. 8 With flaming fire he will punish those who do not know God and do not obey the gospel of our Lord Jesus. 9 They will be punished with the judgment of eternal destruction, separated from the presence of the Lord and from the glory of his might 10 when he comes, on that day to be glorified among his saints and to be marveled at by all those who have believed because our testimony to you was believed. (2 Thess. 1:3-10)

Reflecting and Thinking

References to the coming of Jesus continue in Second Thessalonians. In these devotional thoughts, the titles that outline the letter all relate to our anticipation of Jesus' coming: persecutions and problems, false claims, and misbehavior within the church.

While we Christians in the United States do not often suffer for our faith, there are many people around the world who suffer gravely because of their efforts to follow Christ. Persecutions often seem to strengthen the resolve of those being persecuted. The nominal or minimal Christian may fall by the wayside, but those with conviction are made stronger by persecution. I remember a quotation: "The same fire that melts the butter hardens the steel." The difference is what we are made of.

Paul reminds the Thessalonians that God is the great equalizer. God is just, and the troubles of this life are temporary. Those who are the troublers will one day be troubled, because at Jesus' coming what will matter is to know God and to obey the gospel of Jesus. Knowing God and obeying the gospel lead to the eternal presence and glory of the Lord. How blessed are those who believe and obey the testimony of the gospel!

What do you think would happen if the contemporary church in the U.S. were to suffer intense persecutions and trials? Would the churches grow larger or smaller? What does it mean to you that the comfort of these verses applies only to believers who know God and obey the gospel? How important is it that we make every effort to know God and obey the gospel? What does it mean to you to obey the gospel?

144

In depth: a concordance will help you research the New Testament meaning of the word "gospel" and find occurrences of the phrase, "obey the gospel."

Prayer
Father God, we want to live worthy of the gospel, and we pray that you will help us live faithfully in the particular situations of our lives, both when the circumstances are difficult and challenging and when they are easy. In Jesus' name and by his power we ask it, Amen.

2 Thessalonians 2: Anticipating His Coming -- False Claims

Selected Biblical Text
1 We ask you, brothers, concerning the coming of our Lord Jesus Christ and our being gathered to him, 2 not to be quickly shaken in your thinking or troubled, whether by a prophecy or by a message or by a letter, as though from us, asserting that the day of the Lord is at hand. 3 Don't let anyone deceive you in any way.... (2 Thess. 2:1-3a)

Reflecting and Thinking
How interesting is it that many in the contemporary church are unsettled by the same things Paul wrote about! Paul wrote to help the Thessalonians overcome the tendency to become unsettled. The Thessalonians, reading Paul's letter in the first century, most likely understood what he wrote. Perhaps he was purposefully obscure -- this section has some of the characteristics of apocalyptic literature.

Even if we do not understand every detail of this chapter, we can understand the conclusion: the coming of Jesus had not yet occurred even though some were asserting that it had. Several things had to occur first -- things Paul had told them about previously.

There always have been and always will be date-setters and those who want to ascertain precisely the time of Jesus' coming. Jesus said that the time of his coming is unknown and will come as a surprise. One can say with relative safety, "I do not know when Jesus is coming, but when someone sets a specific date, I can be almost certain that the date is wrong." Our challenge is not to ascertain the date of Jesus' coming but to live in a state of readiness for his coming.

His coming is imminent -- it could occur at any time. It may occur in our lifetime or it may not. In reality, when our lifetime on earth is over, the time of his coming does not matter to us anymore. We will have exited this temporal world and will have entered eternity. While here on earth, we should combat false claims. We should live every day for our Lord.

What is your personal attitude toward "date-setting" and "date-setters?" Are you troubled or comforted by the possibility of Jesus' immediate return? What changes could or should you make today to be ready for his coming? Why not do what you need to do?

Prayer

Dear God, help us live faithful lives in your service. Help us know how to encourage others who are troubled or distraught by the date-setting tendencies of our day. Help us stand firm in God's choosing, the gospel of the glory of Christ, and the sanctifying work of the Holy Spirit, we pray in Jesus' name, Amen.

2 Thessalonians 3: Anticipating His Coming -- Misbehaving Brothers

Selected Biblical Text

6 We command you, brothers, In the name of the Lord Jesus Christ, to keep away from every believer who lives an undisciplined life, not according to the teaching which you received from us. 7 For you yourselves know how you ought to imitate us, and that we were not undisciplined among you. 8 We did not eat anyone's food without paying, instead we worked night and day in labor and toil so as not be a burden to any of you. 9 It was not because we do not have the right, but in order to give ourselves as a model for you to imitate. 10 For even when we were with you, we commanded you this: If anyone is not willing to work, neither shall he eat. 11 We hear that some among you live without discipline. They are not working; they are playing around at working. 12 To such people, we command and exhort in the Lord Jesus Christ to work quietly and to eat their own food. 13 And you, brothers, do not grow weary as you do what is good.
14 If anyone does not obey our instruction in this letter, take note of that one and do not associate with him, so he will be ashamed. 15 Yet do not regard him as an enemy but admonish him as a brother. (2 Thess. 3:6-15)

Reflecting and Thinking

The possibility of Jesus' imminent coming apparently caused some in Thessalonica to quit some of their normal daily activities. Paul warns against idleness, saying that it is a contradiction of his teaching. Paul was not idle among them as he worked to provide for his own needs. The problem with idleness is twofold: the idle are not busy doing the Lord's work as they could be, and they too easily become busybodies.

This chapter may at first reading appear to have little to do with the modern church. When we observe carefully the situation in many churches today, the application becomes clearer. I wonder if the modern church fails to be busy in God's work because we are busy with the wrong things. I wonder, especially when we spend time talking about one another, if we have too much spare time on our hands and are spending too little time in God's work. I wonder if we are too dependent on others for things that we could do for ourselves.

When you think about your involvement in church, are you mostly a receiver or a giver? If idleness were to include those who idle with regard to actively doing the Lord's work, what percentage of the members of the church would belong in the "idle" category? What will you do this week for the work of the Lord (not counting attendance and personal activities such as Bible reading or prayer)?

Prayer

Dear God, help us be busy in the things that you want us to be busy in. Help us to be busy in things that bring you glory and advance the cause of Jesus Christ. Help us encourage one another and lift up the weak. Help us reach out to those who are troubled. May our lives this day be what you want them to be, we pray in Jesus' name, Amen.

1 Corinthians 1: The Gospel Message -- God's Wisdom

Selected Biblical Text

18 For the message of the cross is foolishness to those who are perishing, but to us who are being saved it is the power of God. 19 For it is written: "I will destroy the wisdom of the wise; the intelligence of the intelligent I will bring to nothing." 20 Where is the wise person? Where is the law expert? Where is the debater of this age? Has not God made foolish the wisdom of the world? 21 For since in the wisdom of God the world through its wisdom did not know him, God was pleased through the foolishness of what was preached to save those who believe. 22 Jews demand miraculous signs and Greeks seek wisdom, 23 but we preach Christ crucified: a stumbling block to Jews and foolishness to Greeks, 24 but to those who are called, both Jews and Greeks, Christ is the power of God and the wisdom of God. 25 For the foolishness of God is wiser than human wisdom, and the weakness of God is stronger than human strength. (1 Cor. 1:18-25)

Reflecting and Thinking

Many Bible students know that the church at Corinth was troubled by factions. Beyond the divisions, Paul was also aware of moral and ethical problems and various misunderstandings. The infant church was immature and unspiritual and in need of advice to correct false teachings and to restore healthy relationships within the church.

Paul writes with a clear focus on Jesus Christ, mentioning Jesus Christ eight times in the first nine verses of the book. Division is not solved by focusing on the division. Division is often a symptom of a deeper problem, as was the case at Corinth. The message of the gospel had been misunderstood.

Paul's solution to the problems at Corinth begins with a focus on Jesus as God's wisdom and power. The wisdom of God is often unrecognized and unappreciated by the world. God's wisdom is wiser than the world's wisdom -- in fact, God's foolishness is wiser than human wisdom! The gospel message of the cross appears to be foolishness. When the message of God's wisdom is misunderstood, problems inevitably result. Throughout the book, Paul will provide specific advice about certain problems, but the beginning point is always Jesus. Christ Jesus has become for us wisdom from God -- righteousness, holiness and redemption (1:30).

When have you seen human wisdom fail to accomplish God's purpose and will? Think about your own observations of or experiences with church divisions. How often is it the case that divisions come from failure to understand God's message? One author has suggested that the church is a major factor in the secularization of society. What happens when the church tries to live by human wisdom and standards rather than God's wisdom and standards?

Prayer
Father God, bind us together in your righteousness and holiness. Help us appreciate the disconnection between the message of the cross and the values of the world. Help us not to depend on our own wisdom as we share and live out the gospel. May our focus and boast be only the Lord, in Jesus' name, Amen.

1 Corinthians 2: The Gospel Message -- Spiritual Power from God

Selected Biblical Text
1 When I came to you, brothers, I did not come with superior speech or wisdom as I proclaimed to you the testimony of God. 2 For I resolved to know nothing among you except Jesus Christ and him crucified. 3 Also I came to you in weakness, in fear, and with great trembling. 4 My message and my preaching were not with wise and persuasive words, but with a demonstration of the Spirit and of power, 5 so that your faith would not be in human wisdom but in the power of God. (1 Cor. 2:1-5)

Reflecting and Thinking
        The gospel of God's wisdom is also the gospel of God's power. The message about Jesus Christ and him crucified can be proven to be true, just as a case can be argued in a court room. The word Paul uses (demonstration) does not refer to miraculous signs, although Paul on occasion did miracles. Paul is saying that the message itself is a demonstration of God's spiritual power. The message is both wisdom and power, available to human beings only by God's revelation by his Spirit. This message of spiritual truth is understood by spiritual minds. It matters not what others may think of the message. God's spiritual message is valid, even though the world does not understand and accept it.
        A helpful bridge to the next chapter is in the unspoken conclusion: those who do not understand the message are not spiritual but are worldly.
        Do you think the modern church is more focused on spiritual power or human power? What evidences can you give to support your answer? What does it mean to you to be spiritual (a word Paul uses several times in this chapter and throughout the book of 1 Corinthians)? How could the church better communicate the simple message of Jesus and his crucifixion? When have you see the church depending on human wisdom? When have you seen the church depending on God's power?

Prayer

Dear God, we confess that we easily get off track, focus our attention on the wrong things and depend on the wrong methods to advance the gospel message in this world. Restore our faith in the simple gospel message, recognizing its internal evidences and proofs, seeing its logic and validity, boldly proclaiming the message of the Spirit even when it is rejected by many in the world. Help us focus on spiritual things so that we can understand and discern spiritual truths. Deliver us from the tendency to focus on the things of the world, we pray in Jesus' name, Amen.

1 Corinthians 3: Worldliness Causes Divisions

Selected Biblical Text

1 Brothers, I was not able to speak to you as people controlled by the Spirit, but rather as people characterized by the flesh, as infants in Christ. 2 I fed you milk, not solid food, for you were not yet ready, and you are still not ready. 3 You are still influenced by the flesh. For since there is jealousy and quarreling among you, are you not influenced by the flesh, living as mere human beings? 4 For when someone says: "I am of Paul," and another: "I am of Apollos," are you not mere human beings? 5 What then is Apollos? And, what is Paul? Servants through whom you came to believe, even as the Lord assigned to each one. 6 I planted, Apollos watered, but God was making it grow. 7 So neither the one who plants is anything nor the one who waters, but God who makes it grow. 8 The one who plants and the one who waters work with one purpose, and each will be rewarded according to his own labor. 9 For we are co-workers in God's service; you are God's field, God's building. (1 Cor. 3:1-9)

Reflecting and Thinking

Paul identifies the source of the division at Corinth as worldliness and spiritual immaturity. He mentions worldliness as the reason for their lack of growth -- spiritual infancy, failure to live by the Spirit, and attitudes of jealousy and quarreling. A focus on human concerns (acting like mere human beings) works against spirituality and spiritual attitudes. The Corinthians still belonged to the realm of the flesh.

The antidote is to see human beings and human efforts through God's eyes. The human leaders whom the Corinthians are following are not to be exalted -- they are only servants working according to the tasks God gave them. "Success" does not come from human efforts; the results come from God. In addition, this way of looking at things affirms that we are all coworkers together, called to cooperation and not to division.

Do you think it is safe to say that church divisions today come from worldliness? How often have you heard worldliness cited as the source of a church division? (This will be for many a rhetorical question, given that the answer will be "never.") What can you do in your life, thinking, and attitudes to move away from worldliness and to move toward spiritual maturity? Paul goes on in the chapter to describe how others are already building on his foundation. What examples can you think of where others are building on a spiritual foundation you laid? What examples can you think of where you are building on a spiritual foundation laid by others? What can the modern church do to grow in its sense of cooperation as coworkers with God and one another in God's work?

Prayer

Dear God, today we want to think correctly and honestly about how you use us in your work, and not to think of ourselves too highly. We do not want to be men-followers or men-pleasers. We want to develop lives of spiritual maturity and to fulfill the specific roles you have given us as a part of your grand scheme. Together we are your dwelling -- your temple and a place where your Spirit lives. Bind us together with that attitude and spirit; help us avoid selfishness and human centeredness, we pray in Jesus' name, Amen.

1 Corinthians 4: Healing Divisions with Changed Thinking

Selected Biblical Text

14 I am writing this not to shame you but to correct you as my dear children. 15 Though you may have ten thousand guardians in Christ, you do not have many fathers, for in Christ Jesus through the gospel I became a father to you. 16 Therefore I exhort you: become imitators of me. 17 For this reason I have sent to you Timothy who is my beloved son, who is faithful in the Lord. He will remind you of my ways in Christ, just as I teach them everywhere in every church. 18 Some of you have become arrogant, as if I were not coming to you. 19 But I will come to you very soon, if the Lord is willing, and I will learn not only the message of these arrogant ones, but the power; 20 for the kingdom of God is not evidenced by talk but by power. 21 What do you want? Shall I come to you with a rod of discipline, or shall I come in love with a gentle spirit? (1 Cor. 4:14-21)

Reflecting and Thinking

A major factor in the division at Corinth was spiritual immaturity. Simply put, spiritual immaturity is a failure to grow and to develop spiritual thinking and spiritual lifestyles. The foundation of life is our thinking, even as the wise man said that we are what we think (Prov. 23:7). In Matthew 12:34, Jesus said our words come out of our heart (referring to our thinking). The Corinthians did not understand the message, the messengers or ministers, the ministry, and other Christians correctly. Paul treats each of these in the first four chapters. The message appears to be foolishness; Christian ministers are mere servants entrusted with God's work and ministry; the Christian life is not an opportunity to receive benefits but to benefit others.

Therefore, Paul urges, heal the divisions (4:14-21). Be willing to be spent for others, avoid arrogance, walk the talk, and demonstrate God's power in your life and not just in your speech. Paul sets himself forth as an example, hoping they can solve the division problem before he arrives for his next visit.

Based on Paul's teachings in this chapter and today's text, what are the most important things the church can do to deal with the problem of division? What teaching is needed? What attitudes need to be developed?

Prayer
Heavenly Father, help us grow up spiritually so that we will become like Jesus. Guard our hearts and thoughts, our lips and our lives. Help us see our own feeble efforts in the context of God's great plan. Help us not to trust in ourselves and our own efforts and power; help us not to depend on others but on you. Guide us as we seek to model consistent lives that reflect Jesus, we pray in his name, Amen.

1 Corinthians 5: A Problem -- Immorality in the Church

Selected Biblical Text
9 I wrote to you in my letter not to associate with sexually immoral people -- 10 not the immoral people of this world, or the greedy and swindlers and idolaters, because then you would have to leave this world. 11 So now [again] I am writing to you not to associate with anyone who claims to be a Christian but is sexually immoral or greedy, an idolater or slanderer, a drunkard or swindler. With such a person, do not even eat. 12 What is it to me to judge those on the outside? Indeed, are you not to judge those on the inside? 13 God will judge those on the outside. "Remove the evil person from among you." (1 Cor. 5:9-13)

Reflecting and Thinking
A major purpose for Paul's first letter to Corinth was to address various moral and ethical problems and questions. One of those matters concerned a man who was involved with his father's wife (apparently his stepmother). Such immorality was beyond bad -- such a thing was not even acceptable among the pagans. An even greater problem was the prideful attitude of the church -- how accepting, tolerant, and enlightened we are! Paul tells the church that they must deal with the situation to stop the sinful

action, to save the brother involved, to avoid the leavening influence of evil, and to be the church God intends.

On a scale of 1 to 10, how well do you think the contemporary church has done in avoiding the acceptance of evil and immorality into its midst? Have you known churches that were proud of their tolerance and open-mindedness? What does this chapter say about such attitudes? What evidences can you cite to show that the attitude of the local church in such matters is important to God? How can we help other Christians find repentance and forgiveness when they are involved in immoral situations?

Prayer

Heavenly Father, give us wisdom as we deal with the temptations and challenges of life. Help us know how to help others through difficult times without compromising our faith and responsibility. Help us call evil evil, even when the world about us may call evil good. Help us not to be influenced by the world around us as we seek to live lives of sincerity and truth in Jesus Christ, through whom we pray, Amen.

1 Corinthians 6: More Problems -- Legal Conflicts and Immorality

Selected Biblical Text

12 "All things are legal for me" -- but all things are not beneficial. "All things are legal for me" -- but I will not be controlled by anything. 13 "Food for the stomach and the stomach for food," but God will do away with both. The body is not for sexual immorality but for the Lord, and the Lord for the body. 14 By his power God raised the Lord and he will also raise us. 15 Do you not know that your bodies are members of Christ? Shall I then take the members of Christ and make them members of a prostitute? May it never be! 16 Do you not know that the one being united with a prostitute is one body with her? For it is said: "The two will become one flesh." 17 But the one being united with the Lord is one spirit with him. 18 Flee from sexual immorality. Every sin a person commits is outside the body, but the one who sins sexually, sins against his own body. 19 Or do you not know that your body is the temple of the Holy Spirit who is in you, whom you have received from God, and you are not your own? 20 You were bought at a price. Therefore, glorify God in your body. (1 Cor. 6:12-20)

Reflecting and Thinking

Two additional problems are addressed in today's chapter: (1) brothers who are taking unresolved legal conflicts before the secular legal courts, and (2) the question of sexual immorality related to (temple?) prostitution. Regarding the first matter, Paul says that legal wrangling ("such wickedness") is in the same category as sexual immorality, idolatry, adultery, prostitution, homosexuality, robbery, greed, drunkenness, slander, and cheating. The lawsuits being presented in the governmental courts are a sign of defeat at the hand of Satan. Such disputes should be settled internally, within the church.

The second question Paul addresses by calling to mind several principles. Some things that are acceptable are not beneficial. Some things that are acceptable may eventually master us. It is true that the body is temporal and is not eternal, but God nonetheless has a higher purpose for the physical body. The resurrection of the physical body demonstrates continuity with the celestial body (see 1 Corinthians 15). We participate in the body of Christ (the church) with our physical bodies, so that in some sense our bodies are members of Christ. That our physical bodies are used to fulfill the spiritual purposes of God demonstrates that sexual immorality is especially heinous because sin is internalized, as opposed to the fact that other sins are outside the body (external). Our bodies are God's temple since his Holy Spirit lives in us. We do not belong to ourselves because we were purchased. Our ultimate obligation is to honor God with our bodies, according to his spiritual purpose.

Christianity has often had a low view of the human body or a dualistic view that separates the body from spiritual concerns. What does Paul say about the importance of our physical bodies? How does the physical body contribute to God's spiritual purposes? Which principles that Paul mentions are most helpful to you? What are some of the ways Christians honor God with their bodies?

Prayer
Father God, help us live holy and pure lives, reflecting your presence and the presence of your Holy Spirit within us. Remind us that we are not our own, in Jesus' name, Amen.

1 Corinthians 7: Another Problem -- Marital Questions

Selected Biblical Text
1 Now concerning the things you wrote about: It is good for a man not to touch [have sexual relations with] a woman. 2 But because immorality abounds, each man should have his own wife, and each woman should have her own husband. 3 The husband should give to his wife the sexual rights she is due, and likewise the wife to her husband. 4 The wife does not have the rights to her own body but the husband; in the same way also, the husband does not have the rights to his own body but the wife. 5 Do not deprive each other except by mutual consent for a time agreed to by both, so that you may devote yourselves to prayer. Then come together again so that Satan will not tempt you because of your lack of self-control.

6 I say this as a concession, not as a command. 7 I wish that all were as I am. But each one has his own gift from God; one this way and another that way. (1 Cor. 7:1-7)

Reflecting and Thinking

Based on the first verses of today's chapter, we know that Paul had received a letter from the church at Corinth. The letter apparently raised questions related to marriage and marital relationships. These questions Paul addresses in this chapter. The basic principle is clear: God desires our sanctification. God provides marriage because of (to avoid) fornication or sexual immorality. The context of marriage provides married couples a partnership to help one another avoid fornication, fulfilling mutual responsibilities in the context of individual needs both physical and spiritual. Paul's personal preference is singleness, but he writes from (personal) concession, knowing that not all have the gift of singleness.

Paul addresses three groups: unmarried and widows (v. 8), married (v. 10), and the rest (v. 12), setting forth a summarizing principle in verses 17-24. In verses 25-38, he answers a question about virgins, and in verses 39-40, addresses the question of marriage for widows and widowers. Paul's teachings in this chapter are not easy to understand and apply, and many volumes have been written to explain his meaning and intent.

What principles are set forth in today's selected text to govern Christian marriage? (Try to identify at least six.) In what way is singleness a gift? What part of the text shows that the concession of v. 6 is a personal comment by Paul?

Prayer

Dear God, we thank you for your wisdom; we thank you for your plan both for singleness and for marriage. We want to be faithful servants and are grateful that you provide our needs and remove potential obstacles in our spiritual walk with you. Help us understand and apply your will in our lives so that we can faithfully participate in and fulfill your purpose for us. Give us humility in the face of those things that are not easily understood. We pray in Jesus' name, Amen.

1 Corinthians 8: Another Problem -- Eating Meat Offered to Idols

Selected Biblical Text

1 Now concerning food sacrificed to idols, we know that "we all have knowledge." Knowledge puffs up but love builds up. 2 If anyone [only] supposes he knows something; he does not yet know as he needs to know. 3 If someone loves God, that person is known by God. 4 Then regarding eating food sacrificed to idols: we know

that "an idol is nothing in this world" and that "there is no God but one." 5 For even if there are so-called gods, whether in heaven or on earth (as there are many "gods" and many "lords"), 6 yet for us there is but one God, the Father, from whom all things came and for whom we live; and there is but one Lord, Jesus Christ, through whom are all things and through whom we live.
9 Be careful that your rights do not become a stumbling block to the weak. 10 For if someone with a weak conscience sees you with your knowledge eating in an idol's temple, will not he be emboldened to eat food offered to idols? 11 So by your knowledge is destroyed the one who is weak, the brother for whom Christ died. (1 Cor. 8:1-6, 9-11)

Reflecting and Thinking

Another problem that was getting in the way of the Corinthians' fellowship in the body of Christ concerned the question of food that had been sacrificed to idols and was afterward sold in the markets. What should a Christian do? Some Christians (Jewish Christians?) found the idea of eating meat that had previously been sacrificed to idols abhorrent, believing they were in some way participating in pagan worship. Other Christians could eat such meat with clear conscience.

Paul's instructions have broad applications. He first warns that one must avoid an attitude of intellectual arrogance that tears others down: "I understand things better than you do." The love principle seeks to build others up. Then to the matter at hand: it is true that idols are nothing in comparison to God. One may correctly claim a "right" to eat such meat, not concerned with the previous use as a sacrifice. Yes, one may even ignore the concerns of a brother or sister with scruples against such a practice, but.... what if your freedom becomes a stumbling block to another Christian? What if that person is emboldened to transgress his or her conscience because of your example? What if your freedom and knowledge destroy another? Remember that Christ died for that person whom you now consider so unimportant that you are determined to claim your rights regardless.

What kind of disagreements among Christians today possibly fall into the same category as "meat eating" in this chapter? (Think of "I have a right to..." vs. "It would be better not to..." or "I cannot in good conscience...") To what extent should the scruples of a brother or sister control my action? Under what circumstances do I have freedom to act according to my conscience? When and how are my "rights" limited? When can I exercise my "rights?" (Think about the importance of your example and influence.)

Prayer

Dear God, help us care for one another and respect one another as Christians. Help us support each other and encourage one another to do right.

Help us have right attitudes toward our brothers and sisters for whom Christ died. Give us wisdom as we live life in allegiance and loyalty to you and your Son Jesus, our Savior, in whose name we pray, Amen.

1 Corinthians 9: Principles to Deal with Problems and Conflicts-1

Selected Biblical Text

19 Being free from all [people], I have made myself a slave to all [people], to gain even more [people]. 20 To the Jews I became like a Jew, to gain the Jews. To those under the law I became like one under the law -- though I myself am not under the law -- to gain those under the law. 21 To those not having the law I became like one not having the law -- though I am not without the law of God, but I am under the law of Christ -- to gain those not having the law. 22 To the weak I became weak to gain the weak. I have become all things to all people so that by all means I may save some. 23 I do all things for the sake of the gospel, that I may be a coparticipant in it.

24 Do you not know that although all the runners in a race run, only one receives the prize? Run hard so you receive it. 25 Every contender exercises self-control in all things. They do it to receive a perishable crown, but we do it to receive an imperishable crown. 26 Therefore this is how I run – not with uncertainty; this is how I fight – not as one beating the air. 27 Rather, I control my body and make it my slave, lest after I have preached to others, I myself be unapproved. (1 Cor. 9:19-27)

Reflecting and Thinking

The questions Paul has addressed thus far in the book -- division and human allegiances, dependence on human wisdom and power, worldliness, tolerating immorality, lawsuits between Christians, sexual immorality, marital concerns, meat sacrificed to idols -- all have the potential for great conflict within the church. In today's chapter, Paul begins to set forth a principle base to deal with the problems. Problems are best resolved by principles -- agreement on the guidelines and norms of the Christian life.

Paul uses the "freedom principle" to guide his life. His freedom allows him to enslave himself for the accomplishment of God's purposes. His freedom he uses to identify with others, not to draw lines and separations. His freedom opens possibilities for saving as many as possible for the sake of the gospel. Paul's freedom depreciates his rights, increases his responsibilities, demands self-discipline, and leads to strict living. This is a different kind of freedom than the self-focused freedom many seek in our world today. The freedom of a Christian is not a freedom focused on self, but a freedom focused on God's will. This is not a demand for rights but a willingness to do whatever is necessary for the sake of the gospel.

How strange is Paul's attitude in contrast to the general attitude of the world today? When have you seen people willing to give up their rights for the benefit of others? Think of a difficult or conflicted situation, perhaps in the church where you attend. How would the principles of this chapter change the dynamic of the situation? What would happen if both sides were willing to give up rights for the opponents?

Prayer

Dear God, give us an unselfish spirit of love toward others. In the attitude of Jesus, help us learn self-emptying and sacrifice for the well-being of others. Help us focus on others more than on self. Help us be willing to pay any price for the advance of the gospel in our world. May we live disciplined lives so that we and others reach the goal. We pray in Jesus' name, Amen.

1 Corinthians 10: Principles to Deal with Problems and Conflicts-2

Selected Biblical Text

23 "All things are legal for me" -- but all things are not beneficial. "All things are legal for me" -- but not everything is edifying. 24 No one should seek his own good, but the good of the other person. 25 Eat anything sold in the meat market without asking questions of conscience, 26 for, "The earth and its fullness are the Lord's."
27 If an unbeliever invites you to a meal and you want to go, eat whatever is placed before you without asking questions of conscience. 28 But if someone says to you: "This is from an idol sacrifice," do not eat it, because of the one who told you and because of conscience. 29 I say conscience, not referring to your own conscience but to the other person's. But why is my freedom being judged by another's conscience? 30 If I share the meal with thankfulness, why am I reproached regarding that for which I give thanks?
31 So whether you eat or drink or whatever you do, do all things for the glory of God. 32 Be inoffensive both to the Jews and to the Greeks and to the church of God -- 33 even as I try to please everyone in every way, not seeking my own benefit but the benefit of many, so that they may be saved. (1 Cor. 10:23-33)

Reflecting and Thinking

The first part of today's chapter uses Old Testament events to illustrate how God cares for his people when they focus on spiritual realities and do his will. The passage also shows the result of selfishness and grumbling. Focusing on our rights does not move us closer to God. Paul returns one more time to the question of "idol meat." A comparison of the idol feasts and the Lord's Supper, along with an example from the Old Testament sacrificial system, shows that the wisest course is to distance oneself from every hint of idolatry.

The principle Paul sets forth has already been stated in the book: everything permissible may not be beneficial. Some things permissible may not be constructive, some may in fact be destructive. Some things permissible do not operate for the good of others. Paul's conclusion concerning the meat offered to idols is interesting. If you eat unknowingly, do not worry, go ahead and eat. If someone makes a point to tell you that it is "idol meat," then do not eat. Do all for God's glory, do not cause others to stumble, seek the good of as many as possible.

What impact would the use of these biblical principles have on Christian relationships in the contemporary church? In a world focused on personal rights, think about how the church could become counter-cultural with the application of these principles and the demonstration of a love that puts others before self. What things in today's world appear harmless to some Christians but cause concern for other Christians? That is, some believe they can participate but others believe it is forbidden? Based on 1 Corinthians 9-10, what is the biblical approach to such matters?

Prayer

Dear God, we are grateful this day that we can approach your heavenly throne and pray in the name of Jesus. We come to you seeking wisdom as we try to understand what is best in those areas that present challenges like the ones addressed in today's section of Scripture, Amen.

1 Corinthians 11: Recognizing the Body -- Worship and the Supper

Selected Biblical Text

23 For I received from the Lord what I also passed on to you: the Lord Jesus, on the night he was betrayed, took bread, 24 and after he had given thanks, he broke it and said: "This is my body, which is for you; do this in remembrance of me." 25 In the same way, after supper he took the cup, saying: "This cup is the new covenant in my blood; do this, every time you drink it, in remembrance of me." 26 Every time you eat this bread and drink this cup, you proclaim the Lord's death until he comes. 27 So then, whoever eats the bread or drinks the cup of the Lord in an unworthy manner will be guilty of the body and blood of the Lord. 28 Let each person examine himself, and in this way let him eat of the bread and drink of the cup. 29 For the one who eats and drinks without recognizing the body of Christ eats and drinks judgment against himself. (1 Cor. 11:23-29)

Reflecting and Thinking

The Corinthian church also struggled with questions related to worship: what is proper, how does one dress, questions of style and fashion and personal grooming customs, sharing the Lord's Supper, and the use of spiritual gifts in worship.

Today's selected text focuses on how some abuses surrounding the Lord's Supper reflected the division at Corinth. Some (richer?) Christians were apparently arriving early and partaking of the Supper and the love feast as part of a limited group of believers. The focus was more on the fellowship meal than on the Supper, perhaps hurrying through the latter in order to eat the former before the poorer members arrived. Paul says that such an attitude demeans and even negates the Lord's Supper. The meaning of the Supper is not only vertical -- it is also horizontal. The remembrance of the Supper demands recognition of the body of the Lord—most likely referring to both the physical body and the spiritual body the church. The Supper reminds us that the body is many members, and that all are needy at the foot of the cross. Therefore, Paul says we are to wait for one another and participate together.

Does the observance of the Lord's Supper in the contemporary church help to bind the spiritual body together? How could this part of the worship assembly help the church recognize and celebrate its unity? In what ways is the usual method of celebrating the Supper exclusive? How could the Supper be more inclusive? Should it be? How could the Supper be less individual-focused and more fellowship-focused? On a scale of 1 to 10, how much like or unlike the Lord's Supper in the first century church is the observance in most churches today?

Prayer

Dear Father God, we want our shared worship to glorify you and honor you and your Son, Jesus Christ. We do not intend to call attention to ourselves; forgive us when we do. In our heart of hearts, we want to be bound more closely together as the body of Christ going forth as your presence into this world. Help us learn acceptance and forgiveness around the Table, as you have forgiven us. Help us see our neediness and frailty and help us appreciate the forgiveness you have extended as you unite us in the body of Christ on earth. We pray in Jesus' name, Amen.

1 Corinthians 12: Honor the Body -- Unity and Diversity

Selected Biblical Text

12 For just as the body is one and has many members, and all the members of the body being many are one body, so also it is with Christ. 13 For we were all baptized in one Spirit into one body, whether Jews or Gentiles, whether slave or free, and we were all made to drink of one Spirit. 14 So the body is not one member but many. 15 If the foot says: "Because I am not a hand, I am not part of the body," is

it for that reason no longer part of the body? 16 And if the ear says: "Because I am not an eye, I am not part of the body," is it for that reason no longer part of the body? 17 If the whole body were an eye, where would the hearing be? If the whole body were an ear, where would the smelling be? 18 But in fact God has placed the members in the body, each one of them just as he wanted. 19 If they were all the same member, where would the body be? 20 So now there are many members, but one body. (1 Cor. 12:12-20)

Reflecting and Thinking

In the previous chapter, Paul wrote that worship recognizes and strengthens the body of Christ, the church. The body is one and yet has many members. That the body exists both in unity and diversity is a source of honor. The misuse of spiritual gifts at Corinth was separating and dividing, devaluing certain parts of the body. Today's chapter is the first of three chapters that seek to correct abuses and misunderstandings related to the use of spiritual gifts. Paul begins with a reminder about the nature and importance of the spiritual body.

Consider these truths from today's text. The body (the church) is incomplete without every member. The one body has many parts; the one church has many members. The members of the church have a common heritage in their baptism in one Spirit into the one body. In this shared spiritual heritage, past separations and divisions are undone and become meaningless history. Every part of the body is important and necessary. God is the one who has placed variety in the body, according to his desires and the needs of the church. The variety and diversity in the church work for its good, not for its detriment. The many parts do not deny the unity of the body. There is still only one body.

How would you describe the difference between a church that gives only lip-service to its oneness and unity and a church that intentionally practices unity? Thinking about the two kinds of churches described in the first question, answer the following. What would be the difference in the involvement of every member in the body? How many uninvolved members would there be? What would be the difference in the attendance practices and habits of the members? How many habitual absentees would there be? What would be the difference in the way the church cares for and attends all of its members without partiality? What would be the difference in the way all the members are honored?

Prayer

Dear Heavenly Father, help us to faithfully live out the reality of unity and diversity in the church. Help us to care more deeply for every member. Help me to find my place and fill it according to the gifts you have given me. Thank you for putting me where you have, in Jesus' name I pray, Amen.

❖ ❖ ❖

1 Corinthians 13: Love the Body -- The Greatest Gift

Selected Biblical Text
1 If I speak in the tongues of men, even of angels, but do not have love, I am only a noisy gong or a clanging cymbal. 2 If I have [the gift of] prophecy and I know all mysteries and all knowledge, and if I have complete faith so as to move mountains, but do not have love, I am nothing. 3 If I give away all my possessions and submit my body to hardship so that I may boast, but do not have love, I gain nothing.
4 Love is patient, love is kind. Love is not jealous, is not boastful, is not proud. 5 It is not rude, it is does not seek its own benefit, it is not easily angered, it does not keep an inventory of wrongs. 6 Love does not rejoice in injustice but rejoices with the truth. 7 It suffers all things, believes all things, hopes all things, endures all things.
8 Love never ends. But where there are prophecies, they will be set aside as useless; where there are tongues, they will cease; where there is knowledge, it will be set aside as useless. 9 For we know in part and we prophesy in part, 10 but when the complete comes, the "in part" [knowledge and prophecy] will be set aside as useless. 11 When I was a child, I talked like a child, I thought like a child, I reasoned like a child. When I became an adult man, I set aside as useless the things of childhood. 12 Up to this present time we are looking at a mirror with obscure images, but then face to face. Up to the present moment I know in part, but then I will know fully just as I was fully known. 13 And now remain faith, hope and love: these three. But the greatest of these is love. (1 Cor. 13:1-13)

Reflecting and Thinking
Today's textual reading is a little longer than normal -- 1 Corinthians 13, the "Love Chapter." The members at Corinth were focused on who had the most important spiritual gift, on who had preeminence, importance, reputation, and position. Paul said, "You have not even considered the greatest gift in the body." Let me show you the most excellent way. *What are some of the ways in which love is the greatest gift?*

As Paul explains in verses 8-10, the things the Corinthians were focused on were temporary. Tongues would cease. Prophecies would be put away, knowledge would be put away, the incomplete (imperfect) would be put away. The same verb is used in each of these statements, even though the NIV translation uses three different verbs. The gifts the Corinthians considered most important would stop. Tongues would cease. Their prophecies and knowledge were partial and incomplete and would be put away when the complete came.

Paul mentions five results of the misplaced focus of the Corinthians. The focus on temporary gifts failed to honor the body and the contributions of every member. The focus on temporary gifts tended to maintain a state of immaturity. The focus on temporary gifts failed to consider the possibility of spiritual development and maturity. The focus on temporary gifts failed to think about the potential for more complete knowledge. The focus on temporary gifts failed to consider what was really lasting -- faith, hope, and love, with the greatest of these being love.

Paul uses the verb "to put away" one more time in the chapter. When I became a man, I put away the things of my childhood. What are some of the things that you need to put away in order to become mature in Christ? What could the church today do to encourage greater maturity among its members?

Prayer
Dear God, help us learn the most excellent way. Help us establish as our priorities the things that matter most to you. Help us focus on things that matter and things that can make a difference. Help us not become distracted by things that call attention to ourselves. We pray in Jesus' name, Amen.

1 Corinthians 14: Edify the Body -- Spiritual Gifts

Selected Biblical Text
1 Pursue love, and desire the spiritual [gifts], and even better, that you may prophesy. 2 For the one speaking in a tongue* does not speak to people but to God, because no one understands him. He speaks mysteries in spirit (or, in the Spirit). 3 But the one who prophesies speaks to people for their building up, encouragement and comfort. 4 The one speaking in a tongue* builds up himself, but the one who prophesies builds up the church. 5 So I am willing that all of you speak in tongues* but even better, that you may prophesy. The one who prophesies is greater than the one who speaks in tongues* unless he interprets so that the church may be edified. (1 Cor. 14:1-5)

[*literally, the Greek word means tongue; in the biblical context, the reference is to a language or dialect, known languages of that time period]

Reflecting and Thinking
The titles of the devotionals from this part of Corinthians reflect Paul's concern for the body, the church. Paul is writing to a church with many challenges. He is concerned about whether they will be the church God desires them to be. In worship, we must recognize the body. We must honor God's plan for the body. We must edify the body. Christianity is not designed as a selfish religion. Christians are concerned about one another; Christians are concerned about others.

In today's text, Paul says that understandable prophecy is more to be desired than unintelligible languages that are not known to the others present. It appears that some of the Corinthians were exercising their language gift even when they did not have the gift of translation (interpretation). Paul says that in such cases no one understands what is said so the utterances are mysteries to all, possibly including the speaker (verse 2). The goal is the edification of the body. The gift of languages is desirable when someone interprets, because it edifies the church (in a two-step process) and has basically the same result as prophecy (a one-step process).

On a scale of 1 to 10, how concerned do you think most Christians today are about the edification of the entire body? On the same scale, how would you rate the selfishness of the average Christian? Do you think most people go to church for what they can get out of it, or for what they can give in worship to God and encouragement to other Christians? What percentage of the classes or sermons you hear are effective in edifying (building up, strengthening) the church? What percentage of the classes or sermons you hear have little impact on edifying (building up, strengthening) the church?

The Corinthians failed in edification because they were focused on themselves and their own spiritual gifts and visibility. Does the modern church ever fail in the same way? When have you see Christians focused on themselves more than on God?

Prayer
Dear God, help us develop concern for others and for the church. Help us get self out of the way so we can genuinely follow Jesus. May our lives and our words build others up, both to develop faith in other Christians and to help unbelievers learn about Jesus. As always, we pray in Jesus' name, Amen.

1 Corinthians 15: The Gospel and the Resurrection

Selected Biblical Text
1 Now I make known to you, brothers, the gospel which I preached to you, which also you received, and on which you stand, 2 through which also you are saved, if you hold firmly to the word I preached to you, lest you believed in vain. 3 For I passed on to you as of first importance what also I received: that Christ died for our sins according to the scriptures, 4 that he was buried, that he was raised on the third day according to the Scriptures....
12 But if Christ is preached, [saying] that from the dead he has been raised, how can some among you say that there is no resurrection of the dead? 13 If there is no resurrection of the dead, then not even Christ has been raised. 14 And if Christ has not been raised, then our preaching is meaningless, and your faith is meaningless. (1 Cor. 15:1-4, 12-14)

Reflecting and Thinking

The last major problem Paul addresses in the book of First Corinthians is a misunderstanding of the gospel, especially as it relates to the resurrection. Jesus' resurrection is an integral part of the gospel. To deny the possibility of resurrection is to deny Jesus' resurrection and to deny the validity of the gospel. Jesus' resurrection is the first fruits (promise) of our own resurrection.

For Paul, the certainty of Jesus' resurrection was undeniable. That resurrection is a possibility is evidenced by those who practice baptism for the dead. (Paul does not condone this practice; he merely says that the practice supports the concept of resurrection.) Jesus' conquest of every authority and power, including death, is the foundation of his victory and reign.

Questions about the nature of the resurrection body do not deny the possibility of resurrection. Our inability to understand the "how" of resurrection does not deny the resurrection. Resurrection is essential to eternal hope, because the kingdom of God is not a flesh and blood kingdom but an imperishable kingdom. In resurrection, mortality gives way to immortality and death becomes once and for all powerless. That is indeed Good News!

Given that Paul identifies Jesus' resurrection as an essential and crowning part of the gospel, how often should the church teach and preach about resurrection? How well do you think the average church member understands resurrection or the teachings of 1 Corinthians 15? Many believe that the early church observed and remembered the resurrection of Jesus in the Lord's Supper every Sunday. Given the importance of the resurrection, why are many churches today hesitant to remember the gospel (death, burial and resurrection of Jesus) weekly? How important is the resurrection in your faith in Jesus? Reflect on this statement from Christian evidences: "the resurrection is THE primary evidence that Jesus is the Son of God." How can we make the resurrection more important to the contemporary church?

Prayer

Dear God, thank you for your promise that the end of this physical life is not the end. Thank you for the confidence you have given us through Jesus' resurrection. Help us appreciate the gospel, help us imitate Jesus in our own death to sin, burial in baptism, and resurrected lives. We pray in Jesus' name, Amen.

1 Corinthians 16: Care for the Body -- The Collection and Final Greetings

Selected Biblical Text
1 Now concerning the collection for the saints, as I directed the churches of Galatia, you do likewise. 2 On the first day of the week, let each one of you by yourself set aside, reserving whatever he has been prospered, so that when I come there will be no collections. 3 Then, when I arrive, I will send those whom you approve with letters to carry your gift to Jerusalem. 4 If it seems advisable that I also go, they will go with me. (1 Cor. 16:1-4)

Reflecting and Thinking
The final chapter of 1 Corinthians contains today's selected text about the collection for the poor saints of Judea (also described in 2 Corinthians 8-9) and various personal references and greetings from Paul to members of the church community in Corinth. Both sections show the level of care that characterized the first century church.

Paul's concern for the church in every place is evident in our text -- the church has an obligation to care for itself, not only locally but globally. This provides today's church the foundation for national and international benevolence. This provides the foundation for global efforts in missions.

Paul is planning another trip to Corinth and will receive on that visit the gifts that have been set aside. He suggests a weekly gift so that it will not be necessary to have multiple spur-of-the-moment collections upon his arrival. Some have mistakenly applied these words to Jesus' coming, but the context clearly references Paul's arrival.

What are some of the ways the church today cares for special needs internally and for special needs in other places? What would you tell someone who asked about the necessity of weekly giving when they receive a monthly paycheck? In the text, each Christian was saving and setting aside funds in what appears to be an individual process. Which, if any, of the applications of the text are valid when applied to a church treasury and the weekly collection practices of the church today?

Prayer
Dear God, help us be more like you as we learn generosity by sharing the resources you have given us and by helping those who are in need. Help us learn unselfishness. Help us appreciate the sacrifice Jesus made as he demonstrated his love for us in his death on the cross. May we imitate him in our generosity and spirit of sacrifice for the benefit of others, in His name, Amen.

2 Corinthians 1: Ministering with Integrity

Selected Biblical Text

12 For our reason for glorying is this, the testimony of our conscience, that with pure motives and sincerity from God, not with worldly wisdom but with the grace of God, we conducted ourselves in the world, and especially toward you. 13 For we do not write you anything other than what you can read and understand. I hope that you will understand completely, 14 just as you understood us in part, that we are your glory just as you are ours on the day of the Lord Jesus.

15 With this confidence, I wanted to visit you first so you might have a double blessing, 16 to visit you going to Macedonia and again coming from Macedonia, and by you to be sent to Judea. 17 In planning this, then, did I use levity? Or do I make my plans like the world so that it is for me both the "yes, yes" and the "no, no"?

18 As God is faithful, our message to you is not "Yes" and "No." 19 For the Son of God, Jesus Christ, who was preached among you by us -- by me and Silas and Timothy -- was not "Yes" and "No," but in him it has been only "Yes." 20 For how many ever be the promises of God, they are "Yes" in him, so through him the "Amen" is spoken by us to the glory of God. 21 Now the one strengthening us together with you in Christ, and anointing us, is God, 22 who also sealed us, and gave the down payment of his Spirit in our hearts.

23 I call God as my witness, upon penalty of my life, that to spare you I did not come back to Corinth. 24 Not that we lord it over your faith, but we are coworkers with you for your joy; you stand firm by faith. (2 Cor. 1:12-24)

Reflecting and Thinking

Integrity is a much sought-after characteristic in today's world. Employers seek people of integrity with ethical standards. Wholeness is essential to self-esteem. Relationships soon unravel without integrity. Christian living is defined by integrity. Ministry demands integrity -- in thought, attitudes, conduct, and relationships. Churches are usually less likely than secular employers to screen ministry candidates by checking references, doing background checks and additional investigation. Churches need ministers who are able to minister out of their own personal wholeness. Churches should want to know if ministers are competent, capable, serious, committed, compassionate and caring.

Paul's actions are being called in question by some at Corinth. Why has he not come? Why has he not done what he planned to do? Today's text explains the situation. Paul has not been fickle; he has been faithful in everything. While it may appear that he has backed out of previous commitments, his desire was to spare them and give them time to correct certain problems.

Why is integrity hard to develop and maintain? When have you seen churches or ministries destroyed by lack of integrity? How do such situations show the importance of integrity?

Integrity is a concept much like consistency. Contrast two versions of consistency – (1) being consistent as the natural result of who we are, or (2) wanting to appear consistent but having to think continually about the actions of life in order to maintain that consistency. Integrity properly describes the consistency that comes from integrated lives that grow out of one's nature. Christian integrity grows out of the nature of Christ within us as we partake in the divine nature (2 Peter 1:3-4). For thought: what is the relationship between integrity and hypocrisy?

Prayer

Dear Heavenly Father God, we want to be like you, we want to live lives of integrity. Help us model integrity to those around us, regardless of our roles -- in our families, in our churches, and in our marketplaces. Help us as we seek to keep our word and do what we promise to do. Help us to speak consistent words. Help us live lives consistent with our claim to be Christ-followers. In Jesus' name and by his power I ask it. Amen.

2 Corinthians 2: Ministering the Knowledge of Him

Selected Biblical Text

12 Now when I came to Troas to preach the gospel of Christ and a door was opened for me by the Lord, 13 I still had no relief in my spirit, because I did not find my brother Titus there. So, I said goodbye to them and went on to Macedonia.
14 But thanks be to God who always leads us in triumphal procession in Christ, and the fragrance of the knowledge of him is made known through us in every place. 15 For we are to God a sweet aroma of Christ among those who are being saved and among those who are perishing, 16 to the perishing we are an odor of death that leads to death; to the saved, an aroma of life that leads to life. And who is competent for these things? 17 We are not like the many who are peddling the word of God for profit, but we speak in Christ before God from sincerity, as those sent by God. (2 Cor. 2:12-17)

Reflecting and Thinking

Paul continues to explain his change of plans in today's reading and textual selection. In Troas he found an open door for the gospel and for that reason he delayed his journey. The challenges of ministry are often overwhelming -- relationships, opportunities, new contacts, people who accept the message and are saved, people who reject the message and are perishing. The challenge of proclaiming the knowledge of Him is ever before the church and its preachers. Did I adequately tell the story of Jesus? Did I communicate the glory of God? Did I focus on knowing Jesus, or only on knowing about him? Did I say something eternal or did I simply tickle ears? With Paul we exclaim, "Who is equal to such a task?"

Today's text brings to view a second aspect of ministry and Christian living. Why do we do what we do? What is our motivation? Paul makes clear that none of what he does is for his own benefit or profit as he serves and ministers. As Christians, our great longing is only to spread the knowledge of Jesus Christ in every place to every person. When others come to know Christ, victory follows by God's power.

Since Paul in this second letter to Corinth is explaining and defending his actions as an apostle, many of the natural applications of the text are about ministry. That does not mean that there is nothing in the text of value for the average Christian. What principles in today's text are especially meaningful to you? (For example, consider principles such as sincerity, being sent and placed by God, sharing knowledge, and the immensity of the challenge.) When have you felt especially triumphant in your Christian walk? When you have been aware of the victory? How could you bring those positive feelings to your life more often? What does God want you to do today?

Prayer

Dear God, help me see the open doors you place before me today, and help me understand what you want me to do to serve others in the knowledge of Jesus. May I see and seize those opportunities. May my life reflect my knowledge of Jesus -- clearly showing that I know him in deep, personal relationship and not in merely superficial, external ways. Thank you for the victory you have given us in Jesus, we pray in His name, Amen.

2 Corinthians 3: Reflecting the Lord's Glory

Selected Biblical Text

1 Are we beginning to commend ourselves again? Or do we need, as some people do, letters of recommendation to you or from you? 2 You yourselves are our letter, written on our hearts, known and read by everyone. 3 making manifest that you are a letter from Christ, the result of our ministry, written not with ink but with the Spirit of the living God, not on tablets of stone but on tablets of human hearts. 4 Such confidence we have through Christ before God. 5 Not that we are competent in ourselves to credit anything as from ourselves, but our competence is from God, 6 who also made us competent ministers of a new covenant, not of the letter but of the Spirit; for the letter kills, but the Spirit gives life....

17 Now the Lord is [the] Spirit, and where the Spirit of the Lord is, there is freedom. 18 And we all, with unveiled faces contemplating [reflecting] the glory of the Lord, are being transformed into his image from [one] glory to [another] glory, just as from the Lord, the Spirit. (2 Cor. 3:1-6, 17-18)

Reflecting and Thinking

Paul's first visit and ministry at Corinth had lasted eighteen months. After his departure, some began to question his message and motives. Doubts were being raised about his authenticity as an apostle and the depth of his relationship and concern for those in the church at Corinth. Given Paul's mention of the contrast between the old and new covenants in today's chapter, perhaps Paul's opponents were urging a return to some aspects of Judaism (as the Judaizing teachers in Galatia).

The climax toward which today's selected reading points is this: The Lord's glory, reflected in our lives, changes and transforms us so that the Lord receives even greater glory, in an ever-increasing upward spiritual spiral empowered by the Spirit. Paul guides his readers toward this conclusion in a series of smaller steps: (1) the evidence of changed lives in Corinth, (2) this evidence is not artificial or manufactured but is visible to all, (3) this is the result of Paul's ministry in Corinth, (4) the results are spiritual and not physical, (5) the changes have been wrought by God's power not Paul's, (6) the changes have come through the new covenant and the Spirit, (7) this is obvious because the new covenant is more glorious than the old -- any glory of the old was temporary and fading and was hidden or veiled from the people, and (8) the new covenant is one of openness and transparency in the Spirit and freedom. Therefore, in Christ we see and reflect and experience an ever-increasing glory!

How can our lives as Christians better reflect the glory of the Lord? What does it mean to you that our transformation into his image brings an ever-increasing glory? How it is true that this glory is from the Lord and not from us? Since our competence (as Paul's) is from God, what things is God competent to do in you and through you today? With God's competence, what things are outside your ability? Why do we sometimes not depend on God's competence in our daily lives? (You may want to think about temptation, sharing your faith, talking about Jesus, prayer, Christian fruits or graces, Bible reading, and other such activities, attributes and attitudes as you contemplate your answers to these questions.)

Prayer

Dear God, give us greater confidence today as we live in awareness that our competence is from you and that our actions are not dependent on our power. Be with us as we seek to live glorious lives -- not in our own glory, but reflecting divine glory, and bringing greater and greater glory to Jesus and his reign, in Jesus' name and for the sake of his kingdom we pray, Amen.

2 Corinthians 4: Ministering out of Human Weakness

Selected Biblical Text

1 Therefore, having this ministry just as God has been merciful to us, we do not grow weary. 2 We have denounced secret shameful ways, not living by trickery nor handling deceitfully the word of God, rather setting forth the truth, commending ourselves to everyone's conscience before God. 3 So if our gospel is veiled, it is veiled to those who are perishing, 4 among whom the god of this age has blinded the minds of the unbelievers so that they do not see the light of the gospel of the glory of Christ, who is the image of God. 5 For we do not preach ourselves, but Jesus Christ as Lord, and ourselves your slaves for Jesus' sake. 6 For God who said: Let light shine out of darkness, is the one who shined in our hearts to give us the light of the knowledge of the glory of God, in the face of Christ. 7 But we have this treasure in jars of clay, in order that the surpassing power may be from God and not from us. (2 Cor. 4:1-7)

Reflecting and Thinking

God has mercifully included us in his plan and given us places and opportunities of service. Paul in today's text is thinking specifically about his own apostolic ministry, but the principles he sets forth are true for every Christian. Every Christian has a ministry from God. Our ministry is designed to encourage us in difficult days. We are called to consistent Christian testimony without deception or distortion. Because we serve with God's power, we are not responsible for the results. Still, our hearts hurt when the gospel is not clearly seen by those to whom we speak. This veiling is the result of Satan's work, blinding unbelievers to such an extent that they cannot see light!

When we try to overcome the blindness of the world by focusing attention on things visible (like us), we unwittingly buy into Satan's deception. No! We must continue to preach Jesus Christ as Lord, because God is powerful enough by his Word to make light shine in darkness, even as the light has shined in our lives through Christ. The most powerful ministry of the knowledge of Christ keeps the focus on the treasure and not on the clay jar. This focus makes it clear that the real power is from God and is not centered in human beings or human efforts.

Paul is in a delicate position as he writes to the Corinthians. In the first letter, he had addressed several problems that had arisen, the result of their desire to be men-followers. The last thing he wants now is to resolve the conflict with his opponents by urging the Corinthians to follow him rather than the false teachers and false apostles. To put the focus on Paul and his ministry would undo much of the foundation he had carefully built in his personal presence and ministry and in his first letter.

The solution Paul advances should boldly catch our attention in today's world where people still tend to be men-followers and many local ministers and preachers call attention to self and attain a type of celebrity-status. The message is invariable -- Jesus Christ is Lord. The glory of God is visible only in Christ; Christ is the light -- the light is not what a certain person may say or write or do. The power is not in persuasive speech or human wisdom -- the power is from God.

To what extent do you see that the church today tends to be "men followers" and "people pleasers?"

Prayer

Heavenly Father, thank you for the opportunities for ministry and service which you have given your people. Help us serve faithfully in our weakness, demonstrating the power of the gospel. Forgive us when we are tempted to call attention to ourselves more than to Christ. May we always call attention to the true light of the world. Thank you for revealing yourself in the light of the knowledge of Christ. Thank you that we have been able to see and to be saved, in the name of the Christ who is Lord and Light, Amen.

2 Corinthians 5: Ministering for Reconciliation

Selected Biblical Text

16 So then from now on we look at no one according to the world [literally, the flesh]. Though we have known Christ according to the world, now we no longer know [him, in this way]. 17 So that, if anyone is in Christ, he is a new created being. The old things are gone; look and see, the new things have come. 18 All these things are from God, who reconciled us to himself through Christ and gave us the ministry of reconciliation. 19 Thus, God was in Christ reconciling the world to himself, not counting people's sins against them, and he has committed to us the message of reconciliation. 20 We then are ambassadors of Christ, as though God were calling you back through us. We beg you on Christ's behalf: "be reconciled to God." 21 The one never having known sin, God made [appointed as] sinfulness instead of us, so that we might become the righteousness of God in him. (2 Cor. 5:16-21)

Reflecting and Thinking

In many places, the contemporary church finds itself involved in more and more ministries that do not directly connect with and do not contribute to reconciliation with God. God's eternal purpose in the world is focused in the reconciling death of Jesus for all humankind. Human thinking cannot fathom the immensity of God's plan. When Paul finally grasped the reality of the ministry of reconciliation and the possibility of newness in Christ, he cast aside the worldly (purely human) point of view. Not only is God at work reconciling us, he has given to us the ministry and message of reconciliation. We are messengers (ambassadors) who speak in such a way that it seems as though God is directly appealing through us. There are lots of ways we can be involved in ministry. Every day offers multiple options of activities for serving, ministering and helping others. We choose those options in the spirit of Jesus and seek to help others as we have opportunity. But above all, we pay attention to the opportunities we have for ministering to others as messengers of God's reconciliation. Paul's imploring call is clear (verse 20): Be reconciled to God! In light of this eternal need, nothing else matters. Verse 21 is not easy: the reading that contrasts sinfulness and righteousness helps communicate the meaning.

What ministries of the church where you attend are focused on reconciliation with God? What ministries of the church may indirectly contribute to the ministry of reconciliation? What ministries of the church have little if any impact on the ministry of reconciliation? What are some reasons the contemporary church does not have a greater focus on ministering for reconciliation with God (evangelism with the express purpose of salvation)? How can you be more involved in ministering or serving in ways that help others toward reconciliation with God?

Prayer
Heavenly Father, help us develop the heart of Jesus. Help us develop the mind and attitude of Jesus who sacrificially gave himself for us, the sinless for the sinful, the holy for the unholy, the righteous for the unrighteous. Help us see others through a heavenly point of view that sees their spiritual needs, and not only through a human point of view that sees their physical needs. Help us be more concerned about the threat of spiritual death than about the threat of physical death. Help us grasp the constraining and compelling love of Jesus so that we will go forth as ambassadors in the ministry of reconciliation, through Jesus the Great Reconciler we pray, Amen.

2 Corinthians 6: Ministering through Relationships

Selected Biblical Text
11 Our mouth has opened to you, Corinthians, and our heart has opened wide to you. 12 You are not being restricted by us, but you are restricting your affection [for us]. 13 As a fair exchange -- I speak as to my children -- open wide your hearts also.
2 Make room for us in your hearts. We have wronged no one, we have corrupted no one, we have exploited no one. 3 I do not say this to condemn you; I told you before that you are in our hearts to die together and to live together. 4 Great is my boldness with you; great is my pride because of you. I have been filled with encouragement; I overflow with joy in all our troubles. (2 Cor. 6:11-13; 7:2-4)

Reflecting and Thinking

We have already observed that Paul's ministry among the Corinthians was being questioned and devalued by some opponents at Corinth. His motives were being questioned. Paul's concern for the Corinthians is clearly seen in today's reading. One outline characterizes this section as the appeal of a spiritual father to his children. Paul is so concerned with the continued faithfulness of his converts that he will endure whatever hardships are necessary to avoid placing obstacles in their way. He appeals for open hearts and transparent relationships, based on his example of ministry through relationships. He is not condemning; he is exhibiting his pride and hope and joy.

None can doubt that there were problems at Corinth. It is unlikely that all the problems addressed in Paul's first letter had been completely resolved. Now Paul is addressing a new set of challenges. In the middle of the problems and challenges of ministry, Paul speaks of his great love and hope and joy and pride in the church he had helped establish at Corinth. Effective ministry and service spring from deep relationships.

What do you think of the statement that people tend to live up to or live down to our expectations? Do you agree or disagree? How is Paul's attitude in today's text a model for effective ministry? How could today's text be applied to other relationships in life, e.g. parenting, friendships, employees, etc.? When have you seen effective ministry or outreach based on meaningful relationships? When have you seen ministry or outreach fail due to the lack of a solid relationship base?

Prayer

Dear Heavenly Father, thank you for showing us the way to loving relationships through your example. Thank you for taking the initiative to establish relationship with us even when we were distanced, unlovable, enemies, and unworthy of your love. May we follow your example as we strive to share your love with others. Help us learn the give and take of dynamic ministry based on relationships. Help us walk with you today in meaningful, close relationship. Thank you, in Jesus' name. Amen.

2 Corinthians 7: Ministering for Changed Lives

Selected Biblical Text

8 Even if I caused you sorrow by my letter, I do not regret it. I did regret it, for I see that my letter caused you sorrow, but only for a short time. 9 Now I rejoice, not because you were made sorry, but because you were made sorry to [the point of] repentance. For you were made sorry with godly sorrow, so you were not harmed in any way by us. 10 Godly sorrow produces repentance that leads to salvation not

to be repented of, but worldly sorrow produces death. 11 See what this very thing, to be sorry with godly sorrow, has produced in you: what great diligence, what defense, what indignation, what alarm, what longing, what zeal, what punishment. In each point, you have proved yourselves to be innocent in this matter. 12 Wherefore, even though I wrote to you, it was neither because of the one who did wrong nor because of the one who was wronged, but rather to make known to you your diligence toward us before God.

13 By this we are encouraged. In addition to our own overflowing encouragement, we rejoiced even more at the joy of Titus, that his spirit has been refreshed by all of you. 14 If in anything I had boasted to him about you, I have not been embarrassed. But just as everything we said to you was true, so our boasting to Titus has proved to be true as well. 15 And his affection for you is even greater when he remembers the obedience of you all, how you received him with fear and trembling. 16 I rejoice that in everything I have complete confidence in you. (2 Cor. 7:8-16)

Reflecting and Thinking

One of the great challenges in the Christian life and in Christian ministry is to understand how to help others change their lives. In today's reading we learn that Paul had written a pointed and difficult letter to the Corinthians. He hoped the letter would have its desired effect, but he anxiously awaited the news of how it had been received. The letter was so pointed that he actually for a time regretted writing it. Now he has learned that the possibly hurtful letter had accomplished its goal. The sorrow it caused led to genuine repentance and changed lives.

It would be wonderful if we could have a guarantee that our intentions would always be understood by others. Or if a crystal ball could indicate when we should be strict and harsh and when we should be giving and forgiving. The goal of biblical ministry is changed lives! The long-term impact and value of ministry can only be measured by whether lives are changed. While there is value in changing the physical circumstances of people's lives, the ultimate goal must be that lives are changed spiritually and eternally. Ministry that does not result in eternally changed lives is meaningless. So also, Christianity that does not change our spiritual lives is valueless.

How does God want you to change your life today? For whom are you restless as you await the outcome of your efforts to be an influence for Christ? (Pray specifically for that person today.) What is the difference between godly sorrow and worldly sorrow according to today's reading (verse 10)? What do you think of this contrast: sorry for what you did vs. sorry that you got caught? Is repentance mental, behavioral, or both? Is repentance that does not change one's life genuine? Why or why not?

Prayer

Dear God, we seek changed lives, first for ourselves and then for others. Teach us godly sorrow so that we can find renewed thinking and renewed living. Give us wisdom as we seek to encourage others to follow Jesus. We pray in Jesus' name, Amen.

2 Corinthians 8: The Need for Generosity

Selected Biblical Text

1 Now, brothers, we make known to you the grace of God given by the Macedonian churches. 2 In a severe trial of affliction, the abundance of their joy and the depth of their poverty overflowed into a richness of their generosity. 3 For I testify that they gave according to their ability, and beyond their ability, voluntarily, 4 with much urging they begged from us the blessing [grace] of participating in the ministry to the saints. 5 And not as we had hoped, but they gave themselves, first to the Lord, and to us by the will of God. 6 So that we urged Titus, just as he had previously begun, so also to complete for you, this blessing [grace]. 7 So as you excel in everything -- in faith, in speech, in knowledge, in all diligence and in the love from us that is now in you – so also excel in this blessing [grace].
8 I do not say this as a command, but through the diligence of others, to prove the genuineness of your love. 9 For you know the grace of our Lord Jesus Christ, that though he was rich, he became poor for you, so that you through his poverty might become rich. (2 Cor. 8:1-9)

Reflecting and Thinking

In two chapters in the book of 2 Corinthians (Chapters 8-9), Paul seems to change the subject as he addresses the topic of giving as it relates to the contribution for the poor Christians in Jerusalem. A careful analysis of the book shows that Paul in this section is still focused on ministry and the results of his ministry among the Corinthians. One of the projects Paul was encouraging was a collection for the Christians in Judea who were suffering from a severe famine. He wanted the church at Corinth to finish the project that they had previously begun, based on his instructions (1 Cor. 16:1-4) and the encouragement of Titus (verse 6). To encourage them, he holds up the Macedonians as an example of gracious generosity, noting that the Macedonians had given beyond their ability, on their own initiative, and beyond expectations. Paul's primary point is not the money involved in the collection. Paul is focused on the importance of keeping one's word. He is focused on the development of attitudes and actions of generosity within the Corinthian church, knowing that nothing makes us more like God than a generous spirit. In the last verse of today's text, Paul sets forth Christ as an example of one who was rich but became poor for the good of others. We have become rich spiritually because of him.

Today's text deals with a subject that is difficult and "touchy" for many Christians: money! What is your attitude toward money? On a scale of 1 to 10, how generous do you consider yourself to be? Have you ever given "beyond your ability" to the church, a charity, or other cause? If so, how did it make you feel? What do you think of Paul's observation that the Macedonians gave generously because they had first given themselves to the Lord? Do you think that some do not give today because they have not first settled the fact that they belong to the Lord? If giving is a test of the sincerity of our love, how does the average North American Christian stack up when we give only 2-3% of our income back to God? What level of giving would you consider an adequate indication of genuine, sincere love? How could the church help its members reach new heights in this difficult area? How could you personally grow in this "grace?"

Prayer

Dear God, help us think correctly about "things" and help us develop attitudes of generosity as we consider the great gift we have received through Jesus. Help us grow in love for you and for one another so that we earnestly desire to share our blessings and help with special projects. Teach us graciousness and generosity. Help us learn to imitate the sacrificial spirit of Jesus, we pray in his name, Amen.

2 Corinthians 9: The Fruit of Generosity

Selected Biblical Text

6 Consider this: "The one sowing sparingly will also reap sparingly, and the one sowing generously will also reap generously." 7 Each one should give as he has decided in his heart, not reluctantly or under compulsion, for God loves a cheerful giver. 8 And God is able to make every blessing [grace] abound to you, so that in everything at all times, having enough of everything, you will abound in every good work. 9 As it is written: "He liberally scattered, he gave to the poor; his righteousness remains forever."

10 Now the one supplying seed for the sower and bread for food will supply and increase your seed-sowing and will grow the harvest of your righteousness. 11 You will be enriched in every way to be generous on every occasion, a generosity which through us produces thanksgiving to God. 12 Your service in this ministry is not only supplying the needs of the saints but is also overflowing in many thanks to God. 13 Through the proof of this service, others will glorify God for your obedience to your confession for the gospel of Christ, and for your generosity in sharing with them and with everyone else. 14 And in their prayers on your behalf, they will long for you, because of the surpassing grace of God upon you. 15 Thanks be to God for his indescribable gift! (2 Cor. 9:6-15)

Reflecting and Thinking

In today's text, Paul reminds the church at Corinth of a principle from the book of Proverbs: our reaping is in proportion to our sowing. We reap what we sow, we cannot reap if we do not sow, we reap according to what we sow, and we harvest more than we sow. Paul mentions five results or fruits of this generosity: needs are supplied, thanks overflows, love is proved, God is praised, and prayers are raised (verses 12-14). No wonder Paul concludes: Thanks be to God for his indescribable gift!

An interesting study of this passage centers around Paul's use of the word "all" and some related words -- each, every, all. Read the passage aloud and put a special emphasis on those words. (You may want to underline them in your Bible.) What do you think is the point of the repetition of this concept? Do you think most Christians today sow generously or sow sparingly? How would you evaluate your own generosity and sharing? As we think about the five fruits of generosity Paul mentions, what should we think if there is no fruit? How could the church be helped to grow in developing the fruits of generosity? What connections do you see between our willingness to share our financial resources and our willingness to share the gospel (or connections between a hesitancy to share resources and a hesitancy to share the gospel)?

Prayer

Dear God, help us be eager to serve; again, we ask that you help us develop attitudes of generosity, concern and compassion. Today we contemplate the indescribable gift of Jesus and we come face to face with the fact that we cannot put into words the immensity of that gift. Overwhelm us with gratitude that we might pass on that which we have received. Bless us today as we bless others. We pray in Jesus' name, Amen.

2 Corinthians 10: Honoring the "Place" of Our Ministry

Selected Biblical Text

12 We do not dare to classify or compare ourselves with some who commend themselves. For when they measure themselves by themselves and compare themselves with themselves, they are not wise. 13 We will not boast about things that cannot be measured but will boast only to the limit [measure] of the territory God gave us, a limit [measure] that reaches even unto you. 14 For we did not overstretch ourselves, as though we should not reach as far as you, because we came unto you with the gospel of Christ. 15 Neither do we boast about unmeasurable things in the work of others, having hope that as your faith grows, our work will greatly be expanded among you, unto a superabundance, 16 so that we can preach the gospel in the regions that lie beyond you, not to boast about things already

done in the territory of others. 17 But, "Let the one who boasts boast in the Lord." 18 For it is not the one who commends himself who is approved, but the one whom the Lord commends. (2 Cor. 10:12-18)

Reflecting and Thinking

In answering those who opposed him at Corinth, in today's text Paul writes about the "place" of ministry God has given him. Paul has no desire to go beyond the limits God has set; he seeks only to honor the place God has provided, which place includes the Corinthians. His claim is that his opponents are out of their place, that is, beyond their boundaries or limits, because they are boasting about the work Paul has accomplished in his area of work. One of the phrases Paul uses may refer to athletes who must run in their own lane.

One of the more difficult questions in ministry and in Christian living concerns our "place." Where does God want us to be? We want to serve where we can be most effective, so the answer we give to the question of "place" is often influenced by our human concerns. A contemporary application of the "place" principle may be seen in analyzing mission reports. Sometimes the same results are reported by several different missionaries who happen to be present when something occurs; each report leaving the impression that most of the credit belongs to the one reporting with little or no mention of the others who were involved and supporting the effort. Can we learn to be content with the work and the results God gives us in our field? Can we learn to honor the value of working together without regard for who receives the credit?

How is Paul's description of his "place" in God's ministry and kingdom an effective antidote to the accusations and activities of the false teachers at Corinth? What does it mean to you to "run in your lane?" Can you think of some examples of ministers or Christians who did not honor the "place" where God put them? Why did Paul not want to build on someone else's foundation or to work in someone else's territory? Why was that important to him?

Prayer

Dear God, help us as we seek to find our unique niche and place in your kingdom work. Give us wisdom as we seek your will and way. Thank you for the place where you have put us, even if it does not seem the best or most desirable place or situation to us. Thank you for your wisdom in working all things for good. Give us patience as we work in our place and help us serve faithfully as we depend on you for the results you desire. Help us avoid conflicts of jealousy and competition. May the Kingdom be advanced in every place around the world, we pray in Jesus' name, Amen.

2 Corinthians 11: Loving the "People" of Our Ministry

Selected Biblical Text

1 I want you to put up with me in a little foolishness, but indeed you are putting up with me! 2 I am jealous for you with a godly jealousy, for I promised you to one husband, to present you as a pure virgin to Christ. 3 But I fear lest somehow as the serpent deceived Eve by his subtilty, so your minds may be corrupted from the sincerity that is in Christ. 4 For if someone who comes preaches another Jesus whom we did not preach, or if you receive a different spirit than the spirit you received, or a different gospel than the one you accepted, you put up with it easily. 5 For I consider myself in no way inferior to those "super-apostles." 6 If I am untrained in speaking, I am not so in knowledge, making everything clear to you in every way. 7 Did I commit sin by humbling myself so you would be exalted, because without charge I preached the gospel of God to you? 8 I robbed other churches, receiving support for ministry to you. 9 And when I was with you and lacked something, I was not a burden to anyone, for the brothers who came from Macedonia supplied my needs, so I kept myself from being a burden to you in any way, and will continue to do so. 10 As the truth of Christ is in me, this same boast will not be silenced in me in the regions of Achaia. 11 Why? Because I do not love you? God knows! (2 Cor. 11:1-11)

Reflecting and Thinking

Paul had an intense love for the church at Corinth. He describes that love as a godly jealousy. Like a bride promised to a husband, Paul has promised the Corinthians to Christ. The ultimate choice, however, does not belong to Paul. He is concerned that the members at Corinth could be deceived and led astray; they could veer from their devotion to Christ. They could be distracted by a different message with a different Jesus, a different Spirit, and a different gospel. Paul is concerned that they would not even notice the difference, and that they would put up with those deceivers who do not act out of motives of love.

Therefore, Paul reminds his readers of his love for the people of his ministry. He worked at a trade so he could preach the gospel without burdening them (free of charge). He accepted support from other churches; he sacrificed for the gospel. Why? Because of his intense love for them!

What happens when a minister or missionary really loves the people he is working with? What is the connection between loving people and evangelism that effectively shares the gospel? Have you known situations where ministers entering a new ministry context failed to appreciate the work and effort that had been expended in the past to bring people to Christ, or where such a minister failed to love the people enough to secure them and protect them and support them in difficult times? We expect ministers to love the people. How can elders or shepherds make clear that they love the people in the flock? How would you know whether an elder loved the people or not? What actions would you expect? How do we act toward people we really love?

Prayer

Dear God, help us to grow in our love for people, learning to love them even as you love them. Help us to love to such an extent that no price is too great to pay for the salvation and faithfulness of those you love. Help your people learn to love like you do, so that the gospel message will echo forth. We pray in Jesus' name, Amen.

2 Corinthians 12: Demonstrating "Perseverance" in Our Ministry

Selected Biblical Text

14 Now I am ready to visit you the third time, and I will not be a burden to you, for what I seek is not your possessions but you. Because children are not obligated to save up for their parents, but parents for their children. 15 So I will very gladly spend and be spent for your lives. If I love you more, will I be loved less? 16 Be that as it may, I have not burdened you; perhaps being a crafty person, I took you in by deceit! 17 Did I take advantage of you through any of the ones whom I sent to you? 18 I urged Titus to go to you and I sent another brother with him. Did Titus exploit you? Did we not conduct ourselves in the same spirit, walking in the same path?
19 Have you been thinking all along that we have been defending ourselves to you? We are speaking before God in Christ; and everything we do, dear friends, is for your strengthening. 20 For I fear lest when I come, I will find you not as I want, and you will find me not as you want. I fear that there may be quarreling, jealousy, anger, selfish ambition, slander, gossip, arrogance and disorder. 21 I am afraid that when I come again God will humble me before you, and I will grieve over many of those who previously sinned and have not repented of the impurity, sexual sin and licentiousness which they practiced. (2 Cor. 12:14-21)

Reflecting and Thinking

Paul is committed to the place God has given him. He loves the people he has brought to Christ through preaching the gospel. He realizes the necessity of persevering in the work God has given him. Although it would be easy to give up, Paul will spend and be spent for those he loves. He will do things that are distasteful; he will go through whatever is necessary. The minister who ministers out of love perseveres even when it is not easy or to his advantage. He will pay whatever price is necessary to save those God has entrusted to him. What an example for today's ministers, shepherds, elders, and Christians! Perseverance is an indicator of love. None are going to easily slip out of God's grasp as long as Paul is on duty. He will persevere in speaking, strengthening, and encouraging. He grieves and is willing to face even more grief. He will not give up; he will persevere in the face of insurmountable odds and continue to reach out to Christians who appear to be irreconcilable, having slipped beyond reach. The selected text hardly tells the story -- I encourage you to find time to read the entire chapter today. Paul's struggle with his thorn in the flesh, his willingness to endure pain and suffering for the Corinthians, and his love and perseverance are challenging examples for the church today that too easily gives up on those who struggle and walk away.

On a scale of 1 to 10, how would you rate the perseverance of the contemporary church (or of the local church where you attend)? How would you rate the efforts of local pastors (shepherds or elders), ministers, and members to reach out to Christians who are struggling with faith issues? (These are not judgmental questions, but sincere efforts to evaluate the current situation and think about needed improvements.) What would help the church learn to persevere longer in its efforts to reach out, both to the unsaved and to fellow Christians who struggle or walk away from God? What advice do you see in this chapter for the contemporary church?

Prayer
Dear God, forgive us when we fail to persevere on behalf of the souls of others. Help us grow in love and perseverance, give us wisdom and helpful words as we seek to touch others and encourage them. Teach us perseverance in prayer, in Jesus' name, Amen.

2 Corinthians 13: Praying for the "Product" of Our Ministry

Selected Biblical Text
1 This will be my third visit to you. "By the mouth of two or three witness, every word will be established." 2 I have predicted and now predict, when I was with you the second time and now being absent, to those who sinned previously and to all the rest, that when I come I will not spare anyone again, 3 since you are demanding proof that Christ is speaking through me. He is not weak with you but is powerful among you. 4 For indeed, he was crucified through weakness, yet he lives through God's power. We are weak in him, but we will live with him because of the power of God among you.
5 Test yourselves to see whether you are in the faith; prove yourselves. Or do not you yourselves realize that Christ Jesus is in you? Unless, of course, you are not approved? 6 And I hope that you will realize that we are not unapproved. 7 Now we pray to God that you will not do anything wrong, not so we will appear to be approved, but so you will do what is good, even if we are unapproved. 8 For we cannot do anything against the truth, but only for the truth. 9 We rejoice when we are weak, but you are strong; and this we pray, that you may be complete. 10 Because of this I write these things being absent, so that when I come, I will not deal harshly, according to the authority which the Lord gave me for building up and not for tearing down. (2 Cor. 13:1-10)

Reflecting and Thinking

Paul's earnest desire was that his ministry might not have been in vain. The church at Corinth was facing extremely difficult days and great challenges, but Paul believed in them. He was praying for them. His greatest joy would be that they passed the test. He wanted only to support and advance their faith in Christ, even if it meant his own weakness (or appearance of weakness).

Paul realized that he might have to be stern with some who were willfully, belligerently opposing him. He was willing to do so if necessary, but hopeful that it would not be necessary. His prayer was for their full restoration and success in Christ. Never was it his intent to tear them down; always he desired to build them up.

What or who is the product of your ministry (whether you have an official position of ministry or are a member who ministers and serves)? For whom do you pray regularly? How does one examine self to see whether one is in the faith (verse 5)? Is it ever necessary today to use harsh authority to call attention to the specific situations in which Christians find themselves? As we conclude the study of the book of 2 Corinthians, take some time today to reflect upon and pray about your role in the kingdom -- the place, the people, your perseverance, and the product (results) of your Christian life.

Prayer

Dear God, we praise and honor you for your wisdom. We want to walk more closely with you. We affirm in faith that you are working in our lives. Bless us this day in your power and purpose as we think about the place where you have put us, the people you have put into our lives, the challenge of faithfully persevering, and the results that you will give in due time if we do not grow weary and faint. Guide us in your paths, we pray in Jesus' name, Amen.

Mark 1: The Beginning of the Gospel

Selected Biblical Text

1 The beginning of the gospel of Jesus Christ, the Son of God.
14 After John was put in prison, Jesus went into Galilee, proclaiming the gospel of God, 15 and saying: "The time has been fulfilled; the kingdom of God has come near. Repent and believe the gospel." (Mark 1:1, 14-15)

Reflecting and Thinking

Mark leaves no doubt as he begins his book: "The beginning of the gospel about Jesus Christ the Son of God." The book of Mark begins as do the other Synoptic Gospels (Matthew and Luke) with a series of "identity stories" -- quotations from the Old Testament, prophecies fulfilled, Jesus' baptism, Jesus' temptation. Matthew and Luke include genealogies and birth narratives as part of these identity stories, but Mark 1 moves directly into a series of "amazement stories" -- an evil spirit driven out, healings, demons silenced, a leper healed, and synagogue preaching. In the early chapters of Mark, the biblical text notes again and again the amazement of the people.

In the midst of this rapid-fire beginning, it is quite easy to overlook the affirmation: "The kingdom of God is near. Repent and believe the good news!" Life-changing, designed to catch our attention, challenging! Should we also notice that the order sounds a bit unusual to our ears: repent and believe?

Why does repentance precede belief in this passage? Can a person have faith without changing their thinking about how the coming of Christ brings the kingdom near? Does this admonition of Jesus still apply today, or would he now say, "Believe and repent"? How do the stories in the rest of the chapter illustrate the sequence of "repent and believe"?

Prayer

Father God, we want to become people of great faith, believing the good news to such an extent that our lives are forever changed. Help us see Jesus afresh in today's reading and in the study of Mark's gospel, in Jesus' name I ask it. Amen.

Mark 2: Amazing Works and Amazing Words

Selected Biblical Text

8 And immediately when Jesus knew in his spirit that they were reasoning thus among themselves, he said to them: "Why are you reasoning these things in your hearts? 9 Which is easier: to say to the paralytic, 'Your sins are forgiven,' or to say, 'Rise up, take your mat and walk'?" 10 But so that you can know that the Son of

Man has authority on earth to forgive sins, he speaks to the man: 11 "I tell you, rise, take your mat and go to your house." 12 So immediately he got up, took his mat and walked out before them all, so that all were amazed, and they glorified God, saying: "We never saw anything like this."

17 Hearing this, Jesus said to them: "The healthy do not need a doctor, but the sick. I did not come to call the righteous, but sinners." (Mark 2:8-12, 17)

Reflecting and Thinking

This chapter contains four short narratives -- a paralytic healed, a tax collector called, a theological question about fasting answered, the Sabbath explained. The healing is amazing, but even more amazing is Jesus' power over sin. He has authority on earth to forgive sins. He came to call and rescue sinners. He came to bring God's ultimate plan for human creation to fruition. Mankind was not made to keep rules; rules were made for the well-being of humankind.

Change is coming -- but there will always be some who resist change. Unfortunately, then as now, some of those who most resist the kingdom and most loudly oppose the new order are religious leaders.

In today's text, what was the significance of Jesus' authority to forgive sins on earth? Why were the people amazed? In your opinion, did seeing the healing cause them to "get it" (that is, to see the bigger picture and understand) or were they only impressed by the healing? Why were the religious authorities so upset? (Note that the teachers of the law and the Pharisees are mentioned in all four of the narratives in this chapter.)

Prayer

Dear God, help us escape the boredom and tedium of hearing the same old stories in the same old ways with little emotional involvement. Help us hear with excitement and amazement as did first century observers. Help us understand the significance of what Jesus did and what he said. Would you please help us restore just a little of the wonder and the amazement? Make us people of principle and not people dependent on mere rote. We pray in Jesus' name, Amen.

Mark 3: Confrontation Stories

Selected Biblical Text

1 Then Jesus entered the synagogue, and there was there a man with a shriveled hand. 2 They watched Jesus closely whether he would heal the man on the sabbath, so they could accuse him. 3 Jesus said to the man having the shriveled hand: "Stand up among these people."

4 Then Jesus asked them: "Is it lawful to do good on the Sabbath or to do evil, to save life or to kill?" And they remained silent.

5 After looking around at them in anger, grieving at their callous hearts, he said to the man: "Stretch out your hand." He stretched it out, and his hand was restored.

6 Then the Pharisees went out and began to plot with the Herodians how they might kill Jesus. (Mark 3:1-6)

Reflecting and Thinking

One can hardly read the early chapters of Mark carefully and analytically without noticing that confrontation between Jesus and the Jewish authorities is introduced early in Mark's gospel. The Pharisees are mentioned in each of the four narratives in Chapter 2. This chapter continues the confrontation. In fact, today's selected reading concludes by noting that the confrontation was so severe that the religious leaders began plotting the death of Jesus.

Despite the opposition, Jesus continues preaching and we are introduced to another of the great mysteries of this gospel. The followers of Jesus, those who should know who Jesus is, do not recognize him, but the evil spirits do recognize him. Jesus forbids the spirits to tell who he is, and he must continually explain to his followers his identity and purpose. This is part of what is known as the "Messianic secret" in Mark's gospel.

In this chapter, Mark also introduces the first of many "follower narratives" that are found throughout the book. Jesus appoints apostles and redefines what it means to be a part of his family.

Have you ever thought that the situation described in Mark is still true today – that those who should know and understand who Jesus is (the Christians) do not, and that some of those who are outside the church seem to understand Jesus better than the Christians do? What reasons can you give to explain this? Jesus through his words and actions brought confrontation. Should Jesus' followers today experience confrontation with some of those around us? If the church is not in clear confrontation with the world today, what could explain the lack of conflict?

Prayer

Dear God, teach us what matters and how we can stand up for those things that matter. Help us understand who Jesus is and the power of that belief in our daily lives. Help us understand discipleship so that we can become faithful followers, we pray in Jesus' name, Amen.

Mark 4: Who Is this?

Selected Biblical Text

35 On that day, when evening came, he said to his disciples: "Let us go to the other side of the lake." 36 Leaving the crowd behind, they took him along in the boat where he was, and other boats were with him. 37 A violent squall came up, and the waves beat upon the boat, so that the boat was nearly swamped. 38 Jesus was in the stern, sleeping on a cushion. They awakened him and said to him: "Teacher, does it matter to you that we are about to perish?"

39 So he got up, rebuked the wind and said to the sea: "Silence! Be quiet!" Then the wind stopped, and it was totally calm.

40 He said to them: "Why are you so intimidated? Do you still have no faith?"

41 They were overcome with great fear and kept asking each other: "Who is this? Even the wind and the sea obey him!" (Mark 4:35-41)

Reflecting and Thinking

One can describe the narratives of the first four chapters of Mark's gospel in several ways -- identity stories, confrontation stories, amazing stories. Today's reading suggests yet another description -- "power stories." In the initial chapters of Mark's gospel, Jesus has power over evil spirits, demons, diseases, sin, leprosy, paralysis, and even nature. It is Jesus' power over nature that ultimately catches the disciples' attention: "Who is this?" Even the waves obey his commands.

Today's text also introduces the continuing tension in Mark's gospel between fear and faith. These two concepts are interwoven throughout this gospel. "Why are you so afraid? Does that mean you still do not believe?"

Chapter 4 is probably most famous for the "amazing words" (the parables of Jesus) that take up most of the chapter. How many of the themes in Mark that we have identified up to this point can you find repeated in the parables?

What connections do you see between fear and faith? How do fear and faith work together (either in tension or in tandem) in your own life? Is it true that the more we believe the less we fear? (Try to put your answer into words and share your thoughts with at least one other person today.) Can faith and unfaith dwell side by side in the same human heart? (This is a thought question for now -- we will come to it again later in the reading of Mark.)

Prayer

Heavenly Father, help us grow in faith and deal with fear in our lives. Help us see more clearly not only who Jesus is, but also the power he can wield in our lives because of who he is. Help us see more clearly. In the name of the powerful Jesus, Amen.

Mark 5: Who Can Follow Jesus?

Selected Biblical Text
18 As Jesus was getting into the boat, the man who had been demon-possessed requested to accompany him. 19 Jesus did not let him but said to him: "Go home to your people and tell them what the Lord has done for you, and that he has had mercy on you." 20 So the man went away and began to proclaim in the Decapolis how much Jesus had done for him. And all the people were astonished. (Mark 5:18-20)

Reflecting and Thinking
Who can follow Jesus? The answer may surprise us. Does Mark purposefully include stories about those who are religiously or ceremonially unclean according to the teachings of the Jews? Is there any significance in including the "unclean stories" of a man who lives among the dead and is possessed by evil or unclean spirits, of a hemorrhaging woman, of a dead girl? Can people the world considers unclean and unfit still follow Jesus today? Can people the church considers unclean and unfit still follow Jesus today? Or is it only those who have already escaped most of the world's problems that make fit church members?

Jesus comes into the world touching the untouchable. He interacts with the undesirable, and the religious leaders question his acceptance of sinners. Perhaps in our evangelistic efforts we are looking in the wrong places! The man in our text left Jesus and began to tell everyone what Jesus had done for him. Perhaps we are also telling the wrong story! What has Jesus done for you?

What percentage of the members in the church where you attend are from what could be described as the "bottom" of society -- those whom many people consider "hands off?" In your opinion, could this be evidence that the U.S. church has practiced selective evangelism? How do you explain that Jesus appealed to the poor and that the contemporary church hardly has any interaction with the poor? What could the church do to increase its outreach to those people our society considers "unclean?"

Prayer
Heavenly Father, help us see our world through your eyes. Help us overcome our biases and prejudices, help us notice the people Jesus would touch if he were walking in our shoes. Lift up our eyes to the harvest. Give us opportunities to speak for Jesus and give us boldness to walk through the doors you open. Through Jesus we pray, Amen.

Mark 6: Do You Want to Touch Him?

Selected Biblical Text

53 Crossing over, they landed at Gennesaret and anchored there. 54 As soon as they got out of the boat, people recognized Jesus. 55 They ran through that whole region and began to bring the sick on mats to wherever they heard that he was. 56 And wherever he went -- into villages, towns or countryside – they placed the sick in the marketplaces. They begged him to let them touch even the edge of his cloak, and whoever touched it was healed. (Mark 6:53-56)

Reflecting and Thinking

How does one summarize the unique flavors of this chapter? Jesus is amazed at the lack of faith of those in his hometown...he sends forth the Twelve with spectacular results...the death of his cousin, John the Baptist...the faith test of the Twelve as Jesus feeds over 5000 people using the limited resources available...Jesus walking on the water.... I chose today's selected text because it is a summary of these events. Who sees? Who does not see? Who believes? Who struggles with faith? Is it possible to struggle with faith immediately after a wonderful, successful effort? The actions of the Apostles in this chapter demonstrate that the answer is "yes." Those who see and believe want to be with Jesus. They want to touch him. They seek help and healing. Some days I wonder why we are so far away from Jesus. I wonder if we know how much we need help and healing.

How would you answer the question in today's title? Would the activities of your life support your answer or deny your answer? How far would you go to have Jesus as a part of your life? What would you give? What would you be willing to give up? With which group would Jesus identify you -- the 'lack of faith' folks in his home town (6:1-6), the followers he sent out (6:6-13), the suffering preacher (6:14-29), the doubting followers who do not understand how the challenge can be met (6:30-44), the fearful followers in the boat (6:45-52), or the genuine seekers (6:53-56)?

Prayer

Father God, in Jesus' name and by his power we want to follow Him more closely. We want to overcome the doubts and faith challenges of our lives. We want to go forth powerfully in His power. Increase our faith, especially in the face of fear. Again, we ask these things in Jesus' name, Amen.

Mark 7: Can't Keep a Secret

Selected Biblical Text

20 He said: "What comes out of a person makes the person unclean. 21 For from within, out of a person's heart, come evil arguments, sexual immorality, stealing, murder, 22 adultery, greed, malice, deceit, ungodliness, envy, slander, arrogance and folly. 23 All these evils come from inside and make a person unclean."
24 When he left that place, Jesus went to the coasts of Tyre. When he entered a house, he did not want anyone to know it; yet he could not keep it secret. 25 In fact, as soon as she heard about him, a woman whose little daughter had an unclean spirit came and fell at his feet. 26 The woman was Greek, Syrophoenician by birth. She asked Jesus to cast the demon out of her daughter.
35 At once, the man's ears were opened, his tongue loosened, and he spoke plainly. 36 Jesus commanded them to say nothing. But as much as he commanded them so, all the more they were proclaiming it. 37 People were completely astonished and said: "He has done everything well. He even makes the deaf hear and the mute speak." (Mark 7:20-23, 24-26, 35-37)

Reflecting and Thinking

In his confrontation with the Pharisees and the teachers of the law, Jesus makes clear that they misunderstand what is clean and what is unclean. Ceremonial definitions will never get at the heart of the question. "This is a matter of the heart, and the heart of the matter." Let us not make the mistake of thinking this is only for then and could never apply now! We obviously have our own mistaken definitions of who is an acceptable follower of Jesus and who is not. Is Jesus in this passage preparing the Jews for more redefinitions? Being an outsider (Syrophoenician) does not make one unclean. Being deaf and mute does not make one unclean. Jewish understandings in the first century would have excluded both of the persons whom Jesus helps.

The biblical text tells us that Jesus wanted to keep his location secret; and also, that Jesus wanted to keep the healing secret. No way! When Jesus is present and powerfully active, secrecy is the one thing that will never happen!

Is the last sentence above a possible explanation of why the contemporary church is so often quiet concerning Jesus? Could it be that he is not obviously present for us? Could it be that we do not see him powerfully at work in our world so that we have little to share?

Prayer

Dear God, thank you for working in our lives in the past to save us and cleanse us. Please continue to work in our lives in powerful ways and unloose our tongues so that we may speak plainly and faithfully of the things that we experience. Help our message about Jesus be a message of overwhelming amazement as we seek to bring others to Jesus. We pray in Jesus' name, Amen.

Mark 8: The Son of Man Will Die --
Confessing Jesus or Challenging Jesus?

Selected Biblical Text

27 Jesus and his disciples went to the villages of Caesarea Philippi. On the way he asked his disciples: "Who do people say I am?"

28 They replied: "Some say John the Baptist; others say Elijah; and others, one of the prophets."

29 And he asked them: "Who do you say I am?" Peter answered him: "You are the Christ."

30 Jesus warned them not to tell anyone about him.

31 Then he began to teach them that the Son of Man must suffer many things and be rejected by the elders, chief priests and law experts, and be killed and after three days rise again. 32 He spoke plainly about this, so Peter took him aside and began to rebuke him.

33 But when Jesus turned and looked at his disciples, he rebuked Peter: "Get behind me, Satan!" he said. "You do not think about the things of God, but the things of men." (Mark 8:27-33)

Reflecting and Thinking

One could describe this chapter as the beginning of the end. In Mark 8 we encounter the first of three "passion predictions" -- predictions of Jesus' suffering. Jesus predicts his death. In the Gospel of Mark these appear in the text in rapid succession (8:31, 9:31, and 10:32).

After Jesus feeds the 4000 and explains the significance of recent events to his disciples, and after the healing of a blind man, Peter boldly confesses Jesus as the Christ. When Jesus warns the disciples to be silent and tells them that he will be killed in Jerusalem, Peter boldly challenges Jesus. The text says that Peter rebuked Jesus.

Poor Peter! He could not see the things of God because his vision was overwhelmed and distracted by the things of men. That seemingly small distraction put him on the opposite side, opposing Jesus! What should we learn?

How often do we consider the things of men more important than the things of God? What are some ways Christians today challenge and confront Christ, for example, when do we think there are other ways or better ways to do his will? In your daily life, how often do you confess Christ? What is the significance of Peter's confession that Jesus is the Christ?

Prayer

Dear God, give us understanding and boldness to follow Jesus wherever he leads us. Give us boldness to confess him daily. Help us focus on heavenly things more than on earthly things. Focus our attention on the things of God more than the things of men. Give us boldness in our dealings with the world. Give us humility in our acceptance of your will and way in our lives as we take up our cross to follow. We pray in Jesus' name, Amen.

Mark 9: Following Jesus Is Not Easy

Selected Biblical Text

30 They left that place and went through Galilee, but Jesus did not want anyone to know, 31 for he was teaching his disciples. He said to them: "The Son of Man will be delivered into the hands of men. They will kill him, and after three days he will rise." 32 But they did not understand what he said and were afraid to ask him. (Mark 9:30-32)

Reflecting and Thinking

Three major themes are now intertwined in Mark's Gospel: the identity of Jesus (focused by the introductory identity stories), confrontation with the Jews which will result in his death (the confrontation stories), and discipleship (the follower stories). Interconnected with these three major concepts are secondary storylines: fear, faith, secrecy, and touch (which is also related to the unclean-clean theme).

In the account of the Transfiguration, we can observe several of these points and counterpoints. Three of Jesus' closest followers are with him; the voice from the cloud identifies Jesus as God's beloved Son; Peter is afraid; Jesus commands secrecy until after his resurrection. In the story that immediately follows, fear and faith exist side by side in the father: "I believe, help me overcome my unbelief."

Today's reading contains the second prediction of Jesus' suffering and death and makes clear the lack of understanding and the fear of the disciples. The remainder of the chapter (and the first part of Chapter 10) is a sequence of follower stories, focused on various dimensions or dynamics of what it means to follow Jesus.

How do you think you would have responded had you been at the Transfiguration? When have you identified with the father in the story of the son with the evil spirit, experiencing the existence of faith and unfaith side by the side in your life? Why did the disciples not understand Jesus' teachings about his impending death? Which of the "follower principles" reflected in this chapter is most difficult for you -- pride/humility, service/prestige, judging/accepting, priorities and influence?

Prayer

Dear God, we again pray for increased faith. We want to be faithful followers, and we ask for your strength so that we will accurately reflect the
priorities and heart of Jesus in our own lives. Teach us His ways. We pray in
Jesus' name, Amen.

Mark 10: To Serve and to Give His Life as a Ransom

Selected Biblical Text

41 When the ten heard this, they became indignant with James and John. 42 Calling
them together, Jesus said to them: "You know that those who are recognized as
rulers of the Gentiles lord it over them, and their high officials have authority over
them. 43 It is not so among you. Whoever wants to be great among you must be
your servant, 44 and whoever wants to be first must be the slave of all. 45 Even as
the Son of Man did not come to be served, but to serve, and to give his life as a
ransom for many." (Mark 10:41-45)

Reflecting and Thinking

This chapter marks a transition point in the Gospel of Mark. We
could label Chapters 1-10 as Part One, and give it the heading, "Jesus' ministry." In Chapter 11, the Triumphal Entry will mark the beginning of Part
Two, "Jesus' death." While the third passion prediction (10:32-34) is an important part of today's reading, the chapter is better summarized as a series
of "follower narratives." Being a follower of Jesus has an impact on our mar-
riages, our families, our attitudes (become like little children, avoid the
negative attitudes of the rich young man), and our desire for prominence.
Becoming like Jesus leads us to a life of service and sacrifice.

It is worthy of note that two blind man stories (see 8:22 and 10:46)
seem to frame the section of Mark that includes the three predictions of
Jesus' death. Does this literary device, providing structure to the book, subtly raise the question of who can see and who cannot see?

*Thinking about the contemporary church, how would you compare
the number of people who are focused on becoming a servant with the number of those focused on becoming important? How would you compare the
number interested in service and what they can give with the number who
are interested in what they can receive? How can we imitate Jesus? How do
we live out the teachings of today's reading? What does it mean to you to
"see" in a spiritual sense? Thinking about the Gospel of Mark to this point,
what could the disciples see and what could they not see? Who are some of
those who have seen most clearly to this point in Mark's gospel?*

Prayer

Dear God, on many days we know that following Jesus is not a simple matter. Some days, it is in fact very difficult. We want to be faithful followers; we want our commitment to Christ to be evident in every area of our lives. We want to be totally available for Jesus' work, withholding no part of our lives. Give us spiritual sensitivity and strength to follow in Jesus' footsteps. We pray in Jesus' name, Amen.

Mark 11: The King is Coming

Selected Biblical Text

4 They went and found a colt tied at a doorway, outside in the street, and untied it, 5 some people standing there said to them: "What are you doing, untying the colt?" 6 They answered as Jesus had told them, and they let them go. 7 Then they brought the colt to Jesus, threw their cloaks on it, and he sat on it. 8 Many people spread their cloaks on the road and others spread branches they had cut in the fields. 9 Those going ahead and those following shouted: "Hosanna! Blessed is the one who comes in the name of the Lord! 10 Blessed is the coming kingdom of our father David! Hosanna in the highest heights!"
11 Then Jesus entered Jerusalem, went into the temple and looked around at everything. Since it was already evening, he went out to Bethany with the Twelve. (Mark 11:4-11)

Reflecting and Thinking

The King is coming! The King has come! The story of the Triumphal Entry solidifies the identity of Jesus -- the One who has all authority has come. Every story in today's chapter relates to that authority. Jesus demonstrates his authority in the temple cleansing, in the teaching which follows the withering of the fig tree, and in the answers given when his authority is questioned. He acts with the authority of the Father who validated him as the Beloved Son at the Transfiguration. The identity of Jesus has been clearly declared. That claim -- that Jesus is the Son of God -- is ultimately what the Jewish authorities cannot allow to stand. If Jesus is who he claims to be, that changes everything!

How has the identity of Jesus, that fact that he is who he claims to be, changed your life? How could it change your life today? How could it change your life tomorrow as you seek to follow him more closely? What would it mean for you to follow him in service and ministry? What would it mean for you to follow him in sacrifice on behalf of others?

Prayer

Dear God, thank you for the salvation that is available to us in Jesus. Thank you for his sacrifice. Thank you for giving him the authority to handle life, and thus the ability to handle the problems of our lives. Thank you for the message and encouragement we are receiving in this reading of Mark's Gospel. May it change us and remake us more and more into faithful followers of Jesus. We pray in Jesus' name, Amen.

Mark 12: The Jewish Leaders Do Not "Get It" -- Do We?

Selected Biblical Text

38 In his teaching Jesus said: "Watch out for the law experts who like walking around in flowing robes, special greetings in the marketplaces, 39 the most important seats in the synagogues, and the places of highest honor at feasts. 40 They devour widows' houses and as a show pray long prayers. These will receive more severe punishment."
41 Sitting down opposite the offering box, Jesus watched how the crowd cast their money into the offering box. Many rich people threw in much. 42 But when a poor widow came, she put in two very small copper coins, worth less than a penny. 43 Calling his disciples to him, Jesus said: "In truth I tell you, this poor widow has put more into the offering box than all the others. 44 They all gave out of their abundance [what they did not need]; but she, out of her poverty, put in everything that she had -- all she had to live on." (Mark 12:38-44)

Reflecting and Thinking

The six narratives of this chapter are connected by their shared focus on what one does in response to Jesus. The Jewish leaders rejected him, as illustrated in the parable of the tenants. They knew he had spoken against them. Then they sought to trap him with questions: a legal question about taxes, a question about Levirate marriage in the resurrection (which was also a divisive point between the Sadducees and the Pharisees), and a question about putting the Old Testament laws in priority order.

In our reading, Jesus says that in their efforts to seek the way of the kingdom, the Jewish religious leaders had focused on and found prestige and personal reward, prominence and power. They had abused the least ones in the society, stealing in the name of religion from those least able to pay. For Jesus, the sacrificial, generous response of the poor widow says it all. This is how one follows Jesus; this is how one responds to Jesus.

Based on the brief explanation given above, what is the real point of the story about the widow's offering? How can Christians today imitate her? Does it require that we give everything? How would you explain the principle Jesus is setting forth and its application in our lives today? Does the modern church ever resemble the questioning Jewish leaders -- trying to settle every detail while missing the overall point of what Jesus is about? If you answered "yes," think of some specific examples from your experience where you have observed this. Pray specifically about how we Christians can more accurately reflect what Jesus is about as we work and live in our communities.

Prayer

Dear God, we ask you to give us generous hearts and to help us as strive to understand the message of Jesus and strengthen our faith. Help us to be about what he was about. Help his reasons to become our reasons, his priorities our priorities, his purposes our purposes. In Jesus' name, Amen.

Mark 13: Keep Watch!

Selected Biblical Text

31 Heaven and earth will pass away, but my words will never pass away.
32 But concerning that day or hour no one knows, neither the angels in heaven nor the Son, but only the Father. 33 Be on guard! Stay alert! You do not know when the time will come. 34 It is like a man taking a trip: He leaves his house and gives his bondservants authority, to each one his assigned work, and commands the doorkeeper to be vigilant.
35 Therefore, watch with vigilance because you do not know when the owner of the house will return --whether in the evening, at midnight, when the rooster crows, or at dawn -- 36 lest coming unexpectedly, he finds you sleeping. 37 What I say to you, I say to everyone: Watch with vigilance! (Mark 13:31-37)

Reflecting and Thinking

Jesus' teachings in this chapter (sometimes referred to as the Olivet discourse, see Matthew 24, Mark 13, Luke 21) are admittedly difficult to understand. The application of specific verses has been variously understood. Some verses seem to have such an obvious application to events we know today that we readily overlook how directly they applied to past events. Some verses seem to have such a clear application to the future that it is hard for us to apply them to past events. Add the fact that many of us have limited understandings of the historical context in which Jesus spoke these words.

There is a general agreement that Jesus is talking about two things: the destruction of Jerusalem and the events at the end of the world. What becomes difficult is understanding how Jesus addresses these two topics. Does he address one and then the other sequentially? Does his response intertwine the two themes? Do some verses have dual application?

Jesus' teaching in today's textual selection is a clear reference to the end of time. The owner is coming back. The time of that coming is unknown. Therefore, be on guard. Keep watch. Be diligent in the tasks you have been assigned.

Thinking of today's textual selection, do you think this teaching of Jesus was intended as a warning or as an encouragement to the disciples? How would you respond to the idea that Jesus raised more questions than he answered? How should Christians today respond to this teaching of Jesus? What does it mean for us to be constantly alert and on guard?

Prayer

Dear God, we marvel at the deep things which only you possess and know. We want to understand when we do not. When we remember that your wisdom is beyond our understanding, we grasp a little bit of the reason for the ambiguities. This day, help us cultivate an attitude of watchfulness, in the name of Jesus, Amen.

Mark 14: Wherever the Gospel Is Preached in the World

Selected Biblical Text

1 Two days before the Passover and the Feast of Unleavened Bread, the chief priests and the law experts were seeking how to arrest Jesus subtly and kill him. 2 But they said: "Not during the feast, lest there be a disturbance among the people." 3 While he was in Bethany in the house of Simon the Leper, reclining at the table, a woman came with an alabaster jar of very expensive perfumed oil, made of pure nard. After breaking the jar, she poured it on his head.
4 Some of those present were complaining indignantly to one another: "Why this waste of expensive oil? 5 It could have been sold for more than 300 denarii [a year's wages] and the money given to the poor." And they were murmuring against her. 6 Jesus said: "Leave her alone. Why are you giving her grief? She has done a good deed to me. 7 The poor you will have with you always, and whenever you wish, you can do good for them, but you will not always have me. 8 She did what she could. She poured perfumed oil on my body in advance for my burial. 9 In truth I tell you, wherever the gospel is preached throughout the world, what she has done will be told in memory of her."
10 Then Judas Iscariot, one of the Twelve, went to the chief priests to betray Jesus to them. 11 When they heard this, they were delighted and promised to give him money. So, Judas was seeking an opportunity betray him. (Mark 14:1-11)

Reflecting and Thinking

After reading for three chapters of the suspense and building conflict with the Jewish leaders, we learn that it was one of Jesus' own who handed him over to the Jewish religious leaders. The suspense is all but over. Jesus has been predicting the events which will now come to pass within the week. His anointing serves as validation. The events are not unfamiliar to most Bible students -- the Lord's Supper with the institution of the new covenant meal, Gethsemane, the first of several trials, Peter's denial as predicted.

Hope shines bright as we read the text -- the gospel will be preached throughout the world. The word "wherever" refuses to place a limit -- everywhere. The events planned by God from eternity are certain; the outcome is never in doubt even though the Jewish leaders will think it was their idea.

The new covenant established with Jesus' blood is superior to the old, and we now share his presence and communion in the kingdom of God. May we see the message of hope in a dark section of Scripture!

What would you have thought about the expense of the anointing oil had you been there? This chapter suggests several different ways to respond to the message of Jesus. Which person in the chapter do you identify with most closely -- the woman who anoints Jesus, those who complain about the expense, Judas, the Jewish leaders, the disciples who cannot watch and pray, or Peter?

Prayer

Dear God, you know our daily struggles as we seek to follow you. You know our weaknesses and failures, and in that we are humbled and ashamed. You know our struggles and needs, and in that we find encouragement. Help us develop hearts of love and adoration so that we honor and praise Jesus continually, as did the woman in today's selected text. We pray in Jesus' name, Amen.

Mark 15: Injustice for Our Justification

Selected Biblical Text

33 Then when it was noon, darkness came over the whole land until three in the afternoon. 34 And at three in the afternoon Jesus cried out in a loud voice: "Eloi, Eloi, lema sabachthani?" (which means, 'My God, my God, why have you left me behind?'). 35 When some of those standing near heard this, they said: "Listen, he is calling Elijah."

36 Someone ran, filled a sponge with sour wine, put it on a reed stick, and gave it to Jesus to drink, saying: "Leave him alone. Let us see if Elijah comes to take him down."

37 Jesus cried out with a loud voice and breathed his last.

38 The curtain of the temple was torn in two from top to bottom. 39 And when the centurion, who stood in front of Jesus, saw the way he breathed his last, he said: "Surely this man was the Son of God!" (Mark 15:33-39)

Reflecting and Thinking

If it were it not for its familiarity, reading this chapter would be difficult. We are desensitized by our frequent exposure to the story. Death on a cross in the first century was horrific. The gruesome nature of what occurred is unimaginable. The insults are bad enough, the mocking; the injustice. The emotional stress, the spiritual stress of forsakenness, the physical suffering -- words cannot adequately speak of such atrocities.

It is done, God's mercy intervenes. Joseph of Arimathea, a Jewish council member provides the gift of a proper burial. The tomb is occupied.

What things grab your attention in the reading today? How important to you is the declaration of the centurion that Jesus was surely the Son of God? How well do you think we today understand the severe and cruel nature of crucifixion? What thoughts or desires does the reading of this text motivate in you?

Prayer

Dear God, help us hear the story of Jesus' sacrifice in fresh ways. Increase our appreciation for the great price that was paid for us. Bring this to our mind when we are confronted with decisions as to whether we are willing to pay the price. We pray in Jesus' name, Amen.

Mark 16: Fear or Faith?

Selected Biblical Text

1 When the Sabbath was over, Mary Magdalene, Mary the mother of James, and Salome bought aromatic spices so that they might go anoint Jesus' body. 2 Very early on the first day of the week, at sunrise, they went to the tomb. 3 They were asking each other: "Who will roll the stone away for us from the entrance of the tomb?"

4 But when they looked up, they saw that the stone, which was very large, had been rolled away. 5 Then as they entered the tomb, they saw a young man dressed in a white robe sitting on the right side, and they were alarmed.

6 But he said to them: "Do not be alarmed. You are looking for Jesus the Nazarene, who was crucified. He has risen. He is not here. See the place where they laid him. 7 But go, tell his disciples and also Peter, 'He is going ahead of you into Galilee. There you will see him, just as he told you.'"

8 Then they went out and fled from the tomb, trembling and bewildered. They said nothing to anyone, because they were afraid. (Mark 16:1-8)

Reflecting and Thinking

Today's selected text is the conclusion of the book of Mark in some manuscripts. It is a fitting conclusion -- fear remains until sight verifies the reality of Jesus' resurrection. The events are unbelievable -- until he appears. The reports of others are hardly enough. We want to see.

Through a combination of the manuscript evidence and the precedents of church history, almost all modern translations contain the "rest of the story" -- verses 9-20. Jesus appeared to his followers, gently rebuking them because they did not believe until they had seen him. We are so much like them!

Jesus commissions his followers to go forth proclaiming the gospel in the world, preaching belief and baptism for salvation of sins. Now there is no doubt. The tomb is empty! The disciples went out and preached the message everywhere!

On this day, which has the upper hand in your life -- fear or faith? What would it take to ease the fear and increase the faith? (Pray to God about this.) Many people today still want to see firsthand and experience God's power personally -- do you think Jesus would also rebuke them as he did the Eleven in verse 14?

How do you want to change your life after reading Mark's gospel? (Pray about your response in your personal prayer today.)

Prayer

Dear God, as we come to end of the Gospel of Mark, we ask you to change our lives according to the specific ways the message has touched our hearts during the last few weeks. We ask you to increase our faith and decrease our tendency to be afraid. Increase our faith, again we pray, in Jesus' name, Amen.

Ephesians 1: God's Eternal Plan

Selected Biblical Text

7 In him we have redemption through his blood, the forgiveness of trespasses, according to the riches of his grace 8 which he lavished on us, in all wisdom and insight, 9 making known to us the mystery of his will according to his good pleasure which he purposed in Christ, 10 for the administration of the fulness of times, to bring together under one head all things in Christ, things in heaven and things on earth. 11 In him also we were chosen, having been predestined according to the purpose of him who works in all things according to the counsel of his will, 12 in order that we might be for the praise of his glory, we who were the first to put our hope in Christ. 13 In him you also, when you heard the message of truth, the gospel of your salvation, in him when you believed, you were sealed with the Holy Spirit of promise, 14 who is a down payment guaranteeing our inheritance until the redemption of God's own possession, to the praise of his glory. (Ephesians 1:7-14)

Reflecting and Thinking

Some think the letter to the Ephesians was intended for circulation among a larger group of churches. The letter focuses on Christ and the church. God is at work, according to his eternal plan which he purposed in Christ, to bring all things together under the umbrella of the lordship of Jesus. This plan encompasses God's provision, God's promise, God's power, and God's presence. According to the last verses of Chapter 1, this plan finds its fulfillment in the church as Christ's body and fullness. The beauty of God's plan is unfolded in the rest of Ephesians; this chapter provides an introduction to God's eternal plan.

How often have you heard someone talk about God's eternal plan? In your experience, is this a common theme in today's religious world, or it is more accurate to say that it is "out of view?" If God has an overarching plan, how important is it that we see the plan from beginning to end rather than analyzing little subsections of his plan?

If you have time, read the entire chapter before you try the following exercise. If not, you can use the selected text printed above. Exercise: take a few moments to put your understanding of God's eternal plan into your own words and write it down for your future reference.

Prayer

Heavenly Father, we are grateful today that you have planned for our spiritual needs from before the world began. We praise you in your glory for the wisdom reflected in your eternal plan. Help us to appreciate the importance of "Jesus as Lord." We pray in his name, Amen.

Ephesians 2: God's Plan for Peace

Selected Biblical Text

14 For he himself is our peace, the one who has made the two into one and destroyed the dividing wall of partition, the hostility, 15 by nullifying in his flesh the law of commandments in decrees, to create in himself out of the two one new humanity, thus making peace, 16 and to reconcile them both in one body to God through the cross, by which he put to death the hostility. 17 He came and preached peace to you who were far away and peace to those who were near, 18 so that through him we both have access by one Spirit to the Father.

19 Wherefore, you are no longer foreigners and strangers, but you are fellow citizens with the saints and members of God's household, 20 built upon the foundation of the apostles and prophets, while Christ Jesus himself is the chief cornerstone. 21 In him the whole building, being joined together, grows into a holy temple in the Lord. 22 And in him you too are being built together into a dwelling of God by the Spirit. (Ephesians 2:14-22)

Reflecting and Thinking

Jesus came to earth to make possible the reestablishment of our vertical relationship with God. He also came to make possible peaceful horizontal relationships. The two groups mentioned in the reading are the Jews and the Gentiles. The divisions that previously existed have been destroyed by the death of Jesus. Reconciliation has come through the cross. The healing of broken vertical relationships with God binds together those who used to be enemies. The result is a new dwelling of God by his Spirit, referring to the church.

How aware have you been that God's plan demands both peace with God and peace among people? What does God think when his children cannot get along with one another? What are some of the sources of our controversies and conflicts? How can those be healed through the cross?

Prayer

Heavenly Father God, today we are grateful for your compassion and grace extended to us when we were still sinners, giving us new life. We are grateful that you are shaping us and molding us for your work. We sadly remember our past, and we are grateful for the new present you make possible. Help us to reflect your will in the life we share with other Christians, through your holiness, presence, and Spirit of power, protection and faithfulness. In Jesus' name we pray, Amen.

Ephesians 3: God's Plan for Power

Selected Biblical Text

16 I pray that he will give you, according to the riches of his glory -- power to be strengthened through his Spirit in your inner being, 17 Christ dwelling in your hearts through faith, you in love being rooted and grounded -- 18 so that you will be able to comprehend, with all the saints, what is the breadth and length and height and depth, 19 to know the love of Christ that surpasses knowledge, so may be filled up with all the fullness of God. 20 Now to him who is able to do all things immeasurably beyond that which we ask or imagine, according to the power that is working within us, 21 to him be glory in the church and in Christ Jesus throughout all generations, forever and ever. Amen. (Ephesians 3:16-21)

Reflecting and Thinking

The shared life of diverse groups in the body of Christ, the church, is evidence of God's wisdom. We are heirs together, members together, and sharers together. This truth, which reflects God's eternal purpose to bring all things together in Christ, is powerful witness to the manifold wisdom of God. This shared life is one of Spirit power, Christ's indwelling, love, and God's energizing power within us, resulting in glory in the church and in Christ. The promise that He can and will do far more than we ask or imagine opens unbelievable doors of opportunity for every Christian.

Most days do you feel empowered or disempowered in your Christian life? What could make you more aware of God's power that is within you and is energizing you? Does the contemporary world see the glory of a church where multitudes of diverse people come together and share experiences as part of the body of Christ? Why or why not? Do most churches reflect this aspect of God's wisdom and glory, that is, do most churches include many different and diverse groups of people? Why or why not? What would you do if you thought it was definitely possible?

Prayer

Heavenly Father, thank you for taking care of us as individuals and as members together in the body of Christ, the church. Thank you for giving us access to your power. Thank you for working in us and through us. Help us to be faithful witnesses to your purpose and wisdom. May all the glory be yours, forever, in the church and in Christ Jesus, in His name, Amen.

Ephesians 4: God's Plan for Personal Growth

Selected Biblical Text

11 Also, he himself gave some to be apostles, others to be prophets, others to be evangelists, others to be pastors and teachers, 12 to equip the saints for the work of ministry, to build up the body of Christ 13 until we all arrive to the unity of the faith and of the knowledge of the Son of God, to maturity, to a measure of stature of the fullness of Christ. 14 So that we will no longer be infants, tossed back and forth by waves, and blown about by every wind of teaching and by the trickery used by people for craftiness in their deceitful scheming. 15 But practicing the truth in love, we will grow in all things unto Christ who is the head. 16 From him the entire body, joined and held together by every supporting ligament, according to the working of each member, causes the growth of the body so that it builds itself up in love. (Ephesians 4:11-16)

Reflecting and Thinking

God did not call us and save us to leave us as we were. His calling places new demands on our lives. He empowers us to live changed lives. We have a new nature and new possibilities. We have new relationships and new strength. One purpose of church leaders is to equip and build up the body of Christ (the church) so that each member reaches her or his full potential. With each member fully functioning, the church becomes a more accurate reflection of the head (Christ), growing, working, building itself up, operating as a unit, declaring God's truth.

How does God intend that his children escape the old nature and develop the new nature in the image and stature of Christ? What responsibilities do we have toward one another? What work has God given you in the church?

Prayer

Heavenly Father, continue this day to change our lives, helping us grow into the image of your Son. Bind us together as part of the church, help us live in the light, help us develop the spirit and mind of Christ as we deal with other people. Please guide and empower us in our efforts to help others find your Son, Jesus, in whose name we pray, Amen.

Ephesians 5: God's Plan for Life

Selected Biblical Text

15 Be very careful, then, how you live -- not as unwise but as wise, 16 making the most of every opportunity, because the days are evil. 17 Therefore, do not be foolish, but understand what the will of the Lord is. 18 Do not get drunk with wine, by which comes debauchery, but be filled with the Spirit, speaking to one another

with psalms, hymns, and spiritual songs, singing and making music with your heart to the Lord, giving thanks always for everything in the name of our Lord Jesus Christ to God the Father, submitting to one another in reverence for Christ. (Ephesians 5:15-21)

Reflecting and Thinking

God's eternal purpose is not theoretical. God's intention to bring together lots of diverse people in the church – recognizing Jesus' Lordship, reflecting Jesus' power, presence, and fullness, people reconciled with a peace that only Jesus brings – is not only theological. God's purpose is practical. It is a guide for life in this world. Doctrine has no value unless it is applied to life. If what we believe does not influence how we live, why believe anything? The last three chapters of Ephesians give us insights into God's plan for our lives.

On a scale of 1-10, how are you doing in your growth toward Jesus' image? How is the church where you attend doing? The chapter says we are to live in love, light, wisdom, and understanding. Which of these is your strong point? Which is your weak point? How can we become more aware of the filling of God's Spirit in our lives?

Prayer

Heavenly Father, help us live out your will in our lives with more than words. Help us to act consistently, lining up our preaching and our practice. Help us to seize opportunities. Make us like Jesus, in his name, Amen.

Ephesians 6: God's Plan in Times of Spiritual Conflict

Selected Biblical Text

10 Finally, be strong in the Lord and in the power of his might. 11 Put on the full armor of God, so that you can stand against the schemes of the devil. 12 For our struggle is not against flesh and blood, but against the rulers, against the authorities, against the world-rulers of the darkness of this world, against the spiritual forces of evil in the heavenlies. 13 Therefore, take up the full armor of God, so you will be able to withstand on the day of evil, and after having fully accomplished everything, to stand. 14 Stand then, by cinching up your waist with truth and putting on the breastplate of righteousness, 15 by putting on your feet the preparedness of the gospel of peace, 16 in everything, taking up the shield of faith with which you can extinguish all the flaming arrows of the evil one. 17 Take both the helmet of salvation and the sword of the Spirit which is the word of God, 18 with every prayer and petition, praying at all times in the Spirit, and unto this being alert, with full persistence and with petitions for all the saints. (Ephesians 6:10-18)

Reflecting and Thinking

Conflict comes in many forms. The kind of conflict Paul addresses in this text is spiritual conflict. God empowers his people for their struggles against spiritual forces of evil. The resources he provides may seem powerless and insignificant to us -- truth, righteousness and justice, the gospel of peace, faith, salvation, and the word of God. These are God's power in the face of opposition. In the last part of the chapter, Paul urges prayer in the Spirit, using all kinds of prayer on all kinds of occasions for all of God's people.

Spiritual conflict or warfare has become an increasingly popular topic in recent years. How often are you aware in your daily life of spiritual conflict? Which of the resources God provides do your find most powerful in your life? Do you use prayer as a first resort or a last resort? While this text seems to have primarily individual applications, what can we do to help one another in our spiritual conflicts?

Prayer

Heavenly Father, we want to be strong, we want to overcome evil and temptation, we want to stand firm for you. May we know your power and presence in our lives. May we depend more on you and less on ourselves. Be with us in all of life, in Jesus' name, Amen.

Philippians 1: Progress and Joy in Faith

Selected Biblical Text

21 For to me, to live is Christ and to die is gain. 22 If I am to go on living in the body, this will mean fruitful work for me, and I do not know what I prefer. 23 I am torn between the two: I have the desire to depart and be with Christ, which is better by far; 24 but to remain in the body is more needful for your sake. 25 Being convinced of this, I know that I will remain and will continue with all of you for your progress and joy in the faith, 26 so that your rejoicing will overflow in Christ Jesus in me, by my presence again with you. (Philippians 1:21-26)

Reflecting and Thinking

Some have suggested that the letter to the Philippians is perhaps the richest of Paul's shorter letters. The first chapter is filled with memorable verses -- choosing what is best (v. 9), advancing the gospel (v. 12), preaching Christ (v. 18), exalting Christ (vv. 20-21), progressing with joy in faith (v. 26), and living worthy of the gospel (v. 27). One of the best-known verses is v. 21: "to live is Christ, to die is gain." Paul reflects his own single-mindedness in this chapter. He has only one thing in mind -- progress, both the progress of the gospel and the progress of God's people in joy and faith.

If other people were asked to identify what is the most important thing in your life, what would they say? What is your top priority? What do you pursue single-mindedly? Paul had numerous personal concerns, but his letters are filled with his care for others. How can we help another person experience progress and joy in the faith?

Prayer

Dearest Father, I want to live for Christ. May the days of my life on this earth be pleasing to you. I pray that I will "die to self" and grow and become more like Christ as I journey toward that day when I will be with you in heaven. Please use me to bless others; to give love, encouragement, help, and guidance where needed; to meet material needs of the needy; and to point people to you. Thank you for all that you have done for me, for all that you are doing in my life right now, and for all you will do in the future. In Jesus' precious name I pray, Amen.

Philippians 2: Here's How You Do It -- Follow Jesus' Example

Selected Biblical Text

1 If then, there is any encouragement in Christ, any comfort of love, any sharing in the Spirit, any compassion and mercy, 2 complete my joy and think about the same thing, having the same love and spirit together, thinking about one thing.

3 Thinking nothing according to selfish ambition or vain conceit, rather with humility esteem others superior to yourselves, 4 not looking out for your own interests but each of you for the interests of the others. 5 Have this thinking in yourselves, which was also in Christ Jesus. (Phil. 2:1-5)

Reflecting and Thinking

Jesus is our example. He humbly and unselfishly emptied himself, rejected his divine position, and obediently sacrificed himself on the cross. The result was his exaltation above all else. This is a hard concept for us to understand and accept. Our human nature wants to push self forward, look out for #1, and make sure others know how good we are. The first few verses of Philippians 2 (today's selected text) tell us how imitating Jesus works out in human experience. The result of the mindset of Jesus is beautiful, Christ-like lives of caring and compassion, joy and love, unity and sharing.

Why are we so disinclined (at least at times) to use the "Jesus principles" of this text in our daily interactions? Is it easy or hard to follow these principles when we interact with other Christians? When have you willingly sacrificed your own self-interest for the benefit of another person? Let us resolve today to follow Jesus' example!

Prayer

Dear Lord, please work through me and guide me so that I will have the mind of Christ in all I do. Help me so that I will not do anything out of selfish ambition or vain conceit, but that I will remain humble, never considering myself better than others. Provide the means and the desire to look after the interests of others as well as my own interests. I pray that I will have a godly attitude in all my actions and decisions, and that your love will flow through me. May I be a blessing to you and to everyone around me. In the name of Jesus, I pray, Amen.

Philippians 3: Becoming Like Jesus

Selected Biblical Text

7 But whatever things were for me gain, those things I consider loss because of Christ. 8 Even more, I consider all things to be loss because of the surpassing value of knowing Christ Jesus my Lord, for whom I have lost all things -- I consider them sewage -- that I may gain Christ 9 and be found in him, not having my own righteousness based on the law, but that which is through the faithfulness of Christ -- the righteousness from God based on faithfulness, 10 to know him and the power of his resurrection, to share in his sufferings, becoming like him in his death, 11 so somehow I may attain to the resurrection from the dead. (Philippians 3:7-11)

Reflecting and Thinking

From the "single mind" of Chapter 1 and the "submissive mind" of Chapter 2, Paul turns in this chapter to describe the "spiritual mind." The world may chase after many things that appear to have value. Even we Christians may wrongly evaluate that which matters. Paul has turned from the things that were formerly considered valuable to focus on one priority -- to gain Christ and be found in him. His great desire is to know Christ and the power of his resurrection, to share the fellowship of his sufferings, to share his likeness in death, and to attain the resurrection from the dead. Paul's goal is to become like Christ, leaving all else behind.

What is God's greatest spiritual desire for you? What is your greatest spiritual desire? How is that desire reflected in your daily life? Paul in this chapter describes his goal as "winning the prize for which God has called me heavenward in Christ Jesus." What do those words mean to you? How would you describe the prize you seek? How would you describe God's heavenward calling in your life?

Prayer

Dear God, we want to become more and more like Jesus. We realize that this will require us to let go of some things that we think are important. Help us as we strive to adjust our priorities and devote ourselves to the things that matter eternally. Help us to develop spiritual minds. Transform us and make us fit for heavenly citizenship. Help us press on when days are difficult. In the name of Jesus our Savior, who also pressed on even in the face of death, Amen.

Philippians 4: Depending on Him

Selected Biblical Text

4 Rejoice in the Lord always. Again, I say, rejoice. 5 Let your gentleness be known to all people. The Lord is near. 6 Do not be anxious about anything, but in every situation, by prayer and petition with thanksgiving, make your requests known to God. 7 And the peace of God, which transcends all understanding, will guard your hearts and your minds in Christ Jesus. 8 Finally, brothers, whatever is true, whatever is honorable, whatever is just, whatever is pure, whatever is lovely, whatever is well spoken of -- if anything is excellent and if anything is praiseworthy -- think about these things. 9 What you learned or received or heard from me or saw in me — practice these things. And the God of peace will be with you. 10 I rejoiced greatly in the Lord that now at last you renewed your concern for me. Certainly, you were concerned, but you lacked opportunity. 11 I am not saying this because I am in need, for I have learned to be contented in all circumstances. 12 I know how to be humbled and how to have abundance. I have learned the secret in each thing and in everything, whether well supplied or hungry, whether living in abundance or in want. 13 I prevail in all things through the one who strengthens me. (Philippians 4:4-13)

Reflecting and Thinking

It is not easy to depend on God. Most of the time, our first choice is to depend on self and to seek God's help only in times of emergency. The "secure mind" is centered on God. God's provision allows us peace regardless of our circumstances. God's provision keeps us focused on excellence. The peace that the world gives can never equal the presence of the God of peace.

When do you find it hardest to depend on God? When has your dependence on God been answered by the help of brothers and sisters in Christ? When has the dependence of others on God been answered by your help? God meets our needs and in this we rejoice!

Prayer

Dear God, we marvel at the love that joins believers together. We find incredible the possibility of forgiveness. We do not understand always rejoicing, lack of anxiety, constant prayer, and peace, but we are grateful for these realities in our lives. We believe your promises, and we depend on your power to do all that you want us to do. May we live to your glory. We pray in the name of Jesus, Amen.

Colossians 1: Jesus Is Our Connection with God

Selected Biblical Text

15 He is the image of the invisible God, the firstborn over all creation, 16 for in him all things were created in the heavens and on the earth, things visible and things invisible, whether thrones or lordships, rulers or authorities; all things were created through him and for him. 17 And he himself is before all things, and in him all things hold together. 18 And he is the head of the body, the church; he is the beginning, the firstborn from among the dead, so that in everything he might be first. 19 For God was pleased to have all his fullness dwell in him, 20 and through him to reconcile all things unto himself, whether things on earth or things in heaven, by making peace through the blood of his cross.

21 Also you at one time were strangers and enemies in your minds because of your evil deeds. 22 But now he has reconciled you by his physical body through death to present you holy and without blemish and blameless before him, 23 if you continue in the faith, established and firm, not moved away from the hope of the gospel which you heard. This gospel has been proclaimed to every creation under heaven. Of this gospel, I, Paul, have become a servant. (Colossians 1:15-23)

Reflecting and Thinking

From the beginning -- or at least from Genesis 3 onward -- humankind has struggled with the question of how to reconnect with God. The truth is this: reestablishing the God-connection is impossible with merely human efforts or plans. God is the great repairer of the relationship that was broken by sin; he is not only creator, his is also re-creator. These basic truths stand behind Paul's description of Jesus' role. Jesus is the visible image of the invisible God; he is creator, reigning one, reconciler and redeemer.

When have you observed human beings wanting or trying to connect with God on their own terms or by their own efforts? Try to put into your own words the significance of Paul's affirmation about Jesus. Paul described the reconnection with God in terms of persevering (continuing) in faith, being established and firm, and being hopeful. What would you say to someone who says they want to reconnect with God but does not seem serious enough to continue faithfully?

Prayer

Heavenly Father, we are overwhelmed at times by our separation from you, by the distance we experience as we see the influence of this world in our lives. Today we praise you and give you thanks for Jesus as the one who reveals you and makes you known to us. We are grateful for his powerful work and words in creation, in holding things together, in leading the church, and in providing redemption and reconciliation so that broken relationships can be healed. May we be faithful servants, and faithful proclaimers of the good news, In Jesus' name, Amen.

❖ ❖ ❖

Colossians 2: Jesus Is Our Escape from Human Wisdom

Selected Biblical Text

2 My goal is that their hearts may be encouraged, having been knit together in love, attaining all the riches of assurance in full understanding, so they may know the mystery of God, which is Christ, 3 in whom are hidden all the treasures of wisdom and knowledge. 4 I say this so that no one will deceive you with enticing arguments. 5 For though I am absent in body, I am present with you in spirit, rejoicing when I see your determination and the firmness of your faith in Christ.
6 As then you received Christ Jesus as Lord, remain in him, 7 rooted and built up in him, strengthened in the faith just as you were taught, overflowing with thankfulness. 8 Be careful that no one captures you through the philosophy, which is an empty delusion, according to human tradition, according to the basic principles of this world, rather than according to Christ. 9 For in him all the fullness of the deity lives in bodily form, 10 and in him you have been filled, in the one who is the head over every ruler and authority. (Colossians 2:2-10)

Reflecting and Thinking

Descriptions of Jesus abound in Colossians. In today's selected text, he is the mystery of God, the holder of the treasures of wisdom and knowledge, Lord, fullness of God, and head over all. How amazing that we continue to be tempted by human wisdom! Despite God's clear revelation of himself in Jesus, hollow, deceptive, vain philosophies continue to hold sway in the minds of many -- even though such philosophies are based on human traditions and worldly principles. Many prefer regulations and false guidelines to freedom in Christ. Incredible!

When are you most tempted to buy into human ways of thinking? When have you seen the temptation to think in human terms exhibit itself in the life of the church? The rest of the chapter talks about the shadows versus the reality. What parts of Christianity seem like shadow to you? What parts of your life would you like to make "more real?"

Prayer

Dear God, as we live in this physical world, we often struggle to think in terms of spiritual wisdom and knowledge. The things we see here seem so much more real than the spiritual things revealed by faith. We are tempted to depend on what we can see and on following rules that make us feel like we are succeeding. Help us as we seek genuine connection with Jesus as the Head and deliver us from the false thought systems of this world. We are thankful that you strengthen our faith by letting us see Jesus, in His name we pray, Amen.

❖ ❖ ❖

Colossians 3: Jesus Is the Way to Find Life

Selected Biblical Text

1 If then you have been raised with Christ, 2 seek the things above, where Christ is, seated at the right hand of God. Think on the things above, not on the things on the earth. 3 For you died, and your life is hidden with Christ in God. 4 When Christ, who is your life, is revealed, then you also will be revealed with him in glory. (Colossians 3:1-4)

Reflecting and Thinking

Jesus is our life. As is the case with many of Paul's letters, the letter to the Colossians can be divided into a doctrinal section and a practical section. The foundational truth upon which the practical admonitions of Chapter 3 are built is the identity of Jesus as our life. We intentionally distance ourselves from the evil that was part of a former way of life because we have new life in his knowledge and image. We live a different kind of life with different attitudes because of his presence in our hearts. We are indwelt by his word which overflows in our teaching and admonition and worship -- in all that we do. Our relationships are changed by his presence.

Our world seeks life in a lot of different places. What are some of the items you would include in a short list of "life essentials?" What does the text mean when it says Jesus is our life? Do you have more difficulty with avoiding evil or with adding goodness? What does it mean to you that Jesus "is all, and is in all?"

Prayer

Dear God, we are thankful that you have not left us on our own in this Christian life. We are grateful that you have let us see and experience newness in Christ, with changed hearts and changed thoughts. Help us focus on things above and things eternal. Protect us from evil and encourage us in Christlikeness. Teach us gratitude, in the name of the Lord Jesus, Amen.

Colossians 4: Proclaiming Jesus

Selected Biblical Text

2 Be devoted to prayer, vigilant in prayer with thanksgiving, 3 praying also for us, that God may open to us a door for the message, to proclaim the mystery of Christ, for which I am in chains. 4 Pray that I may make it clear as I should. 5 Walk in wisdom toward outsiders, make the most of every opportunity. 6 Let your words be gracious always, seasoned with salt, so that you may know how to answer everyone. (Colossians 4:2-6)

Reflecting and Thinking

Much of the last chapter of Colossians is devoted to greeting various persons in the church at Colossae. In our brief selected text, Paul seems to have one focus -- the proclamation of the gospel. Pray for open doors for the message, pray for our proclamation, pray for clarity, pray to be able to answer everyone. Proclamation is supported by lifestyle. Our words lose power when our lives do not match. Here is Paul's echo of 1:28 -- our goal is to proclaim him!

Colossians is usually characterized as a Christ-centered book. How many different descriptions of Jesus do you remember from the book? (Review the book briefly if you need help in answering.) Which are most significant for you in your life at this time? How is God calling you to change your life as a result of your commitment to Jesus?

Prayer

Thank you, Father, for taking care of what we could never handle in our own lives by our own power. Thank you for Jesus. May our lives reflect him, may our lips proclaim him, may our actions bring him to life so that others can see him. We pray for the spread of the gospel, and we ask you to help us see how we are a vital part of your eternal plan to bring others to Jesus, in His name, Amen.

Philemon: Understanding Forgiveness

Selected Biblical Text

4 I always thank my God as I remember you in my prayers, 5 because I hear about your love and faith which you have for the Lord Jesus and for all the saints. 6 I pray that the sharing of your faith may be effective in deepening understanding of every good thing that is yours in Christ. 7 I have had great joy and encouragement because of your love, because the hearts of the saints have been refreshed through you, brother. (Philemon 4-7)

Reflecting and Thinking

The book of Philemon is Paul's great treatise on forgiveness. Forgiveness is contagious. Forgiveness establishes and reestablishes broken relationships. Even in a quick overview of today's reading, the key words of this book pile up: love, holiness, faith, partnership, goodness, joy, encouragement, refreshment.

How is our forgiveness of others dependent on God's forgiveness of us? (Think of the Lord's Prayer.) How is our forgiveness ultimately dependent on God's forgiveness? Think about the unique relationships detailed in this book -- Paul, Philemon, and Onesimus. What parallel applications can you think of in your own life? What impact would it have in the church if church members came to understand and apply the message of the book of Philemon?

Prayer

Dear God, thank you for forgiving us in Christ. Thank you for making us whole in the midst of our difficulties and interpersonal conflicts. Help us learn patience and forgiveness in our relationships with others. Thank you for your written word and your living Word, and for making forgiveness real in our lives, in Jesus' name, Amen.

1 Timothy 1: Protect and Proclaim the Gospel

Selected Biblical Text

17 Now to the king eternal, immortal, invisible, the only God, be honor and glory for ever and ever. Amen. (1 Timothy 1:17)

Reflecting and Thinking

This chapter instructs Timothy regarding his tasks in ministry, especially as they relate to the gospel message. Following an introductory purpose statement, Paul breaks into a brief autobiography in which he celebrates God's grace poured out in his life in the midst of his sinfulness. Faith and love can be developed in the worst of sinners because Christ's patience is greater than the human predicament. This is good news indeed! Paul cannot help but break into praise. Paul's apostleship was dedicated to protecting and proclaiming the gospel, precisely because it had made all the difference in Paul's own life.

When have you been so overcome by your own weakness that you broke into praise to God for his strength in the midst of your human failures? Do you think that a greater awareness of sin would motivate you to speak more often on behalf of the gospel? What do you think Paul had in mind when he urged Timothy to hold on to faith -- how does one do that?

Prayer

Heavenly Father, we pray for your help and strength as we overcome daily -- overcoming our past, overcoming our weaknesses, overcoming our disappointments, overcoming our tendency to disbelief. We praise you this day, in Jesus' name, Amen.

1 Timothy 2: Instructions Concerning Prayer

Selected Biblical Text

3 This is good and pleasing before God our Savior, 4 who wants all people to be saved and to come to knowledge of the truth. 5 For there is one God and one intermediary between God and people, the man Christ Jesus, 6 who gave himself a ransom for all – the testimony to his proper time. (1 Timothy 2:3-6)

Reflecting and Thinking

This chapter provides a guide for Timothy's work with and instructions to the church. The last part of the chapter contains several things that are difficult to interpret. Too often the reading and study of the chapter focuses on the difficult verses and misses the importance of the first part of the chapter. The chapter begins with a focus on prayer: the church's prayers should be offered on behalf of all people (2:1-2), God's desire for salvation concerns all people (2:3-4), Christ's death concerns all people (2:5-6), and therefore the church's proclamation must concern all people (2:7).

How often do the prayers offered in the public assembly include all people? To what extent do your personal prayers concern all people? How often do you pray to God for the salvation of the world? How do you understand the idea that it is good to live godly and holy lives, but that lifestyle alone is not an adequate measurement of the Christian life?

Prayer

Thank you, Jesus, for being our mediator, for your willingness to be our ransom, and for your great love for all human beings. I pray today for those who govern our world, and for all people everywhere, knowing that you love them and desire their salvation. Help me today to develop that same love for all people, beginning with those I meet today. Help me know how to pray for them, how to speak with them, and how to act. In the precious name of Jesus, Amen.

1 Timothy 3: Church Leaders with Integrity

Selected Biblical Text

14 These things I write to you, hoping to come to you soon. 15 But if I am delayed, you will know how people should conduct themselves in the household of God, which is the church of the living God, the supporting pillar and foundation of the truth. (1 Timothy 3:14-15)

Reflecting and Thinking

This chapter contains instructions about church leaders. Many times, the study of this chapter revolves around the qualities or characteristics of church leaders. (I like these words better than "qualifications.") In many studies of this chapter, too little attention is paid to the results of effective church leadership. The words of today's selected text, "these instructions," may refer to the contents of the first three chapters or to the contents of the entire book. It is also possible that the specific reference is to the context immediately preceding. That is, appointing appropriate church leaders results in appropriate conduct among God's people. Spiritual leaders must lead with integrity. Their lives must be examples of teaching, evangelistic outreach, prayers for all, gratitude for God's grace, and influence beyond the local church.

When you read the paragraph immediately above about church leaders, did you think of formal church leaders or did you consider that every

Christian is in a sense a spiritual leader? While the chapter clearly focuses on formal leaders, consider how the instructions can be applied to other leaders -- teachers, parents, neighbors, and friends. Is your life a reflection of the principles set forth in 1 Timothy 1-3? Let us pray today about the specific areas of our life that we want to change.

Prayer

Heavenly Father, we honor and adore and say "thank you" for all you are and do. We want to live powerful lives that lead and influence others. We want to strengthen our example, our words, and our desire for reaching out with the gospel. We want to be strong prayer warriors focused on your desire for the salvation of all. Strengthen me this day in the places that are especially weak, in the name of Jesus I pray, Amen.

1 Timothy 4: Integrity in Ministerial Leadership

Selected Biblical Text

12 Let no one look down on you because you are young but set an example for the believers in speech, conduct, love, faithfulness, and purity. 13 Until I come, give attention to public reading, preaching, and teaching. 14 Do not neglect your gift which was given you with prophetic teaching and with the laying on of the hands of the elders. 15 Contemplate these things, be totally involved in them, so that everyone will see your progress. 16 Give attention to your life and teaching, persevere in this, for by doing so you will save both yourself and those who hear you. (1 Timothy 4:12-16)

Reflecting and Thinking

The charge to Timothy that is included in today's selected text concerns Timothy's personal life in ministry. Ministers who would serve with integrity must consider their example, their preaching and teaching of the Scriptures, their diligence, and their personal lives. While the passage is primarily about ministers, the principles apply to every Christian. All Christians are called to minister to those around them, and the principles can be applied more broadly. We will not reach out and touch others for Jesus until our own personal lives have been changed by him.

Paul urges Timothy not to neglect his gift. What gift has God given you to serve others? On a scale of 1 to 10, how would you measure your diligence? your wholehearted commitment? your progress?

Thought question: Do your friends and your enemies describe you in the same way?

218

Prayer

Our God and Father, holy be your name. Help us be people of integrity. May that integrity be an influence on those we know and serve. Help me be more diligent in action, more faithful in perseverance, and more concerned about others. In the name of Jesus, the one who demonstrated the greatest love through his sacrifice, Amen.

1 Timothy 5: Ministry Without Favoritism

Selected Biblical Text

21 I charge you, before God and Christ Jesus and the elect angels, to observe these things without preference, doing nothing by partiality. (1 Timothy 5:21)

Reflecting and Thinking

This chapter contains instructions for Timothy concerning various groups in the church -- how he is to interact with and treat the older men, the older women, the younger men, the younger women, and the widows. Along the way, we learn about the roles and responsibilities of these groups. In conclusion, our text tells Timothy to act without favoritism. Partiality is a killer in the life of the church. Having favorites wrecks the church. Regardless of our roles in the church, you and I are called to interact with a lot of different people and with a lot of different groups and subgroups. There is a right way to treat people. Treating people in the right way will make all the difference in the success or failure of the local church and of our own service and ministry.

When have you served someone that others would not serve? When have you reached out and touched someone that others considered unworthy? If others could see your heart, would they think you are partial? Would they see favoritism? Do you serve all and love all, or do you tend to serve those who can repay the favor?

Prayer

Heavenly Father, teach us your heart, with love for all, compassion for all, hope for all, and service to all. Help us share the message of hope with all, in His name, Amen.

1 Timothy 6: Practice the Principles of the Gospel

Selected Biblical Text

11 But you, man of God, flee these things, and pursue righteousness, godliness, faith, love, endurance, and gentleness. 12 Fight the good fight of the faith, take hold of the eternal life to which you were called when you confessed the good confession before many witnesses. 13 I charge you, before God who gives life to everything, and before Christ Jesus who testified unto Pontius Pilate the good confession, 14 to keep the command without spot or blame until the appearing of our Lord Jesus Christ, 15 which at the right time, God will reveal -- God, the blessed and only Ruler, the King of kings and Lord of lords, 16 the only one having immortality, living in unapproachable light, whom no one has seen or can see. To him be honor and eternal power, Amen.

20 Timothy, guard the deposit entrusted to you. (1 Timothy 6:11-16, 20)

Reflecting and Thinking

The last chapter of 1 Timothy includes various instructions. One way to summarize the chapter is to note the focus on the importance of practicing the principles of the Christian faith. Godliness has its own reward, a reward greater than any other. The controversies, conflicts, and treasures of the world are temporary at best. The sure foundation points to what is yet to come, and ultimately leads to life that is truly life.

How would you describe "life that is truly life?" What is the connection between controversies, worldly ideas, and getting caught up in things that are opposed to Christianity? Consider the phrase that says God provides us everything for our enjoyment. How does this help you toward an integrated view of Christianity, living in this world but focused on a world yet to come?

Prayer

Heavenly Father, help me establish right priorities today and to focus on the things that really matter. Help me experience life that is truly life. Help me not to be drawn away from you by the siren songs of the world. Thank you for who you are -- blessed and only Ruler, King of kings and Lord of lords, immortal, living in unapproachable light, the one whom no one has seen or can see. My prayer is that you will have all honor and might forever and ever, in the name of Jesus, Amen.

Titus 1: Unfit for Doing What Is Good

Selected Biblical Text

15 All things are pure to those who are pure: but to those who are corrupt and unbelieving, not one thing is pure, but both their minds and consciences are corrupted. 16 They profess to know God, but by their actions they deny him, being detestable, disobedient and unfit for any good deed. (Titus 1:15-16)

Reflecting and Thinking

Titus faced very difficult problems on the island of Crete. Few problems challenge the church more than the problem described by the Old Testament prophet, that people call good evil and evil good. Church leaders must love what is good. In fact, Titus calls every Christian to do what is good. Some of the Cretans -- even while they claimed to know God -- were so rebellious, immoral, corrupted, and unbelieving that they are described as "unfit for doing anything good."

Are you familiar with the phrase, "good for nothing?" What happens in a local church when the commitment to doing what is good is lost? What happens in the life of a Christian when that commitment is lost? What can you personally do to equip yourself today for being more capable of and committed to doing what is good?

Prayer

Father God, deliver us from our focus on the things of this world, our desire to protect ourselves, our tendencies to warp the truth and to become enmeshed in countless peripheral details of Christian teaching. Guide us to purity of thought and life. Empower us for consistent living so our actions and beliefs match. Help us do what is good, in the name of our Savior who went about doing good, Amen.

Titus 2: Eager to Do What Is Good

Selected Biblical Text

11 For the grace of God has appeared, bringing salvation to all people. 12 It instructs us to deny ungodliness and worldly passions so we will live self-controlled, upright and godly lives in this present age, 13 while we wait for the blessed hope and glorious appearing of Jesus Christ, our great God and Savior, 14 who gave himself for us to redeem us from every lawlessness and to purify for himself a people for his own possession, eager to do good works. (Titus 2:11-14)

Reflecting and Thinking

Many Bible students are familiar with the first part of the text above; fewer continue to the conclusion of the thought. We are blessed by God's saving grace demonstrated in Jesus Christ; we are equally blessed by the possibility of moral godly lives. We rejoice in our blessed hope for the return of Jesus. We are less likely to focus on the truth that Jesus has called to himself and claimed as his possession a people who are to be eager to do what is good. Life is not only measured by our obedience to the gospel, our worship, passion, faith, and hope. Life is measured by our attitudes and actions -- are we eager to do what is good, do we do what is good?

What does it mean to you to be "eager to do what is good?" When have you known hesitant Christians? What do you think Titus had in mind when he wrote about "what is good?" What do you think of the idea that we define goodness too broadly so that everything not immoral becomes good? How could you today demonstrate to yourself, to God, and to others that you are "eager to do what is good?"

Prayer

Heavenly Father, help us to have a clearer vision of your will for us in every area of our lives. Help us to see our commitment and relationship with you, made possible through Jesus, as a factor and influence in every part of life. Grant us an eagerness to do good, place in us the desire to do good, and teach us goodness. We pray in the name of Jesus, Amen.

Titus 3: Devoted to Doing What Is Good

Selected Biblical Text

This is a trustworthy saying, and I want you to thoroughly confirm these things so that those who have put their faith in God may be intent on practicing good works. These things are excellent and advantageous for everyone. (Titus 3:8)

Reflecting and Thinking

Today we conclude our brief trip through the book of Titus. Some are unfit for doing good; Jesus calls us to be eager to do good; Christians are challenged to devote themselves to doing what is good. Based on the first part of today's chapter, doing good encompasses such things are civil obedience and watching our tongues and our attitudes. Our readiness to do good represents a reversal of our previous experiences when we were foolish and worldly. We have been blessed by his righteousness, our rebirth in baptism, and the renewing presence of God's Spirit within us. Trust in God changes our lives -- not just our status before God as saved or lost. The book of Titus says that devotion to doing good is not optional. In fact, it is something to which children of God devote themselves constantly.

How could the modern church demonstrate a greater devotion to doing good? What are some good things the church typically fails to become involved in? How does devotion to doing good connect with accurate understandings, Christian attitudes, and lifestyle decisions? Describe how these three factors are integrated in the life of a devoted Christian.

Prayer

Our Heavenly Father, help your people find strength in their devotion to goodness. May our lives reflect the generosity of Jesus Christ our Savior, and we pray through Him, Amen.

2 Timothy 1: A Ready Spirit

Selected Biblical Text

3 I am thankful to God, whom I serve with a clear conscience as my ancestors did, as I constantly remember you in my prayers, night and day. 4 I long to see you, remembering your tears, so that I may be filled with joy. 5 When I remember your sincere faith which first lived in your grandmother Lois and in your mother Eunice, I am convinced that it now lives in you also. 6 Based on this faith, I remind you to fan into flame the gift of God which is in you through the laying on of my hands. 7 For God did not give us a spirit of fear but of power, love, and self-control. 8 So do not be ashamed of the testimony of our Lord or of me his prisoner but share our suffering for the gospel by the power of God. (2 Timothy 1:3-8)

Reflecting and Thinking

Few things are of greater value in ministry and Christian service than a ready spirit. Reading between the lines of Paul's letter, some have presumed that Timothy was hesitant or timid. Paul reminds Timothy of his strong heritage of faith, that others have believed in him, and that God bestows a spirit of power, love and self-discipline. A ready spirit will be prepared to testify, even in the face of sufferings. A ready spirit comes from confidence in God's faithful mercy. A ready spirit accepts God's gift, guards it, and lives it out daily.

As a Christian, are you always ready to serve? What are some of the areas in which you are hesitant? What would it take for you to overcome your hesitation? Read again Paul's encouragement to Timothy. Personalize the message and consider how God has blessed you to prepare you for ready service. Evaluate the presence of God's blessings in your life and pray for strength.

Prayer

Father God, we depend on ourselves when we should depend on you. Help us find confidence as we enumerate the blessings we have received from your hand. Bring into our lives a new awareness of your purpose and grace and help us hear and answer your call. Thank you for the Holy Spirit who lives in us. May his presence strengthen our lives, and may we be ready always, in Jesus' name, Amen.

2 Timothy 2: Ready to Teach Others

Selected Biblical Text

1 You then, my son, be strong in the grace that is in Christ Jesus. 2 And the things you have heard from me through many witnesses, these things entrust to faithful people who will be qualified to teach others also.

22 Flee from the passions of youth and pursue righteousness, faith, love, and peace, with those who call on the Lord out of a pure heart. 23 Avoid foolish and stupid questionings, because you know they produce controversies. 24 And the Lord's servant [slave] must not quarrel but must be kind to all, given to teaching, and patient. (2 Timothy 2:1-2, 22-24)

Reflecting and Thinking

This chapter begins and ends with instructions about sharing the message. In the well-known passage of 2 Timothy 2:1-2, four generations are described: Paul, to Timothy, to reliable men, to others. Must we assume that the "reliable men" and "others" are all ministers? Christianity does not seek to establish a protective repository (although the church is composed of the saved). The church is not a repository of the message -- the message is to be spread. Christianity is the delivery system designed to take the message of Jesus to the entire world. God's people are called to a unique manner of life, changed attitudes, and servant hearts, always being ready to teach. Servants of the Lord are called to kindness and to sharing and teaching the message.

In the modern church, the task of sharing the message and teaching others is usually left to a few. Why do you think this is? What you have thought in the past about the "reliable men" and the "others" with whom the gospel was to be shared? What reasons can you give for applying these teachings to designated church leaders? What reasons can you give for applying the teachings to Christians in general?

Prayer

Father, we pray today for the church, for the ability of the church to take the message into the world, and for those who faithfully share your message across generations. Help each of us find our place and part in your eternal plan. Strengthen us with endurance. Fortify our love for the lost, and our compassion for those ensnared by Satan. Make us ready for the tasks at hand, in Jesus' name, Amen.

2 Timothy 3: Ready for the Challenges

Selected Biblical Text

10 You, however, have followed my teaching, way of life, purpose, faith, patience, love, [and] endurance, 11 the persecutions [and] the sufferings, such things as happened to me in Antioch, Iconium, and Lystra, what sort of persecutions I endured, yet from them all the Lord rescued me. 12 In fact, all who want to live a godly life in Christ Jesus will be persecuted, 13 and evil people and impostors will go from bad to worse, deceiving and being deceived. 14 But you, continue in the things you have learned and are assured of, knowing from whom you learned them, 15 and that from infancy you have known the holy writings, which are able to make you wise unto salvation through faith in Christ Jesus. 16 All scripture is God-breathed and useful for teaching, for reproof, for correction, for instruction in righteousness, 17 so that God's person may be complete, fully equipped for every good work. (2 Timothy 3:10-17)

Reflecting and Thinking

Living as a Christian in the United States seems easy -- not too many challenges or challengers, few real persecutions, certainly little suffering. Life as a Christian in the first century was different. Endurance was essential -- Paul had a clear sense of God's rescue. Limited challenges make us less ready to sacrifice. Limited challenges make us less dependent on God and more certain we can make it on our own. God calls us to godly living, training, and good works. The easy life is not the Christian life.

Have you ever been challenged for your Christian faith? Based on Paul's words to Timothy, have you ever wondered where the persecutions are for the U.S. church? What do you think would happen if the faith of the contemporary church were challenged? How many of those who attend church and call themselves Christians would remain faithful? Do you think the church is stronger or weaker in times of persecution?

Prayer

Dear God, we desperately want not to be weak and unfaithful. We think we would be ready for intense challenges if they were to come, but we are not sure. Make us more dependent on you, more willing to sacrifice all that we have, to be all that we can be for our Lord. Thank you for the precious gift of the God-breathed words of truth that meet our every need and equip us for service. Make us servants like Jesus, in whose name we pray, Amen.

2 Timothy 4: Ready for the End

Selected Biblical Text

1 I charge you before God and Christ Jesus who will judge the living and the dead, and by his appearing and his kingdom: 2 Preach the word; be ready in season and out of season; reprove, admonish, and exhort, with all patience and teaching. 3 For the time will come when people will not tolerate sound teaching, but in accord with their own desires, with "itching ears," they will gather around the many teachers who will satisfy their "itching ears." 4 They will turn their ears away from the truth and turn aside to myths. 5 But you, be level-headed in every situation, endure hardship, do the work of an evangelist, fulfill your ministry. 6 For I am already being poured out like a drink offering, and the time for my departure is at hand. 7 I have fought the good fight, I have finished the race, I have kept the faith. 8 Finally the crown of righteousness is reserved for me, the crown which the Lord, the righteous judge, will give to me on that day, and not only to me, but also to all those who have loved his appearing. (2 Timothy 4:1-8)

Reflecting and Thinking

Have you considered why and how Paul so confidently faced the end of his life? What was it about him? Was it not that he had lived out the advice he was giving to Timothy -- preach and teach constantly and consistently, patiently encourage, stay focused, endure, do the work to which God calls you. The conclusion of a life well spent is confident readiness.

Reflect on the journey you have completed to this point in life. How are you doing with the calling and claim of God in your life? Selfishness is the tool of Satan. Evaluate how often you suit your own desires rather than doing what God wants. Consider how easy it is to hear what we want to hear rather than what God is trying to communicate to us. Finally, consider the meaning of the phrase, "to long for his appearance." What does it mean to long for something? Are we eagerly anticipating Jesus' return, longing for his appearing?

Prayer

Dear God, thank you for all you have done to make our faith possible. Give us courage, confidence, and renewed compassion. Hear our hearts, mold us and renew us as we seek to be ready for all that comes, and as we long for His appearing, in His name, Amen.

1 Peter 1: Faithful, Holy Obedience

Selected Biblical Text

13 Therefore, with your minds prepared, and being watchful, set your hope completely on the grace to be brought to you at the revelation of Jesus Christ. 14 As obedient children, not being conformed to the evil desires you had before in your ignorance, 15 but as the one who called you is holy, you also be holy in all your conduct; 16 for it is written: Be holy, because I am holy.

17 And if you call on a Father who impartially judges according to the work of each person, live out the time of your sojourn here in reverence. 18 You know that you were redeemed from your empty way of life inherited from your ancestors, not by corruptible things such as silver or gold, 19 but with the precious blood of Christ, as of an unblemished and spotless lamb. 20 He was foreknown before the foundation of the world, but was revealed in these last times for your sakes, 21 you who through him believe in God who raised him from the dead and gave him glory, so your belief and hope may be in God.

22 Having purified your lives by obeying the truth, unto a sincere and mutual brotherly love, now love one another intently from a pure heart, 23 having been born again, not from perishable seed but from imperishable, through the living and enduring word of God. (1 Peter 1:13-23)

Reflecting and Thinking

Bible students have identified many different themes in Peter's first letter. Some of the more obvious themes are suffering, persecution, courage, glory, hope, and grace. As is common with the General Letters, this letter deals with Christian living and duties. Peter encourages his readers to maintain faith and pure conduct in the midst of trials. The letter is obviously a pastoral exhortation (5:1-3) and contains a series of imperatives (grammatical command forms).

A brief summary could look something like this. Because God has a plan for those who put their faith in Jesus, faith is precious and leads to salvation (1:3-12). Conduct consistent with faith is an essential part of having a new life (1:13-2:3) and receiving a new identity (2:4-10). Christians should act in such a way as to be examples in every relationship of life, even when their good conduct is incomprehensible in the eyes of the world and results in hostility and persecution (3:13-17). Remaining firm in the faith makes a person like Jesus -- participating in his suffering and knowing freedom from sin (4:1-6). Ultimately, God is the one who establishes, strengthens, and perfects our faith (5:10-11).

Peter introduces his letter by mentioning new birth, living hope, eternal inheritance, and faith that leads to salvation, glory and honor. Hope focused on grace motivates faithful obedience that leads to holiness. This new life is based on the message of Jesus and his redeeming blood. It separates Christians from empty religion and immature attitudes, and results in sincere brotherly love among Christians.

Which of the concepts mentioned above is most meaningful to you in your Christian walk?

How often do you meditate each day on these concepts as motivations for Christian living?

Explain to someone you encounter today how you understand the relationship between grace, faith, obedience, holy conduct, and hope (1:13-16).

Prayer

Father God, use my time of reading and study to strengthen and perfect my faith. Give me more complete understanding of your will in my life. Thank you for the blessings of your grace in my life--new life, living hope, and certain inheritance. Help me endure during times of difficulty, keeping my mind focused on your grace exhibited in Jesus, in whose name and by whose power I pray, Amen.

1 Peter 2: Living Stones -- A New Identity for God's People

Selected Biblical Text

5 ...and you yourselves, like living stones, are being built into a spiritual house unto a holy priesthood, to offer spiritual sacrifices acceptable to God through Jesus Christ. 6 For in Scripture it says: "Look, I lay in Zion a stone, a cornerstone chosen and precious, and the one who believes in him will by no means be put to shame." 7 Now the preciousness is for you who believe, but to those who do not believe the stone which the builders rejected has become the cornerstone, 8 both a stone for stumbling and a rock for falling down. Those unbelievers stumble because they disobey the word, unto which also they were destined.

9 But you are a chosen race, a royal priesthood, a holy nation, a people for his own possession, that you may declare the virtues of the one who called you out of darkness into his marvelous light. 10 Then you were not a people, but now you are the people of God; you had not received mercy, but now you have received mercy. (1 Peter 2:5-10)

Reflecting and Thinking

The result of God's work in the lives of Christians -- his work to develop faith, love, and hope -- is a new identity in Christ Jesus. God is forming a new people who are part of a new spiritual house. Those who come to Jesus, the living Stone, are built together as living stones in the new spiritual house. The text describes this new people of God as chosen, special, royal priesthood, holy nation, and the declaration of his praises. God's mercy has been poured out afresh.

1 Peter 2:11-12 is sometimes described as the "hinge" upon which the entire book turns. What comes before may be characterized as teaching

and what follows as application. Because God's eternal plan in Christ Jesus has changed our lives and given us a new identity and new hope, Christians live a different kind of life -- a life of submission that imitates Jesus. This life does not make sense to the world that tends to retaliate and get even, but this life is the calling of those who would walk in the example and steps of Jesus. Our identity motivates our lifestyle and separates us from the world, identifying us also as aliens and strangers in this world.

How do you try to live out the "separated" identity of God's people in your daily life?

When have you submitted in the name of Jesus, not demanding your "rights" and displaying an attitude that some around you thought was unreasonable because you gave in too readily?

When have you wanted to retaliate but did not?

How do you declare the excellencies or praises of God, declaring what he has done in your life? What could you say to make clear that you live as you do because of your allegiance to Christ?

Describe the difference between grudging submission and respectful submission (2:18).

Try for one day to live life according to the well-known question, "What would Jesus do?"

Prayer

Dear God, today I ask you to help me be aware of my new identity in Christ. Help me use my knowledge of who I am in Christ to alter the way I live my life. Help me not to shrink from those times when I am called to be different and to live by different values and a different worldview. Open my mouth when opportunities come to declare praise. Help me die to sin and live for righteousness. I pray in Jesus' name, Amen.

1 Peter 3: Suffering for Doing Good

Selected Biblical Text

13 Now, who is going to harm you if you are committed to what is good? 14 But even if you should suffer for righteousness, you are blessed. Do not fear them or be troubled. 15 But, in your hearts, set Christ apart as Lord, ready continually to answer anyone who asks you the reason for the hope that is in you, 16 but with gentleness and respect, keeping a clear conscience, so that those who falsely accuse your good conduct in Christ may be ashamed of what they say against you. 17 For it is better, if God so wills, to suffer for doing good than for doing evil. (1 Peter 3:13-17)

Reflecting and Thinking

When Christians act in such a way as to be examples in every relationship of life, such good conduct is incomprehensible in the eyes of the world. Incredibly it often results in hostility and persecution. Although not many people in this world are going to hurt those who try to do good, there are exceptions. Sometimes Christians suffer because they do what is right. Such suffering in the first century was often physical; we today may think also of emotional, relational, social, and economic suffering that comes when we do what is right. When Christians do what is right, even when it works against them, the world considers such behavior ridiculous, but Peter says that it is also an opportunity to share gently and respectfully the reason for our hope (3:15-16). A question: is this a part of declaring his excellencies or praises (see 2:10)?

Christians have the opportunity to do what is right and live good lives in all of life's relationships (2:12-3:12) -- with unbelieving neighbors, governments and authorities, masters or employers, husbands and wives, and other Christians. Such behaviors are evidence of our total separation from sin, even as Christ died for sins once for all (3:18). Many people today reject the message and only a few believe. This was the case in the days of Noah and is still the case today. Baptism saves because of our submitted hearts and the promise that is ours through Jesus' resurrection.

Have you ever suffered for doing what is good or for doing what is right?

When have others thought your behavior did not make sense, because you were guided by a different standard?

When has your example given you the opportunity to express the reason for your different life, or the reason for your hope in Christ?

Describe the connection between baptism and Jesus' resurrection. In your opinion, is this connection emphasized enough in the church's teaching concerning baptism? Why do you answer as you do? How could we work together to make clear the connection?

Jesus submitted himself during his earthly sojourn; now authorities and powers are in submission to him. Is this a model that teaches Christians what will happen as a result of our submission? Why or why not?

Prayer

Dear God, our humanity gets in the way sometimes of our imitation of Jesus. It is not easy to be submissive when others are mistreating us. Help me know the right and do the right. Help me seize the opportunities you provide to share my hope. Separate us from sin, because Jesus died for sin to bring us to God. Help me not to get so involved in difficult or unknowable parts of this text that I miss the real point -- the blessing that comes to those who seek God in good conscience in order to know the salvation He provides through our conscientious obedience. Forgive me when I find relationships difficult and challenging. Forgive me when I have failed to use relationships to your glory and honor. In Jesus' name, Amen.

1 Peter 4: Living for God

Selected Biblical Text

1 Therefore, since Christ suffered in the flesh, arm yourselves also with the same attitude, because whoever suffers in the flesh has finished with sin, 2 so that he lives the rest of his time in the flesh, not for human passions but for the will of God. 3 For sufficient is the time that has passed for you to do what the Gentiles desire, having gone along with licentiousness, passions, drunkenness, carousing, drinking parties, and abominable idolatry. 4 They think it strange that you do not run with them into the same excessive excess, so they speak evil of you. 5 They will give an account to the one who is ready to judge the living and the dead. 6 For this purpose the gospel was preached even to those who are now dead, so that though they may be judged according to human standards in the flesh, they may live according by God's standards in the spirit.

16 But if any suffer as a Christian, let him not be ashamed, but let him glorify God in this name. 17 For it is time for judgment to begin from the household of God; and if it begins with us, what will be the end result for those who do not obey the gospel of God? 18 And, if the righteous are hardly saved, where will the ungodly person and the sinner appear? 19 So then, let those who suffer according to God's will entrust themselves to a faithful Creator as they do good. (1 Peter 4:1-6, 16-19)

Reflecting and Thinking

The connection may seem obscure to the modern reader -- suffering separates us from sin. The will of God becomes supreme and is our greatest desire. The preaching of the gospel judges all according to the body, that is, it judges human beings for emphasizing physical realities and pleasures more than spiritual things, and it judges humans for the things done in the body. The alternative is clear for God's people -- when we live for God in the spirit, even while we exist in the body, we are genuine imitators and followers of Jesus. This is the goal of God's judgment.

This spiritual life for God alters our conduct toward others but does not eliminate the possibility of suffering. Suffering because we deserve it may be expected. Suffering as a Christian declares God's praise. Commit yourself to him and keep on doing what is right!

Do you think modern Christians would be less prone to sinful behaviors if we lived in persecution?

What unique challenges do today's Christians have in the matter of avoiding sin?

What does this text say about peer pressure?

How could you each day commit your life to God more fully?

How do we proactively do what is right, and not merely avoid what is wrong? What is the difference between these two ideas in your mind? Does one who merely avoids wrong automatically do what is right?

Prayer

Heavenly Father, help us live life for your desires and not for our own desires. Help us use our existence in the body on this earth for spiritual purposes, and not for physical pleasures. Strengthen us as we strive to live according to your will in the Spirit. Help us as we seek to arm ourselves with Jesus' attitude and to avoid sin. In the name of Jesus, the Christ, Amen.

1 Peter 5: Strong, Firm, and Steadfast

Selected Biblical Text

6 Humble yourselves, then, under the mighty hand of God, that he may lift you up in the opportune time. 7 Cast all your cares on him because he cares for you.

8 Be sober; be alert. Your enemy the devil, like a roaring lion, goes about looking for someone to devour. 9 Resist him, being strong in the faith, because you know that the same kinds of sufferings are being faithfully endured by the brotherhood throughout the world.

10 And the God of all grace, who called you to his eternal glory in Christ, after you have suffered a little while, will himself restore, make firm, strengthen, and establish you. 11 His is the power for ever and ever. Amen. (1 Peter 5:6-11)

Reflecting and Thinking

The message of Peter's letter can be summarized in five phrases: <u>our faithful holy obedience</u> in responding to God's grace <u>gives us a new identity</u> as the people of God, so that even <u>as we suffer for doing good</u> we are <u>committed to living for God</u>, thus being <u>made strong, firm and steadfast</u> in his grace and glory.

Peter began his letter focusing on God's gracious work. He concludes with the same theme. Here are the reflections and instructions of an elder-pastor. Here are the words of a shepherd who is diligently concerned about the glory of his flock when the Chief Shepherd returns. He reminds us that Christian living is not about human effort but is about human response to God's grace. God's initiative empowers our obedience and changes our identity, resulting in changed lives. What previously mattered doesn't matter now. Living according to the Spirit replaces living according to the body. This text makes clear that human response is essential: resist the devil, stay strong. But God is ultimately in control. Suffering is temporary but living for God is eternal.

How would your life change if you could you live according to grace?

Do you depend more on yourself and your own efforts to attain spiritual steadiness, strength, and firmness, or do you depend on God's gracious activity in your life? How could you live out God's promise more fully (see 5:10)?

How does an awareness of God's power humble us?

On a scale of 1 to 10, how aware are you each day of God's care and provision?

Prayer

Heavenly Father, we marvel at the wisdom of your plan, and at how much you are involved in our daily lives so that we can reach the goal of living for you and being done with sin. We are journeying daily toward a goal we have not yet attained, yet you call us and claim us according to a new identity and not according to our moments of weakness. We are grateful for your promise of new life, new hope, and eternal glory, even as our faith is tried and tested and perfected through trials and difficulties. Thank you for your gift of Jesus, for your patience, and for the salvation and cleansing you provide through our faithful, conscientious response to and participation in Christ's resurrection through our baptism. We want to follow in Jesus' steps, we want to imitate his example, and we ask your presence and power, through Jesus we pray, Amen.

2 Peter 1: Remembering Jesus

Selected Biblical Text

8 For if you have these things and they are increasing continually, they will keep you from being ineffective and unfruitful in the knowledge of our Lord Jesus Christ. 9 But whoever does not have these things is blind, nearsighted, having forgotten the cleansing of his past sins. 10 Therefore, brothers, be diligent to make your calling and election sure. For if you do these things, you will never stumble, 11 for in this way an entry into the eternal kingdom of our Lord and Savior Jesus Christ will be richly supplied to you.

12 So I will always remind you of these things, even though you know them and are firmly established in the truth you now have. 13 And I think it is right, as long as I am in this tabernacle, to stir up your memory, 14 because I know that the laying aside of my tabernacle is soon, as our Lord Jesus Christ has revealed to me. 15 And I will be diligent, that after my departure you will always have a way to remember these things.

16 For we did not follow cleverly devised fables when we made known to you the power and coming of our Lord Jesus Christ, but we were eyewitnesses of his magnificence. 17 For he received honor and glory from God the Father when the voice came to him down from the majestic glory, saying, "This is my beloved son, with whom I am well pleased." 18 We ourselves heard this voice that came down from heaven when we were with him on the holy mountain. 19 Now we have the prophetic word, completely reliable, and you will do well to pay attention to it as to a light shining in an obscure place, until the day dawns and the morning star rises in your hearts. (2 Peter 1:8-19)

Reflecting and Thinking

Peter's message in his second letter is clear. The chapter divisions set forth three distinct but related thoughts: (1) Remember Jesus, so you can (2) avoid false teachers who spread false ideas about Jesus, and so you can (3) joyfully anticipate the Day of the Lord. Today's first chapter contains many different descriptions of Jesus. You may want to underline the descriptions in your own Bible.

Knowing Jesus helps us grow spiritually and gives life meaning and depth. Knowing Jesus reminds us of our calling, promises, protection, and new nature. Failing to know Jesus holds us back and enslaves us in guilt because we cannot accept his forgiveness. Failing to know Jesus explains our stumbling and falling. Because remembering Jesus is so important, Peter says he will keep reminding his readers about Jesus until he dies. Peter gives his own personal testimony. The message of Jesus is not a clever story but reflects Jesus' power and greatness as God's Son. This message was secured by the voice on the mountain (at the Transfiguration) and makes certain the message of the prophets, even though they could not see clearly. The prophets spoke with certainty and waited expectantly. When we hear their message and pay attention, we also we come into light and God's prophesied Morning Star becomes for us reality.

On a scale of 1 to 10, how well do you think your church does in emphasizing Jesus?

What things sometimes replace Jesus in the emphasis of the modern church? (Think about the classes, teaching, sermons, and preaching you have heard recently.)

Do we know Jesus, or do we merely know about Jesus? Consider a scale where 3 is neutral, 1 represents "knowing Jesus well", and 5 represents "only knowing about Jesus." Where would you put yourself? Where would you put the church you attend?

According to this chapter, why is knowing Jesus important?

Does a person who only knows about Jesus have faith? Tell someone you encounter today how you understand your faith.

Prayer

Father God, we want to know Jesus, to participate in his divine nature, to experience his calling to glory, and to know his goodness within us. We want to escape the ways of the world and live productive lives in his eternal kingdom. Help us focus on Jesus and see Him in the words of Scripture. In Jesus' name and by his power I ask it, Amen.

2 Peter 2: Warning Against False Teachers

Selected Biblical Text

18 For by speaking pompous useless words, by the passions of the flesh and with lasciviousness, they entice people who are just escaping from those who live in delusion. 19 They promise them freedom, while they themselves are slaves of corruption, for by whatever someone is overcome, to that he is enslaved. 20 For if, after having escaped the contaminations of the world with full knowledge of our Lord and Savior Jesus Christ, these are again entangled and overcome, the last state has become for them worse than the first. 21 It would have been better for them not to have known the way of righteousness, than after having known it to turn away on the holy commandment that was passed on to them. (2 Peter 2:18-21)

Reflecting and Thinking

The false teachers Peter describes are saying false things about Jesus (denying the sovereign Lord, 2:1). It is probable that they were formerly Christians, or at least they professed to know Christ, but now they have gone astray by failing to develop a correct knowledge of Christ Jesus. God's judgment against them is certain, and their influence should be visible to all. Unfortunately, they are able to ensnare new Christians who have barely

escaped the world's corruptions. The false teachers enslave people, not realizing that they themselves are also enslaved because they have turned
their back on God's message, the knowledge of Jesus, and the holy commandments that point to Jesus.

What happens when God's people lose sight of who Jesus is?

*Have you ever known a Christian who was vulgar and crude? How
did you explain the apparent inconsistency? What does this text say about
that?*

*What are some of the false ideas about Jesus that threaten the
church today? (Think about a too strict gospel, a too loose gospel, failure to
recognize the truth of Scripture, cultural accommodation, etc.)*

*What are some of the unhealthy results of failing to recognize who
Jesus is?*

Prayer

Dear God, we want to teach right and live right. Help us recognize the connection between these two ideas. Help us as we seek to know the truth
about Jesus and his way, and help us speak truth in all we say, both directly
and indirectly. May we value the message God has given us about Jesus.
May we apply that message as motivation to imitate and live for Jesus. In
His name we pray, Amen.

2 Peter 3: Anticipating the Day of the Lord

Selected Biblical Text

8 But do not be unaware of this one thing, beloved: that one day with the Lord is
like a thousand years, and a thousand years are like one day. 9 The Lord is not slow
concerning his promise, as some understand slowness, but is patient toward you,
not wanting anyone to perish, but everyone to come to repentance. 10 But the day
of the Lord will come like a thief, on that day the heavens will disappear with a
whirring sound; the celestial bodies [literally, basic building blocks] will be destroyed being burned up, and the earth and the works in it will be disclosed
[revealed].

11 Since all these things will be destroyed in this way, what kind of people ought
we to be, living holy and godly lives 12 looking forward to and hastening the coming
of the day of God? On that day the heavens being burned up with fire will be destroyed, and the elements being set on fire will melt away. 13 But according to his
promise, let us wait for a new heaven and a new earth, where righteousness
dwells.

14 Therefore, dear friends, since you are waiting for these things, be diligent to be
found spotless and blameless in him, and at peace. 15 Consider the patience of our
Lord as salvation, just as our dear brother Paul also wrote you according to the
wisdom that God gave him, 16 also in all his letters speaking of these things. In his

letters are some things that are hard to understand, which untaught and unstable people twist, as also the rest of the scriptures, to their own destruction. 17 Therefore, beloved, since you have been forewarned, be on guard so that you are not seduced by the deceit of these wicked men and do not fall away from your steadfastness. 18 But grow in the grace and knowledge of our Lord and Savior Jesus Christ. To him be glory both now and on that eternal day. Amen. (2 Peter 3:8-18)

Reflecting and Thinking

Knowing Jesus is the antidote to false teachers who twist the Jesus message. Knowing Jesus is also the key to understanding God's patience and the certainty of his promise. The certainty of God's promise motivates pure, peaceful living. Some would twist the truth about what will happen in the future, scoffing at the delay in Jesus' return and questioning God's promise. They use the delay as an excuse to continue in evil. They refuse to recognize that God's patient delay means salvation. Failing to understand who Jesus is brings error and lawlessness, so Christians must be on guard and grow in grace and knowledge of Jesus as Lord and Savior.

Considering the importance of the concept of "knowing Jesus" in 2 Peter, how do you understand the admonition to "grow in knowledge" (3:18)?

This chapter says that one result of failing to know Jesus is a failure to understand God's patient nature. What are other results of failing to know Jesus, as set forth in this chapter?

How could Christians be more certain of Jesus' return by knowing Jesus (by understanding Jesus' nature and identity) more clearly?

Prayer

Dear God, thank you for revealing yourself in your holy written word. Thank you for revealing yourself in Jesus, the living word. Help us to know him better, so we can avoid the snares of misunderstanding. Keep us firmly planted in wholesome thinking, the words of the prophets, and the apostolic commands and teachings. Keep us in your care and give us wisdom and insight to identity false concepts about Jesus. In Jesus' name, Amen.

Jude: Ungodly!

Selected Biblical Text

4 Certain people have secretly slipped in among you, those who were long ago written about for this condemnation, godless people who change the grace of our God into a license for lasciviousness, denying the only sovereign and our lord, Jesus Christ.

15 [The lord is coming] to render judgment for everyone, and to convict every person concerning all their ungodly acts which they committed in ungodly ways, and of all the harsh words that ungodly sinners have spoken against him. (Jude 4, 15)

Reflecting and Thinking

No room for doubt -- Jude clearly states his primary concern. He had first wanted to write about the faith entrusted to God's people; I presume he had hoped to encourage his readers. But he decided that he needed to write about godlessness. Godlessness is rooted in misunderstanding Jesus and in using grace as an excuse rather than a blessing. When ungodliness takes hold, it overpowers. Ungodly people commit ungodly acts in ungodly ways and speak ungodly words against God himself. Ungodliness is rooted in denying God and Christ. Ungodliness is subtle, because the denial of God and Christ is not always in word -- it can be by action. One definition of sin is "acting as though there were no God."

What are some of the fruits of ungodliness, according to Jude? Carefully examine this little chapter for references to division, actions based on human instincts, and Spirit-less lives. How is it possible that such influences could infiltrate the church? How should this chapter guide our prayer lives? What obligations do we have toward others – other Christians, those outside of Christ?

Prayer

Dearest Father, give us hearts of mercy, especially for those who doubt. Give us hearts of compassion for those who are in danger; help us find strength for the rescue and heaviness of heart for those in danger. May we know a holy fear of the things that could wreck our lives. We depend on you for security when we would fall and for lifting us up when we are not so glorious. Through Jesus Christ our Lord -- who is glory, majesty, power, and authority -- we pray, Amen.

John 1: Introducing Jesus

Selected Biblical Text

1 In the beginning was the Word, and the Word was with God, and the Word was God. 2 This one was in the beginning with God. 3 All things through him were made; and without him was made nothing that has been made. In him was life, and that life was the light of men. (John 1:1-3)

Reflecting and Thinking

Word. God. Light. Life.

In these short verses John begins the process of piling on descriptions of Jesus, one after another, as he introduces Jesus and identifies him as the Cosmic Christ. Jesus comes to give order (the Greek word is "cosmos") to an unorderly world (also "cosmos"). The world does not realize that it exists in chaos (a Greek word that is basically the opposite of cosmos).

Jesus is the Cosmic Christ because He transcends normal boundaries. He is divine. He is creator. He enters creation as Word and flesh, dwelling among humanity. He reveals glory, grace, and truth.

Unique Son of God ("only being" is a more likely reading than "only begotten"). Lamb of God. Son of God. Jesus of Nazareth, son of Joseph. Rabbi. King of Israel. Son of Man.

Each of the gospels begins with what I like to call an "identity section." John 1 serves that purpose in the Gospel of John. How many different descriptions of Jesus can you find in John 1? in the entirety of John's gospel?

Prayer

Father God, make known to me afresh this day the presence and power that you give to those who believe, to those who are your children. Help me see your glory in your Presence, in your Creation, and in other people. Thank you for making your grace known, the grace of second chances, and third, and fourth chances, ever without limit so that we, living by faith, can never run out of your favor because of our foolishness. In Jesus' name and by his power I ask it. Amen.

John 2: Revealing Glory -- Building Faith

Selected Biblical Text

11 This, the first of his miraculous signs, Jesus did at Cana in Galilee. He revealed his glory and his disciples believed in him. (John 2:11)

Reflecting and Thinking

Human nature changes slowly -- if at all. We seek the spectacular as the foundation of faith, somehow thinking it better than the constant and the dependable. We can be duped by one unexplainable event and assume we have seen a pattern for all time. In John's gospel, miracles are "signs." Something is happening and it has a meaning. The action communicates a truth; something is revealed. Jesus' signs are always needs-meeting. They are marvelous, but the focus is not on the miraculous. It is possible to believe without seeing -- think about the story of Thomas in John 20. Jesus' first miracle at the wedding in Cana revealed his glory and his disciples believed.

Afterward, the Jews desired another sign from Jesus -- something that would demonstrate his authority and authorize his actions. Some saw his actions and believed; others saw the same actions and did not believe.

How did the events of this chapter (the wedding feast with the "water to wine" miracle and the clearing of the temple with Jesus' prophetic statement) reveal Jesus' glory? How did these events build faith in the disciples? Why does it take them so long to "get it?" When have you seen Jesus' glory? What would be required for us to "get it" -- to put our entire trust in Jesus?

Prayer

Dear God, help me today to see and recognize and honor Jesus' authority in this world and in my life. Help my faith to be less dependent on external circumstances and more focused on the reality of Jesus' identity and his presence in my life. As I read Scripture, bless me with a faith that develops even though I have not seen irrefutable physical evidence. Please wrap me in your presence and help me not to let go of You. In Jesus' name, Amen.

John 3: Plainly Seeing the Work of God

Selected Biblical Text

19 This is the basis of judgment: Light has come into the world, but people loved the darkness instead of the light because their deeds were evil. 20 Everyone who does evil deeds hates the light and does not come into the light so that his deeds will not be exposed. 21 The one who practices the truth comes into the light, so his deeds may be clearly seen, that they have been done in God. (John 3:19-21)

Reflecting and Thinking

Listen for the key words and phrases in John 3: Jesus came from God, light, truth, testimony, faith, eternal life, testifying about what he has seen and heard. No human effort can stand in the face of God's presence, truth, and testimony. Accepting God's truth declares that God is truthful. Accepting God's truth means accepting God's Son as God's spokesperson and authority. No life is possible except through the Son. Rejecting the Son cuts one off from life. Eternal life is possible only through believing in Jesus.

Why are we afraid of light and truth? One reason is that it exposes us for what we are. Living in light and truth exposes us, but because of Jesus what is seen is not our feeble, frail and even sinful human actions. What is seen is that God is at work in our lives, renewing us through a new birth of water and Spirit, drawn to Jesus, saved through Jesus.

How would it make you feel if you were sure that people saw only God's work in you when they looked at you? What kind of renewal (rebirth) would be required to make that kind of change a reality -- to turn your life completely around? Would such a change be enough motivation for you to live in truth and light?

Prayer

Dear God, help me today to live by truth and to walk in light. Help me overcome the fear of being found out. Give me confidence of your forgiveness and motivation to right living. Help me be honest with myself rather than hiding and hoping that my weaknesses and sins can be hidden by staying close to the darkness. Bring me into the light where I can see myself, depend on you, be transparent with others, and find confidence and forgiveness. In Jesus' name, Amen.

John 4: Developing Faith -- Seeing for Yourself

Selected Biblical Text

40 So when the Samaritans came to him, they urged him to stay with them; and he stayed there two days. 41 And many more believed because of his words. 42 They said to the woman: "We no longer believe because of what you said: We have heard for ourselves, and we know that this man really is the Savior of the world." (John 4:40-42)

Reflecting and Thinking

Understanding Jesus is no easy thing. Some Christians seem to think faith is easy. Faith is difficult. In today's chapter, the disciples misunderstand Jesus. The woman at the well fails to understand. The Samaritans find faith only after two days of careful listening. In the middle of a familiar story, do we miss the real point? The second narrative in the chapter finds a father and his house believing because he is convinced of Jesus' power. The Bible says that Jesus' promise and his son's healing occurred "at the exact time."

Have you really listened to Jesus? Have you heard him? Have you seen the foundations of faith for yourself, or are you trying to survive with an inherited, secondhand, proxy faith? Let us pray today that we will be aware and able to see when God shows up.

When have you seen the glory and certainty of God's presence in this world? What would it feel like if your faith was definitely yours and was based on the essence and certainly of hope and evidence and conviction of the invisible?

Prayer

Heavenly Father, open my eyes today -- to living water springing from within me, to confidence in Jesus, to seeing the harvest, to finding faith in life's 'coincidences.' In the name of Jesus who is the Christ, the one who explains everything, Amen.

John 5: Developing a Faith that Brings Healing, Life, and Confidence

Selected Biblical Text

19 Then Jesus answered: "In truth I tell you, the Son can do nothing by himself; except what he sees his Father doing, for whatever the Father does, these things the Son also does. 20 For the Father loves the Son and shows him all he does. And he will show him even greater works than these, so that you will be amazed. 21 For just as the Father raises the dead and gives them life, even so the Son gives life to whomever he wants. 22 Furthermore, the Father judges no one, but all judgment has been given to the Son, 23 that all may honor the Son just as they honor the Father. Whoever does not honor the Son does not honor the Father who sent him. 24 In truth I tell you that the one hearing my word and believing him who sent me has eternal life and will not be judged but has crossed over from death to life." (John 5:19-24)

Reflecting and Thinking

The uniqueness of the question must not escape us: "Do you want to be well?" Some people enjoy ill health. Some never find the healing, life, and confidence Jesus provides. John 5 can be thought of in three acts. First, Jesus heals the invalid by the pool. Second, Jesus declares that there is no life apart from him. Third, Jesus declares that multiple witnesses make his claims certain. It is one thing to have faith -- it is another to have faith that makes a difference in our lives, a faith that buoys our spirits, empowers our living, and instills confidence. Some versions of faith are not worth having -- all mental acceptance but no changed lives and no changed actions.

On a scale of 1 to 10, how would you rate your spiritual health right now? How would you rate your overall spiritual life? How would you rate your confidence? What testimony or witnesses are most powerful for you when you wonder about Jesus' identity?

Prayer

Heavenly Father, we want healing from our infirmities and weaknesses. We desire life that feels like life, confidence that overwhelms doubt. Thank you for giving us all of the things we need. Bring us closer to you today, through Jesus we offer this prayer, Amen.

John 6: Dimensions of Faith -- Physical or Spiritual?

Selected Biblical Text

26 Jesus answered them: "In truth I tell you, you seek me, not because you saw the signs but because you ate the loaves and were satisfied. 27 Do not work for food that spoils, but for food that endures to eternal life, which the Son of Man will give you. For on him God the Father has put his seal of approval." (John 6:26-27)

Reflecting and Thinking

Living out the reality of spiritual faith in a physical world is not easy. The two realms get intertwined because we humans live in both realms simultaneously. Unfortunately, too often we begin to measure God by what we see and experience. The people in John 6 made the same mistake -- disciples who did not see a way to feed the people, fearful disciples, a sinking Peter on an uncertain sea, people who came back for more food, Jews who sought a military leader and a physical kingdom, Messianic Jews anticipating a Messiah in the image and heritage of Moses -- one who would restore the manna so that no one would ever hunger again. This is a chapter of misunderstandings, false hopes, and spiritual insensitivity. When Jesus says that following him requires spiritual connectedness (communicated in figures of speech that the Jews found repulsive, "chewing his flesh" and "drinking his blood"), many rejected him. There are still many who follow Jesus because of what they see and experience physically, with little interest in experiencing the full dimensions of the spiritual kingdom Jesus came to establish.

When has your faith become dependent on success in the physical realm? What do you think about Christians or churches that focus on externals more than internals? What could we do to participate more fully in the cause of Christ? How do we today "eat his flesh and drink his blood?" (The context of John 6 makes it highly unlikely that Jesus' use of these phrases had anything to do with the communion meal.)

Prayer

Father God, we seldom find our version of Christianity difficult. We wonder sometimes what we would do if it became hard to be a follower of Jesus. We wonder how we would respond to persecution; we wonder if we have an authentic understanding of faith in view of the Bible teaching that those who faithfully follow will suffer. Help us today to live out an authentic spiritual life in this physical world. Help us not to become overly enamored or impressed by that which is seen; help us to focus on what is unseen. We pray in the name of Jesus, who makes the invisible visible, Amen.

John 7: Faith Brings God's Presence and Power

Selected Biblical Text

37 On the last day, the greatest day of the feast, Jesus stood and said in a loud voice: "If anyone is thirsty, let him come to me and drink. 38 Whoever believes in me, as Scripture has said, rivers of living water will flow from within him." 39 This he spoke about the Spirit, whom those who believed in him were to receive later. For until that time the Spirit was not yet given, since Jesus had not yet been glorified. (John 7:37-39)

Reflecting and Thinking

This chapter reveals one result of faith. Those who believe will receive God's presence through the Holy Spirit. It had not happened yet because Jesus had not yet been glorified. Later in John's gospel, Jesus will say that the Holy Spirit cannot come until he goes away.

Why do many Christians live powerless lives devoid of a sense of God's presence? Genuine faith brings into our lives a power that gushes forth as living streams of water. John says that such an experience is the fulfillment of Scripture, but we can identify no Old Testament passage that provides a clear reference. Perhaps the reference is to the water that flowed from under the temple (as in Ezekiel 40-48), foreshadowing God's presence within the Christian so that we are temples of the Holy Spirit. Regardless of the Old Testament prophetic foundations, Jesus promises something new as God's Spirit comes to dwell within his people so that his presence might flow into the world.

On a scale of 1 to 10, how aware are you of God's presence in your life? How aware are you of the presence of the Holy Spirit within you? God's presence within us is not just for us, it is for the world into which God's presence and Holy Spirit can flow through us. Let us pray today about how we can be instruments of God for his purpose.

Prayer

Dear God, we desperately need your presence and your power. We know that we cannot fulfill your purpose by our own human efforts. We are grateful for the confidence we find in the promise that you are continually walking alongside us. We pray for your presence to gush forth from us and not merely to drip slowly. We pray for more awareness of our temple status as a dwelling of your Spirit. May we bless others by being your presence in their lives. In Jesus' name, Amen.

John 8: Developing Faith that Brings Freedom

Selected Biblical Text

54 Jesus answered: "If I glorify myself, my glory is worth nothing. My Father is the one who glorifies me, the one you claim to be your God. 55 Though you do not know him, I know him. If I said that I do not know him, I would be a liar like you, but I do know him, and I obey his word. 56 Your father Abraham rejoiced to see my day; he saw it and was glad."
57 Then the Jews said to him: "You are not yet fifty years old, and you have seen Abraham?"
58 Jesus said to them: "In truth I tell you, before Abraham was, I am!" (John 8:54-58)

Reflecting and Thinking

Glory, life, light, truth! What exalted concepts! To think that Jesus is all of these! In this chapter, Jesus confronts the Jews. The Jews were depending on legalistically following their traditions and their heritage as descendants of Abraham. They were too little interested in God's purpose and too much interested in fulfilling the letter of the law while missing the spirit. They claimed to know God but did not. They pretended to be obedient but were not.

Their attitude -- being all wrapped up in themselves and their little, narrow understanding of God and his Word -- kept them from experiencing God's ultimate desire for his human creation. They were so busy interpreting laws, defining boundaries, and describing the "thou shalt" and the "thou shalt nots" that they fell short -- they lacked integrity, they had missed any meaningful relationship with God, they were inadvertently buying into Satan's agenda. Perhaps worst of all -- rather than finding true freedom, they were returning to slavery, a slavery worse than that from which God had delivered them in Egypt.

God wants us to be free. God desires our freedom. Freedom comes from knowing the truth. The verb "to know" is rich and broad -- not mere intellectual knowledge so that we know about the Word, but personal experience that shows that we truly know God.

Are you genuinely free in Christ? Jesus says freedom comes from obedience, from knowing and honoring God's word and dealing with sin in our lives. Freedom is possible because of who Jesus is. Seeing Jesus clearly will generate greater faith -- faith that will bring the freedom God provides.

Prayer

Dearest heavenly Father, we praise you for your wisdom and for your desire and your ability to deliver us from the power of Satan, from our own misunderstandings, from our weaknesses, and from our hard hearts. Bring us into the glorious light of your freedom. Help us use freedom not for license but to fulfill your purpose in our lives. In the name of Jesus, we pray, Amen.

John 9: Developing Faith that Empowers Spiritual Sight and Insight

Selected Biblical Text

35 Jesus heard that they had thrown him out, and when he found him, he said: "Do you believe in the Son of Man?"
36 The man answered: "Who is he, sir? Tell me so that I may believe in him."
37 Jesus said: "Now you have seen him; he is the one speaking with you now."
38 Then the man said: "Lord, I believe, and he worshiped him."
39 Then Jesus said: "For judgment I came into this world, so that the ones not seeing will see and the one seeing will become blind."
40 Some Pharisees – those who were with him -- heard him say this and asked him: "We are not blind, are we?"
41 Jesus replied to them: "If you were blind, you would not be guilty of sin; but now that you say you can see, your guilt remains." (John 9:35-41)

Reflecting and Thinking

Here are two amazing things. Those who were blind can now see; those that could see are now blind. Spiritual blindness is a terrible thing, frightening because it is so hard to recognize. Today's reading, the story of the blind man healed by Jesus, is for many one of the more familiar chapters in the New Testament. If you do not know the story, I encourage you to read the entire chapter. Lots of people are blind (in some sense) in the story. In addition to the blind man (who is physically impaired), one can note the blindness of the disciples, the townspeople, the man's parents, and the Jewish leaders. The saddest lesson to be learned is that some people are intentionally blind.

Are you ever intentionally blind? Have you ever ignored an opportunity because you caught only a fleeting glimpse of a possibility? Have you ever failed to act on your better motives? Have you ever seen, only to quickly turn away? All of these situations can indicate spiritual blindness.

Prayer

Heavenly Father, help us see. Help us see what you want us to see. Help us so that we do not ignore your urgings, turn away from opportunities, or openly work against your involvement in this world. Give us spiritual insight to see and believe, to worship, and to act. We pray for your presence and help today so that we can see and act, in Jesus' name, Amen.

John 10: The Good Shepherd Provides Abundant Life

Selected Biblical Text

7 Then Jesus said again: "In truth I tell you, I am the entry door for the sheep. 8 All who came before me are thieves and robbers, but the sheep did not listen to them. 9 I am the entry door; whoever enters through me will be saved, will come in and go out and will find pasture. 10 The thief comes only to steal and slaughter and destroy; I have come that they may have life and may have it abundantly. 11 I am the good shepherd." (John 10:7-11a)

Reflecting and Thinking

The words in today's selected reading were spoken to the Jews on behalf of a man who needed encouragement. Rejected, cast out, belittled and demeaned -- it seems that his healing from a life of blindness had gained him little. But then again, life is not to be measured in externals. Not everyone who is rich in this world's goods has an abundant life; in fact, surveys show that many rich people still feel that something is missing from their lives.

The question is not, "What are your circumstances?" The question is, "What will you do with your circumstances?" A blind man sees and believes. Jews who have a long history with God fail to see: "How long will you keep us in suspense? If you are the Christ, tell us plainly" (John 10:24). In a chapter where many remain in unbelief, the last verse of the chapter says, "many believed." Read, think, understand. Familiar texts must be read more closely. What is going on here?

To what extent is it true that "we see what we want to see?" If you are among those who have seen and believed in Jesus, why do you believe? If you are among those who have not believed in Jesus, why do you not believe? Can we be honest with ourselves? Unless we are willing to answer questions like these, we may never experience abundant life -- life to its fullest.

Prayer

Thank you, Jesus, for your obedience to the Father. Thank you, God, for your loving sacrifice. Thank you, Holy Spirit, for your comforting guidance. My life is so much richer and sweeter because of the hope I have in you,

Lord. I am glad that you have provided the way for me to have eternal life in your presence -- in a place where there will be no more tears and no more suffering; a place where there will be unimaginable joy, praise, worship, and peace. I praise you for who you are and for what you have done. In Jesus name, Amen.

John 11: Jesus' Identity -- "I Am" the Resurrection and the Life

Selected Biblical Text
21 Then Martha said to Jesus: "Lord, if you had been here, my brother would not have died. 22 But I know that even now, whatever you ask, God will give you."
23 Jesus said to her: "Your brother will rise again."
24 Martha answered him: "I know he will rise again in the resurrection at the last day."
25 Jesus said to her: "I am the resurrection and the life. The one who believes in me, even though he dies, will live; 26 and anyone who lives and believes in me will never really die. Do you believe this?"
27 She replied: "Yes, Lord, I believe that you are the Christ, the Son of God, the one coming into the world." (John 11:21-27)

Reflecting and Thinking
Much of John's gospel is devoted to making clear who Jesus is. Even casual readers have noticed the numerous "I am" statements. In these statements, Jesus identifies himself with God the Father. In today's selected reading, Martha is confident of Jesus' connection with God: "you could have averted this death, and God will respond even now if you ask." She confidently affirms that Jesus is the Messiah (Christ), the Son of God.

The larger context provides an enlightening contrast because the disciples, especially Thomas, are not so quick to believe. Jesus says that through Lazarus' death the disciples will have another opportunity to believe. (See verses 14-15.) When Jesus raises Lazarus from the dead, he demonstrates his power over death ("I am the resurrection") and his power over life ("I am the life"), thus pointing to the abundant life that fully conquers the fear of death.

When have you been overwhelmed by the power of death? When have you caught a glimpse of Jesus' power over life and death, either in your own experience or in that of others?

Prayer
Heavenly Father, we are grateful that Jesus conquered death. May we find assurance and calm in our faith in him -- power to live life fully on this earth, to be confident of resurrection from the grave, and to anticipate eternal life

with you thereafter. Thank you for showing us these truths through your Son. Thank you for your sacrifice -- and for his sacrifice. Help us to enjoy the morning as though it were the first day of our lives, and to enjoy the evening as though it were our last. In Jesus' name we praise and honor and adore and say "thank you," Amen.

John 12: Jesus' Glory: Demonstrated, Affirmed, Explained, Rejected

Selected Biblical Text

23 Answering them, Jesus said: "The hour has come for the Son of Man to be glorified. 24 In truth I tell you, unless a seed of wheat dies when it falls upon the ground, it keeps on being only a single seed. But if it dies, it produces many seeds. 25 The one who loves his life will lose it, and the one who hates his life in this world will keep guarding it for eternal life. 26 If anyone would serve me, let him follow me. Where I am, there also my servant will be. If anyone serves me, the Father will honor him. 27 Now my soul is troubled, and what shall I say? 'Father, save me from this hour'? But for this purpose, I have come to this hour. 28 Father glorify your name."
Then a voice came from heaven: "I have both glorified it and will glorify it again." (John 12:23-28)

Reflecting and Thinking

Today's chapter contains many smaller narrative sections. One way to tie together the multiple storylines is suggested in today's title. Jesus' glory is demonstrated at the Triumphal Entry, affirmed and explained by Jesus' teachings and by the voice from heaven, and rejected by the Jews who continue in their unbelief. The question posed by today's reading is this: "What will we do with Jesus' glory?"

How often do you think "glory" when you think of Jesus? Have you seen his glory? When? Where? How? Consider the various groups described in this chapter -- what did they think of Jesus' glory? What do you do in your daily life to demonstrate how glorious Jesus is? (Consider this: the risen Jesus is in one sense even more glorious than the incarnate Jesus!) Make a special effort today to look for and see Jesus, just as the Greeks did in today's chapter.

Prayer

Our God and Father, thank you for glorifying the name of Jesus. Give us greater respect for his name and authority; help us see his glory in this world, in our lives, and in the lives of others. Help us reflect that glory, in the name of the One who reflects your glory, Amen.

❖   ❖   ❖

John 13: The Fullness of Love

Selected Biblical Text

1 Just before the feast of the Passover, Jesus knew that the time had come for him to leave this world in order to go to the Father. Having loved his own who were in the world, now to the very end he loved them. (John 13:1)

Reflecting and Thinking

John 13 is a familiar chapter to many Bible students. It is at the same time unknown and unfamiliar. References to the chapter often focus on only one verse -- verse 35: "love is how the world will know we are disciples." Have we missed the point? Have we failed to see that the chapter is more about the attitude of service and sacrifice than it is about love? In fact, the text affirms that love is reflected in service. The question is not how often we affirm our love, or for how many we proclaim our love. The question is how often and for how many we demonstrate our love through service. Love is action -- not mere affirmation. The love Jesus describes is self-sacrificing, willing to give one's entire lifetime, and even one's life if necessary. "Love as I have loved you. Love one another to the fullest, love to the end." We are to love as Jesus has loved us -- making supreme sacrifices. Suddenly, love is not nearly so much fun. Jesus' example is more than words -- he demonstrates his love in an action that foreshadows the sacrifice he will ultimately make for all humanity.

When have you loved someone unlovable? When have you loved someone you did not know? When have you loved someone undeserving? When have you loved another Christian? When have you experienced love, not as an emotion, feeling or a sharing of fellowship, but through genuine service that required you to make a sacrifice and go out of your way?

Prayer

Heavenly Father, teach us to love as Jesus loved. Help us to show our love by what we do, and not merely in our words. Give us a loving spirit of humility and compassion, a willingness to serve whomever wherever and whenever you give us the opportunity, a spirit of forgiveness and love even when we have been wronged and rejected. Help us to follow Jesus' example, in His name, Amen.

John 14: Faith Sustained --
Words of Comfort and the Promise of Another Advocate

Selected Biblical Text

1 "Do not let your heart be troubled. You believe in God; believe also in me. 2 In my Father's house are many residences; if it were not so, would I have told you that I am going to prepare a place for you? 3 And if I am going and will prepare a place for you, I will come back and take you to be with me, so that you can where I am. 4 You know the way to where I am going."

5 Thomas said to him: "Lord, we do not know where you are going, how can we know the way?" 6 Jesus answered: "I am the way and the truth and the life. No one comes to the Father except through me."

15 "If you love me, keep my commands. 16 And I will ask the Father, and another Advocate he will give to you to be with you forever – 17 the Spirit of truth…" (John 14:1-6, 15-17)

Reflecting and Thinking

The Jews of the first century thought they knew God, but they did not know him accurately. They had built protective fences around God. They could not see him clearly. In today's chapter, Jesus says that seeing him is like seeing God. If we can trust God, we can trust Jesus. If we can trust Jesus, we can trust God. They are one.

Trust is not easy. Going where we cannot see; going places we do not know; doing what we do not understand; living in hope when we cannot see. For many years in the early 20th century, mission work involved going to places that people did not know. Today, imitating Jesus by following his example and obeying his teachings to be baptized is a stumbling block for many. Make no mistake: faith goes into places that are unseen and unknown. Faith is hoping for what we cannot see, making visible the invisible.

Fortunately, when Jesus went away and was no longer present to speak words of comfort to his followers, he sent a Comforter to be his presence in our lives and in our world. The Comforter, the Holy Spirit, speaks the words of Jesus even as Jesus spoke the words of God. The Holy Spirit's words can be trusted because they received from Jesus and they are all truth. Why do some people continue to reject the clear teaching of inspired Scripture, the sword of the Spirit?

When have you struggled with something you thought God wanted you to do, but you preferred not to do? Have you ever been purposefully disobedient? What role does lack of faith or lack of trust play in such experiences? Where is God calling you to go? What is Jesus calling you to do so that you can be totally obedient?

Prayer

Heavenly Father, we are grateful for the unity shared by Father, Son and Spirit, a mystery that is beyond our comprehension. Thank you for the words of comfort in Scripture. Thank you for the constant presence of the Comforter in my life. Help me today to do what you want me to do, to put you and your will at the top of my list. Help me to be obedient to everything you say and desire. Help me to obey, even when I cannot see the reason, the sense, or the purpose. Teach me trust. In the name of Jesus, the Way, the Truth, and the Life, Amen.

John 15: Faith Connections -- Connected to the Word or the World?

Selected Biblical Text

16 You did not choose me, but I chose you and have appointed you, so you will go and bring forth fruit -- fruit that lasts, and so that whatever you ask in my name the Father will give you. 17 These things I command you, so that you will love one another. 18 If the world hates you, keep in mind that it hated me before you. 19 If you were of the world, it would love you as it loves its own. But you are not of the world for I chose you out of the world. For this reason, the world hates you. (John 15:16-19)

Reflecting and Thinking

When I think of John 15, I think first of Jesus' teaching about the vine and the branches. But there is another very important teaching in John 15. The "rest of the story" tells us why the world hates followers of Jesus. The common point between these two sections is found in the word "connections."

What are your connections? Who are your connections? What are the primary connections of your life? Is your primary connection to Jesus (the vine) or is your primary connection to the world? Is your connection to the Word or to the world? When you are more comfortable with the world than with Jesus, it is evident in your life. Because we live in the world, we are tempted every day to buy into the world -- to become "of" the world and to become like the world. One connection yields eternal fruit -- the other yields fruit that will soon be gone.

When have you experienced the hatred, disdain, or rejection of the world? How does it feel to know that Jesus calls you his friend? Does it make you want an even closer friendship? What can you do today to be a fruitful branch, firmly connected to the vine?

Prayer
Father God, thank you for your care and your desire to comfort me as I live in this world. Keep me firmly connected to the vine. Help me avoid the temptation to be tightly connected to the world. In Jesus' name I pray for strength and power, protection and faithfulness, Amen.

John 16: Empowering Faith -- The Holy Spirit

Selected Biblical Text
7 I tell you the truth, it is better for you that I go away. Because if I do not go away, the Advocate will not come to you; but if I go, I will send him to you. 8 When he comes, he will prove the world concerning sin, righteousness, and judgment.
13 But when he, the Spirit of truth, comes, he will guide you into all the truth. He will not speak from himself; but whatsoever he hears he will speak, and he will tell you about the things that are to come. 14 He will glorify me, because he will receive from me and tell it to you. (John 16:7-8, 13-14)

Reflecting and Thinking
The Holy Spirit empowers our faith in several ways. He accompanies us -- in fact, he is with us forever. He teaches and reminds and instructs. He testifies that Jesus' claims are valid; he empowers our testimony as we boldly live out our faith. He is our confidence -- affirming that we are children of God, that we are heard in prayer, and that the future is secure. He helps us have a right understanding of and attitude toward sin, righteousness and judgment.

Some think that faith is a "do it yourself" proposition -- just hear and accept the word of God. Biblically, faith is a mysterious combination of God's initiative and my response, just as mysterious as God's grace. God's initiative ultimately finds its power and meaning in the human response of faith.

When have you felt lonely in your faith? When you feel spiritually alone, how aware are you that Jesus has promised his presence and comfort through the Holy Spirit? Is faith for you more like a mental exercise, or is it more like an experience that is lived out? (Biblically it is both -- that which I come to know and understand and accept to such an extent that I apply it and live it out in my life.)

Prayer
Heavenly Father, increase our faith. Help us see the story of Jesus clearly; help us listen to the testimony of your inspired word and Spirit. Help us live out what we intellectually believe, so that faith becomes real and vibrant and useful. In the name of Jesus who demonstrated faithfulness to us, Amen.

❖ ❖ ❖

John 17: Jesus' Glory and Faithful Followers -- The Power of Unity

Selected Biblical Text

20 I am not praying only concerning them, but also for the ones who will believe on me through their message, 21 that all of them all may be one, Father, just as you are in me and I am in you, so that they might be in us, so that the world may believe that you sent me. 22 And the glory which you have given to me I have given to them, so that they may be one as we are one – 23 I in them and you in me -- so that they may be perfectly one. Then the world will know that you sent me and have loved them just as you have loved me. (John 17:20-23)

Reflecting and Thinking

During his earthly ministry, Jesus prayed many times. He taught his disciples to pray. The longest recorded prayer of Jesus is in John 17. He prays for himself, he prays for his followers, he prays for believers, and he prays for the world. Jesus came into the world for the world. He came to save the world. He died for the world. He prays for the world, realizing that his influence in the world will be determined by how his followers act and how they reflect the divine oneness. Scary thought!

How could the modern church reach the unity Jesus prayed for? Jesus says that the world's belief or lack of belief is dependent on how well his disciples relate to one another in love and unity. Through our unity the world will recognize and know that God sent Jesus and that God loves the world. As you think this through, how would you describe it in your own words? How are such unity and such influence possible in the life of the church?

Prayer

Heavenly Father, help your people find the way to unity. Help us understand Jesus' prayer and make it a reality in our lives. Help us live powerful lives that declare God's existence, God's power, God's love, and the truth that God sent Jesus. In the name of your Son, Jesus, Amen.

John 18: Jesus' Identity -- Who in the World Is this Man?

Selected Biblical Text

33 Then Pilate went back into the praetorium [governor's court room], he summoned Jesus and spoke to him: "Are you the king of the Jews?"

34 Jesus replied: "Do you say this as your own idea, or did others talk to you about me?"

35 Pilate replied: "I am not a Jew, am I? The people of your own nation and the chief priests handed you over to me. What did you do?"

36 Jesus answered: "My kingdom is not of this world. If my kingdom were of this world, my servants would fight to keep me from being handed over by the Jewish leaders. So, my kingdom is not from here."

37 Then Pilate said to him: "Then you are a king!" Jesus answered: "You say that I am a king. I was born for this, and for this I came into the world, so I may testify to the truth. Everyone who is on the side of truth listens to me."

38 Pilate said to him: "What is truth?" (John 18:33-38a)

Reflecting and Thinking

John's gospel uses a lot of space and spends a lot of time telling us who Jesus is. It does this through telling us about his experiences, his human interactions, his conversations, and his teachings. Jesus' conversation with Pilate is telling. Pilate asks about Jesus' identity: "Who are you?" Pilate thinks he has the upper hand. Faithful believers know differently. Pilate does not know what truth is because he does know the One who is truth. Do we?

As we anticipate reading about the crucifixion of Jesus, the identity of Jesus becomes a crucial point. We are approaching the end of the Gospel of John. At this point in the book, how would you describe who Jesus is? What aspects of his identity are most meaningful to you? How would you answer someone who asked you the question of our title, "Who in the world is Jesus?"

Prayer

Father God, we come to you in the name of Jesus, by his authority, depending on who he is and what he did so that we could have access to you. We are grateful for his demonstration of your love. We feel our frailty, our fragility. We feel our humanness. We want to be better and to do better. May we commit ourselves to knowing and acting on truth. Make us like Jesus, in his name, Amen.

John 19: Faithful Testimony Leads to Faith

Selected Biblical Text

35 The one who saw it has given testimony and his testimony is true. He knows that he speaks the truth, so that you also may believe. 36 These things happened so that the scripture would be fulfilled: "Not a bone of his will be broken," 37 and, again another scripture says: "They will look on the one whom they have pierced." (John 19:35-37)

Reflecting and Thinking

The man in our selected textual reading is unidentified. Perhaps John is referring to himself. Perhaps he refers to another disciple who could serve as a reliable witness. What matters is not who the witness is, but who Jesus is. The testimony reaches its climax in Jesus' death. The testimony is certain: these things are true. The foundations for belief are established. Scripture is fulfilled.

Is faith easy for you or is it hard? Does the testimony of the Bible carry sufficient weight with you, or do you often wish for something more? Can you figure out the "why" of these first two questions? John writes so that people will believe. He writes so that people will have faith, and thus have life. How can we develop faith based on John's gospel?

Prayer

Heavenly Father, we barely understand the cruelty, pain, and suffering of crucifixion. We marvel at the immensity and complexity of your plan. We do not understand, but we accept by faith, because of who Jesus is. Increase our faith and trust. We pray in Jesus' name, Amen.

John 20: Faith When One Does Not See

Selected Biblical Text

24 Now Thomas (also called Didymus), one of the Twelve, was not with them when Jesus came. 25 Then the other disciples told him: "We have seen the Lord." But he said to them: "Unless I see in his hands the wounds of the nails and put my finger into the wound of the nails, and put my hand into his side, I will not believe."
26 A week later his disciples were again in the house and Thomas was with them. Even though the doors were locked, Jesus came and stood among them and said: "Peace be with you!" 27 Then he said to Thomas: "Put your finger here; look carefully at my hands. Reach out your hand and put it into my side. Quit your unbelief and believe."
28 Thomas said to him: "My Lord and my God."
29 Then Jesus said: "Because you have seen me, you have believed; blessed are those who have not seen and yet believe."
30 Jesus did many other miraculous signs in the presence of the disciples, which are not recorded in this book. 31 But these have been written so that you may believe that Jesus is the Christ, the Son of God, and so that in believing you may have life in his name. (John 20:24-31)

Reflecting and Thinking

Has Thomas gotten a bad rap? What do you think? It is true that he was not present at that first Sunday night meeting. It is true that he wanted personal proof -- that he wanted to see for himself. But after all, isn't that what the other apostles had received? Hadn't they seen for themselves? Jesus himself talks about the difficulty of faith, and he blesses those who do not see and yet believe. In one sense, I would like to think he is talking about me. I have not personally seen. I depend on testimony and witnesses, historical accounts and things written. Perhaps I can be blessed for believing!

When have you believed something you have not seen? (For example, what major world city have you not visited, yet you believe such a city exists. You can develop a long list of things you believe even though you have not seen and do not have firsthand proof.) Is seeing always believing? What aspect of Jesus would you most like to see or experience firsthand?

Prayer
Heavenly Father, bless us in our faith journey as we contemplate the road that we have traveled by hearing the story of Jesus afresh through the eyes and pen of John. Help us believe that Jesus is the Christ, the Son of God. Help us have life through that faith. In His name, Amen.

John 21: Faithful Living in a Post-Resurrection World

Selected Biblical Text
24 This is the disciple who testifies to these things and has written these things. We know that his testimony is true. 25 There are also many other things which Jesus did. If every one of them were written, I suppose the whole world would not have room for the books that would be written. (John 21:24-25)

Reflecting and Thinking
Have you considered that the world after the resurrection of Jesus was significantly different than the world that existed before? Have you considered all that Jesus' resurrection makes possible? Have you thought about what can be known after the resurrection that could not be known with certainty prior to the resurrection? Some think John 21 stands as a complete unit -- an epilogue that is disconnected from what precedes it. Others have observed that the final chapter is introduced by the well-known text of 20:30-31.

I like to think that John 21 as an overview or summary of the Gospel of John. Consider these lessons.

* First, Jesus meets our needs; he is interested in our needs. He is the Word who became flesh and dwelt among us, experiencing our life with its hurts and sorrows.
* Second, Jesus is interested in the success of his disciples as they return to fishing. He interacts with them in the present moment of their lives.

Jesus does the same for us. He is interested in our spiritual life; he is interested in our life in this world.

- Third, Jesus reinstates us, forgives us, and blesses us with real forgiveness. The story of Peter's reinstatement is not for Peter only. It is our story. It is the reflection of our sometimes-misdirected love, our twisted priorities, and our self-doubts. Our response is to accept his forgiveness and pardon.
- Fourth, Jesus walks beside us; he is present in our lives. The invitation of Jesus is repeated: Follow me. Jesus still wants us as followers, even after our failures and frustrations. Jesus is willing to work in our lives to complete his purpose.

Reflect on the journey you have taken through the Gospel of John. What were the high points? What things have you remembered as most helpful? What identity of Jesus most catches your attention? Which identity does John focus on most? How would you summarize the main message of this gospel?

Prayer

Dear God, thank you for showing us our possibilities. Thank you for being there, providing our needs, being aware of our weaknesses, forgiving us, reaffirming us, and working through us. Through the name of Jesus who has made our faith possible, Amen.

1 John 1: A Sure Message of Hope

Selected Biblical Text

5 This is the message that we have heard from him and proclaim to you, that God is light, and in him is no darkness at all. 6 If we say we have fellowship with him while we walk in darkness, we lie and do not practice the truth. 7 But if we walk in the light, as he is in the light, we have fellowship with one another, and the blood of Jesus his Son cleanses us from every sin. (1 John 1:5-7)

Reflecting and Thinking

Some people have turned the good news into bad news. A word of hope has become a word of doom; a word of forgiveness a word that speaks failure. A word of certainty has become unsure. The message must be restored. Christian living depends on understanding the message (truth) and practicing it. Our certain hope is that Jesus' blood cleanses us and keeps on cleansing us from all sin.

How often do we try to deserve forgiveness? How often we try to earn it, merit it, and guarantee it? Have you ever struggled with the certainty of forgiveness? When do you feel least forgiven? When has forgiveness felt certain? Why? Meditate for a moment on the message of this chapter: When Jesus who is the light (remember John's Gospel) walks beside us, it is certain that we also walk in light, and that we have fellowship and forgiveness.

Prayer

Father God, help us find certainty in this world of doubt. Let us confidently affirm the truth that is Jesus. Walk beside us and help us know and accept truth, so that we may we celebrate the continual cleansing of Christ's blood. In Jesus' name and by his power I ask it, Amen.

1 John 2: Knowing How to Live

Selected Biblical Text

3 And by this we know that we have come to know him, if we keep his commandments. 4 The one who says, I have come to know him, while not keeping his commandments, is a liar, and the truth is not in him, 5 but whoever keeps his word, in him truly the love of God has been perfected. By this we know that we are in him. 6 The one who says that he abides in him ought to walk in the same way that Jesus walked. (1 John 2:3-6)

Reflecting and Thinking

We want to know. We like assurance. John writes about our assurance of forgiveness. He says that such assurance is based on Jesus' advocacy, the forgiveness of the sins of the whole world. It is evidenced by our response -- how we imitate Jesus, how we treat one another in love, how we live above the world, how we live in the anointing and knowledge of Jesus as the Christ. Not all accept this truth, but for those who do, it is a source of confidence and righteousness.

Do you ever feel uncertainty in your Christian life? Reflect on the following truths. Some uncertainty comes as a result of the tumultuous times in which we live. Some uncertainty comes from uncertain messengers, even as false teachers twisted the truth near the end of the first century. John wants believers to know assurance of salvation. This assurance depends on Jesus, not on us.

Prayer

Dearest Heavenly Father, some days are strong testimony to your presence in my life and in the world; other days are difficult at best. Be in my life to even out the emotional rollercoaster and to help me live above the world even as I live in the world. Help me walk as Jesus walked, and forgive me when I do not, in Jesus' name, Amen.

1 John 3: Children of God

Selected Biblical Text

1 See what great love the Father has given us, that we should be called children of God, which we are. This is why the world does not know us, because it did not know him. 2 Beloved, now we are children of God, and what we will be has not yet has appeared. But when it [he] appears, we will be like him, because we will see him as he is. 3 Everyone who has this hope in him purifies himself, just as Jesus is pure. (1 John 3:1-3)

Reflecting and Thinking

Children of God. Perhaps we have heard it so often and said it so much that its uniqueness and power have been lost. Children of God -- doing what is right because he is righteous. Children of God -- loving one another as he has loved us. Children of God -- loving with actions and with words of truth. Children of God -- condemning ourselves in our weakness when God who knows our hearts would instill confidence. Children of God -- he lives in us, and we know the certainty of his life within us through the Spirit he gave us.

Wow! The evidences that we are children are numerous and strong. We may not give them much weight -- we tend to measure life by a different, human standard. God says life can be measured by our clean break with sin, our love, and our compassionate sharing. Focusing on us is discouraging and condemning. Focusing on him is cleansing and brings confidence. Children learn to imitate their parents by watching them closely. Identify and commit to two or three things (at least one!) that you can do today to focus on your status as a child of God.

Prayer

Dear God, we cherish the exalted position you have made possible for us, that we can be your children. Some days we do not feel the closeness of relationship with you, and we do not live out the reality of that relationship. Thank you for your constant, forgiving presence made certain by your Spirit. In Jesus' name, Amen.

1 John 4: Prove It!

Selected Biblical Text

4 You are from God, dear children, and have overcome them, because greater is the one in you than the one in the world. 5 They are of the world; therefore, they speak from the viewpoint of the world, and the world listens to them. 6 We are from God, the one who knows God listens to us; whoever is not from God does not listen to us. By this we know the spirit of truth and the spirit of deceit. (1 John 4:4-6)

Reflecting and Thinking

Even young children understand the principle. Someone makes a claim, and the group echoes back, "Prove it!" John gives us a series of tests by which we prove truth. You can recognize God's Spirit and know which spirits are not from God by listening to what is said about Jesus. You can recognize and distinguish truth and falsehood by noticing who pays attention to which claim -- the world only listens to those who speak according to the ways of the world. You can understand genuine love by contemplating what it means that God sent his Son among us. You can know your relationship with him through his Spirit. You can know, and you can respond.

Truth is easily spoken, easily forgotten. We love because he loved us. We would not know what love is without having witnessed it in the actions of God. Only one response is possible -- I will love him as he has loved me. My love for him so changes me that I cannot love God and at the same time hate his creation (my brother). Is it possible to love your brother without first loving God? What can you do today to reflect your love for God?

Prayer

Father God, help me overcome the world with its claims, its message, its values, and its actions. I believe you are greater than that which surrounds me, but I sometimes have trouble fighting through the surroundings to see you and depend on you. Thank you for the reminder that truth can be recognized and is knowable. Thank you for the proofs that overcome all my fears. In the name of Jesus who is the Christ, the ultimate proof, Amen.

❖   ❖   ❖

1 John 5: Confident of Eternal Life

Selected Biblical Text

13 These things I have written to you, the ones who believe in the name of the Son of God, so that you may know that you have eternal life. 14 And this is the confidence we have before him: if we ask anything according to his will, he hears us. (1 John 5:13-14)

Reflecting and Thinking

Faith in the Son of God is powerful -- loving God, carrying out his commands, obeying, enjoying freedom from burdensome rules, overcoming the world. Faith overcomes the world! God does not leave us on our own to figure out the faith or no faith options. His testimony is greater, dependable, and secure. God gives eternal life in his Son. We see life, and we recognize the Son of God who is life.

Eternity is a long time. Eternal life is unbelievable, whether one thinks of quantity (length), quality, or both. Long ago John wrote a message that is still needed today – "so that we might know that we have eternal life." John's message of certain hope grows out of the gospel. The message empowers our lifestyles, identifies us as children of God, and provides certain proofs by which we can know about Jesus, life, and our future. Spend some time today contemplating the connection between your belief and your future eternal life.

Prayer

Heavenly Father, we marvel at the way you address our weaknesses. Without doubt, one of our problem areas is lack of confidence. Frankly, we know ourselves well, and we worry whether the reality is what we see in our daily lives or what you promise as our potential in you. Thank you for confidence -- in assurance of salvation, and in the ability to approach you according to your will so that you hear us. Bring us closer to you today, through Jesus we offer this prayer, Amen.

2 John: Joy and Watchfulness

Selected Biblical Text

4 I rejoiced greatly that I have found some of your children walking in truth.... 8 Watch out for yourselves, that you do not lose what we have worked for, but that you receive a full reward.... 12 Having many other things to write to you, I do not want to write with paper and ink, but I hope to come to you and speak face to face, so that our joy may be completed. (2 John 4, 8, 12)

Reflecting and Thinking

The two short one-chapter letters of John give a hint as to why the General Letters are called general. Probably written to a specific church, the letter touches a variety of topics. Two of my favorites are joy and hope. John rejoices when others succeed spiritually. He urges caution in securing the future and considers his relationship with his readers a special joy.

When have you rejoiced in the success of another person? When has the cause of your rejoicing been spiritual? What would it mean for you to be watchful so that you do not lose what you have worked for? What have you accomplished that you could lose? To whom would you say the words of verse 12? Why not contact that person or persons today -- by phone, email, or in person!

Prayer

Father God, it is easy for us to lose track of the things that matter in our busy world. It is easy for us to miss the things that really matter. We misplace our priorities and misuse our time. Help us to relish spiritual things. Help us as we seek faith and watch diligently. Bind us together with other Christians in your great love. We pray these things in the name of Jesus, Amen.

3 John: Joy and Faithfulness

Selected Biblical Text

3 For I rejoiced greatly when the brothers came and testified in truth about you, just as you walk in truth. 4 I have no joy greater than this, that I hear that my children are walking in the truth. (3 John 3-4)

Reflecting and Thinking

The third letter of John was written to a Christian named Gaius, probably a convert of John, based on the information we have. That Gaius is faithfully following Christ was a source of great joy for John. Rejoicing when others continue as faithful servants is not just for those we know -- we can love and serve those we do not know. The servant spirit is essential, but in some places, it is far from alive and well. In fact, John was concerned about a Christian named Diotrephes who appears to be the opposite of Gaius. Diotrephes was malicious, a gossiper, an isolationist, a bossy controller, and an opponent of good works. Evil can be recognized, as can good. John urges Gaius to imitate what is good.

Thinking about the relationship between Gaius and John, if you are Gaius, who is your John? Have you said "thank you" lately? How could you be a more faithful servant to other Christians? What does it mean in your life to walk in truth?

Prayer

Dear Father, help us connect joy and faithfulness in our lives. Sometimes the world tells us that joy comes from other sources. The connection between joy and faithfulness sometimes seems weak. Strengthen our commitment to good and help us avoid evil. May our lives evidence that we are yours, we pray in Jesus' name, Amen.

Revelation 1: The Alpha and the Omega -- The First and the Last

Selected Biblical Text

8 I am the Alpha and the Omega, says the Lord God, the one who is, and who was and who is to come, the Almighty.

12 I turned around to see the voice that was speaking to me. And when I turned, I saw seven golden lampstands, 13 and in the midst of the lampstands was one like a son of man, dressed in a robe reaching down to his feet and girded with a golden sash around his chest. 14 His head and hair were white like wool, as white as snow, and his eyes were like a blazing flame of fire. 15 His feet were like lustrous bronze refined in a furnace, and his voice was like the sound of many waters. 16 In his right hand he held seven stars, and from his mouth extended a sharp, double-edged sword. His face was like the sun shining in full strength.

17 When I saw him, I fell at his feet as though dead and he placed his right hand on me and said, do not be afraid. I am the first and the last. 18 I am the one who lives; I was dead, and look, I am alive forever and ever. I hold the keys of death and hades. 19 Therefore write what you saw, both [and] what is now and what will happen after these things. 20 The mystery of the seven stars that you saw in my right hand and of the seven golden lampstands: the seven stars are the messengers of the seven churches, and the seven lampstands are the seven churches. (Rev. 1:8, 12-20)

Reflecting and Thinking

We must not spend much time in introductory comments, but it should be noted that the book of Revelation belongs to a literary genre known as apocalyptic literature. Because the characteristics of apocalyptic literature should be kept in mind as one reads Revelation, some of those characteristics will be noted from time to time in the reflections.

The introduction or prologue to the vision introduces us to Jesus, one like a Son of Man. The book reflects the word of God and the testimony (witness) of Jesus Christ. "Witness" is an important theme in Revelation. The doxology of 1:8 gives praise to God -- the one who was, who is, and who is to come. Revelation was written to first-century churches to encourage them. One way to summarize the message of the first three chapters of Revelation is that Christ is walking among the persecuted churches to comfort the persecuted Christians.

John is told to write "what you have seen, what is now and what will take place later" (1:19). This may be a past-present-future reference, but grammatically and contextually, it is more likely an appositive construction. The meaning is this: "Write what you have seen—both what currently is and what will soon take place."

What New Testament descriptions of Jesus are most impressive to you? What is the reader to learn from the first part of the vision that John receives? Make a list of all of the descriptions of Jesus in Chapter 1. What truths are being communicated about Jesus?

Prayer

Father God, as we begin this reading of the book of Revelation, we ask your guidance and insight. We want to understand the message you have for us. We want to hear you speak about things that matter to us every day, just as this book provided a word of comfort and encouragement to first-century readers. In Jesus' name and by his power we ask your presence in our study, Amen.

Revelation 2: Understanding the Patterns in Revelation --
The Letters to the Churches

Selected Biblical Text

1 To the angel of the church in Ephesus write: These things he says, the one who holds the seven stars in his right hand, the one who walks in the midst of the seven golden lampstands. 2 I know your works, your labor and your perseverance, and that you cannot endure evil people; you have tested those who claim to be apostles but are not and have found them false. 3 You have persevered and endured for my name and have not grown weary.

4 But I have this against you, that from your love, the first love, you have departed. 5 Remember from where you have fallen, repent and do the first works. If not, I will come to you and remove your lampstand from its place. 6 But you have this one thing: you hate the works of the Nicolaitans, which works I also hate.

7 The one who has an ear, let him hear what the Spirit says to the churches. To the one who conquers, I will give to him [the right] to eat from the tree of life, which is in the paradise of God. (Rev. 2:1-7)

Reflecting and Thinking

The letters to the churches (Revelation 2-3) follow a general pattern. The elements of the pattern are not always in the same order, but the letters to the churches include at least the following five items: (1) what Jesus knows about the church, (2) a reference to their work and attitude toward the word of God, (3) a summary of their current "life situation," (4) an admonition to continue faithfully, and (5) a promise to those who overcome.

In the same way that the letters to the churches have a pattern, the book of Revelation also follows a pattern. This pattern can be seen in the groups of seven seals, seven trumpets, and seven plagues. Each of these follows a pattern of "6 + additional information + 1." (Some scholars identify the additional information as an interlude or pause; others identify it as part of the sixth item.) The patterns and the parallel constructions suggest a possible chiastic structure for the book. This will be explained later.

Let us review what we know thus far. In Chapters 2 and 3, Christ is walking among and present with the persecuted churches, sending similar messages to each through the designated messengers.

What would you want God to say to you during difficult times? How and why would the messages of Chapter 2 be helpful to the churches? How would these messages provide comfort? What parts of the messages are surprising to you?

See if you can find the five items mentioned above in each of the letters in Chapter 2.

Prayer

Dear God, we are grateful that you know our situation and circumstances. We are glad to know that you understand our situation -- even when we have failed and gotten there through our own weaknesses. Guide us in your ways and help us overcome the challenges before us so that we will live faithfully. Thank you for your provision and promise for those things we cannot do for ourselves, through Jesus we pray, Amen.

Revelation 3: Promises to the One that Overcomes

Selected Biblical Text

5 The one who conquers will be dressed the same way in white clothing, I will never wipe out his name from the book of life but will confess his name before my Father and before his angels. 6 The one who has an ear, let him hear what the Spirit says to the churches.

12 The one who conquers I will make a pillar in the temple of my God, and he will never leave it anymore. I will write upon him the name of my God, and the name of the city of my God, the new Jerusalem, which is coming down out of heaven from my God, and my new name. 13 The one who has an ear, let him hear what the Spirit says to the churches.

21 To the one who conquers I will give [the right] to sit with me on my throne, just as I was also conquered and sat down with my Father on his throne. 22 The one who has an ear, let him hear what the Spirit says to the churches. (Rev. 3:5-6, 12-13, 21-22)

Reflecting and Thinking

Today's chapter contains the letters to the churches in Sardis, Philadelphia, and Laodicea. The selected reading includes the "overcoming promises" from these three letters, promises which have parallels in the other four letters of Revelation 2 and 3. As we read the various promises to the one that overcomes, we should ask ourselves about the meaning of the promises and the phrases used. Remember how we summarized the message of these letters: Christ is walking alongside his persecuted church. Christ controls the ultimate outcome. Victory is possible. Even in difficult days, the power of the opponents is not insurmountable.

Why are we Christians not more confident of our power to overcome? What obstacles stand in your way when you want to be positive in the midst of problems? How do you think the seven churches would have received the letters of Chapters 2-3? Do you think they were comforted, encouraged, reprimanded, motivated....? What words would you use to describe their thoughts and feelings as they received these letters?

Prayer

Dear God, give us the courage and faith to stand firm in difficult situations. The dangers are as real today as they were twenty-one centuries ago. We need Jesus' presence as he walks alongside his church. Help us grasp the reality of his presence, in Jesus' name, Amen.

Revelation 4: The Throne Room of Heaven (1) -- Holy, Holy, Holy God

Selected Biblical Text

8 Each one of the four living creatures had six wings and was full of eyes all around and within. Day and night, they never rest, saying: "Holy, holy, holy, is the Lord God Almighty, who was, and is, and is to come."
9 And whenever the living creatures give glory, honor and thanks to the one seated on the throne, the one who lives forever and ever, 10 the twenty-four elders fall down before the one seated on the throne and worship the one who lives forever and ever. They cast their crowns before the throne, saying: 11 "You are worthy, our Lord and God, to receive glory and honor and power, because you created all things, and by your will they exist and were created." (Rev 4:8-11)

Reflecting and Thinking

After the introduction (Chapter 1) and the letters to the seven churches (Chapters 2-3), the vision of Chapters 4-5 gives us a change of scenery and entrée to the throne room of heaven. The writer tells us that the purpose of this view of heaven is to make clear what is going to take place. We should note that God was on his throne even when the church was experiencing difficulties and persecution. His authority, power, glory and honor were in place and secure. God's deity does not waver. He is holy God, sitting on his throne and receiving worship.

This is a good time to note the initial parallel elements in a possible chiastic structure of Revelation. First, the prologue of Chapter 1 is paralleled by the epilogue of Chapter 22. Second, Christ walking with his persecuted church (Chapters 2-3) finds a parallel in Christ walking with his victorious church (Chapters 21-22). Third, the initial heavenly scene (Chapters 4-5) has a parallel in the heavenly scene of Chapters 19-20. More chiastic parallels will be noted in future devotional readings.

Why do we sometimes think that God has abdicated his throne, or at least given some part of his power to other forces? How can we reconcile the presence of problems in our world and the continuing control and love of God? How do you think you would personally respond if you were to have a vision such as this one? What would be your response if you were able to peer into the throne room of God?

Prayer

Heavenly Father, we praise you and worship you in your holiness, splendor and grandeur. We give you glory, honor and gratitude. We declare that you are worthy, and we ask you to strengthen our faith. In the name of Christ, the Lamb, Amen.

Revelation 5: The Throne Room of Heaven (2) --
The Lamb Is Worthy to Open the Scrolls

Selected Biblical Text

6 Then I saw in the middle of the throne and of the four living creatures, and in the middle of the elders, a Lamb, that appeared to have been slain. He had seven horns and seven eyes, which are the seven spirits of God sent out into all the earth. 7 Then he went and took the scroll from the right hand of the one seated on the throne, 8 and when he had taken the scroll, the four living creatures and the twenty-four elders fell down before the Lamb. Each one had a harp and golden bowls full of incense, which are the prayers of the saints. 9 And they sang a new song, saying: "You are worthy to take the scroll and to open its seals, because you were slain, and with your blood you purchased for God persons from every tribe and language and people and nation, 10 and you made them for our God to be a kingdom and priests, and they will reign on the earth."

11 Then I looked and heard the voice of many angels all around the throne and the living creature and the elders, and the number of them was thousands of thousands, and ten thousands of ten thousands, 12 saying in a loud voice: "Worthy is the Lamb who was slain, to receive power and wealth and wisdom and might and honor and glory and praise."

13 Then I heard every creature in heaven and on earth and under the earth and in the sea, and all that is in them, saying: "To the one seated on the throne and to the Lamb be praise and honor and glory and power, forever and ever." 14 And the four living creatures were saying: "Amen," and the elders fell down and worshiped. (Rev. 5:6-14)

Reflecting and Thinking

The continuation of the vision of the heavenly scene introduces us to the Lamb who is worthy to open the seals of the scroll. This is the first of two scrolls that are mentioned in the book. John hears a lion and sees a lamb. The Lamb refers to Jesus. Opening the seals indicates control of the events represented by the contents of the scroll. The contents of this first scroll are revealed in Chapters 6-11.

The opening of the seals reveals historical events or realities, but the descriptions are general rather than specific. The events are not necessarily or obviously sequential. When we read about the seals in the next chapters, we will be reminded of the "6 + additional information + 1" pattern that characterizes the groupings of "seven."

For today, let us enjoy the beautiful description of the Lamb. Through the eye of faith, try to envision the scene being described. Hear the songs of praise and worship. Soak up the fact that all the earth declares his praise, and that even heaven worships the Lamb.

What does it mean to you that Jesus controls the events of this world? When does it appear that he may not be in control? How do you explain his "control" when things seem out of control? What aspects of the worship scene are most impressive to you?

Prayer

Heavenly Father, help us see the Lamb afresh as we read today's biblical text. Generate in us hearts of praise and worship as we see and understand. We stand in awe at such unbridled majesty; we join the thousands and millions to declare his power and riches and wisdom and strength and honor and glory and praise. We give thanks that we can approach you through Jesus, Amen.

Revelation 6: The First Scroll Revealed --
Historical Overview, Six Seals Opened

Selected Biblical Text

1 Now I watched as the Lamb opened one of the seven seals, and I heard one of the four living creatures saying with a voice like thunder, Come. 2 And I looked, and there was a white horse, and the one seated on it had a bow, and he was given a crown, and he went forth, conquering and to conquer.

3 Now when the Lamb opened the second seal, I heard the second living creature saying, Come. 4 Then another horse, fiery red, came out, and to the one seated on it was given power to take peace from the earth and to make people kill each other, and to him was given a large sword. 5 Now when the Lamb opened the third seal,

I heard the third living creature saying, Come. I looked and there was a black horse, and the one seated on it had a balance scale in his hand....

7 When the Lamb opened the fourth seal, I heard the voice of the fourth living creature saying, Come. 8 I looked and there was a pale green horse, and the name of the one seated upon was Death, and Hades was following right behind him....

9 When he opened the fifth seal, I saw under the altar the souls of those who had been slain because of the word of God and the witness they had....

12 Then I watched as he opened the sixth seal, and there was a great earthquake.... (Rev. 6:1-5, 7-9, 12)

Reflecting and Thinking

In today's chapter, the first six seals are opened. Remember that the Lamb controls the contents of the scroll as he opens the seals. The four horses with riders represent conquest, war, famine, and death. The descriptions are general and not specific. The message of assurance for the first-century readers was that when these occur, God is on his throne and the Lamb is in control of history.

The fifth seal reveals souls under the altar—those who have died for their witness, and the sixth seal reveals an earthquake. Since we are reading apocalyptic literature, we expect the use of symbols. We must not be content to describe what we see in the vision. We must also ask, "What do the symbols mean?" The souls under the altar and the earthquake are representations—what do they represent? What is the message?

Is there a message other than that God is in control? Is God still God when his people die for their faith? Can God work his will through the death of martyrs? Do natural disasters mean that God has turned his back on his people? Can natural events ever be evidence of the wrath of God and the wrath of the Lamb? What events in history have caused people to think about the existence of God, either to doubt or to affirm the existence of God (for example, the Holocaust)? What difference does it make whether we take a long view or a short view of history? What if we are called to live our entire lives in one of the "faith valleys" of history where Christianity is under attack? What difference would the message of today's reading have made for first-century readers?

Prayer

Father God, help us see your presence in the world about us, both in good times and bad times, blessings and difficulties. May we follow faithfully regardless of the circumstances in which we are called to live -- regardless of the historical times in which we are born. Thank you for the assurance that you are working all things toward your ultimate goals and ends. In Jesus' name and by his power we ask these things, Amen.

Revelation 7: A Message of Protection and Deliverance --
144,000 Sealed and a Great Multitude in Heaven

Selected Biblical Text

1 After this I saw four angels standing at the four corners of the earth, holding back the four winds of the earth so no wind would blow on the land or on the sea or on any tree. 2 Then I saw another angel coming up from the east, having the seal of the living God. He called out in a loud voice to the four angels to whom power had been given to harm the land and the sea, 3 Do not harm the land or the sea or the trees until we have sealed the servants of our God on their foreheads. 4 Then I heard the number of those who were sealed: 144,000 from all the tribes of Israel.... 9 After these things I looked, and there was a great multitude that no one was able to count, from every nation, tribe, people and language, standing before the throne and before the Lamb, clothed in long white robes with palm branches in their hands. 10 And they cried out in a loud voice, saying: "Salvation belongs to our God, to the one seated on the throne, and to the Lamb." 14 ..."These are they who have come out of the great affliction; they have washed their robes and made them white in the blood of the Lamb. (Rev. 7:1-4, 9-10, 14)

Reflecting and Thinking

The sixth seal was opened at the end of Chapter 6. In today's chapter we learn what occurs after the earthquake of the sixth seal and before the opening of the seventh seal. Remember the "6 + additional information + 1" pattern that we previously noted. The seventh seal (Chapter 8) will usher in seven trumpets which will also follow the "6 + additional information + 1" pattern.

In Chapter 7, we read two descriptions of God's people -- the 144,000 and a great multitude who have come through a great affliction (Greek, *thlipsis*). There are five occurrences of this word in Revelation (see 1:9; 2:9, 10, 22). The "additional information" in Chapter 7 reveals that the servants of God are given a seal of protection. God's faithful will not be subject to the harm that is coming. All of God's faithful are sealed. John hears the number of those sealed – 144,000, but he sees a great multitude (as he heard a lion and saw a lamb in 5:5-6). The number 12 represents the people of God, 1000 magnifies the number to completeness, 12 x 12 x 1000 = 144,000. The number is symbolic not literal. Then John sees those who have endured affliction and have been delivered; they are now in the presence of the Lamb. Some scholars suggest the two descriptions are of the same group. Some think the chapter describes both the situation and events on earth (with God's people protected, represented by the 144,000) and in heaven (where a great multitude is before the throne of God).

The great multitude is of "every nation, tribe, people, and language." This phrase also appears in 5:9, 7:9, 11:9, 13:7, and 14:6, with similar wording in 10:11 and 17:15. What do these parallel verses suggest about the great multitude? Does God deliver and protect his people today? Is God's protection at times unseen? What is the purpose of sealing God's people in this chapter? What is the significance of the seven characteristics mentioned in worship (v. 12)?

Prayer

Dear God, we praise you for your salvation power, and we confidently affirm that you yet sit on your throne. Protect us and deliver us as we live for you, we pray in Jesus' name, Amen.

Revelation 8: The Seventh Seal Introduces Trumpets of Judgment -- The First Four Trumpets

Selected Biblical Text

1 Now when he opened the seventh seal, there was silence in heaven for about half an hour. 2 And I saw the seven angels who stand before God, and seven trumpets were given to them.
3 Another angel with a golden censer came and stood at the altar. He was given much incense to offer, with the prayers of all the saints, on the golden altar before the throne. 4 The smoke of the incense, with the prayers of the saints, went up before God from the hand of the angel. 5 Then the angel took the censer, filled it with fire from the altar, and threw it on the earth; and there were peals of thunder, rumblings, flashes of lightning and an earthquake. 6 Then the seven angels who had the seven trumpets prepared to blow them. (Rev. 8:1-6)

Reflecting and Thinking

The opening of the seventh seal ushers in seven trumpets (remember the pattern: "6 + additional information + 1"). Clearly, the trumpets communicate God's judgment. Chapter 8 describes the events that accompany the first four trumpets. The trumpets should be remembered, for the same sequence of judgments will appear again in the bowls of wrath, impacting (1) the earth or land, (2) the sea, (3) the rivers and waters, (4) the heavenly bodies, (5) the seat of Satan, and (6) the Euphrates.

A review will be helpful. What have we seen? The heavenly vision reveals that God is on the throne and the Lamb is in control of history (Chapters 4-5). The history revealed in the first six seals is controlled by the Lamb as he opens the seals (Chapter 6) -- a history of conquest, war, want, and death, a history of persecution and God's limited judgment. Then God's servants are sealed (protected) and a great multitude that has already experienced affliction (often translated as "tribulation") is seen before God's throne.

In Chapter 8, the opening of the seventh seal finalizes the judgment of God that was described in the sixth seal, introducing a sequence of the trumpets that pronounces judgment on the earth, sea, waters, sky, and evil forces from the abyss, capped by calling angels from the Euphrates (a reference which introduces good forces from the East). These six trumpets are eventually followed by the seventh trumpet of victory (Chapter 11).

The judgment of the trumpets is not total; notice the smaller fractions. This judgment is partial or limited, perhaps allowing time for repentance. The sad commentary after the sixth trumpet sounds (9:20-21) is that those not affected by the plagues still did not repent.

How does God come in judgment on the world today? Since these descriptions occur in symbolic apocalyptic literature (containing figurative language), how should one apply these symbolic concepts to our world today? How do they apply to our Christian lives at the beginning of the 21st century? Do these judgments come upon everyone, or are some protected (note in the text the references to the inhabitants of the earth and those whom God is protecting)?

Prayer

Dear God, we wish that all would turn to you and accept salvation in Christ, but we understand that such will never be, not because of any weakness or incapacity on your part, not because of the impotence of the gospel, but because of the nature of our world and the human condition. We pray for your continued protection, guidance, and strength. Help us share the good news that delivers from judgment. Help us listen and learn. In Jesus' name, Amen.

Revelation 9: The Seventh Seal Continues --
Two More Trumpets of Judgment

Selected Biblical Text

20 And the rest of humanity, who were not killed by these plagues, still did not repent of the works of their hands; they did not stop worshiping demons and idols made of gold, silver, bronze, stone and wood, idols that cannot see or hear or walk. 21 Nor did they repent of their murders, their magic, their sexual immorality or their stealing. (Rev. 9:20-21)

Reflecting and Thinking

The description of the fifth and sixth trumpets of God's judgment sets forth the work of the forces of evil as well as the work of the forces of good. The forces of evil work against the good of mankind but cannot touch those who are sealed and protected by God. The forces of good are God's instrument of judgment and kill one-third of human beings. Still the rest do not repent.

Considering the parallels between the trumpets of Chapters 8-9 and the plagues which will appear in Chapters 15-16, it is interesting to note that the activity unleashed by the sixth trumpet (9:13-19) is described as plagues in verse 20.

In an apocalyptic book, written to a people who were in distressing circumstances near the end of the first century, what was the meaning these figurative representations? What was the message for them? What is the message for us?

What would it take for people committed to evil to repent? Are some people beyond repentance? Based on the protection God provided to his people to protect them from evil (8:4), do you think God still protects his people from evil today? If God is protecting us, why are we sometimes en-trapped by evil activity and temptations?

Prayer

Dear God, we marvel that you so often withhold judgment when it is due. We are grateful for your care and protection. Help us to seek you so that Satan will flee from us. Help us to seek the ways of escape that you provide. Give us understanding as we study difficult Bible texts like the book of Revelation, we pray in Jesus' name, Amen.

Revelation 10: The Sixth Trumpet --
A Second Scroll Is Introduced

Selected Biblical Text

5 Then the angel that I saw standing on the sea and on the land raised his right hand to heaven 6 and he swore by the one who lives for ever and ever, who created heaven and what is in it, the earth and what is in it, and the sea and what is in it, "There will be no more delay, 7 but in the days when the seventh angel is about to blow his trumpet, the mystery of God will be fulfilled, just as he announced to his servants the prophets."
8 Then the voice that I heard from heaven spoke to me again: "Go take the open scroll that is in the hand of the angel who is standing on the sea and on the land."
9 So I went to the angel and asked him to give me the little scroll. He said to me: "Take it and eat it. It will make your stomach sour, but in your mouth, it will be as sweet as honey." 10 Then I took the little scroll from the angel's hand and ate it. It was as sweet as honey in my mouth, and when I had eaten it, my stomach became sour. 11 Then they told me: "You must prophesy again about many peoples, nations, languages and kings." (Rev. 10:5-11)

Reflecting and Thinking

Six trumpets sounded God's judgments in Chapters 8-9. We antici-pate the seventh trumpet, but before the seventh trumpet sounds, we again encounter a pause or interruption. (Remember the "6 + additional information + 1" pattern.) The trumpets were introduced by the opening of the seventh seal (8:1) which came after the first six seals (Chapter 6) and some additional information (Chapter 7). In Chapter 10, an open scroll is introduced and seven thunders sound. The message of the seven thunders is sealed and not revealed.

Immediately after these events comes a declaration that the delay is over, that the sounding of the seventh trumpet is near, and that God's mystery will be brought to completion. John is also told that he is to take the open scroll and eat it, after which he is told he must prophesy again. It seems likely that John's is being called to share the prophecy that was written on the open scroll. The scroll already open may indicate immediacy.

Looking ahead, Chapter 11 and the sounding of the seventh trumpet (11:15-18) would be a fitting conclusion to the book were it not for the fact that John has received a second scroll with instructions that he must prophesy again about many peoples, nations, languages and kings. Some scholars believe that the contents of the second scroll are revealed in the second part of Revelation. In this case, the outline and presentation of the contents of the second scroll may closely parallel the patterns we have seen in the first scroll. Others believe the contents of the second scroll are found in 11:1-14.

Chapter 10 is preparatory for the seventh trumpet which will also conclude the seventh seal of the first scroll (see 10:7). The preparations continue in Chapter 11 where we will be able to understand more about the significance of the information presented in Chapters 10-11.

The mystery of God (10:7) was announced by the prophets. That mystery is about to be accomplished. In the Bible, mystery often refers to something previously unknown but now revealed. That is likely the meaning here. God is in control and working toward his purpose, a purpose he was making known to the recipients of the book of Revelation. How do you feel about the truth that God is at work and in control? Do you think the first-century readers were able to accept that truth? Why or why not? Why is it significant that the second scroll is already open? What does it mean that John eats the scroll, experiencing both sour and sweet? What applications can you make to our lives today?

Prayer

Dear God, we await the ultimate accomplishment of your will in this world. We struggle and hurt, and we seek understanding. We eagerly await your return and our deliverance from this world. In the meantime, we want to be faithful witnesses for you. Strengthen us, we pray in Jesus' name, Amen.

Revelation 11: Two Witnesses Confirm God's Victory --
The Seventh Trumpet Completes the Seventh Seal of the First Scroll

Selected Biblical Text
15 Then the seventh angel blew his trumpet, and there were loud voices in heaven, saying: "The kingdom of the world has become the kingdom of our Lord and of his Christ, and he will reign forever and ever." 16 And the twenty-four elders, seated before God on their thrones, fell on their faces and worshiped God 17 saying: "We give thanks to you, Lord God Almighty, the One who is and who was, because you have taken your great power and have begun to reign. 18 The nations were angry, and your wrath has come and the time to judge the dead and to reward your servants the prophets and the saints and those who revere your name, both great and small, and to destroy those who destroy the earth."
19 Then the temple of God in heaven was opened, and the ark of the covenant was seen within his temple. And there were flashes of lightning, rumblings, peals of thunder, an earthquake and a great hailstorm. (Rev. 11:15-19)

Reflecting and Thinking
The figurative language of this chapter presents some of the most difficult symbolism we have thus far encountered in the book. Many readers of Revelation easily work through the introductory prologue and letters to the churches (Chapters 1-3). The heavenly scene that reveals God on the throne and the Lamb who can open the seals is not too troublesome (Chapters 4-5). The seals, declaring that God and the Lamb control all of history, including martyred witnesses and judgment, are more difficult (Chapter 6) but we are comforted by promises of protection and deliverance (Chapter 7). The trumpets of judgment introduced by the opening of the seventh seal present difficult details but the judgment of God against evil is comforting (Chapters 8-9). Chapters 10-11 are more challenging. We meet two witnesses, both of whom are martyred and then resurrected. What does this mean? Some of the confusion clears up when we remember that witness, martyr, and testimony are translations of only one Greek word. Witness has been an important concept in Revelation – 1:2, 5; 2:13; 3:14; 6:9.

The two witnesses in Chapter 11 testify to the power and holiness of the Lord (11:3-6). They also testify to the resurrection power of the Lord by their own resurrection and by being taken to heaven. Everything is not as it seems -- God is the God who works to reverse irreversible situations. In the face of an all-powerful God, Satan's power is limited and temporary.

The completion of the second woe (the sixth trumpet) opens the way for the final victory, but the judgment of God convinces only a few to give glory to God. Today's selected text contains the theme statement of the book: "The kingdoms of the world have become the kingdom of our Lord and of his Christ, and he reigns forever."

The book of Revelation could close, and the celebration could begin immediately were it not for John's command to prophesy again. The brief view into God's temple (11:19) reminds us of Chapters 4-5. More important is that it gives us orientation as we start down a road not unlike the road we have just traveled – a road that advances the story of God's actions in this world even further.

Spend a few minutes today thinking about your journey through the book of Revelation. Think about how God may want this story to change your life and pray about those things that come to mind.

Prayer
Dear God, help me see where and how you want me to change, and empower my life, I pray in Jesus' name, Amen.

Revelation 12: The Second Scroll -- The Rest of the Story

Selected Biblical Text
10 Then I heard a loud voice in heaven saying: "Now have come the salvation and the power and the kingdom of our God, and the authority of his Christ, because the accuser of our brothers, who accuses them before our God day and night, has been cast down. 11 And they conquered him by the blood of the Lamb and by the word of their testimony; and they loved not their lives, even to the point of death. 12 Therefore you rejoice, the heavens and those dwelling in them. Woe to the earth and the sea, because the devil has come down to you with great wrath, because he knows that he has only a short time." (Rev. 12:10-12)

Reflecting and Thinking
Today's text continues where the seventh trumpet concluded: "the kingdom of God has broken forth in the world." In one sense, Revelation 12 begins where the book of Revelation began – the second scroll retells the story of the first scroll with specific attention to Rome. The second scroll tells the "rest of the story." The second section of Revelation, beginning in Chapter 12, frequently uses symbolism and personification. In Chapters 12-13, we encounter six characters -- a woman, a man-child, Michael, the dragon or Satan (already having been judged, based on the message of the first scroll in Rev. 1-11), a sea beast, and an earth beast. The text in Rev. 12-18 has interesting parallels to the seals and trumpets (Rev. 6-11). We have already mentioned the parallel between the trumpets and the plagues.

The identity of the four persons in Chapter 12 is easy to determine, with the exception of the woman. The child is the Christ, we know Michael the archangel from other Bible passages, and the dragon is Satan. The cosmic description of the woman may represent God and his eternal purpose, perhaps symbolizing the people of God. These personages and the events described are figurative or symbolic ways of communicating God's plan, the conflict, God's protection, and God's judgment.

These ideas are reflected in today's selected poetic text. In summary, one could say that the first scroll showed the victory of God's kingdom over all opposing forces and enemies, while the purpose of the second scroll is more specific -- to show the victory of God over Rome. But that is getting ahead of ourselves and prematurely anticipating "the rest of the story."

In what sense are the appearances of the woman and the dragon "signs?" What are they signs of? How can the writer say that the things mentioned in 12:10 have already come? How would you explain that Satan continues to battle against God's people even after the cross and the resurrection of Jesus has declared his defeat? What parts of today's text are most encouraging to you?

Prayer

Dear God, we are easily discouraged as we look at the world around us and see increasing hostility toward Christianity. We easily lose sight of your work in this world, and some days we wonder how long things can continue as they are. We are grateful for your promises of deliverance and for the assurance that you are actively involved in the world as you combat evil. We are grateful that you have made it possible for us to be identified with the side of good through the death of Jesus on the cross. Keep us strong, we pray in Jesus' name, Amen.

Revelation 13: Historical Realities -- Some Oppose God

Selected Biblical Text

1 And I saw a beast coming up out of the sea, having ten horns and seven heads, and on its horns ten crowns, and on its heads a blasphemous name. 2 The beast that I saw was like a leopard, but its feet like a bear and its mouth like the mouth of a lion. The dragon gave to the beast his power and his throne and great authority. 3 One of the heads of the beast was as if it had been slaughtered to death, but the deadly wound had been healed. The whole world was amazed and followed after the beast 4 and worshiped the dragon because he had given authority to the beast, and they also worshiped the beast, saying: "Who is like the beast? Who can wage war against it?"

5 The beast was given a mouth to utter proud and blasphemous words and could exercise authority for forty-two months. 6 It opened its mouth to blaspheme God, to blaspheme his name and his dwelling, those who dwell in heaven. 7 It was given to power to wage war against the saints and to conquer them, and it was given authority over every tribe, people, language and nation, 8 and all those who live

on the earth will worship the beast, everyone whose name has not been written in the Lamb's book of life, the Lamb who was slain from the foundation of the world.... 10 This calls for patient endurance and faithfulness from the saints.
11 Then I saw another beast, coming up from the earth. It had two horns like a lamb and was speaking like a dragon. 12 It exercised all the authority of the first beast on its behalf and made the earth and those living in it worship the first beast, whose deadly wound had been healed. 13 And it performed great signs....
18 This calls for wisdom. Let the one who has insight calculate the number of the beast, for it is man's number, and his number is 666. (Rev. 13:1-8, 10, 11-13a, 18)

Reflecting and Thinking

This chapter introduces the fifth and sixth personages -- the sea beast and the earth beast. These beasts are empowered by and are instruments of the dragon, Satan. As such, they represent evil forces, most likely political Rome and religious Rome. Their presence calls for "endurance and faithfulness" and "wisdom." Endurance and faithfulness are required when political forces demand emperor worship and enforce their demands with God-like powers. Wisdom is required when false religions entice and tempt toward syncretism.

Translation note: in today's selected text (verse 18), I have translated generically, "the number of man," that is "man's number." The number 666 most likely refers to human beings as less than perfect, less than 777. In another document from the same historical timeframe, Christ is referred to as 888. Even if one understands the 666 number as a specific application to a certain individual, a major point of the text is the application to all human beings, thus the "number of [a] man" more accurately means "the number of any or every man."

What parallels to the two beasts do you see in the world today? What political or religious forces work against Christians today? How could we apply this text in our daily lives? When are we called upon to endure in faithfulness? What things in our lives require wisdom?

Prayer

Dear God, we rejoice that you are able to defeat all enemies, and we confidently affirm that truth even when it appears that evil is winning. Help us persevere and give us wisdom. Help us understand the principles communicated in this text even when we do not understand every detail. We pray in Jesus' name, Amen.

Revelation 14: God Controls --
144,000 in Heaven and Warnings and Judgment on Earth

Selected Biblical Text

1 Then I looked, and there was the Lamb, standing on Mount Zion, and with him 144,000 who had his name and his Father's name written on their foreheads. 2 And I heard a voice from heaven like a voice of many waters and like a strong thunder. The voice which I heard was like that of harpists playing their harps. 3 And the 144,000 are singing a new song before the throne and before the four living creatures and the elders. No one could learn the song except the 144,000 who had been redeemed from the earth.

6 Then I saw another angel flying high in the air, and he had the eternal gospel to proclaim to those who remain on the earth, to every nation, tribe, language and people....

8 A second angel followed, saying: "Fallen, fallen is Babylon the great city, which made all the nations drink from the wine of her sexually immoral passion."

9 A third angel followed them, saying in a loud voice: "If anyone worships the beast and its image and receives its mark on their forehead or on their hand, 10 that person will drink the wine of God's anger, which has been poured undiluted into the cup of his wrath, and will be tormented with fire and sulfur in front of the holy angels and in front of the Lamb. 11 And the smoke of their torment will go up forever and ever, and those who worship the beast and its image will have no rest day or night, and anyone who receives the mark of its name." 12 This calls for patient endurance from the saints, those who keep the commands of God and the faith of Jesus....

14 I looked, and there was a white cloud, and seated on the cloud one like a son of man, having on his head a crown of gold on his head and in his hand a sharp sickle. 15 Then another angel came out of the temple, calling in a loud voice to him who was sitting on the cloud: "Put forth your sickle and reap because the time to reap has come, for the harvest of the earth is ripe." 16 So the one seated on the cloud put forth his sickle upon the earth, and the earth was harvested. 17 And another angel came out of the temple in heaven, also having a sharp sickle. 18 And another angel, being in charge of the fire, came from the altar and called in a loud voice to him [the angel] who had the sharp sickle: "Put forth your sharp sickle and gather the clusters of grapes from the vine of the earth, because its grapes are ripe." (Rev. 14:1-3, 6, 8-12, 14-18, selected verses)

Reflecting and Thinking

Today's text presents several elements from the previous pauses. Especially notable are parallels to the information which followed the sixth seal. (To help you get a better grasp on the book of Revelation, this would be a good day to read the entire chapter in your own Bible if time permits.)

In Chapter 7, we read about 144,000 who were sealed or protected and a great multitude in heaven who had endured affliction. Today we again meet 144,000. This time they are in heaven having been redeemed from the earth. Three angels (verses 6-12) show us the gospel which is being proclaimed as broadly as the authority of the sea beast (cf. 13:7), the fall of Babylon, and judgment against the beasts (which again calls for endurance among God's people). Afterward three angels support the work of one like a son of man, one who is sitting on a cloud as an indication of authority, to harvest the earth. The judgment of the earth is near.

While some of the symbols in this section of Revelation are difficult to interpret, based on the reflections, thoughts, and comments in this devotional series, what do you understand to be the basic message? Who is in control? Whose purpose and will are being fulfilled on earth today? Whose purpose and will are being fulfilled in your life?

Prayer

Dear God, help us live by faith and believe the outcomes you have promised. We pray in Jesus' name, Amen.

Revelation 15: The Seven Plagues Introduced

Selected Biblical Text

1 Then I saw in heaven another great and marvelous sign: seven angels having the final seven plagues, final because with them God's wrath is completed. 2 And I saw something like a sea of glass mixed with fire, and those who had conquered the beast and its image and the number of its name standing on the sea of glass having the harps of God, 3 and they sang the song of Moses the servant of God and the song of the Lamb, saying: "Great and marvelous are your deeds, Lord God Almighty. Just and true are your ways, King of the nations. 4 Who will not fear you, Lord, and glorify your name? For you alone are holy. All nations will come and worship before you, for your righteous acts have been revealed."
5 After these things I looked and the temple, the dwelling place of the covenant, was opened in heaven, 6 and seven angels came out of the temple, with the seven plagues. They were dressed in clean, shining linen and wore golden sashes around their chests. 7 Then one of the four living creatures gave to the seven angels seven golden bowls filled with the wrath of God who lives forever and ever. 8 And the temple was filled with smoke from the glory of God and from his power, and no one could enter the temple until the seven plagues of the seven angels were completed. (Revelation 15)

Reflecting and Thinking

After reading about six symbolic personages (Chapters 12-13), followed by Chapter 14 with its parallels to previous pauses, we come to the introduction of the seven plagues of God's wrath and judgment. Thinking about the pattern ("6 + additional information + 1"), the question arises, "What is the seventh item in this series?" Several possibilities exist. It may be that the "wrath of God" is personified in Chapter 14 or it may be that

God himself is the seventh personage. Another possibility is that the seventh personage in the series is Babylon (Rome), introduced in Chapter 14 and soon to be the recipient of God's judgment (Chapters 17-18). Finally, it is possible that this section does not follow the previous pattern.

The contents of the second scroll are remarkably similar to the message of the first scroll, only with a more specific application in view -- the judgment of God against the city of Rome in its service as an instrument of Satan.

How hard is it for you to see God at work in difficult situations? Given that many of the verses in Revelation are references or allusions to Old Testament texts, what Old Testament events come to mind as you read this chapter? Who is on the throne? How does that make you feel?

Prayer

Dear God, today again we are grateful that you are in control and on the throne. We praise and magnify your name as we contemplate your great and marvelous deeds, both in creation and in the events of this world. We believe even when we cannot see you or understand your ways. Thank you for delivering us through Jesus, in whose name and by whose authority we pray, Amen.

Revelation 16: Seven Plagues (Bowls of Wrath)

Selected Biblical Text

1 Then I heard a loud voice from the temple saying to the seven angels, "Go, and pour out the seven bowls of God's wrath on the earth." 2 Then the first angel went forth and poured out his bowl on the land, and ugly, ulcerated sores appeared on the people who had the mark of the beast and worshiped its image.

3 Then the second angel poured out his bowl on the sea, and it turned into blood like that of a dead person, and every living thing in the sea died.

4 The third angel poured out his bowl on the rivers and springs of water, and they turned into blood.

8 The fourth angel poured out his bowl on the sun, and the sun was allowed to scorch people with fire.

10 The fifth angel poured out his bowl on the throne of the beast, so that its kingdom was darkened....

12 The sixth angel poured out his bowl on the great river Euphrates, and its water was dried up to prepare the way for the kings from the East.

13 Then I saw, [coming] out of the mouth of the dragon, out of the mouth of the beast, and out of the mouth of the false prophet, three impure spirits like frogs. 14 They are spirits of demons, performing signs; they go out to the kings of the whole earth, to gather them for the battle of the great day of God Almighty. 15 Look, I come like a thief. Blessed is the one who stays alert and keeps his clothes on, so he

does not have to walk around naked, so others see his shame. 16 Then they gathered them to the place that in Hebrew is called Armageddon.

17 Then the seventh angel poured out his bowl into the air, and out of the temple came a loud voice from the throne, saying, it is done. (Revelation 16, selected verses)

Reflecting and Thinking

The seven bowls of wrath which bring God's plagues on the earth follow the same pattern as the trumpets ("6 + additional information + 1"). These are bowls or vials of judgment and wrath. The pause that follows after the sixth bowl is poured out is very brief (16:13-16) and tells about the gathering of the three frogs, likely representing opposing kings, for battle.

The sequence of the bowls of wrath is earth, sea, waters, sky, throne of the beast, and Euphrates, followed by the victory announced by the seventh bowl. Sound familiar? Hint: check out the sequence of the judgment of the trumpets -- the sequence is the same!

In the context, this chapter pictures the completion of God's wrath against Rome, meaning that those who are persecuted by this enemy are being delivered. The wording of the seventh plague indicates that judgment is being rendered against Babylon (Rome).

What do you make of the parallel between the trumpets and the plagues? Is this a way of saying that God's judgments are complete or total -- that is, what is being represented is the completeness of God's judgment? Where can we see God's judgment at work today? What problems come when we think "end of time" every time we read about God's judgment? Can you think of some judgments of God in the Bible that do not involve the end of time? (Remember that Jesus promised to come quickly --in judgment? -- upon the churches who did not repent in the letters of Chapters 2-3.)

Prayer

Dear God, guide our thoughts and study as we contemplate your magnificent and marvelous ways. Instill in us faith, confidence and hope as we think about your great work in this world. Show us your ways so that we will walk by your side and on your side, we pray in Jesus' name, Amen.

Revelation 17: Result of Seventh Plague --
The Great Prostitute Brought to Ruin

Selected Biblical Text

1 Then one of the seven angels who had the seven bowls came and spoke with me, saying: "Come, I will show you the judgment of the great prostitute who sits on many waters. 2 With her the kings of the earth committed sexual immorality, and the inhabitants of the earth became drunken with the wine of her immorality."

3 Then he carried me away in the spirit to a wilderness. And there I saw a woman sitting on a scarlet beast that was covered with blasphemous names, having seven heads and ten horns. 4 And the woman was dressed in purple and scarlet, glittering with gold, precious stones and pearls. She had a golden cup in her hand, filled with detestable things and the uncleanness of her immorality. 5 On her forehead was written a name, a mystery, BABYLON THE GREAT, THE MOTHER OF PROSTITUTES AND OF THE DETESTABLE THINGS OF THE EARTH.

6 I saw that the woman was drunk with the blood of the saints and the blood of those who testified about Jesus. And I marveled greatly when I saw her. 7 Then the angel said to me: "Why are you astonished? I will tell you the mystery of the woman and of the beast who carries her, the one with seven heads and ten horns. 8 The beast which you saw was, is not, and is about to come up out of the abyss and go to its destruction. The inhabitants of the earth whose name has not been written in the book of life from the foundation of the world will be astonished when they see the beast that was, is not, and is coming."

9 This calls for a mind with wisdom. The seven heads are seven hills on which the woman sits. (Rev. 17:1-9)

Reflecting and Thinking

Chapters 17-18 reveal God's judgment on Rome; the city is identified by the seven hills in verse 9. Are the seven plagues described in Revelation only against Rome? Perhaps so, but in principle these truths about God's judgment apply to all of his enemies. Take careful note of the connection between Rome and the beasts and the repeated call for wisdom. Again, some details of this figurative section are difficult to discern, but it seems safe to say that the historical details being communicated could be understood by the first-century readers. Sometimes, even the forces of evil work inadvertently to accomplish God's purpose (17:17). The certainty of God's purpose is always secure.

In your opinion, what or who are some of God's enemies today, those that he will judge? How are those enemies working on Satan's side? Do we ever misidentify the enemies? When and how do we fail to see that God is working through what we consider negative events?

Prayer

Father God, again we ask for wisdom so that we will stand for good and oppose all that is evil. Help us as we seek to live within your purpose. Guide us, in Jesus' name and by his power we ask it, Amen.

Revelation 18: Result of Seventh Plague -- The Fall of Babylon

Selected Biblical Text

1 After these things I saw another angel coming down from heaven, having great authority, and the earth was illuminated by his glory. 2 With a mighty voice he shouted saying, Fallen, fallen is Babylon the great. She has become a dwelling place for demons, a haunt for every unclean spirit, a haunt for every unclean bird, a haunt for every unclean and detestable beast.
3 For all the nations have drunk the wine of her sexually immoral passion. The kings of the earth committed immorality with her, and the merchants of the earth grew rich from the power of her sensual excess. (Rev. 18:1-3)

Reflecting and Thinking

The fall of Babylon is described in four movements. The lament of the selected text communicates the fall of Babylon in dirge style (verses 1-3). Given the certainty of Babylon's fall, the people of God are warned to escape and have nothing to do with such sins (verses 4-8). Three paragraphs of "woes" (verses 9-20) are followed by a concluding poetic section portraying the finality of Babylon's doom (verses 21-24).

The result of the seventh plague is the fall of Babylon. The victory is won, as will be seen in the heavenly scene and the visions of the next chapters in the book. Regardless of the seeming strength of any enemy, God will prevail. How would you apply this chapter to your daily life? What prayer concerns come to mind as you read this chapter? [Include those in your prayer today.]

Prayer

Dear God, we rejoice in the certainty of your way, and we trust you to accomplish your will and to bring your vengeance upon those who deserve it. Help us to see the ways you wish us to join you in your great work, in Jesus' name, Amen.

Revelation 19: Heavenly Scenes (1)

Selected Biblical Text

1 After these things I heard what sounded like a loud voice of a great multitude in heaven, saying: "Hallelujah. Salvation and glory and power belong to our God, 2 for true and just are his judgments. He has judged the great prostitute who corrupted the earth with her sexual immorality. He has avenged the blood of his servants, [shed] by her hand." 3 And again they shouted: "Hallelujah. The smoke from her goes up forever and ever."
4 The twenty-four elders and the four living creatures fell down and worshiped God, the one seated on the throne, saying: "Amen, hallelujah."

5 Then a voice came from the throne, saying: "Praise our God, all his servants, those who fear him, both great and small."

6 Then I heard what sounded like a voice of a great multitude, like the sound of many waters and like the sound of strong thunder, saying: "Hallelujah. For our Lord God Almighty reigns. 7 Let us rejoice and be glad and give him glory. For the wedding of the Lamb has come, and his bride has made herself ready. 8 Fine linen, bright and clean, was given her to wear." (Fine linen is the righteous actions of the saints.)

9 Then the angel said to me: "Write, blessed are those who are invited to the wedding supper of the Lamb." He also said: "These are the true words of God." 10 And I fell at his feet to worship him. But he said to me: "Do not do that. I am a fellow servant with you and with your brothers who hold to the testimony about Jesus. Worship God, for the testimony about Jesus is the spirit of prophecy." (Rev. 19:1-10)

Reflecting and Thinking

An analysis of the text may suggest a series of seven "heavenly" scenes (19:11-21:1), each introduced by the phrase "I saw" or similar wording. With victory assured, we are given a final overview of God's power and work, including declarations of praise and majesty and worship by the heavenly host.

The heavenly scenes and visions cause us to think of similar events and wording in Chapters 4-5. The return to the heavenly scene signifies the end of the story of God's victory over Babylon (Rome). Not only is the Lamb present, the bride of the Lamb has arrived.

How encouraging! As we near the end of the book, we see that both the Lamb and the bride of the Lamb are present in heaven! God is on the throne and in control as he judges and overcomes his enemies. The heavenly visions provide us one more look backward at the glory and majesty of God that were reflected in the stories of the second scroll, and also a preview of God's continuing power to judge. John's visions give us an inclusive overview of the accomplishment of God's purpose.

Looking ahead, we see the end of the book approaching. The visions given to John include Jesus the conqueror, an angel issuing a "supper call," the beastly opponents gathered and conquered, the temporary binding and inactivity of Satan with regard to deceiving the nations, the saints and martyrs (witnesses) in heaven participating in the second resurrection, an all-inclusive judgment on God's enemies including Satan and his future activity, and the blessings of the new heaven and new earth.

In what ways do the heavenly visions summarize God's work in the world? What do you think about the idea that these visions provide a summary of the second scroll and point to the ultimate outcome? How well does this summary honor the fact that we are dealing with apocalyptic, figurative language from which we must seek to understand a general message and not specific details?

Prayer

Dear God, help us so live that our names are in the book of life, in Jesus' name, Amen.

Revelation 20: Heavenly Scenes (2)

Selected Biblical Text

11 Then I saw a great white throne and the one who was seated on it. The earth and the heaven [sky] vanished from his presence, no place was found for them. 12 And I saw the dead, great and small, standing before the throne, and books were opened. Another book was opened, which is the book of life. The dead were judged by the things written in the books, according to their deeds. 13 The sea gave up the dead that were in it, and death and hades gave up the dead that were in them, and each person was judged according to his deeds. 14 Then death and hades were cast into the lake of fire. This is the second death, the lake of fire. 15 If anyone's name was not found written in the book of life, that person was cast into the lake of fire. (Rev. 20:11-15)

Reflecting and Thinking

The heavenly perspective continues in today's chapter. While the vantage point is heaven, some of the scenes seem to refer to earthly events. The certainty of victory has already been proclaimed, even though Satan is still active on the earth. God's people are protected, and the destruction of evil is certain.

Today's text recounts the ultimate judgment of evil and the ultimate rescue of those whose names are written in the book of life. God's purpose is secure!

This chapter is troublesome to many. It is beyond the scope of this devotional series to try to answer the many questions that have been raised. Suffice it to say that we are reading or seeing symbols, and the question must always be, "What do the symbols represent?"

Here is a brief summary. For 1000 years (a symbolic number), Satan is bound and unable to deceive the nations as he had done through Rome. The 1000 years are not literal but symbolic. From the text, we understand that the 1000 years begin when Rome falls. The binding of Satan during the 1000 years is only with regard to deceiving the nations. There has never been a time in history when Satan was not active. The vision reveals the victory of those who have endured as they opposed evil and tells of the defeat of Satan and his forces. The vision ends with the judgment of the dead, just as did the first scroll (compare 11:18).

What is the purpose of today's text in the larger context of Rev. 19-20? What questions or thoughts come to mind as you think of the summary of the visions: Jesus the conqueror, a "supper call," the beastly opponents gathered and conquered, the temporary binding and inactivity of Satan, saints and martyr-witnesses in heaven, an all-inclusive judgment on God's enemies (including Satan and his future activity), and the future blessings of the new heaven and new earth? Do these seven concepts provide a summary of the prophecy of the second scroll and the judgment against Rome and all future opponents?

Prayer

Heavenly Father, we are relieved that you are working out your will, capable of restraining and opposing Satan's work as needed for your purposes, protecting your people, securing our ultimate presence and fellowship with you. Thank you for making our rescue possible, in the name of the resurrected Christ, Amen.

Revelation 21: Christ Is Present with His Victorious Church

Selected Biblical Text

1 Then I saw a new heaven [sky] and a new earth, for the first heaven [sky] and the first earth had passed away [ceased to exist], and the sea was no more. 2 I saw the holy city, new Jerusalem, coming down out of heaven from God, prepared as a bride beautifully dressed for her husband. 3 And I heard a loud voice from the throne saying: Look, the dwelling place of God is among the people, and he will dwell with them, and they will be his people, and God himself will be with them. 4 He will wipe away every tear from their eyes, death will no longer exist, neither mourning nor crying nor pain, for the former things have passed away [ceased to exist].

5 The one seated on the throne said: I am making all things new. Then he said: "Write, these words are trustworthy and true."

6 He said to me: "It is done. I am the Alpha and the Omega, the beginning and the end." To one who is thirsty I will give water without cost from the spring of the water of life. 7 The one who conquers will inherit these things, and I will be his God and he will be my son. 8 To the cowardly, the unbelieving, the detestable, the murderers, the sexually immoral, those who practice magic, the idolaters and all liars – their share [inheritance] will be in the lake burning with fire and sulfur, which is the second death.

9 Then one of the seven angels who had the seven bowls full of the seven final plagues came and said to me: "Come, I will show you the bride, the wife of the Lamb." 10 And he took me away in the spirit to a mountain great and high, and showed me the holy city, Jerusalem, coming down out of heaven from God. (Rev. 21:1-10)

Reflecting and Thinking

The coming of the new Jerusalem pictures Christ with his bride. He is present with and walking with the victorious church, just as the letters of Chapters 2-3 showed us Christ present and walking among the persecuted churches. Many questions have been raised about whether the application of this last part of Revelation is to the church as it exists on earth or to the church in heaven. The easiest, and perhaps the best, answer may be that it is both. Jesus' presence ensures victory, and that victory is spoken of in Scripture as already existing and having already been won, even though the church on earth faces continuing challenges. Yes, some aspects of Revelation 21-22 do not seem to apply to the church on earth, but we remember again that we are reading symbolic language and should not expect that every detail will be literal. We also remember that parallel language was used by the Old Testament prophets to describe the coming of the Messiah in his kingdom, referring to the earthly church.

With either application, the victory is secure. God protects and delivers his faithful people. Numerous Christian authors and speakers have summarized the message of Revelation like this: "We win!"

Read today's text (or the entirety of Chapter 21) carefully and devotionally, thinking about how the various descriptions can be applied to the church today. How encouraging is this message! Note that the angels who were involved in the last seven plagues are also involved in this chapter -- what does this suggest about the application of this chapter?

Prayer

Heavenly Father, we anticipate anxiously the final victory and ultimate blessing of continuing perpetual fellowship with you and Jesus and the Spirit. We marvel at the continuity of the message of Revelation -- the parallels, the summaries, the message to John from the Alpha and Omega, instructions to write down the message. Thank you for the certainty of your promises, through Jesus we pray, Amen.

Revelation 22: Jesus Is Coming

Selected Biblical Text

6 Then the angel said to me: "These words are faithful and true. The Lord, the God of the spirits of the prophets, sent his angel to show his servants the things that must soon take place. 7 Look, I am coming soon. Blessed is the one who keeps the words of the prophecy of this book." 8 And I, John, am the one who heard and saw these things. And when I had heard and seen them, I fell down to worship at the feet of the angel who was showing them to me. 9 But he said to me: "Do not do that. I am a fellow servant with you and with your brothers the prophets and with

all who keep the words of this book. Worship God." 10 Then he said to me: "Do not seal up the words of the prophecy of this book, because the time is near."

12 Look, I am coming soon. My reward is with me to pay to each person according to what he has done. 13 I am the Alpha and the Omega, the first and the last, the beginning and the end....

16 I, Jesus, have sent my angel to testify to you about these things for the churches. I am the root and the descendant of David, the bright morning star. 17 The Spirit and the bride say: "Come." And let the one who hears say: "Come." Let the one who is thirsty come; and the one who wishes, let him take the free gift of the water of life.

18 I testify to everyone who hears the words of the prophecy of this book: If anyone adds to these things, God will add to that person the plagues written in this book. 19 And if anyone takes away from the words of this book of this prophecy, God will take away his share of the tree of life and from the holy city, of the things written in this book.

20 The one testifying to these things says: Yes, I am coming soon. Amen. Come, Lord Jesus. 21 The grace of the Lord Jesus be with all. Amen. (Rev. 22:6-10, 12-13, 16-21)

Reflecting and Thinking

We end where we began. The things we have been reading in the book of Revelation are things which must soon come to pass; the time is near. The enemies of the church have been conquered; they will never prevail. Jesus is coming and every eye will see him. May it be so. Amen.

When does the promise of Jesus' coming provide you the most comfort? When is the promise most challenging? How often have you heard the prayer, "Come, Lord Jesus?" Why or why not do we pray those words?

Prayer

Father God, we come because we are thirsty and seek water, because we are in need of your blessings and forgiveness. We ask you to provide, and we eagerly await Jesus' coming. Come, Lord Jesus. In Jesus' name and by his power we pray this prayer, Amen.

Name _____   Beginning Date _____

❑ Mat 1	❑ Lk 2	❑ Ac 2
❑ Mat 2	❑ Lk 3	❑ Ac 3
❑ Mat 3	❑ Lk 4	❑ Ac 4
❑ Mat 4	❑ Lk 5	❑ Ac 5
❑ Mat 5	❑ Lk 6	❑ Ac 6
❑ Mat 6	❑ Lk 7	❑ Ac 7
❑ Mat 7	❑ Lk 8	❑ Ac 8
❑ Mat 8	❑ Lk 9	❑ Ac 9
❑ Mat 9	❑ Lk 10	❑ Ac 10
❑ Mat 10	❑ Lk 11	❑ Ac 11
❑ Mat 11	❑ Lk 12	❑ Ac 12
❑ Mat 12	❑ Lk 13	❑ Ac 13
❑ Mat 13	❑ Lk 14	❑ Ac 14
❑ Mat 14	❑ Lk 15	❑ Ac 15
❑ Mat 15	❑ Lk 16	❑ Ac 16
❑ Mat 16	❑ Lk 17	❑ Ac 17
❑ Mat 17	❑ Lk 18	❑ Ac 18
❑ Mat 18	❑ Lk 19	❑ Ac 19
❑ Mat 19	❑ Lk 20	❑ Ac 20
❑ Mat 20	❑ Lk 21	❑ Ac 21
❑ Mat 21	❑ Lk 22	❑ Ac 22
❑ Mat 22	❑ Lk 23	❑ Ac 23
❑ Mat 23	❑ Lk 24	❑ Ac 24
❑ Mat 24	❑ Jn 1	❑ Ac 25
❑ Mat 25	❑ Jn 2	❑ Ac 26
❑ Mat 26	❑ Jn 3	❑ Ac 27
❑ Mat 27	❑ Jn 4	❑ Ac 28
❑ Mat 28	❑ Jn 5	❑ Rom 1
❑ Mk 1	❑ Jn 6	❑ Rom 2
❑ Mk 2	❑ Jn 7	❑ Rom 3
❑ Mk 3	❑ Jn 8	❑ Rom 4
❑ Mk 4	❑ Jn 9	❑ Rom 5
❑ Mk 5	❑ Jn 10	❑ Rom 6
❑ Mk 6	❑ Jn 11	❑ Rom 7
❑ Mk 7	❑ Jn 12	❑ Rom 8
❑ Mk 8	❑ Jn 13	❑ Rom 9
❑ Mk 9	❑ Jn 14	❑ Rom 10
❑ Mk 10	❑ Jn 15	❑ Rom 11
❑ Mk 11	❑ Jn 16	❑ Rom 12
❑ Mk 12	❑ Jn 17	❑ Rom 13
❑ Mk 13	❑ Jn 18	❑ Rom 14
❑ Mk 14	❑ Jn 19	❑ Rom 15
❑ Mk 15	❑ Jn 20	❑ Rom 16
❑ Mk 16	❑ Jn 21	❑ 1 Co 1
❑ Lk 1	❑ Ac 1	❑ 1 Co 2

❑	1 Co 3	❑	Col 3	❑	1 Pet 4
❑	1 Co 4	❑	Col 4	❑	1 Pet 5
❑	1 Co 5	❑	1 Th 1	❑	2 Pet 1
❑	1 Co 6	❑	1 Th 2	❑	2 Pet 2
❑	1 Co 7	❑	1 Th 3	❑	2 Pet 3
❑	1 Co 8	❑	1 Th 4	❑	1 Jn 1
❑	1 Co 9	❑	1 Th 5	❑	1 Jn 2
❑	1 Co 10	❑	2 Th 1	❑	1 Jn 3
❑	1 Co 11	❑	2 Th 2	❑	1 Jn 4
❑	1 Co 12	❑	2 Th 3	❑	1 Jn 5
❑	1 Co 13	❑	1 Tim 1	❑	2 Jn
❑	1 Co 14	❑	1 Tim 2	❑	3 Jn
❑	1 Co 15	❑	1 Tim 3	❑	Jud
❑	1 Co 16	❑	1 Tim 4	❑	Rev 1
❑	2 Co 1	❑	1 Tim 5	❑	Rev 2
❑	2 Co 2	❑	1 Tim 6	❑	Rev 3
❑	2 Co 3	❑	2 Tim 1	❑	Rev 4
❑	2 Co 4	❑	2 Tim 2	❑	Rev 5
❑	2 Co 5	❑	2 Tim 3	❑	Rev 6
❑	2 Co 6	❑	2 Tim 4	❑	Rev 7
❑	2 Co 7	❑	Tit 1	❑	Rev 8
❑	2 Co 8	❑	Tit 2	❑	Rev 9
❑	2 Co 9	❑	Tit 3	❑	Rev 10
❑	2 Co 10	❑	Philm	❑	Rev 11
❑	2 Co 11	❑	Heb 1	❑	Rev 12
❑	2 Co 12	❑	Heb 2	❑	Rev 13
❑	2 Co 13	❑	Heb 3	❑	Rev 14
❑	Gal 1	❑	Heb 4	❑	Rev 15
❑	Gal 2	❑	Heb 5	❑	Rev 16
❑	Gal 3	❑	Heb 6	❑	Rev 17
❑	Gal 4	❑	Heb 7	❑	Rev 18
❑	Gal 5	❑	Heb 8	❑	Rev 19
❑	Gal 6	❑	Heb 9	❑	Rev 20
❑	Eph 1	❑	Heb 10	❑	Rev 21
❑	Eph 2	❑	Heb 11	❑	Rev 22
❑	Eph 3	❑	Heb 12		
❑	Eph 4	❑	Heb 13		
❑	Eph 5	❑	Jas 1		
❑	Eph 6	❑	Jas 2		
❑	Phil 1	❑	Jas 3		
❑	Phil 2	❑	Jas 4		
❑	Phil 3	❑	Jas 5		
❑	Phil 4	❑	1 Pet 1		
❑	Col 1	❑	1 Pet 2		
❑	Col 2	❑	1 Pet 3		

Name _____   Beginning Date _____

☐ Mat 1	☐ Lk 2	☐ Ac 2
☐ Mat 2	☐ Lk 3	☐ Ac 3
☐ Mat 3	☐ Lk 4	☐ Ac 4
☐ Mat 4	☐ Lk 5	☐ Ac 5
☐ Mat 5	☐ Lk 6	☐ Ac 6
☐ Mat 6	☐ Lk 7	☐ Ac 7
☐ Mat 7	☐ Lk 8	☐ Ac 8
☐ Mat 8	☐ Lk 9	☐ Ac 9
☐ Mat 9	☐ Lk 10	☐ Ac 10
☐ Mat 10	☐ Lk 11	☐ Ac 11
☐ Mat 11	☐ Lk 12	☐ Ac 12
☐ Mat 12	☐ Lk 13	☐ Ac 13
☐ Mat 13	☐ Lk 14	☐ Ac 14
☐ Mat 14	☐ Lk 15	☐ Ac 15
☐ Mat 15	☐ Lk 16	☐ Ac 16
☐ Mat 16	☐ Lk 17	☐ Ac 17
☐ Mat 17	☐ Lk 18	☐ Ac 18
☐ Mat 18	☐ Lk 19	☐ Ac 19
☐ Mat 19	☐ Lk 20	☐ Ac 20
☐ Mat 20	☐ Lk 21	☐ Ac 21
☐ Mat 21	☐ Lk 22	☐ Ac 22
☐ Mat 22	☐ Lk 23	☐ Ac 23
☐ Mat 23	☐ Lk 24	☐ Ac 24
☐ Mat 24	☐ Jn 1	☐ Ac 25
☐ Mat 25	☐ Jn 2	☐ Ac 26
☐ Mat 26	☐ Jn 3	☐ Ac 27
☐ Mat 27	☐ Jn 4	☐ Ac 28
☐ Mat 28	☐ Jn 5	☐ Rom 1
☐ Mk 1	☐ Jn 6	☐ Rom 2
☐ Mk 2	☐ Jn 7	☐ Rom 3
☐ Mk 3	☐ Jn 8	☐ Rom 4
☐ Mk 4	☐ Jn 9	☐ Rom 5
☐ Mk 5	☐ Jn 10	☐ Rom 6
☐ Mk 6	☐ Jn 11	☐ Rom 7
☐ Mk 7	☐ Jn 12	☐ Rom 8
☐ Mk 8	☐ Jn 13	☐ Rom 9
☐ Mk 9	☐ Jn 14	☐ Rom 10
☐ Mk 10	☐ Jn 15	☐ Rom 11
☐ Mk 11	☐ Jn 16	☐ Rom 12
☐ Mk 12	☐ Jn 17	☐ Rom 13
☐ Mk 13	☐ Jn 18	☐ Rom 14
☐ Mk 14	☐ Jn 19	☐ Rom 15
☐ Mk 15	☐ Jn 20	☐ Rom 16
☐ Mk 16	☐ Jn 21	☐ 1 Co 1
☐ Lk 1	☐ Ac 1	☐ 1 Co 2

- [ ] 1 Co 3
- [ ] 1 Co 4
- [ ] 1 Co 5
- [ ] 1 Co 6
- [ ] 1 Co 7
- [ ] 1 Co 8
- [ ] 1 Co 9
- [ ] 1 Co 10
- [ ] 1 Co 11
- [ ] 1 Co 12
- [ ] 1 Co 13
- [ ] 1 Co 14
- [ ] 1 Co 15
- [ ] 1 Co 16
- [ ] 2 Co 1
- [ ] 2 Co 2
- [ ] 2 Co 3
- [ ] 2 Co 4
- [ ] 2 Co 5
- [ ] 2 Co 6
- [ ] 2 Co 7
- [ ] 2 Co 8
- [ ] 2 Co 9
- [ ] 2 Co 10
- [ ] 2 Co 11
- [ ] 2 Co 12
- [ ] 2 Co 13
- [ ] Gal 1
- [ ] Gal 2
- [ ] Gal 3
- [ ] Gal 4
- [ ] Gal 5
- [ ] Gal 6
- [ ] Eph 1
- [ ] Eph 2
- [ ] Eph 3
- [ ] Eph 4
- [ ] Eph 5
- [ ] Eph 6
- [ ] Phil 1
- [ ] Phil 2
- [ ] Phil 3
- [ ] Phil 4
- [ ] Col 1
- [ ] Col 2

- [ ] Col 3
- [ ] Col 4
- [ ] 1 Th 1
- [ ] 1 Th 2
- [ ] 1 Th 3
- [ ] 1 Th 4
- [ ] 1 Th 5
- [ ] 2 Th 1
- [ ] 2 Th 2
- [ ] 2 Th 3
- [ ] 1 Tim 1
- [ ] 1 Tim 2
- [ ] 1 Tim 3
- [ ] 1 Tim 4
- [ ] 1 Tim 5
- [ ] 1 Tim 6
- [ ] 2 Tim 1
- [ ] 2 Tim 2
- [ ] 2 Tim 3
- [ ] 2 Tim 4
- [ ] Tit 1
- [ ] Tit 2
- [ ] Tit 3
- [ ] Philm
- [ ] Heb 1
- [ ] Heb 2
- [ ] Heb 3
- [ ] Heb 4
- [ ] Heb 5
- [ ] Heb 6
- [ ] Heb 7
- [ ] Heb 8
- [ ] Heb 9
- [ ] Heb 10
- [ ] Heb 11
- [ ] Heb 12
- [ ] Heb 13
- [ ] Jas 1
- [ ] Jas 2
- [ ] Jas 3
- [ ] Jas 4
- [ ] Jas 5
- [ ] 1 Pet 1
- [ ] 1 Pet 2
- [ ] 1 Pet 3

- [ ] 1 Pet 4
- [ ] 1 Pet 5
- [ ] 2 Pet 1
- [ ] 2 Pet 2
- [ ] 2 Pet 3
- [ ] 1 Jn 1
- [ ] 1 Jn 2
- [ ] 1 Jn 3
- [ ] 1 Jn 4
- [ ] 1 Jn 5
- [ ] 2 Jn
- [ ] 3 Jn
- [ ] Jud
- [ ] Rev 1
- [ ] Rev 2
- [ ] Rev 3
- [ ] Rev 4
- [ ] Rev 5
- [ ] Rev 6
- [ ] Rev 7
- [ ] Rev 8
- [ ] Rev 9
- [ ] Rev 10
- [ ] Rev 11
- [ ] Rev 12
- [ ] Rev 13
- [ ] Rev 14
- [ ] Rev 15
- [ ] Rev 16
- [ ] Rev 17
- [ ] Rev 18
- [ ] Rev 19
- [ ] Rev 20
- [ ] Rev 21
- [ ] Rev 22

Name _____   Beginning Date _____

❏ Mat 1	❏ Lk 2	❏ Ac 2
❏ Mat 2	❏ Lk 3	❏ Ac 3
❏ Mat 3	❏ Lk 4	❏ Ac 4
❏ Mat 4	❏ Lk 5	❏ Ac 5
❏ Mat 5	❏ Lk 6	❏ Ac 6
❏ Mat 6	❏ Lk 7	❏ Ac 7
❏ Mat 7	❏ Lk 8	❏ Ac 8
❏ Mat 8	❏ Lk 9	❏ Ac 9
❏ Mat 9	❏ Lk 10	❏ Ac 10
❏ Mat 10	❏ Lk 11	❏ Ac 11
❏ Mat 11	❏ Lk 12	❏ Ac 12
❏ Mat 12	❏ Lk 13	❏ Ac 13
❏ Mat 13	❏ Lk 14	❏ Ac 14
❏ Mat 14	❏ Lk 15	❏ Ac 15
❏ Mat 15	❏ Lk 16	❏ Ac 16
❏ Mat 16	❏ Lk 17	❏ Ac 17
❏ Mat 17	❏ Lk 18	❏ Ac 18
❏ Mat 18	❏ Lk 19	❏ Ac 19
❏ Mat 19	❏ Lk 20	❏ Ac 20
❏ Mat 20	❏ Lk 21	❏ Ac 21
❏ Mat 21	❏ Lk 22	❏ Ac 22
❏ Mat 22	❏ Lk 23	❏ Ac 23
❏ Mat 23	❏ Lk 24	❏ Ac 24
❏ Mat 24	❏ Jn 1	❏ Ac 25
❏ Mat 25	❏ Jn 2	❏ Ac 26
❏ Mat 26	❏ Jn 3	❏ Ac 27
❏ Mat 27	❏ Jn 4	❏ Ac 28
❏ Mat 28	❏ Jn 5	❏ Rom 1
❏ Mk 1	❏ Jn 6	❏ Rom 2
❏ Mk 2	❏ Jn 7	❏ Rom 3
❏ Mk 3	❏ Jn 8	❏ Rom 4
❏ Mk 4	❏ Jn 9	❏ Rom 5
❏ Mk 5	❏ Jn 10	❏ Rom 6
❏ Mk 6	❏ Jn 11	❏ Rom 7
❏ Mk 7	❏ Jn 12	❏ Rom 8
❏ Mk 8	❏ Jn 13	❏ Rom 9
❏ Mk 9	❏ Jn 14	❏ Rom 10
❏ Mk 10	❏ Jn 15	❏ Rom 11
❏ Mk 11	❏ Jn 16	❏ Rom 12
❏ Mk 12	❏ Jn 17	❏ Rom 13
❏ Mk 13	❏ Jn 18	❏ Rom 14
❏ Mk 14	❏ Jn 19	❏ Rom 15
❏ Mk 15	❏ Jn 20	❏ Rom 16
❏ Mk 16	❏ Jn 21	❏ 1 Co 1
❏ Lk 1	❏ Ac 1	❏ 1 Co 2

- ❏ 1 Co 3
- ❏ 1 Co 4
- ❏ 1 Co 5
- ❏ 1 Co 6
- ❏ 1 Co 7
- ❏ 1 Co 8
- ❏ 1 Co 9
- ❏ 1 Co 10
- ❏ 1 Co 11
- ❏ 1 Co 12
- ❏ 1 Co 13
- ❏ 1 Co 14
- ❏ 1 Co 15
- ❏ 1 Co 16
- ❏ 2 Co 1
- ❏ 2 Co 2
- ❏ 2 Co 3
- ❏ 2 Co 4
- ❏ 2 Co 5
- ❏ 2 Co 6
- ❏ 2 Co 7
- ❏ 2 Co 8
- ❏ 2 Co 9
- ❏ 2 Co 10
- ❏ 2 Co 11
- ❏ 2 Co 12
- ❏ 2 Co 13
- ❏ Gal 1
- ❏ Gal 2
- ❏ Gal 3
- ❏ Gal 4
- ❏ Gal 5
- ❏ Gal 6
- ❏ Eph 1
- ❏ Eph 2
- ❏ Eph 3
- ❏ Eph 4
- ❏ Eph 5
- ❏ Eph 6
- ❏ Phil 1
- ❏ Phil 2
- ❏ Phil 3
- ❏ Phil 4
- ❏ Col 1
- ❏ Col 2
- ❏ Col 3
- ❏ Col 4
- ❏ 1 Th 1
- ❏ 1 Th 2
- ❏ 1 Th 3
- ❏ 1 Th 4
- ❏ 1 Th 5
- ❏ 2 Th 1
- ❏ 2 Th 2
- ❏ 2 Th 3
- ❏ 1 Tim 1
- ❏ 1 Tim 2
- ❏ 1 Tim 3
- ❏ 1 Tim 4
- ❏ 1 Tim 5
- ❏ 1 Tim 6
- ❏ 2 Tim 1
- ❏ 2 Tim 2
- ❏ 2 Tim 3
- ❏ 2 Tim 4
- ❏ Tit 1
- ❏ Tit 2
- ❏ Tit 3
- ❏ Philm
- ❏ Heb 1
- ❏ Heb 2
- ❏ Heb 3
- ❏ Heb 4
- ❏ Heb 5
- ❏ Heb 6
- ❏ Heb 7
- ❏ Heb 8
- ❏ Heb 9
- ❏ Heb 10
- ❏ Heb 11
- ❏ Heb 12
- ❏ Heb 13
- ❏ Jas 1
- ❏ Jas 2
- ❏ Jas 3
- ❏ Jas 4
- ❏ Jas 5
- ❏ 1 Pet 1
- ❏ 1 Pet 2
- ❏ 1 Pet 3
- ❏ 1 Pet 4
- ❏ 1 Pet 5
- ❏ 2 Pet 1
- ❏ 2 Pet 2
- ❏ 2 Pet 3
- ❏ 1 Jn 1
- ❏ 1 Jn 2
- ❏ 1 Jn 3
- ❏ 1 Jn 4
- ❏ 1 Jn 5
- ❏ 2 Jn
- ❏ 3 Jn
- ❏ Jud
- ❏ Rev 1
- ❏ Rev 2
- ❏ Rev 3
- ❏ Rev 4
- ❏ Rev 5
- ❏ Rev 6
- ❏ Rev 7
- ❏ Rev 8
- ❏ Rev 9
- ❏ Rev 10
- ❏ Rev 11
- ❏ Rev 12
- ❏ Rev 13
- ❏ Rev 14
- ❏ Rev 15
- ❏ Rev 16
- ❏ Rev 17
- ❏ Rev 18
- ❏ Rev 19
- ❏ Rev 20
- ❏ Rev 21
- ❏ Rev 22

Name _____   Beginning Date _____

❑	Mat 1	❑	Lk 2	❑	Ac 2
❑	Mat 2	❑	Lk 3	❑	Ac 3
❑	Mat 3	❑	Lk 4	❑	Ac 4
❑	Mat 4	❑	Lk 5	❑	Ac 5
❑	Mat 5	❑	Lk 6	❑	Ac 6
❑	Mat 6	❑	Lk 7	❑	Ac 7
❑	Mat 7	❑	Lk 8	❑	Ac 8
❑	Mat 8	❑	Lk 9	❑	Ac 9
❑	Mat 9	❑	Lk 10	❑	Ac 10
❑	Mat 10	❑	Lk 11	❑	Ac 11
❑	Mat 11	❑	Lk 12	❑	Ac 12
❑	Mat 12	❑	Lk 13	❑	Ac 13
❑	Mat 13	❑	Lk 14	❑	Ac 14
❑	Mat 14	❑	Lk 15	❑	Ac 15
❑	Mat 15	❑	Lk 16	❑	Ac 16
❑	Mat 16	❑	Lk 17	❑	Ac 17
❑	Mat 17	❑	Lk 18	❑	Ac 18
❑	Mat 18	❑	Lk 19	❑	Ac 19
❑	Mat 19	❑	Lk 20	❑	Ac 20
❑	Mat 20	❑	Lk 21	❑	Ac 21
❑	Mat 21	❑	Lk 22	❑	Ac 22
❑	Mat 22	❑	Lk 23	❑	Ac 23
❑	Mat 23	❑	Lk 24	❑	Ac 24
❑	Mat 24	❑	Jn 1	❑	Ac 25
❑	Mat 25	❑	Jn 2	❑	Ac 26
❑	Mat 26	❑	Jn 3	❑	Ac 27
❑	Mat 27	❑	Jn 4	❑	Ac 28
❑	Mat 28	❑	Jn 5	❑	Rom 1
❑	Mk 1	❑	Jn 6	❑	Rom 2
❑	Mk 2	❑	Jn 7	❑	Rom 3
❑	Mk 3	❑	Jn 8	❑	Rom 4
❑	Mk 4	❑	Jn 9	❑	Rom 5
❑	Mk 5	❑	Jn 10	❑	Rom 6
❑	Mk 6	❑	Jn 11	❑	Rom 7
❑	Mk 7	❑	Jn 12	❑	Rom 8
❑	Mk 8	❑	Jn 13	❑	Rom 9
❑	Mk 9	❑	Jn 14	❑	Rom 10
❑	Mk 10	❑	Jn 15	❑	Rom 11
❑	Mk 11	❑	Jn 16	❑	Rom 12
❑	Mk 12	❑	Jn 17	❑	Rom 13
❑	Mk 13	❑	Jn 18	❑	Rom 14
❑	Mk 14	❑	Jn 19	❑	Rom 15
❑	Mk 15	❑	Jn 20	❑	Rom 16
❑	Mk 16	❑	Jn 21	❑	1 Co 1
❑	Lk 1	❑	Ac 1	❑	1 Co 2

❑ 1 Co 3
❑ 1 Co 4
❑ 1 Co 5
❑ 1 Co 6
❑ 1 Co 7
❑ 1 Co 8
❑ 1 Co 9
❑ 1 Co 10
❑ 1 Co 11
❑ 1 Co 12
❑ 1 Co 13
❑ 1 Co 14
❑ 1 Co 15
❑ 1 Co 16
❑ 2 Co 1
❑ 2 Co 2
❑ 2 Co 3
❑ 2 Co 4
❑ 2 Co 5
❑ 2 Co 6
❑ 2 Co 7
❑ 2 Co 8
❑ 2 Co 9
❑ 2 Co 10
❑ 2 Co 11
❑ 2 Co 12
❑ 2 Co 13
❑ Gal 1
❑ Gal 2
❑ Gal 3
❑ Gal 4
❑ Gal 5
❑ Gal 6
❑ Eph 1
❑ Eph 2
❑ Eph 3
❑ Eph 4
❑ Eph 5
❑ Eph 6
❑ Phil 1
❑ Phil 2
❑ Phil 3
❑ Phil 4
❑ Col 1
❑ Col 2

❑ Col 3
❑ Col 4
❑ 1 Th 1
❑ 1 Th 2
❑ 1 Th 3
❑ 1 Th 4
❑ 1 Th 5
❑ 2 Th 1
❑ 2 Th 2
❑ 2 Th 3
❑ 1 Tim 1
❑ 1 Tim 2
❑ 1 Tim 3
❑ 1 Tim 4
❑ 1 Tim 5
❑ 1 Tim 6
❑ 2 Tim 1
❑ 2 Tim 2
❑ 2 Tim 3
❑ 2 Tim 4
❑ Tit 1
❑ Tit 2
❑ Tit 3
❑ Philm
❑ Heb 1
❑ Heb 2
❑ Heb 3
❑ Heb 4
❑ Heb 5
❑ Heb 6
❑ Heb 7
❑ Heb 8
❑ Heb 9
❑ Heb 10
❑ Heb 11
❑ Heb 12
❑ Heb 13
❑ Jas 1
❑ Jas 2
❑ Jas 3
❑ Jas 4
❑ Jas 5
❑ 1 Pet 1
❑ 1 Pet 2
❑ 1 Pet 3

❑ 1 Pet 4
❑ 1 Pet 5
❑ 2 Pet 1
❑ 2 Pet 2
❑ 2 Pet 3
❑ 1 Jn 1
❑ 1 Jn 2
❑ 1 Jn 3
❑ 1 Jn 4
❑ 1 Jn 5
❑ 2 Jn
❑ 3 Jn
❑ Jud
❑ Rev 1
❑ Rev 2
❑ Rev 3
❑ Rev 4
❑ Rev 5
❑ Rev 6
❑ Rev 7
❑ Rev 8
❑ Rev 9
❑ Rev 10
❑ Rev 11
❑ Rev 12
❑ Rev 13
❑ Rev 14
❑ Rev 15
❑ Rev 16
❑ Rev 17
❑ Rev 18
❑ Rev 19
❑ Rev 20
❑ Rev 21
❑ Rev 22

Name _____   Beginning Date _____

❑ Mat 1	❑ Lk 2	❑ Ac 2
❑ Mat 2	❑ Lk 3	❑ Ac 3
❑ Mat 3	❑ Lk 4	❑ Ac 4
❑ Mat 4	❑ Lk 5	❑ Ac 5
❑ Mat 5	❑ Lk 6	❑ Ac 6
❑ Mat 6	❑ Lk 7	❑ Ac 7
❑ Mat 7	❑ Lk 8	❑ Ac 8
❑ Mat 8	❑ Lk 9	❑ Ac 9
❑ Mat 9	❑ Lk 10	❑ Ac 10
❑ Mat 10	❑ Lk 11	❑ Ac 11
❑ Mat 11	❑ Lk 12	❑ Ac 12
❑ Mat 12	❑ Lk 13	❑ Ac 13
❑ Mat 13	❑ Lk 14	❑ Ac 14
❑ Mat 14	❑ Lk 15	❑ Ac 15
❑ Mat 15	❑ Lk 16	❑ Ac 16
❑ Mat 16	❑ Lk 17	❑ Ac 17
❑ Mat 17	❑ Lk 18	❑ Ac 18
❑ Mat 18	❑ Lk 19	❑ Ac 19
❑ Mat 19	❑ Lk 20	❑ Ac 20
❑ Mat 20	❑ Lk 21	❑ Ac 21
❑ Mat 21	❑ Lk 22	❑ Ac 22
❑ Mat 22	❑ Lk 23	❑ Ac 23
❑ Mat 23	❑ Lk 24	❑ Ac 24
❑ Mat 24	❑ Jn 1	❑ Ac 25
❑ Mat 25	❑ Jn 2	❑ Ac 26
❑ Mat 26	❑ Jn 3	❑ Ac 27
❑ Mat 27	❑ Jn 4	❑ Ac 28
❑ Mat 28	❑ Jn 5	❑ Rom 1
❑ Mk 1	❑ Jn 6	❑ Rom 2
❑ Mk 2	❑ Jn 7	❑ Rom 3
❑ Mk 3	❑ Jn 8	❑ Rom 4
❑ Mk 4	❑ Jn 9	❑ Rom 5
❑ Mk 5	❑ Jn 10	❑ Rom 6
❑ Mk 6	❑ Jn 11	❑ Rom 7
❑ Mk 7	❑ Jn 12	❑ Rom 8
❑ Mk 8	❑ Jn 13	❑ Rom 9
❑ Mk 9	❑ Jn 14	❑ Rom 10
❑ Mk 10	❑ Jn 15	❑ Rom 11
❑ Mk 11	❑ Jn 16	❑ Rom 12
❑ Mk 12	❑ Jn 17	❑ Rom 13
❑ Mk 13	❑ Jn 18	❑ Rom 14
❑ Mk 14	❑ Jn 19	❑ Rom 15
❑ Mk 15	❑ Jn 20	❑ Rom 16
❑ Mk 16	❑ Jn 21	❑ 1 Co 1
❑ Lk 1	❑ Ac 1	❑ 1 Co 2

- ❑ 1 Co 3
- ❑ 1 Co 4
- ❑ 1 Co 5
- ❑ 1 Co 6
- ❑ 1 Co 7
- ❑ 1 Co 8
- ❑ 1 Co 9
- ❑ 1 Co 10
- ❑ 1 Co 11
- ❑ 1 Co 12
- ❑ 1 Co 13
- ❑ 1 Co 14
- ❑ 1 Co 15
- ❑ 1 Co 16
- ❑ 2 Co 1
- ❑ 2 Co 2
- ❑ 2 Co 3
- ❑ 2 Co 4
- ❑ 2 Co 5
- ❑ 2 Co 6
- ❑ 2 Co 7
- ❑ 2 Co 8
- ❑ 2 Co 9
- ❑ 2 Co 10
- ❑ 2 Co 11
- ❑ 2 Co 12
- ❑ 2 Co 13
- ❑ Gal 1
- ❑ Gal 2
- ❑ Gal 3
- ❑ Gal 4
- ❑ Gal 5
- ❑ Gal 6
- ❑ Eph 1
- ❑ Eph 2
- ❑ Eph 3
- ❑ Eph 4
- ❑ Eph 5
- ❑ Eph 6
- ❑ Phil 1
- ❑ Phil 2
- ❑ Phil 3
- ❑ Phil 4
- ❑ Col 1
- ❑ Col 2

- ❑ Col 3
- ❑ Col 4
- ❑ 1 Th 1
- ❑ 1 Th 2
- ❑ 1 Th 3
- ❑ 1 Th 4
- ❑ 1 Th 5
- ❑ 2 Th 1
- ❑ 2 Th 2
- ❑ 2 Th 3
- ❑ 1 Tim 1
- ❑ 1 Tim 2
- ❑ 1 Tim 3
- ❑ 1 Tim 4
- ❑ 1 Tim 5
- ❑ 1 Tim 6
- ❑ 2 Tim 1
- ❑ 2 Tim 2
- ❑ 2 Tim 3
- ❑ 2 Tim 4
- ❑ Tit 1
- ❑ Tit 2
- ❑ Tit 3
- ❑ Philm
- ❑ Heb 1
- ❑ Heb 2
- ❑ Heb 3
- ❑ Heb 4
- ❑ Heb 5
- ❑ Heb 6
- ❑ Heb 7
- ❑ Heb 8
- ❑ Heb 9
- ❑ Heb 10
- ❑ Heb 11
- ❑ Heb 12
- ❑ Heb 13
- ❑ Jas 1
- ❑ Jas 2
- ❑ Jas 3
- ❑ Jas 4
- ❑ Jas 5
- ❑ 1 Pet 1
- ❑ 1 Pet 2
- ❑ 1 Pet 3

- ❑ 1 Pet 4
- ❑ 1 Pet 5
- ❑ 2 Pet 1
- ❑ 2 Pet 2
- ❑ 2 Pet 3
- ❑ 1 Jn 1
- ❑ 1 Jn 2
- ❑ 1 Jn 3
- ❑ 1 Jn 4
- ❑ 1 Jn 5
- ❑ 2 Jn
- ❑ 3 Jn
- ❑ Jud
- ❑ Rev 1
- ❑ Rev 2
- ❑ Rev 3
- ❑ Rev 4
- ❑ Rev 5
- ❑ Rev 6
- ❑ Rev 7
- ❑ Rev 8
- ❑ Rev 9
- ❑ Rev 10
- ❑ Rev 11
- ❑ Rev 12
- ❑ Rev 13
- ❑ Rev 14
- ❑ Rev 15
- ❑ Rev 16
- ❑ Rev 17
- ❑ Rev 18
- ❑ Rev 19
- ❑ Rev 20
- ❑ Rev 21
- ❑ Rev 22

BIOGRAPHICAL NOTES

 **Dr. Bob Young** directs an international ministry committed to providing Christians and churches around the world with teaching resources for ministry and mission work.

Bible resources are made available through a dedicated website (www.bobyoungresources.com), social media, written materials, books, and videos. Young speaks frequently in local churches and in regional and national conferences across Latin America and in the United States.

He has authored a number of books. His most recent books are five volumes in a series of Bible Study Guides (*Early Letters, Prison Letters, Pastoral Letters, Hebrews, and General Letters*). He also authored a book in Spanish designed to energize and equip churches for evangelism. These books are currently available in paperback and Kindle editions on Amazon.

His master's thesis focused on the role of Baby Boomers in the church, and his doctoral project was titled *Building Cohesion in Church Leadership*. As part of his work in Christian higher education, he wrote five books (*Biblical Perspectives for the Adult Learner, Integration of Biblical Principles for the Adult Learner, Life Applications of Biblical Values for the Adult Learner, Supplement to MLA 4th Edition*, and *Handbook to the Practicum Experience at Ohio Valley College*.)

During more than 25 years of ministry, he authored several adult Bible study books (*The Major Prophets; Proverbs: Vertical Wisdom for Horizontal Living; Acts: The Savior, the Spirit, and the Struggle; First Corinthians: Developing Spiritual Maturity; First Thessalonians: Spiritual Living in a Secular World; Expectant and Encouraged—Confident That Christ Is Coming Again;* and *James: Authentic Living in a Shadowy World*).

He served on the editorial committee and contributed a chapter to a festschrift in honor of Howard Norton, *A Handbook on Leadership: As Exemplified in the Life of Howard Norton.* He wrote a Bible survey book for teens, *Time Travelers.*

He has e-published several books, including *An Easy Model for Doing Bible Exegesis, Moving from the Text to the Sermon,* and *Developing a Planning Model for the Smaller Church,* plus three books in Spanish.

After thirty years of preaching and twelve years in Christian higher education, Bob retired in 2007 and has devoted his time to strengthening and empowering churches. For the last eleven years, he has traveled extensively in Latin America teaching Bible seminars and providing training for evangelism, discipleship, leadership development, and church planting.